Couples

Couples

SCENES FROM THE INSIDE

Sally Cline

THE OVERLOOK PRESS
Woodstock • New York

First published in the United States in 1999 by
The Overlook Press, Peter Mayer Publishers, Inc.
Lewis Hollow Road
Woodstock, New York 12498

Library of Congress Catalog-in-Publication Data

Cline, Sally.
Couples : scenes from the inside / Sally Cline
p. cm.
Includes bibliographical references.
1. Couples--United States--Interviews. 2. Gay couples--United States--Interviews.
3. Interpersonal relations--United States. 4. Interpersonal conflist--United States.
5. Interpersonal communication--United States.   I. Title.
HQ801.A3C55   1999   99-11456
306.7--dc21

Manufactured in the United States of America

Originally published in Great Britain by Little, Brown and Company

ISBN: 0-87951-946-0

This book is dedicated to
EM MARION CALLEN

This book goes also with love to
BA SHEPPARD

Contents

ACKNOWLEDGEMENTS

This book could not have been written without the many women and men in Great Britain and North America who talked to me at length and offered their accounts of coupledom. Their names have been altered but their voices weave through these pages.

My principal acknowledgement is to Rosemary Smith, my meticulous, creative and hardworking research assistant who helped organise the research, transcribed tapes, read and proof-read endless drafts, cut chapters and compiled the bibliography. Her professional expertise and intellectual clarity, matched by her generous spirit, literally kept me going.

In the USA I have a particular debt of gratitude to my researcher Julie McClusky who conducted a series of West Coast interviews with the same skill and sensitivity with which she undertook the library research.

Additional audio-typing was done by Beth Callen, Kathryn Pedersen, Nicki Moretta and at great speed for long hours by Stephanie Croxton-Blake, to all of whom I extend my gratitude.

For research space, hospitality, networking, information, stimulating discussions and professional and personal support in the USA I thank Anne Gurnett, Elizabeth Dunn, Abe Polonsky and most especially Martha Campbell. In Canada I thank Peggy Harris of the Ottawa Women's Bookstore, Geoff and Josette Tesson, Kathy Mullen, Robert Hess, Alisa Hornung Weyman, and in particular Kate McKenna for her comments and analysis and

Cheryl Lean and Graham Metson for their constant encouragement and many weeks' accommodation.

Special thanks go to Margaret Drabble and Michael Holroyd, Davina and Larry Belling, Edna and Denis Healey, Nicci Gerrard and Sean French, Nancy Kline and Christopher Spence for the time they gave me and their dedication to the project.

I am indebted to the following individuals, organisations and libraries for their help: Relate, Tavistock Marital Studies Institute, One Plus One Marriage and Partnership Research Charity, British Association of Sociology and Social Policy Section, Family Policy Studies Centre (London), Harry Ransom Humanities Research Center (Texas), Stephanie Macek at the Social and Political Sciences Library, Cambridge, the staff at the Cambridge University Library, Chris Avery at Arbury Court Library, Cambridge, and most especially Olga Foottit and the project team at the 92 Stretten Avenue Family Centre, Cambridge, for their participation, guidance and networking.

For networking, writing space, research accommodation, financial understanding, medical help, literary criticisms, draft reading, encouragements of many kinds, I thank: Jean Adams (at glorious Sunset Heights), Alice Ball, Sue Benson, Bob Biderman, Kathy Bowles, Bunny Catterall, Anne Christie, Gwynneth Conder, Cheryl Day, Zena Denne, Kay Dunbar and the *Ways With Words* Literary Festival team, Ro Fitzgerald, Dr Katherine Grimshaw, Caroline Hill, Jane Jaffey, Joel Jaffey, Stella King, Caroline Knox, Josie McConnell, Linnie Price, Nick Price, Barbara Rodbard, Vera Segal, Aliye Seif Al Said, Julia Smith, Alison West, Hilda Wynne; for sharing knowledge, experience and insights Carol Jones and Michelle Stanworth; and Dale Spender whose unfailing creative, critical and provocative ideas enriched this manuscript.

Throughout the project Caroline Middleton, Angie North, Ralph and Maggie Ward strengthened my spirits and cared for my house and cat while I was on research trips abroad. For their consistent literary guidance, ideas and editing advice I thank Wendy Mulford, and the Cambridge Women Writers – Geraldine Ryan, Joy Magezis, Marion Callen and most particularly Chris Carling without whose assistance Chapter 3 would never have been completed.

I thank my editors Richard Beswick and especially Antonia

Hodgson for their enthusiasm and understanding throughout the project. My appreciation too to Jean Maund for her caring and careful copy-editing.

My literary agent Barbara Levy has read and analysed every chapter. The changes she has suggested have improved the text as dramatically as her joyous support improved my spirits.

My family and extended family have yet again strengthened my writing life. My personal experience of coupledom has been enhanced by children, so a big thank you to the Young Ones (Marmoset, Vic, Helen, Manda, Beth and Aaron) for their professional gifts and personal help. My daughter Marmoset Adler has networked interviewees, retrieved cuttings, ransacked libraries, photocopied articles, found books, listened to drafts. Vic Smith has mailed encouragement from Costa Rica and Japan; Beth Callen has achieved scholarly transcriptions; Manda Callen has faxed articles and affection; Helen Bamford and Aaron Callen have offered consistent cheer.

Despite severe illness and hospitalisation Elsie Sheppard and Larry Adler have both been stalwart; Jane Shackman has read endless drafts with wondrous patience; Joan and Jonathan Harris have discussed, listened, criticised and helped; Aunt Het (Harriet) Shackman has photocopied articles, debated the project, turned her London apartment into an interviewing centre, been of particular research help with the Denis and Edna Healey interviews, and never failed to encourage me.

Ba Sheppard generously shared her insights into coupledom and offered me wise guidance on the book's shape. My appreciation of her enduring friendship, now in its twentieth year, and her challenging ideas runs deep.

Last but first my deep gratitude to Em Marion Callen who for the last two and a half years has had to share me with hundreds of other couples! I thank her for her skill at Interdependence which allows me the space to write and for her talents at Commitment, Communication, Coping with Change, Compromise and above all Cherishing.

Sally Cline
Cambridge, England
January 1998

CHAPTER 1

The 5 Cs and the Big I

SINGLEHOOD OR COUPLEDOM?

Becoming a couple is seen as a serious matter. *Not* becoming a couple is seen as even more serious.

Or so it appears in our couple-oriented culture.

In the late 1990s, despite changing family patterns, and despite the fact that more women who are financially independent are selecting a highly satisfying life without a partner, coupledom is still the norm. The marketing model assures us all is well. Social and cultural life revolves around coupledom. In some countries there is tax relief for married couples. In the Western world restaurant tables are laid for two. Single supplements are slapped on hotel rooms. Property taxes in some countries assume at least two adults live in each house, and those who live alone have to apply for a discount. Evidence suggests that more married couples than single people eat breakfast, suffer fewer depressions, and sustain lengthier passages of stress-free health.

For many women and men coupledom is an enviable state. It beckons as an elusive goal.

Madge, a 54-year-old health researcher whose ten-year partnership broke up several years ago, now lives on her own:

> I have a fascinating job, primary care is where it all begins. I've paid off my mortgage. My daughters often stay here. I go on

sailing and walking holidays with good friends. In many ways I
am very content.

She looks out at 100 feet of beautifully tended garden:

> Yes, I spend hours poking about out there. And I have chosen to
> live on my own, not share with anyone. I like the feeling that
> when you put down the shampoo it stays just where it is. But . . .
> yes there is a but . . . I still miss that 'someone', that person you
> rush home to and tell all those boring details about the day at
> work. Then suddenly they are not boring any more! It is the
> proximity of a live-in relationship, the fact that they are near
> enough to touch, you just have to reach out your hand, that's
> what made it valuable to me.

Those live-in partnerships, preferably heterosexual, are still promoted as the most desirable family form. However, a new
development in the 1990s is the number of live-out partnerships
between women and men, two women or two men, who see
themselves as a committed couple but choose to reside in separate houses, cities or even countries.

Gay couples, once seen as unspeakable, gay marriages, once
seen as impossible, now seem unstoppable. They are on the political and social agenda in the USA, Great Britain and Canada
where, at least in large urban cities, partnerships between gay
men and women are becoming more socially acceptable.

Nevertheless, 'straight' live-out lovers or gay partnerships
(whether they live together or apart) are not yet perceived as an
'ordinary couple'. Instead they are viewed as outré, cranky, or in
some way 'improper'.

As for single people, even when surviving successfully in a
couple society, unjustly they are denigrated as failures.

Sometimes single people internalise that feeling. Rose, a white
British writer, 36, is in her small apartment in downtown Los
Angeles, waiting in high spirits for her new partner, a black
American sales executive, to fly in from Chicago:

> I've been single all my adult life . . . and couples looked to me
> like cosy people who'd got their own support system. I've

always detested being single. I always felt excluded from what I thought couples were enjoying. They got support. They got sex on tap. That's what I thought. I have been unintentionally celibate for the last six years. I've never known whether that would be *it*. I've thought I might never sleep with anyone again in my whole life!

Rose used to stand on the sidelines watching couples, and making notes for short stories:

Couples looked more sleek to me, they were kind of cared for. Like the difference between an indoor cat and a farmyard cat that is just fed by having its food put out so it has to go ratting. That's the difference between single people and couples. Single people of the world have to struggle. Being alone has been a real struggle. I never thought I would be alone for as long as this.

Rose is now in a tempestuous couple which has its share of problems. 'We live thousands of miles apart in different time zones so we only meet at weekends, and row all the time about money. Bobby earns a whole lot more than I do which can become a real power conflict.'
Money is not the only issue for Rose and Bobby:

We face racism here in a frightening way. There are far fewer inter-racial couples here than back home. When we are in Dallas, Bobby won't let us hold hands.

Despite these conflicts, Rose makes excitable global telephone calls to keep her family informed of the partnership's progress:

I love my family's recognition. My mother will ask: 'How is Bobby?' I feel I have increased my value by having somebody . . . that I am now of worth . . . I am capable of attracting somebody and having somebody love me. I feel secure so I can go out to work, come back and no matter how hard my life is I've got that fact to bolster me up. At the end of the day that protects you against everyone.

Whether or not coupledom in practice *does* offer protection, Rose's view suggests that there is a high status set on coupledom irrespective of what goes on inside a particular partnership. Her view also echoes and reflects the problems many women and men have in coming to terms with not being in a couple.

Part of that problem is that in Western society we have had scant guidance on how to live alone fruitfully, whilst simultaneously we are subjected to pressure to be enclosed in an intimate partnership, a pressure that is hard to resist.

That singlehood, celibacy and solitude can be a profoundly productive and positive state has already been well documented by Anthony Storr in his book on *Solitude* and in an earlier book of mine, *Women, Celibacy and Passion*.[1]

But despite the fact that singlehood is on the increase – in the USA between 1970 and 1995 the proportion of people who had never married rose from 16.2 per cent of the population to 22.9 per cent, and the projection for the year 2010 is nearly a quarter of the population[2] – its status is woefully low.[3]

The abyss into which single people feel they have fallen is satirised by Nick Hornby in *High Fidelity*, a novel about the consistent demise of couples, where Rob, the seriously-below-average narrator, is dumped by his girlfriend. At 35 Rob is reduced to the ignominy of going to the pictures with his Mum and Dad 'and their insane friends'. Whilst waiting for the insane friends to purchase the entire contents of the Pick-'n'-Mix counter, Rob, all self-esteem gone, receives the boneshaking chilling smile of recognition from the world's Most Pathetic Man (that is other than himself) a similarly coupleless soul in a dirty fawn anorak who in his late twenties is also being taken by his parents to see *Howards End* on a Sunday night.

Being in a state of unchosen singleness in London has severely crippled Rob. But being spotted as that kind of cripple by a fellow man who sees him as a kindred spirit is an unendurable humiliation. From his lamentable situation the pathetic Rob generalises about the life of the uncoupled:

> All of us, old and young, men and women: we need someone to save us from the sympathetic smiles in the Sunday night cinema

queue, someone who can stop us from falling down into the pit where the permanently single live . . .[4]

The philosophy behind such satire is less that being in a couple is seen as positive than that the reverse is seen as blightingly negative. Not being in a couple it appears can open people up to curiosity, pity, or ridicule.

As for a positive desire for a lifetime's solitude, it is regarded as the consequence of an emotional trauma, an inability to make relationships or a sign of immaturity.

Remember Madge and her wistful phrase: 'I still miss that "someone".' Cultural messages assure us that we 'need someone' to feel complete. Few messages indicate that 'the someone' could be oneself, a healthy, optimistic, sane, strong and sensitive self. I have seen many sane, strong, single people suddenly weaken, become vulnerable to the ideology that they are emotionally incomplete and set off in a crazed and determined mate-search.

Young girls, perhaps more than boys, learn early – as much from literature as from life – that pairing-off, being part of an intimate twosome, could be seen as a means of escape. Take the case of Joanna, Lisa St Aubin de Teran's downtrodden heroine of her novel by the same name, who grew up in London during the Thirties, the years of the Depression that 'pinched the bones and sapped the marrow'.[5]

Red-headed Joanna, huge and gangly, a servile human giraffe, a physical abomination to her violent and bitter mother, flees the cruelty of home for the haven of young people. She giggles with the girls, meets a number of boys, feels less of a giraffe, and later recalls:

We stayed up until late into every night, and after the dancing finished a group of us girls would lie in a heap on one of the canopied beds and discuss love and sex . . . Each night, as we lay in bed, we paired each other off with one or other of the brothers or friends.[6]

Pairing off for Joanna released her from an unbearable life, it became a way forward.

Pairing off in society is seen as the emotional routine and rhythm of life. That there is a well-documented psychological need for attachment often expressed as sexual desire in all of us means that when this is maintained by intense media persuasion, it is difficult to desire a life that is *not* to be spent in a couple.

Certainly the myth of coupledom offers an attractive prospect. It represents love, intimacy, emotional security and often financial stability. An ideal of coupledom is eulogised as an erotic arena where sex is wild, or a safe haven where interests are shared, allowances are made, and support is constant. At its best it allows for growth, development and space. The desire for intimacy (being close, sharing, feeling loved, understood, accepted, known and appreciated) is a major reason for wishing to be in a couple relationship. Recent research suggests that where couples have a healthy intimacy they create an environment where each individual can be herself or himself, where the couple can become a jointly fulfilled unit, and where both individuals as well as the partnership can grow, change and develop.[7]

Who would not want this?

Too often, however, the reality of coupledom belies the myth, or the partners themselves are unsure how to achieve a healthy intimacy. Thus what transpires within the couple may be claustrophobia, possessiveness or tension. At least one partner may feel she or he is stunted, or that instead of the predicted joy and comfort they are beset by an unexpected loneliness.

The current insistence on fulfilment through coupledom may lead to the swift cycle of the mate-search, where people believe they have 'fallen in love' often before they have become acquainted; sometimes they may move in together after a very short time, only to discover their partner is quite different from their fond imaginings. They may adapt, change and come gracefully to terms with the reality of what a challenging partnership can be about; or they may become disillusioned, a prey to unresolved conflicts, feel trapped, look for an escape route, break up, grieve, then start the partner-search cycle again.

Part of the problem lies in the fact that we have not known from the inside what contemporary couples in the 1990s genuinely want or how far their needs match up to what they have been led to expect by the current cultural definitions of coupledom.

What we do know from previous studies is that whether we see the institution of 'the couple' as positive or negative we almost never see it as problematic. We may regard certain partnerships with amazement, envy or horror, but rarely do we call into question the institution of coupledom. It is viewed as the norm against which other situations are measured.

What I have tried to do in this study is to separate the institution of coupledom from the experience of individual couples, to question the current context for coupledom, to throw a fresh light on couples' goals and motives, and to redefine and enlarge our existing definitions of heterosexual, lesbian and male gay couple relationships.

I wanted to find out whether intimacy in its most healthy aspect (which included emotional security and the growth and development of both partners) actually took place inside our contemporary Western model of coupledom; and if it did, on what it depended.

The model however has a new style, for there have been major changes in family structure including less frequent and later marriages, an increase in divorce, and a significant rise in the popularity of cohabitation. Have these changes affected what couples want or how they behave in practice? Do couples even wish to live up to the cultural myths created for them or do women and men today, in heterosexual and homosexual partnerships, desire and design something quite different?

The theme of this major and detailed study on couples is a radical reinterpretation of what it means to be a couple in the USA, Canada and Great Britain in the late 1990s. As the subtitle of this book *Scene from the Inside* suggests, I have spent two years conducting interviews and analysing *from the inside* differences in couple perceptions held by female and male partners and by gay, straight and bisexual partners.

I focused on three areas.

Firstly I asked what we mean by 'a couple'. Is there a difference between the *institution* of 'the couple' and the social and emotional *experience* of an intimate partnership? I discovered that the institution of coupledom can (though not necessarily) take over, limit, even control the lives or behaviour of the two people concerned.

The couple as an institution is subject to severe over-protection. Loyalty to the partnership, for instance, often forbids discussion with family or friends of important issues when matters go wrong between the partners. Sometimes one or even both partners become isolated.

When the institution brings about those kind of restrictions it is often due to the way contemporary coupledom has been defined. Because I believed that coupledom is due for a redefinition, based more accurately on the partners' own needs and wishes, my second aim was to try to understand what these needs were.

I investigated the definition of 'the couple' by asking people inside an intimate partnership how they defined themselves as a pair and whether that definition matched up to how people outside the pair defined them.

I discovered many couples were heavily influenced by what outsiders thought of them or how outsiders expected them to behave. What *they* wanted from their relationship was often in conflict with contemporary cultural expectations or labelling. Many couples told me of their struggles 'to do things differently' or 'make up their own rules'.

Lesbian and gay male partners' wishes and fears were often quite different from heterosexual partners' hopes and demands, and where this occurred the importance of inventing new guidelines cannot be over-estimated.

Women's needs and expectations often differed from men's, which if not communicated adequately produced arguments and tensions. Sometimes the interviews with each partner separately clarified for them the underlining meaning of the arguments, and by the time of a second interview these had often been aired and on occasion some headway had been made.

One couple said: 'We are getting more out of these interviews than we got out of going to therapy. Talking to you has helped us talk to each other.'

Another couple said:

These interviews are a bit like Couples Therapy without all that stigma! We would never go to that sort of thing, because you're embarrassed to tell people, but saying it's for a book is cool!

My third aim was to discuss with each couple the major practical, psychological and emotional issues they faced and the conflicts they needed to resolve. As well as reporting the views of couples in three countries I have also used certain pieces of literature to illustrate the most important themes the couples raised. The precise subjects tackled and themes explored are given in the final chapter, *Background to the Research*. My underlying interest was in asking women and men how their coupledom was constructed, whether it was as beneficial as it is publicised to be, whom it benefited and how.

I am fascinated by the ways in which the lives of the two sexes can be enhanced or damaged by intimate partnerships. It became clear how gender, colour, sexual orientation – and more significantly institutionalised sexism, racism, anti-Semitism and homophobia – can affect the partners' behaviour and emotions and raise issues for the mental health of the couples concerned.

These were all issues which interviewees were eager to talk about, and they formed the backdrop to many of the taped stories running through the rest of the book.

THE RELATIONSHIP REVOLUTION

In the last forty years we have witnessed a Relationship Revolution which meant my questions were designed to fit radically altered partnerships.

In Europe and the USA marriage rates per thousand of population have reached an all-time low: in the USA the marriage rate has gone down from 10.6 in 1970 to 9.1 in 1994.[8] A parallel situation has taken place in Great Britain where marriage is occurring later and less often.

In both the USA and Europe there has been an increase in divorce. In the USA the number of divorces had risen from 708,000 in 1970 to 1,191,000 in 1994.[9] The marriages do not last long either. During the twenty years between 1970 to 1990, those marriages in the USA which ended in divorce lasted less than seven years.[10]

A growing number of these divorce proceedings are being

initiated by women, despite the fact that it is women who are almost inevitably worse off as a consequence of a legal breakup. In Britain recent figures showed 71 per cent of divorces were initiated by women, three-quarters of them granted on the basis of 'male misconduct'.[11] Although figures are only part of a story, and when it comes to divorce partners often collude on a method to hurry one through, nevertheless those high numbers are not insignificant.

Though divorce rates remain expectably low in the Catholic countries of Italy, Spain and Greece, throughout the rest of Europe they have increased, with the UK having Europe's highest divorce rate. Forty per cent of marriages in Great Britain now end in divorce.[12]

These divorce and separation rates offer significant clues to the view that financial stability is no longer grounds for staying together. The trigger in this situation is women's more prominent entry into the global labour market.

Today in the USA there are more than three times as many women in the labour force as there were thirty-five years ago. Recent figures show that the female participation rate has gone up from 37.7 per cent in 1960 to 58.9 per cent in 1994, and it has affected both single and married women.[13, 14]

Yet new figures and old feelings are often in curious contradiction. Despite the falling marriage rate, most of the couples I interviewed, including those who deliberately chose to live together rather to marry, held the status of a married couple to be both 'more acceptable' and 'somehow more committed' than the status of an unmarried couple. That the number of weddings at least in Britain is still very high, currently 300,000 a year, no longer surprises me.

One couple who had lived comfortably together for nineteen years decided at the start of this research to celebrate their twentieth year by taking a train to the Outer Hebrides, telling no one and having a quiet four-person wedding: bride and groom and two witnesses from the public library. 'We decided not to tell even our families because we were worried that people might regard us differently,' explained the bride. Their concern is borne out by evidence in this study which conclusively suggests that outsiders' perceptions of a couple's status can affect and change the insiders' viewpoint.

Another couple, in a lesbian relationship, had each been previously unhappily married to men who gave them a hard time
when the marriages broke up. The two women had five daughters between them, all of whom had been badly affected by the
strains and tensions. All five girls vividly recalled the misery of
their childhood spent inside a destructive marital environment.
All five were delighted at their respective mothers' new-found
happiness. I could find no evidence of homophobia when talking
to any of the daughters. Yet last year four of the young women
got married all within a three-month period. One daughter said:
'We know what marriage can be like but we want to try for something better.' Another one commented: 'Our Mums are in a
committed relationship, living together and everything, but we
want to be *really* committed, marriage gives you that.'

That there is a contemporary gloss on the traditional notion
that marriage offers 'real commitment' may be one reason for the
increasing popularity of remarriage. In Great Britain one third of
all marriages are now remarriages – the attempts to 'try for something better' – which has led to a sharp increase in the number of
stepfamilies and stepchildren.[15] In Britain an estimated 8 per cent
of all families are now stepfamilies or 'reconstituted' families,
and a similar 8 per cent of children are estimated to be living in
such families.[16]

How couples deal with the children of their partner is an issue
confronted by many I interviewed. Divorced or separated heterosexual couples in new partnerships increasingly face the
challenge of an 'existing family', where the 'other parent' regularly sees the children. 'Every time the boys go away with their
"real Dad",' one man told me, 'they come back to us after their
away-day with the "real" father or mother, grumpy, or tense or at
best unsettled.'

The boys' mother said: 'I and my ex-husband and my new
lover all try and show patience and understanding, we try and
keep the two "families" absolutely separate, but because the boys
didn't want a stepdad he finds it particularly hard.'

For lesbian couples that challenge is extended and made more
difficult because, far from attempting separation, the lesbian
ethos is to include ex-lovers and ex-lovers' children into a new
extended family. This means that many new female partners may

have the responsibility of their own children, their partner's children, and the regular part-time care of the children of their new partner's former partner whom they may not know or may not even like.

Hester, a 42-year-old white senior advertising executive, and her black woman partner Earlene who works in the same company, are struggling with some of these childrearing difficulties. For ten years Hester had lived as a celibate single mother with her 10-year-old daughter Lizzie, who now felt resentful at having to share her mother:

> It has not been an easy ride for Lizzie because she has never seen me in a relationship before. She is very close to her father and I have worked hard at maintaining that. This is my first lesbian relationship, so she is having to come to terms with me not only having a relationship but a gay relationship. It is not surprising that sometimes she feels excluded. Earlene doesn't live with us but she is here most of the time. I try to keep one day free, when she doesn't come, just for Lizzie.

Earlene has no doubts about the strength of Lizzie's jealous feelings towards her. 'She resents me and is very angry if I am there when she feels I am not supposed to be.'

The situation is further complicated by Earlene's problems in trying to continue co-parenting Dwight, the two-year-old son of her previous partner Betty with whom she lived for eleven years:

> I adore him. I am committed to helping bring him up if my ex-partner is agreed to that. So far she has but I do see him less now, only every other weekend, since I've been with Hester.

Hester herself is prepared to welcome the two-year-old but admitted:

> Dwight's mother is a bit nervous about me, about letting Dwight stay here with us. She is protective about her son and about my involvement with him.

Another feature of the Relationship Revolution is that young people are more likely to postpone marriage in favour of living together. Many couples defer childbearing and population researchers point to declining fertility. The availability of reliable contraception allows women both to marry earlier and to postpone the birth of their first child. This has led to more couples marrying with the intention of not having children, and also to more couples cohabiting before subsequently having children.[17] Interestingly, almost one third of births in the UK now occur outside marriage.

Another issue raised in this research was the difficulty young lesbian women had in deciding what path to take in order to bear children. 'I used to be totally in favour of anonymous insemination,' said Katy, a young lesbian, 'but now I don't feel that I have the right to decide for my unborn child that they will never know where they sprang from or who their father is. So it has become much harder.' Katy's partner, Anne, found this change of plan threatening. 'I feel the decision to involve a man, no matter who it is, has threatening implications. At the moment we have not found a way to resolve it.'

For gay male couples who wanted to raise children, issues of surrogacy and 'moral welfare' of offspring confused and complicated what they had hoped would be a simple decision.

Another challenge faced by live-out couples is how to survive as a single parent with the partner not on hand. Scandinavia has led the way in this much heralded rise in lone parents caused by increases in divorce, cohabitation breakdown and non-marital births, with a substantial following in all other European countries.

In Great Britain 20 per cent of all families with dependent children are today headed by a lone parent. In the USA in the early 1980s men who acted as single parents only numbered 616,000, but by the early 1990s they had increased their numbers to 1,153,000.[18] Where households with dependent children under 18 in the USA are headed by a woman, the numbers are substantially larger and the increase greater.[19]

On both sides of the water, where the lone head is a mother she is considerably more likely to be in paid employment, which has decisive implications for any live-out couple relationship she may be in.[20]

Repeatedly I heard the old mother/career woman issue in new guises. It was an issue heatedly discussed by couples where the father lived in a separate residence and the mother, in full- or part-time employment, raised their children. But it also proved a problem for several women who lived in the same house as their partners, when they both worked full-time, but where it was the women who were still largely responsible for the child care.

Social attitudes towards living together have changed drastically across the globe. As marriage rates decline, cohabitation rates rise steadily. Where 'living in sin' was once a stigmatised minority state, now many counsellors and partnership agencies advise younger respondents to live together before marriage as a sensible prelude to marital commitment.

Where 'engagements' were once the tradition for couples who courted, they have been replaced by cohabitation, now an institutionalised part of the mating process. In the USA alone there has been an enormous rise amongst heterosexual cohabiting couples. In the first year of the Seventies decade they numbered a mere 523,000. The figures for 1995 showed a leap to 3,858,000.[21] This escalation has been matched in both Canada and Great Britain.

Cohabitation, no longer perceived as deviant, is widely accepted as either a prelude or an alternative to marriage; or in the cases of most of the couples I interviewed, as virtually indistinguishable from marriage in practical terms if not in status.

These changes in family formation and dissolution are considerable, closely interlinked, and may be due to a number of causes. In the West we have made major scientific gains over reproduction, recent years have seen a strong move towards individualism, and increased opportunities and equality are available to women.

Although these trends seem to reflect a rejection or at least a postponement of marriage, there is no evidence at all that men and women are abandoning intimate one-to-one relationships.

Far from it.

Coupledom is not under collapse, but it is under constraint. The pressure is to meet the needs of re-formed families and restructured partnerships. As women's new freedoms and decisions reshape relationships, as mixed race partnerships grow in number (in the USA we see that the number of married inter-racial couples alone has increased from 310,000 in 1970 to 1,392,000 in 1995),[22] as gay relationships become more socially acceptable, coupledom is in a state of flux and change. Old models cannot be relied on. Couples themselves are asking challenging questions.

I interviewed 160 women and men who represented straight and gay couples of different ages, social classes, races, ethnic groups and religious persuasions; some who lived together, some who lived apart, some with children, some childless. My interest lay in what they saw as the value of coupledom in general and in what values each particular unit held, and whether patterns could be drawn between and amongst couples.

FIVE Cs AND AN I

The most significant finding of this study is that from the point of view of the couples themselves certain consistent key elements are needed to ensure the making rather than the unmaking of a couple.

These features, mentioned by every partner in the couples in this study, can be broken down into six elements, **five which I have characterised by C:** *Commitment, Communication, Coping with Change, Cherishing,* **and** *Compromise;* **and one indicated by I:** *Interdependence:* **the balance between dependence and independence.**

Commitment was seen by the couples as an emotional (and sometimes legal) pledge of love and faith in the relationship. It always carried undertones of dedication, safekeeping and trust, and sometimes hinged on fidelity or building up a lifelong relationship.

Communication was understood by couples to mean a connection through language, which included an exchange of conversation, body language or sexual intimacy.

Many women and men agreed with Dale Spender and Deborah Tannen[23] that the two sexes speak 'two different languages' and thus find communication hard. This proved to be a persistent stumbling block.

Coping with Change included any radical alteration in a couple's particular situation, either in the present or one they recalled from the past. Changes included new jobs, new forms of study, raised or lowered income, the birth of children, taking on other people's children, illness, disability, bereavement, depression, change in sexual habits, affairs, retirement, moves to another location or country, any of which changes could have negative or positive consequences for the couple.

Cherishing was defined as the feeling and the expression of *care* for a partner. This included lovemaking, offering them emotional protection, laughing with them, remembering romance, looking after their welfare, accepting responsibility, offering support time and energy, being considerate, taking the partner into account, demonstrating appreciation and gratitude, looking out for them, and being on their side. It also covered understanding their partner's needs, recognising that the other person's point of view might be valid, focusing attention on them and their concerns as well as on one's own. It was often rooted in compassion.

Compromise, the element that couples in this study found the most difficult to sustain in their partnerships, was defined as a midway path between two different ideas or values or codes of behaviour. Compromise was the settlement of disputes and discussions by negotiation, adaptation, understanding and a constant willingness to see the other person's point of view.

Interdependence is an equilibrium or state of harmony between identity as an individual and connection as a couple. Achieving a balance between these two states was seen as a complex juggling act by most couples. Younger couples in particular had very high expectations about maintaining a personal sense of self and not getting lost inside their couple.

An opposing view was taken by several middle-aged and older couples who suggested that interdependence, unlike the other five elements, was a 'luxury item'. One woman voiced their view: 'It would be wonderful to be able to afford a sense of self, but in a couple, a harmonious couple, you have to be prepared to sacrifice it when necessary, I mean for the good of the unit.'

Most couples, however, believed that the best interests of the unit were served when individual identity and the couple's joint well-being were in balance.

In this book I consider each of the six elements in turn and discuss the couples' responses to these issues.

In the final section of the book I look at a seventh element, the notion of *Creativity* and its relationship to coupledom. I am interested in how two creative people live together in a society which sets up two apparently clashing ideas. There is a dominant belief that suggests literature or art is produced by individuals in solitude, yet this is set against the standard social structure which sets marriage, partnerships and families as the norm. There is also the notion that every creative artist, whether male or female, needs a 'wife'. If this idea has any credence, what happens if there are two creative people inside a couple?

Among my interviewees were several professional novelists, biographers, screen-writers, artists, politicians, film-makers and musicians who agreed to discuss both the specific issues related to creativity and also the general issues relevant to most partnerships such as children, money, love, sex, freedom, which find expression or restriction under the categories of commitment, communication, change, cherishing, compromise and interdependence. Unlike the other participants in the study, all of whom remain anonymous, with their names coded and fictionalised, the Creative Couples, as public figures, use their own names.

They include the novelist Margaret Drabble and her husband biographer Michael Holroyd; the British politician and writer Denis Healey and his writer wife Edna Healey; the film producer Davina Belling, who co-produced the exceptional *Gregory's Girl*, and her American writer/computer publicist husband Larry Belling; writer Christopher Spence, the founder and director of London Lighthouse (the 'place of safety' for people facing the challenge of HIV/AIDS) and his American wife, writer and consultant Nancy Kline; and the successful husband-and-wife writing partnership Nicci Gerrard and Sean French. It is the stories of their unusual coupledoms with which I close the book.

I open the book as I opened each interview with the question: Why be in a couple?

NOTES

1   Sally Cline, *Women, Celibacy and Passion*, André Deutsch, London, 1993; *Solitude*, Anthony Storr, Fontana, London, 1989.

2   The projection for year 2010 is that 50,747,000 people over 18 years (more than 22.5 per cent of the population) will never marry.

3   Population Statistics. Marital Status of the Population by Sex, Race and Hispanic Origin: 1970 to 1995. Chart 58. Source: US Bureau of the Census. 1970 Census of Population vol. 1, part 1, and Current Population Reports, pp. 20–450, and earlier reports and unpublished data. Also Marital Status Statistics. Chart 60. Marital Status of the Population – Projections, by Age and Sex: 2000 and 2010. Source: US Bureau of the Census, Current Population Reports pp. 25–1129. The projection statistics also indicate that by the year 2000 the projected number of people in the USA who will never marry will be 44,459,000 of the population over 18 years. This is 21.8 per cent of the US population.

4   Nick Hornby *High Fidelity*, Indigo, London, 1996, pp. 117, 118.

5   Lisa St Aubin de Teran, *Joanna*, Virago, London, 1991, p. 19.

6   Ibid, p. 97.

7   Janet Woititz, *The Struggle for Intimacy*, Impact Publications, California, 1980.

8   The marriage rate in the USA is per thousand of the population. Chart 146. Marriages and Divorces 1970 to 1994. Vital Statistics of the United States, p. 104.

9   In the USA the divorce rate shot up from 3.5 people per thousand in 1970 to 4.6 twenty-four years later. Chart 146. Marriages and Divorces 1970 to 1994. In Health Statistics, Vital Statistics of the United States, p. 104.

10 USA Marriage and Divorce Statistics. Chart 150, p. 105. Divorces and Annulments – Duration of Marriage, Age at Divorce and Children Involved. 1970 to 1990. The median duration in years of those marriages which ended in divorce was 6.7 in 1970 and 7.2 in 1990.

11 Figures from Jill Radford, 'Breaking Up is Hard to Do' in *Trouble and Strife*, 34, Winter 1996/97, pp. 12–20. Divorce figures for 1994. Of the 71 per cent divorces initiated by women in the UK, 76 per cent were granted on the basis of male 'misconduct', 22 per cent adultery and 54 per cent unreasonable behaviour.

12 In 1995, in the UK 175,000 divorces were granted. In 1995 two in five marriages in the UK ended in divorce. Figures from Jill Radford, op. cit.

13 Looking back to the 1960s there were 12,893,000 married women in the work-force and 5,410,000 single women. But by the 1990s, the female work-force numbers had risen to 33,358,000 married women in 1994, matched by a similar rise that same year of 15,467,000 single women.

14 USA Bureau of Labor Statistics. Bulletins 2217 and 2340 and unpublished data. Chart 624, p. 399, Labor Force Participation Rates – by

Marital Status, Sex and Age: 1960 to 1995. Also Chart 625, Marital Status of Women in the Civilian Labor Force, 1960 to 1995.

15 Britain's General Household Survey, 1996.

16 J. Haskey, 'Stepfamilies and stepchildren in Great Britain' in *Population Trends* No. 76, pp. 17–28, 1994.

17 Peter Selman, 'The Relationship Revolution: Is the family collapsing or adjusting to a new world of equal opportunities?' in *Families Behind the Headlines*, ed. Robin Humphrey, British Association of Sociology and Social Policy Section/Department of Social Policy, University of Newcastle, 1996, pp. 1, 2. Using research from D. van de Kaa, 'Europe's Second Demographic Transition', *Population Bulletin*, 42 (1), pp. 1–59, D. van de Kaa, 'Emerging Issues in Demographic Research for Contemporary Europe' in M. Murphy and J. Hobcraft (eds), *Population Research in Britain*, Supplement to *Population Studies*, vol. 45, 1991.

18 Figures for 1980 and 1990.

19 In 1980 there were 5,445,000 women acting as lone parents, but ten years later we saw a massive increase to 6,599,000. USA Bureau of the Census. Current Population Reports, pp. 20–447, and earlier reports and unpublished data. Page 65 Chart 80. Family Households with own children under age 18 by type of family 1980 to 1995 and by age of householder, 1995.

20 Janet Walker. 'Changing Families. Great Expectations in Hard Times', in *Families Behind the Headlines*, ed. Robin Humphrey, British Association Sociology and Social Policy Section/ Department of Social Policy, University of Newcastle, p. 50. Walker is using research from D. Utting, *Family and Parenthood: Supporting families, preventing breakdown*, Joseph Rowntree Foundation, York, 1995.

21 US Bureau of the Census. Current Population Reports, pp. 20–450 and earlier reports and unpublished data. Chart 61: Unmarried Couples by Selected Characteristic 1970 to 1995. It is interesting to note the definition of an 'unmarried couple' at March 1995 which is 'two unrelated adults of the opposite sex sharing the same household'. So in US Census terms, unmarried couples cannot be gay.

22 Figures given are for black/white interracial couples. US Bureau of the Census. Current Population Reports pp. 20–450, and earlier reports and unpublished data. Chart 62, p. 56, Married Couples of Same or Mixed Races and Origins, 1970 to 1995.

23 Dale Spender, *Man Made Language*, Routledge & Kegan Paul, London, 1980; Deborah Tannen, *You Just Don't Understand: Women and Men in Conversation*, Virago, London, 1991; *That's Not What I Mean*, Virago, London, 1992.

CHAPTER 2

What is a Couple?

What exactly is a couple, and how do we recognise when two people are in one? The men and women to whom I talked found it easier to discuss recognition than definition, so I shall start with that.

How do we know that two people are in a couple? Most interviewees decided the giveaway signals were the couples' body movements:

> If you *want* to be in a couple, if you want to be dating somebody, you're definitely sending out that message by body language or flirting . . . it says 'I'm still on the market!' but if two people are IN a couple they do not send out that signal. You can still be kind of flirty with somebody who's in a couple but there is this line that you don't cross and they don't cross, so you know, it's like an animal sense.

> It is the chemistry that is between the two of them. If you can see how they are looking at each other or the vibes they are bringing out between each other, that is the definite way to tell if they are in a couple.

> It is the intimate body language between two people. The way they talk to each other easily. They don't have to get on. Even if they are angry they still have an intimacy.

I can tell a couple by their intimacy, their body language. People react differently together when they are being intimate. I can tell at work if colleagues are seeing each other in that way, it's just the interaction, the way the body relaxes with the other body.

There is a sense when I see two people in a couple in how they look at each other and how they relate, whether it is loving or whether there's this argumentative tone. There's a certain aura that you can sense around two people. You know there's something a little bit deeper than just a superficial friendship.

There is a small scene in Doris Lessing's novel *Love, Again* which shows vividly how this works. Sarah, the novel's heroine, is having dinner with her friend Stephen, his wife Elizabeth, their three sons, and Norah, who unknown to Sarah was Elizabeth's lover. Later Sarah relives the dinner-table scene:

> . . . There was something bothering Sarah, and she couldn't put a finger on it. . . . She was remembering a scene at the table of Norah handing Elizabeth a glass of wine, and Elizabeth's smile at Norah. Well, yes, that was it. And she shut her eyes and replayed the scene. Stephen was at one end of the table, Elizabeth at the other, Norah beside Elizabeth. The women's bodies had carried on a comfortable conversation with each other, as well-married bodies often do. . . .[1]

'Well-married bodies' is an interesting phrase because it is Stephen and Elizabeth who are the married pair and who at least legally are the well-established couple. However those 'comfortable conversations' of bodies that are or have been intimate are often clues to coupledom that may not be legally or openly recognised. As one woman said, being in an intimate couple allows one to continue with interrupted conversation.

Guidelines to recognising couples were much easier to establish than answers to the central question 'What *is* a couple?' When I tried it out on the women and men in this study, initially they all said 'It is obvious!' but when pressed to define a couple, they floundered. There appeared to be a tricky area between what they thought couples 'ought to be' or had been 'set up to be' and what in practice couples were.

I went to the dictionary for hints. The first meaning given is that a couple are two people who regularly associate with each other or live together.[2] Yet in this study at least a third of the couples did not live together and many irregularly associated, yet all were emphatic about being considered a couple.

I tried again. The second meaning offered by the dictionary is two people who are considered as a pair.[3] Again this definition could not uniformly be adopted because to be widely considered as a pair requires self-disclosure and acceptance which is not always possible.

When a man and a woman decide they are 'a couple', their expectation is that friends and family will also see them as a pair. In general heterosexual couples do not have to deal with issues about acceptance in the wider world. Occasionally they may find difficulties over self-disclosure to immediates or employers, as in the case of two mixed-race heterosexual couples in this study who found disclosure impossible to racist relatives, and in the case of one heterosexual woman who had decided to marry a man in prison for life but felt unable to tell her family. These are however relatively rare situations, whereas gay couples encounter this problem consistently.

In this research, whether gay male or lesbian couples were considered as 'a pair' depended on how far out of the closet they had come. Sometimes they were deemed 'a pair' by their close friends or by the gay community, but not by their office colleagues and in some cases not by their children or parents.

Some interviewees believed firmly that disclosure is an integral part of being a couple:

> Being a couple is inevitably something to do with the world.
> The two people usually, or eventually, are happy for the world
> to know they are a couple.

This was the view of Christopher Spence. Founder and former director of London's Lighthouse (interviewed fully in Chapter 9), Spence had spent more than twenty years in a couple with a male partner and for the last seven years has been contentedly married to American writer and consultant Nancy Kline. In both partnerships Spence was 'happy for the world to know' he was in a couple.

People's 'happiness', or ease, at disclosure of their coupledom varied widely in this study but for most interviewees, coupledom *was* 'something to do with the world'. How two people behave inside their partnership is a peculiarly private practice, but 'a couple' is not simply a personal phenomenon. As a societal institution, coupledom, rife with myths and often intangible rules, ensures that each intimate pair has complex associations with the wider community:

> That word 'couple' is odd but it does have something to do with longevity and public perceptions. At least it has if you're not married. It was many many years before I thought of Jacob and I as a couple. Though we had bought a house because of finances, for the first ten years that we lived together we still always assumed that we wouldn't be living together, so we would buy separate copies of exactly the same books, kind of feeling that we had separate lives.
>
> It changed . . . this sounds stupid . . . when there was this particular sofa that was quite expensive that we bought for the house, the most expensive piece of furniture we ever bought. Individually we couldn't afford it so we actually had to buy it together and that was the turning point. I relaxed about not quite knowing if it belonged to Jacob or to me. Now we have been together, not married, for 24 years and people have noticed! So now I think it's reasonable to start describing us as a couple. But it's because it's got something to do with some kind of *public perception* of you as 'together', what my nieces would describe as 'an item'.
>
> *(Natasha, 44, British. Partner to Jacob, 50, Australian.)*

Many couples who felt coupledom was rooted in an emotional understanding also believed it improved if it was validated from outside:

> You *can* be a couple even if other people don't see it, if you know it in your own heart and mind but what makes a couple

work long-term is getting along, communicating, showing others, and letting people see.

(Jeff, 48, Interior decorator. Los Angeles, USA. Partner to Pete, 31.)

I think being in a couple is as much self-defined as other-defined. Once you live with a person or spend a lot of time with another person, then in a sense, you start to think of each other as a couple. Then other people start treating you as a couple and I guess that reinforces it.

(Kurt, 55. Austrian university lecturer. Canadian resident. Married to Caitlin.)

Before I was in this couple I signed my Christmas cards 'Love, Sarah'. When I started to think of Emily as my partner I signed them 'Love, Sarah and Emily'. Then other people took notice and sent us joint cards. The only exception I make is for my ex-lover where I still sign with my name!

(Sarah, 55. British partner to Emily, 56.)

These were all couples who were happy for the world to know it. But can there be couples who are not happy for the world to know it?

Not for long. Because we are members one of another. A relationship is a relationship between two people but it is also a relationship between those two people and the wider society. I think secret coupledoms probably usually perish or become public.

(Christopher Spence.)

Although the relationships of few 'secret couples' to whom I talked had not perished, the secrecy – usually on the part of one partner and against the wishes of the other – led in each case to distressing and destructive rows.

This emphasis on a public dimension to coupledom was borne out by those whose partnership was not open to everyone but who, *with no exceptions*, told me they wanted it to be. Many were working toward that end.

How do you continue to see yourself as a couple if the world does not view you in that way?

Heterosexual couples living apart geographically, if they were on good terms with each other, said they consistently communicated information about long-distance partners to those in their professional or social circle:

> About two days after starting at the New York radio station, I told the women in the office about Anne, my English fiancée. That way they knew I wasn't available so they flirted with the other guys.
>
> *(Vince, 36, New York, USA. Partner to Anne, 28, in England.)*

Some gay couples found such a stand harder to take. Despite the fact that Roy and Jack recently committed themselves to each other in a gay Christian wedding ceremony, they still encounter bureaucratic problems.

> Even though Roy and I got married in Los Angeles, society doesn't recognise us, every day we have to believe in our couple without outside support. Roy's employer recognises us as a couple because that firm chooses to accept same-sex couples. My employer does not. Simple things like spousal benefits I can't take advantage of even though I consider Roy my spouse. So there is this uneasiness when I look at my documentation. When it says 'Do I want spouse life insurance?' my first response is 'Yes I do!' But I can't do that. I can't put that. I can't get that.
> Simple things like getting car insurance are not simple. In order for us to get car insurance and discounts on more than one car, we have to register both cars in both our names and get insurance in both our names on both cars. It is so convoluted. We are saying 'We are a couple.' Our community is saying 'You are a couple, we recognise you as a couple.' But society says 'You guys are room-mates and nothing more.'
> *(Jack, 36, insurance computer analyst, married in Los Angeles, USA to Roy, 34, sales director).*

Roy, unlike Jack, saw his definition of a couple grounded in the personal rather than the public. He felt this made it psychologically easier:

Coupledom to me is defined by a personal commitment; if I'm committed to another person I see myself as part of a couple and whatever other people think is irrelevant.

Social changes on both sides of the Atlantic have however benefited many couples in Roy and Jack's situation. Sarah and Emily are a case in point:

It isn't hard for me to think of myself as part of a couple because the process is becoming more open. Where it said on an insurance form 'Who is your beneficiary?' and 'How are they related to you?' I put 'significant other' and Emily put 'partner'. Every time you do something like that it becomes a little easier. I'm sure, if you make a stand, it helps other people in our situation.

That the institution of coupledom, if not necessarily each personal experience, is subject to public scrutiny and assumptions, was well established by interviewees in this study. But the precise definition of what made up a couple remained more problematic.

The dictionary definition of a couple closest to those I was offered is 'a connector or link between two members'.[4] Connection and link were words used by everyone I talked to. But what *is* the connection, what *is* the link which turns two individuals into a couple?

Is it shared residence?

Do you have to live together to be considered a couple? Many interviewees lived apart but considered themselves and were considered by others as 'a pair'. Several couples lived separately but had had children together and still brought them up jointly as a family. In those cases the shared nature of the childrearing contributed to the unanimity with which the live-out parents were considered a couple.

Is it shared finance?

If the varied range of budgeting amongst those who considered themselves couples is a guide, it would appear not.

System One: The One-Pot Shared System. This was a single joint account usually held in both names and used by both partners.

System Two: The Two-Pot Separate System. This was where partners operated two independent accounts. In this system one group elected to pay individually but in equal shares; a second group decided that the partner with the greatest income should pay proportionately more; a third group allocated major bills to one partner, whilst the other partner contributed towards 'treats', holidays, or consumer goods.

System Three: The Three-Pot Budget System. Here partners held two individual accounts from which they fed an agreed amount of money to cover mortgages or rent and bills into a third shared account. This system was very popular with couples in their twenties to forties where each partner had a reasonable income, and particularly popular if the woman had a higher income .

System Four: The One-Pot-One-Person System. This was a single account in one partner's name operated by that person (in this study mainly men) on behalf of the couple. This was rare and was found only in a few couples where the man was employed but the woman had no income. (Interestingly, in cases where the women were employed or self-employed while the men were either unemployed or had taken on the role of 'housefathers', joint accounts were used even though all contributions came from the women's incomes.)

Sometimes a couple changed from one system to another as in the case of Sebastian, a British illustrator, and Georgina, a British advertising agent, who plan to marry. During their first three years together they adopted System Two: The Two-Pot Separate System, ran separate accounts but shared all communal expenditure in equal shares:

> That was like our levels of commitment. We have just now opened a joint account which could be tricky as I work, have my own income, earn twice what Sebastian does. Yes, tricky, but yes we are showing our commitment, you see we have just bought a house together, have a mortgage together, our life insurances are in each other's names, we are getting married, so it kind of seems a sensible point to have a joint account.
>
> *(Georgina, 33. Partner to Sebastian, 29. Illustrator.)*

However, in order for each of them to maintain a sense of their own financial identity, Sebastian and Georgina have now decided to adopt System Three which gives them two individual accounts which feed their new joint account.

Is it a sexual connection?

Participants in this study heatedly debated the question of whether sexual activity is necessary either to be considered a couple, or more significantly to consider yourself as part of a couple.

Leonora, 49, and Phil, 69, a British couple who have been married 26 years, were typical of a large vociferous group who felt sexual activity was one of three central elements, the other two being an emotional connection and shared finance.

> We ended up being quite conventional, actually went through a legalised form of partnership for people who wished to have a sexual emotional relationship. Also a relationship based on economy, because you know finance has to come into it. Sex is definitely a very significant part of it.
>
> *(Leonora.)*

This group saw sexual desire as the initial bonding element and sexual activity as, in the words of several interviewees, 'exciting' and 'inspiring'. Several couples were purposefully celibate either through their partnership or for sustained periods during it. Where their 'no sex' rule was intentional and mutual, and where it existed alongside affection and emotional intimacy, both partners reported deep satisfaction with the arrangement.

As a society we have become highly pressured to be sexual even when we don't want to be, and to make sexual activity the yardstick of a good relationship. That sexual activity does not have to be the measure of a fulfilling relationship was shown again in this study, as it had been shown in a previous study I conducted.[5]

Trouble for couples began in relationships where the 'no sex' plan was instituted by one person, without open or adequate discussion. Often the other partner understandably felt hurt or rejected.

Ironically, several couples who were no longer sexually active with each other (and who expressed personal contentment with this situation) nevertheless expressed anxiety as to whether they would still be considered a 'proper couple' by outsiders if those outsiders knew this fact.

Such anxiety, which is widespread, is triggered by two key assumptions about the institution of coupledom:

1) The assumption that 'proper couples' are sexually active. This is a myth. Many couples are not.

2) The assumption that if one or both partners do not want sex then 'something is wrong' with the partnership. This too is a myth. Nothing may be wrong with the partnership. Take the case of Tommy and Tina:

Sex used to be great but after she had our first child her cunt had a terrible smell. Sweet and sour and almost rancid. I couldn't bear to go down on her and that's what she liked best. So gradually I just eased off. Of course I didn't tell her the reason. There is no way I would want to hurt her. When anyone else is around I'm extra lovey-dovey so there are no fears on that score. Funnily enough we are just as close, maybe closer than before, it hasn't made any difference to the way we feel about each other. I'll jerk off if I feel the need and I guess she does, though never in front of me, but really we have so much going on in our lives that it's not a thing we miss.

(Tommy, 35, British salesman. Married for 11 years to Tina, 28, secretary.)

Tommy used to get off on sex much more than me. I more or less put up with it. It was the best way of getting cuddles. Then something happened around my pregnancy. I got tired and scratchy. Far too tired to make love. Then I became hugely involved with the baby. Breast-feeding turned me on in a way sex never did. Tommy, far from withdrawing, became much more affectionate, all the time, not just when we were in bed, he really seemed to want to show my Mum and Dad how much he cared for me and the baby. Sex just faded out. All that pressure went. It was like we had a new lease of life.

(Tina.)

Although Tommy and Tina appeared equally content with low or no sexual activity, the fact that they had not discussed the issue with each other could lead to conflict if their attitudes changed.

By contrast Americans Oswald and Terry discussed at length their no-sex-yet programme. On Oswald's suggestion the couple had decided to postpone sexual activity until he had fully recovered from poor childhood and religious experiences relating to sex. In conversation the two men show genuine understanding of each other's viewpoint as well as an awareness of the attitudes of outsiders:

> I was involved with a church that viewed homosexuality as a psychological defect so I went through years of therapy till finally I realised it wasn't working. Because of those experiences and having a lot of trouble with my sexuality, Terry and I have been dating seven months but haven't slept together yet. Terry wants to be sexually involved and I can't yet. It is my goal. I'm working on being able to express that in a healthy way and not feel guilty and torn up about it. Like we have full body massage but I don't let Terry touch my penis. He is very understanding so it is not a big source of conflict. Though when he says, 'I think you're so hot', I'm a bit uncomfortable.
>
> I don't feel peer pressure to have sex but I don't feel that a lot of gay men, well any men, understand my position . . . or lack of position! This culture is so dripping with sex, it's so important, and here I am saying well it's not a part of this relationship with my boyfriend.
>
> *(Oswald, 32, office administrator. Los Angeles, USA.)*

Oswald's observations reveal outsiders' expectations of the institution of coupledom:

> I think I may be viewed as some sweet naïve thing. Or a prude. And I'm not a prude. I can be as risqué as anyone else. But I think a lot of gay friends just assume Terry and I are having sex, just because we are in a couple . He spends the night and stays over and people know that so our friends just assume we are having a very active sex life.
>
> Maybe I resent the fact that I can't be honest. It's another prejudice. You always assume that the gay community would be

the most understanding as far as this is the way you want to live your life. Queer activism you know, being able to do whatever you want. Be whatever you want to be. But when you say 'I want to be this virginal celibate princess' they won't let you!

Terry was attentive to how others viewed his support of Oswald's unusual stance:

We are seen as different from other couples by those who know because we have not had a sexual relationship yet. We are just getting to really know each other. Some friends think that's ridiculous, others think that's wonderful because it's real and solid. I see it as building a good solid relationship. Part of me wishes we would, but I have to be patient, and I think it has been good for me and it's been good for him, it's making the couple stronger.

(Terry, 50, mechanic. Los Angeles.)

If the connections which define a couple are not sexual, financial or residential, does the connection rest instead on each partner's decision to consider the other as their primary intimate? In other words, are you a couple simply and only because that is what the two of you say you are?

The way interviewees defined what a couple was to some extent conditioned by the way they responded to the six goals of *Commitment, Communication, Coping with Change, Cherishing, Compromise* and *Interdependence*, which they saw as the crunch points for successful coupledom.

If for instance monogamy was part of their basic definition for their couple, then if one person had an affair, the way they coped with that *change* might make or break their couple. Similarly if the partners' definition of a 'proper couple' was living together in one residence, when one partner was offered a job abroad and the other partner was unable to move, how they effected a *compromise* could have severe implications for a continuing successful coupledom.

Most people defined a couple on the basis of their *commitment* to each other:

What makes me say that two people are in a couple is not if they are living together in one place, it is only their sense of some kind of lifelong spiritual, social, physical commitment. We belong to the Baha'i faith which gives us the spiritual element. I'm not kidding myself any more that marriages are for ever. Though at 20 I never thought for a moment I would leave a relationship, I left my first marriage. Even though I've always thought this second marriage to Kurt, it's now 18 years, would last for ever, I'm not that naïve. So what it needs to be defined as a couple, is the *intention* that this will be a life-long commitment to live together.

(*Caitlin, 45, Welsh New Zealander resident in Canada. Second marriage to Kurt.*)

A sense of commitment can operate even within a tense or hostile partnership.

The relationship doesn't need to be a harmonious one (though one would hope for that), it can even be aggressive. I do think of people as being a couple although they have not lived together for extended periods, but they must have this sort of commitment, this relationship, this communication. As I am frankly old-fashioned, I feel if two people are married it makes them more of a couple. The commitment seems greater.

(*Kurt. Second marriage to Caitlin.*)

American writer Nancy Kline enlarged on the definition of commitment.

A couple are two people who love to be with each other more than anybody else, and who are committed to each other. I think it has to do with the primary person in your life who is not a blood relation – the one with whom you *choose* to spend the most time and also to do the most significant things with and of course to communicate with.

That definition, although positive, has certain problems. It works for happy couples who appreciate time with each other and communicate well. But we all know couples who may spend a great deal of time together but may not enjoy it, and who may be poor at communication.

Nancy's husband Christopher Spence pointed out that for the first seven years of their 14-year relationship, Nancy lived in America while he lived in London: 'We spent most of our time apart but undeniably we were a couple.' Then Nancy hastily repaired her definition:

Hmm! Yes. That's right. We were definitely a couple when we spent most of our time apart because of the Atlantic Ocean. So being a couple isn't necessarily the amount of time. It must be to do with focus. It is two people who focus on one another more than they focus on anyone else.

Several men and women described how that focus worked. For some the focus is a shared daily life:

The fact that I'm in a couple means that the two of us have chosen to make a commitment of love, a commitment to share, a commitment to help. Like when the noise is gone and the party's over, this is who I want to be with. This is who I do the dishes with!
  (Coralie, 49, Canadian. In partnership with Renate for 26 years.)

For others the focus is on mutual cherishing and nurturing. It is a desire to improve a partner's self-esteem:

If you live with a person then it is important that you don't do something that really threatens or weakens that relationship. Sometimes it is easy if you are intimate to know what someone hates, it is hard sometimes to avoid doing what they hate.
  My first wife for instance, who was from Fiji, was extremely jealous which is something I hate. She constantly watched me for slips. If she just saw me look at another woman . . . It made it virtually impossible to live with. It wasn't a matter of being unfaithful or playing around, I did not do those things, but when she thought I would even see another female, for a talk or coffee, she would run amok. I had to live this stifled life and felt undermined. It is terrible to do something that the person you love or live with really hates that you do.
  So in my second marriage to Caitlin I try and find out what

she hates; then somehow, even if you feel provoked, you don't
do it, you try, however hard, to think of something else to do!
(Kurt.)

Often children provide the impetus for commitment or become
part of its focus. Ruth and Lou, a white Texan lesbian couple who
have lived together for five years, have now adopted an African-
American baby:

I know I am in a couple because the couple is our life.
Everything we do is for us and our child. We wanna be together
for the rest of our lives. We have made that commitment to each
other. With little Dale coming home to us and it being a haven
for him and being filled with love, when we walk through that
door, we're just like any other family. We call each other 'dear'
in the day, if we're not in the office or we're some place else
we'll call each other 'dear' in the day and talk and tell each
other that we love each other. That's our commitment.
(Ruth, 37, care worker. Texas.)

Making the commitment does not necessarily mean it is easy to
carry it out in practice, as Lou and Ruth have discovered. Despite
Ruth's brave words they are not treated 'just like any other family'.

My family haven't talked to us since we adopted Dale. They
talked to me before but never to Lou. They didn't want anything
to do with her. My sister and brother-in-law wrote and told me
after Christmas that Lou wasn't welcome back in their house. I
was welcomed but their four children were never welcomed to
come down and see us because we were contaminated and
probably going to cause the kids to become lesbians. It was
made worse because I was in a couple. Sure if I'd been single
they'd think I'd get over it and get married to some man. My
mother used to invite us to their house. But oh no, not now!
    When I adopted a black baby that's when they stopped
talking to me. Here in Texas we live in a retired community with
a lot of conservative Republicans, which hasn't exactly helped.
But it's more to do with we are from Mississippi. It's to do with
the baby was black. He is the bright light of our lives, but all

they see is he's black. They don't see what a real committed couple we are, what a family we are.

If a 'real commitment' as a couple is seen as being strengthened by offspring, then a woman's (or a man's) inability to bear children can diminish her (or his) perception of 'proper coupledom'. Take the case of Georgina, who was told at 16 she could not have children:

> For me a way of dealing with my infertility was to join a celibate meditation group. I was kind of into the spiritual religious life. I was celibate for ten years. I found it more secure to be surrounded by people who weren't trying to have families and be in relationships because I saw my infertility as an obstacle to being in a relationship.

Georgina had long desired a partner. 'At the back of my mind being in a couple is what I always wanted.' Her perception of coupledom when viewed from the outside is that of exclusivity and intimacy, a similar perception to that held by Rose in Chapter 1 who saw couples as indoor cats, well fed and sleek, and singles as outdoor cats who were forced to go ratting. Believing, like Rose, that coupledom was an impossible target – 'I never thought I would find anyone prepared to take me on, knowing what my situation was' – to Georgina's surprise she now finds herself in a couple with Sebastian, whom she plans to marry this year. Her own distress over her inability to bear children, as well as her belief that a couple is strengthened by child-rearing, has impelled her towards marriage and new possibilities:

> I was perfectly content cohabiting for three years, but now I want to get married in case we decide to adopt children. Marriage has definitely become a commitment before having children. It will provide a framework within which to raise a family as a committed couple.

Both Ruth in Texas and Georgina in London, like many others, used the label 'a committed couple'. It was a phrase which proved to be another tripwire.

To some, 'a committed couple' could only mean a male-female

partnership. The notion of partnerships outside this parameter, such as Ruth and Lou's, seemed curious or shocking. To others, the phrase 'a committed couple' could only mean those who were married. However, when I asked couples who defined it as a marital relationship if they knew any unmarried twosomes whom they would consider as a couple, many admitted they did. At that point they changed their definition and said there were 'couples' (unmarried) and 'proper couples' (married).

In the USA and Canada many interviewees saw commitment ceremonies in the same way as marriage contracts, as formalising an emotional relationship. In general, however, interviewees saw formal or legal contracts as *deepening* the notion of a couple but *not* defining it.

From responses to the question 'What is a couple?', I have drawn up a list of the fourteen most significant points. Obviously nobody felt that a definition of coupledom had to include all fourteen elements, but most interviewees included five or six of these elements in their definitions.

Couples are seen as:

1. *Two people linked by emotional commitment.*

2. *Two people linked by emotional commitment to make the relationship long-lasting or for a lifetime.*

3. *Two people who cherish each other, support each other, protect each other, who are on the same side.*

4. *Two people who are prepared to compromise for the best interests of the couple, especially when change occurs, and who keep communicating.*

This feature was mentioned over and over again, and was seen as a major stumbling-block for many couples.

5. *Two people with a 'united viewpoint' who see life events as a twosome instead of or as well as seeing them as individuals.*

This united viewpoint can be the bedrock of a couple's definition, as it is for Marie-Claire and Rupert:

It is forgetting about just yourself and seeing things as a two instead of just a one. This is what being a couple is and it is hard work. Having to compromise, all the time. Knowing you have to work it out. That is the work of being a couple. With our two kids' education, bringing them up, we had to have this united viewpoint. I would have been tempted to follow the French system where everything is structured, very defined. Rupert would have been on the British system, much softer, more lenient over their spending money or their going-out rules, or their study rules.

So here in Canada we have to come to some understanding. We decided that I would have some rules and Rupert, he would have other rules and that we must not interfere the one with the other one and their way of operating. So for the children and for anyone who sees us we have the one viewpoint from two different philosophies. But it is a whole series of work to think about it, plan it, find time to sit and talk about it.

(Marie-Claire, 53, French, resident in Canada; married to Rupert for 32 years, having known him for 40 years.)

6. *Two people who make up a whole unit.*

A couple is seen as an entity that is more than the sum of its parts:

Being in a couple makes a person more whole. More than they are alone. I see myself as a bit, you know, as some energy, some this, some that, and the other one is the complement to those highs and lows. It makes a kind of wholeness, a circle.

(Marie-Claire.)

Sometimes parental example can confirm this belief:

I saw how much my parents got from being with each other. I was brought up with this notion that one plus one equals more than two, that there's so much more you can achieve by teaming up with someone and pooling resources and creativity and ideas and energy and making something bigger than you could make on your own . . . I'd go to a party and I'd see a man take the glass out of her hand and go and fill it. He didn't have to ask whether she wanted red or white; there was that unspoken bond between them that I felt was tangible. As someone not in a relationship for ten years, that was something I envied and wanted.

(Georgina.)

7. *Two people with a desire for intimacy.*
Intimacy can work on several levels. For some it is intense emotional closeness, for others it is an easy physical familiarity:

I piss in front of Helen while she's doing her make-up at the bathroom mirror. I guess that's intimate. Most of the time she takes no notice, just squints at her mascara. But once in a while she'll draw back from the sink and watch me take a leak, just making me feel good about it.
(Mick, 27, British, accountant. Married to Helen, 28, waitress, New Zealander resident in England.)

Jacob will see me without make-up, with my legs unshaven, ill, you know, being sick, all sorts of really disgusting things. I think the intimacy is to do with accepting each other as you really are.
(Natasha, partnered to Jacob for 24 years.)

In my second marriage I lived 34 years without intimacy, without being touched. He couldn't bear to touch me, to touch anyone. He wouldn't even put his hand out in the car just to sort of touch. Once he'd died I came to live in a village and got to know a young woman. One day we were crossing the road together and she took my hand. It was such a strange feeling to have my hand held. It was as though it belonged to somebody else. I wouldn't have believed it.
   The same thing, this is quite extraordinary, happened when I first met Charles, now my third husband. As we crossed a road together in Paris he went to take my hand and he was very trembly. It was so nice to have my hand held. When we got to the other side of the road I said: 'You needn't worry about holding my hand, it doesn't commit you to anything!' He laughed but whenever we crossed roads on that trip, even though we were strangers, he kindly held my hand. He was a widower, he must have been used to doing it for his wife. It was

a natural intimacy with him. Now we are together we have that intimacy, I don't mean necessarily sex, but a lot of touching. We are almost the whole time in contact. It would break my heart to be separate again.

(Lillian.)

Genuine intimacy requires a high level of trust and respect. **In this study, heterosexual and lesbian couples appeared to find this easier to achieve than certain gay male couples whose similar social scripting pointed to masculine competitiveness as a possible barrier to intimacy**. I noticed that the heterosexual and lesbian couples who reported a good level of intimacy also believed in the goals of cherishing and equality.

8. *Two people who want to share a life and its many activities.*

A couple must do more things together than they do apart. Doing things together and supporting each other kind of mysteriously binds you into a kind of whole that is a couple.
    (Evie, 32, housewife, British. Married to Matt, 32, unemployed.)

She turns round and says I'm to go down the supermarket with her. So I turns round and says well if that's what's being a couple, well, I'll go. So she turns round and says she don't like me going down the pub on me own. Later I turns round and says I don't mind that, but she's not having any. We're a couple she says.

(Matt.)

Some people who establish a convivial pattern of sharing in their first couple relationship repeat it almost exactly in a second or third marriage or partnership:

Lillian, my third wife, and I do absolutely everything together. It was exactly the same pattern with my second marriage which ended in the sudden death of my wife. She had this clot of blood on the lung and it carried her off. I don't know how many buckets of tears I shed. For twenty years we were together, we liked each other, we loved each other, we went places together,

terribly boring really, but it was very nice. Now I do it with
Lillian.

*(Charles, 72, British, retired, former radio executive and writer. Third
marriage to Lillian, 73, retired, former linguist.)*

For Lillian this sharing ideal is new:

Sharing is more than falling in love, it is the real bond. We are
both in our seventies and we share everything. We do
everything together. That's why there is no time to do anything
else. We trot about together. I trot along and Charles trots along.
He seems to want me trotting with him all the time. After two
previous marriages when I was independent but alone most of
the time, it is absolutely incredible to find this happiness in the
later years of one's life.

9. *Two people who have a shared sense of history.*
Several interviewees decided that the word 'couple' implied an
acknowledgement of their long-term personal history together.

We were in a long-term partnership for fifteen years. Sometimes
we thought we might get married. We had our three kids, but
the boy was born badly disabled, and the next year the eldest
girl got run over and died before they got her to the hospital.
After that we never talked of marriage. The life had gone out of
our lives. Eventually we split up. It was a terrible break-up
because of all that history. I wanted us at least to try and carry
on as friends. I think when you've known a person as long as
we knew each other, and shared so much and had so much
history, I couldn't see how you could discard that type of
relationship. But he found a new woman, he said he needed a
new life. But choosing to give up on our history was almost as
painful for me as the break-up. It was like losing a bit of my
blood line, for our families were enmeshed too.

(Theresa, 36, British. Formerly partnered to Kevin for 15 years.)

A couple are definitely two people who have a sense of history.
Renate and I have been together 26 years ever since we started
as room-mates, then fell in love at a time when you had to stay

in the closet. Suddenly a few years ago I fell for another woman, Ellie. That was bad, but worse was she fell for Renate my partner. So Renate and I talked and decided to try and move from our twosome to a threesome. Being in a three had been one of my secret fantasies, you know, wouldn't it be neat to try, then bingo, oh, wow it's here! So we both had a sexual relationship with Ellie for eighteen months and we all lived together, group sex, all of it, we did it all! Three working women and three dogs. We would all pitch in and do the chores and all three make love together. That's how we ran. The highs were high but the lows were quite low because we couldn't explain to our friends. They would have been shocked, so having come out of the closet as a lesbian couple – and that was mighty tough – now after nearly 30 years Renate and I were back in the closet as a threesome.

It was complicated because Renate and I had this long, long history as a couple. We tried to forget we were a couple and make our three work as a new family group, a new creation. It didn't work in the end because we had too much history, too many memories; we'd been together too long, there was too much couple bonding between us. I always saw my relationship with Renate as primary even though I was in love with Ellie. I loved the different kind of energy a three brings, I loved what Ellie's presence brought, but a part of me knew it was doomed. In the end Ellie felt she'd never be able to crack this completely. We were too much a historical couple and eventually Ellie left.

(Coralie.)

10. *Two people whose ideal is to be good friends.*

This contemporary notion of coupledom where the partner is seen as the 'best friend' was adhered to despite the recognition that some couples behaved like enemies! This definition was offered more frequently by heterosexual couples (usually under 35) and lesbian couples (of any age) than by older heterosexuals or gay men:

Companionship is part of being a couple, just as much as passion. Kinda what friendship means is that you can be somewhere else doing something totally different, but that

person's part of you in your heart. You take them with you.
(*Lou, Texas, partner to Ruth.*)

First and foremost, in a good friend you have somebody who knows you better than anyone. Your partner is your real friend, your companion. If you want to talk about work, they will want to see it from your point of view rather than from your boss's point of view. In my case, apart from my sister and school-friends, Bram is my oldest friend and in some way is my best friend as well as partner-husband.
(*Rita, 37, British, TV researcher. Married to Bram, 44,*
British, social worker.)

11. *Two people committed to an ideal of equality.*

Most couples under 40 saw the notion of equality as an ideal, and much discussion evolved around ways to promote equality within partnerships.

Traditionally women in opposite-sex couples – whether through oppression, religion, biology or social expectations – have expected to be dependent on male partners. Males in both the USA and Great Britain still have greater earning power, and financial inequity often brings other inequities in its wake. Though several heterosexual couples had made considerable changes over roles and tasks (particularly where the women had the higher income) almost all of them, men as well as women, reported how ingrained was their internalisation of traditional male-female expectations. Feminists in heterosexual couples said one of their constant challenges was 'to combat sexism every day'.

Though equality (specifically shared tasks) was a goal in most relationships between two women, where one (or both) of them had previously been in a heterosexual relationship they some-times fell into traditional male-female patterns over domesticity. However, in the area of sexuality all lesbian couples expressed feelings of equality.

An outstanding finding of this research was the *assumption* of equality between two men in a partnership. Many gay men main-tained separate finances, at least during the early years of their partnership and explained that this aided or exemplified their equality. Several gay male couples expressed their feelings of equality in these phrases:

Roy is the spiritual leader while I am the financial leader and I lead in cleaning and organisational parts of the relationship.
(Jack, 36, USA. Note the consistent use of the term 'leader'.)

I wanted an equal partner, not someone to fulfil a role. So we both share the cleaning, we both take out the garbage, we both drive the car, he does the cooking, I do the dishes. He hates to do dishes, I hate to cook. We work it all out equally as we go along.
(Roy, 34.)

We both cook, we share a pretty high-powered job in a computer software company, we don't have those assigned roles, so we do feel like equal. A lot of gay guy couples are like us.
(Martin, 45, New York. Partner to Mervyn, 44.)

Male couples who do not behave like Martin and Mervyn concentrate on their differences in order to feel equal:

We stay equal and independent because I make sure I stay focused on who I am. Keep my own profession, and keep that in one perspective. I am the interior decorator, he is the writer. We don't merge. I have to be myself.
(Jeff.)

12. *Two people for whom sex is seen as cement.*
Many couples regarded sex as being a crucial bonding that had taken place early in the relationship but might be very important, unimportant or entirely absent later on.

Whether the couple had sex with each other, or sexual involvements with other people, was not seen as part of the definition of what a couple was. What was important was an agreement between the partners as to whether the relationship should be monogamous or open, celibate or sexual.

My study confirmed what McWhirter and Mattison found in

1984, that the expectation of outside sexual activity was the exception for heterosexual couples but the rule for male couples.[6] However, I noticed some changes. Though gay male partnerships more often built non-monogamy into their theoretical definition of a couple than did heterosexual or lesbian couples, in practice many male couples were monogamous, while sexual affairs often occurred in heterosexual and lesbian partnerships which offered monogamy in their definition.

For some couples monogamy was essential. For some it was used to define and maintain their own partnership but was not used in defining couples in general. Where non-monogamy took place in other partnerships, if the partnership remained primary and the sexual affairs secondary those outside saw the partners as 'a couple'.

13. *Two people living together in one space.*

I have termed this **The Proximity Model** of Coupledom.[7] I widened it slightly to include couples who live in separate residences but within a few minutes' walking distance from each other. For some people this is an essential part of the definition of a couple. Many of those who lived together found it hard – even impossible – to accept that a couple who lived apart had the same kind of commitment.

The advantages were reported as a sense of security, a feeling that 'home is where the heart is', an appreciation of the fact that if one partner received good or bad news, the consequent excitement or distress could be communicated instantly, and comfort or support was on hand. The other asset frequently mentioned was the growing intimacy which can come from shared daily experience.

Disadvantages were seen as being 'joined at the hip', a feeling of insufficient space or privacy, or in bad situations claustrophobia and 'having nowhere to run'. Habit or over-familiarity was seen as breeding disrespect or lack of interest in the partner's independent activities. Romantic and sexual feelings were said to wane within a couple of years. The two disadvantages mentioned most frequently were first, 'setting the partners in concrete' – not allowing for change and using phrases like 'you *always* do it this way' or 'you *never* drink coffee'; and secondly, other people's perceptions of the two people as a single unit with no separate ideas.

14. *Two people living separately but committed emotionally.*

I have termed this **The Intimate Commuter Model.** It encompasses couples who live in different residences geographically distant in the same town, or in different towns or different countries. Because this phenomenon has become so frequent, particularly in France, the media have already labelled such couples as LAT (Living Apart Together) couples.

In general the interviewees, whether Proximity Couples or Intimate Commuters, did not see residence as a defining characteristic although some felt that the Proximity Model appeared to the outside world as 'more of a couple' than the Intimate Commuter Model.

These views were occasionally internalised even by couples who lived apart by choice, such as Pete and Jeff in Los Angeles:

> I think it is easier to think of two people as a couple if they live together. Funny that I'm saying that because we don't live together, and at this stage I don't want to. We are both very comfortable with living apart. We certainly are a couple.
>
> *(Pete.)*

Sometimes one partner felt it more strongly than the other, as in the case of Canadians Blake and Jimmy. Blake was the more relaxed:

> Being in a couple means having somebody in your life, somebody you care for, somebody you want to share things with, that you don't want to share with other people. It could be sharing your home but it doesn't have to be.
> *(Blake 46. Canadian. Partner to Jimmy.)*

Jimmy, whose idea it had been to live separately, paradoxically felt that sharing a home was the crux of 'a proper couple':

> I see us as a couple in some respects, but maybe not entirely because we haven't made that final commitment of living together and sharing our lives in the same way.

Jimmy's hesitancy about his Intimate Commuter status, though voiced by a few couples, was not common in this study. Most of those men and women who lived apart felt positive about it. Several long-term Intimate Commuters who had lived apart for between eight and twenty years saw their situation as highly satisfactory. They reported significant advantages. Living in different homes enabled them to show more interest in each other's activities, conversation and well-being than was often seen in those couples for whom a decade of day-to-day familiarity had deadened freshness. Lack of boredom, a sense of adventure, the maintenance of romance, and the renewed excitement of sex, were all mentioned as assets. When rows took place most Intimate Commuters found it helpful to have their own space to retire to temporarily. Difficulties were the travel, the lack of spontaneity because planning is an integral part of an Intimate Commuter relationship, and the need for easy cheap communication methods during periods apart.

Intimate Commuter relationships fit easily into the Nineties decade with its strong emphasis on individual fulfilment. For two people who want independence as well as emotional bonding, such a relationship which offers personal space as well as security makes a great deal of sense.

After talking about these fourteen elements to more than 160 people, most of whom focused on the notion of commitment, I have evolved a working definition of a couple:

> **Two partners who are committed in a primary way to each other. This commitment has to be for a longer continuous period than any commitment to other people. The couple commit themselves to sharing emotions, activities or time more intensely or more often than with anyone else. A committed couple is one which desires *intimacy* and at one time, whether in the past or present, has professed love. Whether the partners live together or apart, whether they share a bed or a bank account, is less significant.**

From definitions of coupledom, I turned to the reasons for being in a couple and the struggles to maintain a successful partnership.

NOTES

1 Doris Lessing, *Love, Again*, Flamingo, London, 1996, p. 66.
2 *Collins English Dictionary*, ed. Patrick Hanks, Collins, London and Glasgow, 1979, 1985, p. 343.
3 Ibid. Another dictionary meaning in *Collins English Dictionary* was 'a pair of collars joined by a leash', a definition ruefully acknowledged as having some merit by a few long-time partners who felt stifled!
4 Ibid, p. 343.
5 Sally Cline, *Women, Celibacy and Passion*, André Deutsch, London, 1993.
6 *The Male Couple. How Relationships Develop*, David P. McWhirter and Andrew M. Mattison, Prentice-Hall Inc., Englewood Cliffs, N.J., 1984, p. 3.
7 This term was coined during a conversation with sociologist Barbara Sheppard, July 1997.

CHAPTER 3

Commitment

Commitment is the first element characterised by 'C' which couples saw as necessary for a satisfying relationship. When their couple floundered, often they blamed it on 'lack of proper commitment'. When their labels for what had gone wrong were more specific, such as 'his temper', 'not enough money', 'her depressions', 'his father not accepting us because we're gay', or 'too much interference from her in-laws', some couples found that beneath diverse labelling lay insufficient commitment or insufficient communication about exactly what each person meant by 'being committed'.

In *general* terms couples understood commitment to mean a pledge of love, loyalty and trust through bad as well as good times, an agreement to depend on their partner for emotional nurturance. Many couples' commitment is inextricably grounded in religious belief. Caitlin and Kurt, members of the Baha'i faith, are typical:

> Being in a couple means a long-term spiritual commitment as well as a social and physical one. Kurt and I assume the reality of every human being is a spiritual essence, that is more important than the physical. The most profound love is spiritual love.
>
> *(Caitlin.)*

Jewish, Muslim, Buddhist and Christian couples echoed these

statements. For couples who were not religious the 'clauses' of their commitment contract varied. Some couples emphasised a Siamese twin togetherness. Others inserted a rider that commitment must be balanced by 'keeping one's independent spirit alive'.

> We are committed but we don't live in each other's pockets.
> *(British lesbian woman in Intimate Commuter couple.)*

> Sure we're a unit but we're also two separate people.
> *(American heterosexual woman in Proximity Model couple.)*

Several dissatisfied couples saw lack of commitment or insufficiently *expressed* commitment as a major stumbling-block to relationship growth.

Just as the institution of coupledom itself is seen as normative and desirable, so the idea of commitment to it is viewed not merely as a goal but also as the norm for 'proper couples'.

> If you're not committed to the relationship there is no point going into it! I'm having problems because being bisexual I also have a woman lover. Committing to two of them is doing my head in!
> *(Married bisexual woman, British.)*

Those who did *not* see themselves as committed long-term or those who felt *less* committed than their partner said they 'felt guilty' or 'somehow lacking'.

This desire for commitment rests on the way the institution of coupledom, primarily heterosexual coupledom, has been set up, which asserts that coupledom is 'normal' and commitment to it imperative. By implication, choosing not to be in a couple or not to feel committed carries with it a lesser status.

DOES PROXIMITY HELP COMMITMENT?

Is commitment strengthened by living together? Proximity Model couples find it hard to accept that those who live in separate places can be 'just as committed'.

People who live separately can't be a couple in the real sense because they are never there when the other one needs them. It's the friends and family who pick up the pieces, not the so-called partner! In my view that's no partnership at all!

(*Married woman.*)

Most Intimate Commuter couples did *not* accept this common assumption that Proximity Couples are more committed. They had no problems with their own sense of commitment, but felt constantly pressured by what they saw as others' hostile attitudes.

Some Intimate Commuters were employed in different cities; a few lived separately, while one resided with dependent children from a previous relationship or cared for an elderly relative; but many Intimate Commuters had given a lot of thought to separate living arrangements. Often their choice was based on the need for space and independence. Commuting couples frequently mentioned logistical problems in arranging to see each other regularly, but few felt they would *feel* more commitment if they lived together.

Earlene, 38, and Hester, 42, a multi-racial couple from Trinidad and England, live in separate houses at opposite ends of London, Hester with her 10-year-old daughter Lizzie. They are unusual in that while they separate their private lives, their professional lives are inextricable.

Hester is a white senior executive in the advertising company where she has worked for twenty years, while Earlene who joined three years ago is considered a dynamic black radical voice:

As lovers we do our Filofax once a month and put in our dates. It's easier for Lizzie to be dropped off to school from their house, so I tend to go there. When Lizzie is at her Dad's, Hester comes to my house. I keep some of my clothes there (but Hester doesn't keep any at mine). I always leave my toothbrush and my hair products. If there's one thing about black people, we have to have our hair products!

Do they think it is harder for Intimate Commuters to establish commitment?

In Hester's world it is harder because her world tends to be more heterosexual. When those people form commitments, they get married or at least live together. So the way they see it is, if we lived together then like yeah it's real! In my world, pah! It doesn't mean anything. Apart, yeah, together, yeah, makes no difference to your commitment. What counts in my world is being seen out together, dinner, cinema, people's houses, being publicly acknowledged as a couple.

(Earlene.)

Hester, now in her first lesbian couple, after the break-up of her previous relationship with Lizzie's father, finds that living separately requires her to make positive statements about their couple in order to confirm their commitment.

Although we go in and out of who we tell about our lesbianism, I have less problem making statements around this relationship than I did when I was with Lizzie's father. But I *do* have to make them. I have to say *we* are going on holiday together, *we* share a life, whereas the friends who live together don't have to make those statements.

WHAT DO COUPLES FEEL AFTER THEY MAKE A STATEMENT?

After making a commitment, most couples expressed positive views. Those under 35 made remarkably similar assertions:

Relief, that's what happens! As soon as I told my boyfriend that I'd make that marriage commitment, I knew I was secure, unavailable to other people. No more taking risks. No more looking about, wondering, hoping, will the next one turn out to be the one? No more 'Will he? Won't he?'

(Janie, 27, British partner to Jonnie, 29, British.)

Being committed to a partner gives you immediate benefits. You always have an escort and somebody to share your life with. I have a high-pressured marketing job. That's where my head is.

If you're in a committed relationship you can both get on with
your careers and feel safe at home. I'd not been in a couple for
eight years, so I'd forgotten how nice it is to have somebody
involved with all the areas of your life including your work.
(Susanna, 33, British, newsreader; engaged to Ivan, 35,
pilot, New Yorker.)

Commitment to us means we call long-distance all the time. I
wanna know how she managed on air. Make it regular she says.
That way she loses the heebies. When I can tune in, you bet it's a
thrill. When she calls she wants to know everything about the
last flight, who the change-over guys were, the politics on the
ground. The way she cares, I tell you, it comes through the
airwaves!
(Ivan.)

You stop feeling pressured. If you're not committed there's a lot
of pressure from guys. You are made to feel your life is lonely
even if it isn't. You're made to feel you should keep looking
around for someone compatible. You want that person to
understand your work as well as understand you!
(Herb, 34, New Yorker; partner to Harry 35, New Yorker.)

The benefits of commitment sometimes sound minor, like
somebody else to do the dishes while you take out the trash; or
not having to do all the womanly things that single women
think they have to do: the make-up, the clothes, the phone calls,
the what-do-I-do-tonight?, the do-I-call-him-do-I-not? Do I want
them to know my personality all the way yet? All that STUFF!
Once you've talked about commitment, it's not even an issue
anymore. When I get home, I take my make-up off, I kick back, I
can fart! I can do whatever I want and Ricardo will love me
anyway.
(Fifi, 25-year-old American graduate student; partner of Ricardo,
24-year-old Italian-American cook.)

I am in a sense religious so I was spiritually better off. I always
had the sense that I wanted to see through a commitment to one
person. So I raced through a whole lot of boyfriends, who

weren't 'good husband material'. They were not people you could see yourself being able to cope with for a lifetime. I wanted to make a commitment to a man who was 'good husband material', someone whose bottom line is that they care about you, whom you can rely on, who is on your side. I was ready to find that kind of husband before I met Gulliver. We have been together twenty years, married nineteen. Of course I've been tempted along the way to look elsewhere but I never took up that temptation. I wouldn't want to start again. The stronger the commitment, the longer the relationship, the richer it becomes.

(*Tess, 46, Canadian lawyer; married to Gulliver, 62, sculptor, British born, Canadian citizen.*)

WHAT MAKES COMMITMENT EASIER TO KEEP?

Making a positive public statement of an initial commitment and attempting to make that commitment work are two very different matters. To succeed, couples rely on certain rituals or lifestyles. Similar expectations, longer courtships and shared interests all facilitated commitment. Communication about individual needs early on was vital, more so if partners had different psychological or emotional needs or did not share value systems, politics, leisure pursuits or work.

Matching Expectations

Commitment was easier when couples talked about expectations and hopes early on:

We had to tear down the misty veil of 'falling in love' in order to accept the real people, US, lurking beneath the image.

Some couples found honesty about their 'rock-bottom selves' difficult which is a predictable finding. One American study showed that even 21 months into a relationship around 20 per cent of couples were still hiding things which they believed spoilt their image.[1] Couples learned the hard way that far from being erotic icons or romantic partners from the pages of a glossy magazine, they were merely two flawed struggling humans attempting to maintain a relationship.

How then to maintain a commitment that survives ups and downs? This study bears out research which reveals that courtships of at least two years give couples greater chances of long-term commitment. Couples who maintained long-term commitments were those who had discovered and accepted what they were being asked for.

Commitment works most successfully as a two-stage process. The first stage is for partners to ask themselves what they feel is most important in a relationship. Is it sexual faithfulness? Is it time to talk? Is it ensuring there is enough physical and emotional space to meet one's own needs? It could be finding someone who is a good financial provider, or who agrees with your wish to share your incomes. Some partners need a lover or spouse who will understand and accept their least endearing characteristics, whilst others, vulnerable to criticism, may need constant cherishing.

Only after analysis and recognition of one's own basic needs is it possible to see if the other person can answer them.

The second stage is to establish the other person's fundamental emotional requirements, then to decide honestly whether you can meet them.

Couples who had this clear understanding but were ready to adapt to change found commitment easier than those who projected their own emotional patterns on to partners or assumed without checking that they shared core values.

COMMITMENT SCENE: MATCHING EXPECTATIONS: LOUISE AND ROBERT

Louise and Robert found commitment easy because at the start of their partnership their expectations matched up:

> We met on my 17th birthday. We married in 1962 when I was 18 and he was 23. I went straight from home to marriage. I was glad because I had incredibly strict conventional parents. My home wasn't happy or free, it was uptight. My father had died when I was three, my mother remarried this strict man. Her main interest was that my brother and I should be grateful to

this kind man for taking on somebody else's family. Therefore we shouldn't be a nuisance. Nobody hugged, it just wasn't done. I wanted a free happy relationship with lots of cuddles and loving, things we didn't do naturally. I wanted to feel important. I think Robert and I were very lucky in that we were both looking for the same thing. He too needed lots of loving. I think we got enough stability in the beginning to give us a good foundation for when we evolved.

(Louise.)

In Robert's family also there was little affection:

Mine was an unfulfilling sort of family. Neither parent was good with children. My father was preoccupied starting up a business. My mother was controlling. She would threaten to kill herself if you didn't behave. My father became ill with arthritis. I was told if I was bad he would have to come after me and would hurt himself! So you had to be good. It was like Louise and I found each other as a life raft.

(Robert.)

Robert felt that their childhoods offered them matching scripts for life:

We both had low self-esteem so we wanted to build each other up. Right from the start Louise reinforced me. I think Louise came from a sort of script of: 'Who do you think you are? Don't get out of your station.' I came from a script about: 'Be good to Mother and Father or you won't get anywhere.' Very powerful stuff, very disabling. We wanted to become freer and let our children grow up as free spirits. We talked about it a lot.

Their commitment strengthened when they continued to talk about individually changing needs as their relationship developed:

At the start we always wanted to be physically close. Thirty-five years later we are still very cuddly even though sex varies from time to time, but we have always slept naked in each other's arms. We have closeness with our two sons too. I've always enjoyed cuddles and kisses with the boys. Robert and I were lucky because we evolved together.

This couple's commitment was very firmly rooted in matching expectations which held until a major change (analysed in Chapter 5) occurred in Robert's life, which meant that his personal evolution streaked ahead of Louise's.

Not all couples are as fortunate as Louise and Robert. Take the cases of Sue and Stella and Gaye and Ricky.

Sue described herself as 'having been single far too long, having taken lonely holidays abroad for years'. She felt strongly that all leisure time should be spent together. Stella, also formerly single for ten years, who had good friends with whom she took vacations, assumed she would have some holidays with Sue but also some time away with other friends.

They suffered a shock when they discovered these basic assumptions were dissimilar. After a short stressful period of sulks and silence, having a reasonable level of communication they compromised by sharing their 'main' vacation but having a few days alone or with others. But each said tension would have been averted had they been open about their needs earlier.

Gaye, who cleaned café tables and made breakfasts from 6 a.m., ten hours a week, which allowed her to look after their two toddlers most of the time, felt that regular child-free times to talk through confrontational issues was important. Ricky, who worked full-time and travelled abroad, adopted a head-in-the-sand approach.

A key danger zone was Gaye's desire to take time away from the children in order to study and retrain for a better job. This could have involved Ricky reducing his work hours or the couple finding extra money for outside help. By using his absences and long work hours as a reason for 'not wanting to talk about anything heavy', the issue got shelved. Frustration went underground, anger slowly built up.

This fundamental difference of how to manage conflict, as well as the underlying social problem of women's relationship to mothering and the market place, led to unresolved tension. Several times during the interviews the possibility of 'breaking-up' was mooted.

In both cases there had been no discussion of essential differences of outlook before they undertook a commitment to live together.

COMMITMENT SCENE: NON-MATCHING EXPECTATIONS: DAVE AND BARBARA
Dave and Barbara discovered far too late, with horror, that there were fundamental values that they did not share.

During their first eighteen months of cohabitation, both were in full employment:

> It was a great time, we shared everything, talk about our jobs, housework, shopping, we enjoyed going to the supermarket together.
>
> *(Barbara.)*

> My work as a salesman wasn't too stressful when we lived together. Barbara and I left our offices at the same time so we often met and did the shopping. I tried to help out at home too. It felt a bit like kids playing house! But really I was bent on getting promotion and we both wanted children. We didn't talk much about future plans.
>
> *(Dave.)*

When Barbara became pregnant, they decided to make what they described as a 'proper commitment' and get married:

> I assumed that after we married we would continue to share all the household tasks. With me pregnant there would be much more to do. Obviously I assumed we would divide up the child care equally.
>
> *(Barbara.)*

Barbara did not talk about her assumptions to Dave; nor were they obvious to him:

> I liked the idea of Barbara being my 'new wife!' I assumed she

would want to look after the child as much as possible. Her thing, you know! Of course I intended to help out whenever I could. But I was now in line for promotion.

Dave did not check out these assumptions with Barbara. He was promoted, the baby was born, he began to work longer hours. He further assumed (without discussion) that 'now things had become difficult Barbara would consider going part-time.' He said: 'Obviously that would give her more time for the child and the house.'

None of his assumptions was obvious to Barbara. None of them pleased her. The marital commitment into which they had so breezily entered suffered bad knocks as they recognised that their individual expectations were not being met.

For two years resentment and rows escalated. The situation was partially aided by Barbara's mother agreeing to do more of the child care, but neither of them felt happy about it. Barbara saw a counsellor who suggested they made huge efforts to communicate their deepest feelings. Neither wanted to break up, so with difficulty they effected some compromises.

Dave changed his work status and hours and joined the company's flexi-time system which enabled him to do considerably more child care. Barbara reduced her work hours to four days a week which relieved her mother of a full day's child-care chores, but they agreed that on that day the husband would vacuum and do the ironing.

One facet of coupledom which this story – like that of Ricky and Gaye – illustrates is the fundamental fact that despite new public policy schemes to offer women flexible working hours, crêches and day nurseries, in the private world it is still assumed by both sexes that women, not men, will take the lion's share of child care.[2] Surveys in the 1990s show that in two-thirds of households where both partners work women take the major share of all chores; women in full-time jobs have an average of ten hours less leisure time per week than men, but when not working women spend that leisure time doing household tasks.[3]

Since the mid-1980s the number of women in the labour force has increased by one million. Each year that number grows! But women spend on average 34 hours per week shopping, cooking and cleaning, whilst men put in only 13 hours![4]

Dave was typical in believing that even today his role was to 'help out' rather than to take an equal share. He was statistically unusual in accepting flexi-time offered by his company, for as Melissa Benn points out, though theoretically many companies today offer family-friendly policies which include flexi-time, part-time working, term-time working, job shares, career breaks or adoptive leave, in practice it is mainly women who take them up. In the late 1990s, society still not merely accepts but also con-firms that a woman's place is to take the largest role in parenthood, whilst being stridently pressured to join the market place.[5] For couples with children, this can become a central issue affecting their commitment.

Early discussion of differing outlooks on critical issues before commitment can go a long way towards ensuring that it will be maintained. Discussion allows each person to participate in deciding whether compromise is possible or whether a partner's needs could be met by someone else. If the relationship is sound, one partner can rely on close family or friends for support in areas lacking in the other partner without harming the relation-ship. Deciding to compromise is harder but, as we see in Chapter 6, with enough good will on both sides, many couples manage effectively to clear the way for commitment.

Similar Interests

In theory it may seem like a breath of freedom if one partner watches a football match with football-addicted cronies twice a week, or sails a boat with a group of sailing friends every week-end, leaving the other partner who cares nothing for football or sailing to enjoy time on their own or with friends. However in many couples, where both partners work full-time and the week-end is the sole occasion for leisure spent together or for family outings, these unshared exclusive hobbies can become a source of irritation.

This study included couples where one partner became actively hostile towards an interest passionately held by the other.

COMMITMENT SCENE: HATE YOUR HOBBY: DERMOT AND MAXINE

At the start of their relationship Dermot, who belonged to the Young Conservatives, went regularly to meetings and drew his friends from amongst their ranks. Maxine initially held no particular political beliefs and would spend her leisure hours shopping with girl-friends or visiting her mother and sister. When Dermot entered politics professionally, Maxine felt insecure: 'I needed to know more about what was going on. I was fearful of being excluded.'

She and her sister enrolled in a local politics evening class. Maxine found this so enthralling that she decided to take an Open University degree in politics.

> That I had the brain to do it at all staggered Dermot. But that I found myself becoming a staunch Labour supporter absolutely appalled him! We began to argue – and I mean argue, not simply discuss. I began to resent the leisure hours he spent away from me with those awful Conservative blokes. How could he be the person I loved but hold those dreadful views, mix with those frightful people? He wanted to get married, but I worried about marrying someone with diametrically opposed views on important subjects like health and education. If we had kids he might want them to go to private schools!

> I felt she no longer understood me. She had become jumped-up, taken on strange ideas. I wanted to marry her, but I needed the right kind of wife.

Dermot and Maxine did not resolve their political differences. Maxine's uncertainties about marriage, Dermot's feeling that he needed a 'particular kind of wife' finally led them to split up.

Many narratives offered to me by couples showed that commitment tends to become easier if at least the problem of widely divergent values or interests is aired early on. Research shows, and this study confirms, that although opposites like Dermot and Maxine initially attract, those couples often do not stay the course. Men and women want partners who will reinforce their view of the world.[6]

COMMITMENT SCENE: SHARED INTERESTS: MAURICE AND DOLLY
Maurice is a tall imposing 76-year-old, with an air of Hollywood power. A former motion picture executive, he now teaches screen-writing at a Los Angeles college. A man used to doing business in public places, he insisted on having his first interview in a restaurant before he taught his class. Waiters hovered round his chair while he proudly discussed the amount he and Dolly had shared for half a century. He glowed every time he mentioned Dolly, a former Hollywood screen-writer, who now lectures in film-writing at the same college.

At 75, Dolly has sleek salt-and-pepper hair, unusual in a dyed-hair city, is fit, zesty, and acts twenty years younger than her age, with a warm bubbly manner. She talks constantly about their matching interests and the ways in which their committed marriage has nurtured her.

Maurice, as enthusiastic about her achievements as about his own, describes their relationship as one of 'total commitment for 54 years'. Over and over again he stressed that this was primarily due to common interests, similar work and shared goals:

> Hollywood doesn't have the reputation for being supportive for long-term relationships so we're unique in that way. I think in life opposites do NOT attract! I think LIKE attracts! If you have the same ideological point of view, the same principles, you're going to get along better. Both being in the same business, we had a kind of shorthand.

Dolly, for whom being a professional working woman – rare in her era – was crucial, also adheres to this view.

> One of the best aspects of our marriage is that we have been able to understand each other's needs professionally. If one person is terribly creative and the other person isn't, that can itself cause conflict. In our cases we have both been creative, we admire each other's creativity, we have given each other the space to do things we want to do and to understand time considerations.

We work very differently, he is more impulsive, quicker-
minded, a faster thinker, I am more of a perfectionist. Maurice
has to recognise, he *does* recognise that I am slower, need more
time. Part of our commitment is learning these things.

Their relationship, which started on a blind date when Dolly
was 20 and Maurice 21, was firmly founded in shared culture:

I had an inkling it would be like that from our first date. We
went to a concert, found we both loved music. The concert
tickets were 50 cents! The cheapest date you could possibly get!
We enjoyed the music, the talk, it grew from there. We enjoy the
same things, we even respond to people the same way. We set
out to build a long-lasting relationship.

(Dolly.)

The idea that a relationship should be 'for ever' was part of
their childhood environment:

We come from the same racial background, our values arise out
of very similar experiences.

(Maurice.)

We were both raised in New York. He was raised in a much
poorer family than I was, mine had middle-class values. For
my mother he was really too poor! I was raised to marry a rich
Jewish doctor! But class was not that significant. You see we
are both Jewish, brought up with Jewish values, Jewish
attitudes, Jewish food! This is a cultural thing where both
families valued similar things like book learning, a good
education, and being caring people. Maurice is very kind and I
know he appreciates the kind of caring I give him and the
children.

(Dolly.)

Dolly's caring was stretched to its limit during a critical illness:

We had a major crisis. Maurice had to have heart surgery. The
only admonition he gave me was not to cry. It was very

frightening but I found I really wanted to take care of him. More recently I had an operation; then of course I wanted to be taken care of. I got the same treatment back except I'm more competent than he is. He doesn't cook! I needed somebody to cook for me. Those qualities have to do with the give and take of people understanding each other's strengths.

The couple saw their commitment grounded in family life. The fact that their core values and upbringing are remarkably similar, rooted in artistic and educational ideas, meant they had identical attitudes towards the upbringing of children:

When we raised children we had few differences. Were there any differences at all? We always appeared as a sort of 'one'. We read. So the children all read. So they see us reading, so they read. Dolly and I would discuss everything! We would have discussions at dinner. With the children that was always the place we would gather. I had a job which could hold me up till 7.30 some nights but they waited till I got home to eat, then we would have big discussions, religion, politics. The kids will hear a discussion about something intellectual or political and they'll react to that. Dolly and I shared those things, then the children shared so that helped our commitment.

(Maurice.)

Dolly sees *her* commitment based on accommodation and understanding the other person's expectations:

It isn't easy to live up to everybody's expectations or for them to live up to yours. One learns to accommodate. It is hard work to tell the truth. You are always adjusting. Either you accommodate being alone or you're accommodating living with somebody, it is a series of healthy exchanges. A big part of our commitment has been our children and I've always found a way to accommodate them and Maurice. He could work while they had the hi-fi on (that dates me!) but I locked myself in a room to work. But I always had jobs I could do at home, or I'd work when they were in school or in bed. Most of life is a question of accommodation. The key to my personality is that I'm a good accommodator. I won't do something unprincipled or unethical, but if it is a question of making things easier for people I will accommodate them.

The couple have an insider's perspective on what happens to those without shared interests:

> I don't even know how people who are opposites can be married! I don't know what they talk about. I saw an example of that in my son and his wife. She was an archaeologist, he was a screen-writer. They never had anything in common. They liked each other. But they always talked past each other.
>
> *(Maurice.)*

> They did not have a great marriage. It wasn't an evil, ugly marriage, but it wasn't a good relationship by MY standards. She HATED the movie business and that was his work. She hated people in the movie business. He was uninterested in her archaeological work. Even when they took a vacation it became an issue because they really preferred different types of vacations.
>
> *(Dolly.)*

Has Dolly's and Maurice's commitment to each other's company lessened with the unfolding years?

> We still have similar ideology, similar philosophy, we *like* each other more!
>
> *(Maurice.)*

> I've reached an age when many people I know are widowed. For me a major advantage of being in this couple is not having to worry about loneliness, which isn't to say I don't like to be alone because I do. But there are many, many benefits of a partnership with another human being where you respond so similarly to so many things, good and bad. I don't care about its sexuality . . . it has to do with two people having some kind of commitment to each other.
>
> *(Dolly.)*

Their joint conscious effort to become what Dolly terms 'well adjusted' appears to have done away with rows.

> We have had very little anger between us. We accept each other, we are both pragmatic, we deal with what we have to deal with, or it may be that there are not many things we really disagree about. I find things in Maurice that I lack in myself, he finds things in me that he lacks, it is a complementary relationship. I never worried at any stage that the relationship might not last.

> There might be a momentary irritation. I'm more impulsive so I'll blow my top, so I probably irritate her more than she irritates me. Maybe the fact that she's more methodical I find trying, but never enough to say 'to hell with it'. Whatever slight anger comes up, it is never a continuing thing. I have never worried it won't last! I can't imagine that!

WHAT STRENGTHENS COMMITMENT?

When couples commit there is often an unofficial agenda about what that commitment entails. Often commitment resides in religion, or in rituals such as marriage, gay marriage, or commitment ceremonies. It may be strengthened by sharing a name (mainly couples over 50), bearing or rearing children, spoken or assumed agreements about sexual fidelity, a conscious decision to build up a long-term relationship, buying or renting a house together, or a belief in equality (of striking importance to couples under 35).

If these are part of the couple's 'commitment contract', then any deviation such as a sudden affair or a decision to live separately may be seen as betrayal, and the commitment lessens. Outside influences over which the couple have little or no control, such as racism or homophobia, may also weaken commitment.

Marriage/Cohabitation/Divorce

Despite the fact that singlehood is on the increase[7] it still has a lower status than marriage, largely because of the cultural notion that marriage carries the highest level of commitment of any paired relationship. For heterosexual partners, marriage has long had a deep symbolic significance which even today – when marriage in practice is less frequent and occurs later – is intricately entwined to the idea of a binding union.

During the last fifty years, motivated by the Women's Movement, there has been a significant change in emphasis within marriages from traditional 'marriage as an institution' to modern 'marriage as a relationship'. Whereas formerly the focus was on marriage roles and structure, today it is on the quality of the partnership. Couples who wed in the 1950s or earlier recall less freedom of choice in marriage partners, greater emphasis on economic aspects and property, stronger links to relatives, less emphasis on mutual sexuality, a sharp division of labour between men and women, and substantial inequality between spouses.

By contrast those who wed today are offered greater freedom of choice in partners (anything from singles clubs to computer dating), a marriage that can be separated from family obligations, an ideal of companionship, a positive emphasis on both partners' sexual activity, a strong focus on emotional and interpersonal fulfilment, and at least lip-service to equality in marriage.

Such changes have made inevitable differences to the goal of commitment. Whereas couples formerly committed themselves to a division of roles or a series of duties, today they commit themselves to an ideology of shared companionship.

Qualitative research evidence suggests that women have moved towards the 'relationship model' of marriage at greater speed than men. Wives' views of 'committed togetherness' focus on shared interests, time alone with the husband, talking about feelings, sharing chores. Husbands' views on 'committed togetherness' still stress their role as worker/breadwinner, and de-emphasise talking and sharing tasks. Problems ensue where one partner (usually female) began their commitment to a traditional marriage plan but now wishes to change the commitment aims to fit the contemporary viewpoint.

The BSA survey of 1986 found that the qualities couples identified as 'very important' in contemporary marital commitment were faithfulness, mutual respect, understanding and tolerance.[8] Ten years later I too found 'no sexual betrayals', 'mutual respect', 'flexibility' and 'having an understanding partner' consistently mentioned as necessary for marital commitment.

Older marriages: 'Marriage as an institution': Early conditioning
For some women now over 50, early conditioning meant that commitment had be founded in marriage. Dolly, Marie-Claire and Lillian are typical:

> I have never once thought I should love to be single. I think that has to do with my early conditioning. You know you are supposed to be married and I always accepted that. I knew I was supposed to have children. I never questioned it. I never even thought about whether I would make a good mother. I think women do that now, which is good.
>
> *(Dolly.)*

> When I was growing up there was pressure on me to get married largely because my father was rather Victorian. I grew up with the feeling that women really had to get married. This was a woman's one aim in life. I didn't think about it; I took it for granted that it had to be! I never contemplated not getting married. It seemed a natural thing to do.
>
> *(Lillian, 73, British, married three times;*
> *second marriage lasted 34 years.)*

Marie-Claire has known Rupert (55, Professor of Astronomy at a Canadian university) for 40 years, and has been married for 32. As a girl from a traditional French family, she – like the American Dolly and the English Lillian – was brought up to believe that only one kind of couple was possible:

> It would have to have been a married couple. Very traditional. In France as soon as you reach a certain age there was social pressure to get into a married situation, not a couple situation. I could not have wanted to be a single person all those years ago because it would have been difficult to be single in that society where I was encouraged to be a married couple.

Some older couples, where the wife is not in paid employment, retain certain characteristics of the traditional '*marriage as an institution*' model. In Louise and Robert's case, this suits Robert better than it does his wife.

COMMITMENT SCENE: MARRIAGE AS AN INSTITUTION: LOUISE AND ROBERT
Louise, a 53-year-old British housewife, feels that in some sense, the fact that she has never held a paid job makes her 35-year marriage to Robert, a senior lecturer, less contemporary in its feel than marriages of their two-income friends:

> The only job I had before we married was working on a farm, cycling three miles and then milking cows at 6 a.m. I couldn't continue with that once the children came along. But I was blissfully happy. I have some strong feminist friends who have not approved. They think I've let the side down. Women who strongly resent being dependent on men can be cruel. I've felt angry because I have never passed judgement on women who preferred to go to work and farm out their children. I resent that they should do that to me!

To outsiders Louise's unemployed status has produced a relationship of financial inequity, but the couple see it as a shared commitment:

> Robert has always brought the money in but I have always looked after it! He hated anything to do with it. Early on when we were practically on the breadline I knew what went in and out. I handled our one account, he would ask me if there was anything in it! I used to get very, very guilty about not making any contribution. I have had big hang-ups about that . . . we know so many couples with two incomes. That felt more equal! But Robert said I did more than my share by looking after him and the money. It's never been a problem for him. It has been a problem for me.

Robert admits that Louise's lack of independence, though hard for her, has been of benefit to him:

> She is a wonderful companion. I guess it would have been

harder if she had had a job. She cooks and she looks after me and she dresses me when I am wearing the wrong things to go to this job or that job. She is there! The benefits of our long-term relationship are a great deal of support, dependency, an acceptable level of dependency. I suppose really just to know she is there. I mean I do have a problem with dependency, but if I'm honest with myself I like it that she is there when I get home.

Louise's version? 'Robert is utterly distraught if I am not there when he gets home!'

More recently Louise has wondered about switching roles:

We have incredibly traditional roles. Robert hates cooking and can't cook and that annoys me. I think it would be nice if he could, because I get bored to tears doing it every day. I've become a person who gets cleaning windows done by swearing I'm bad at it, so he does it. Fairly manipulative I suppose.

Had Robert ever encouraged Louise to take up a career or earn money?

I've never discouraged her. I mean I haven't. I've never wanted to put pressure on her to do that because the deal we had originally was that she didn't want to work and I was happy that she shouldn't. So we have always had a one-income relationship. On the other hand, if she wanted to do something I'm sure I would have encouraged her. It would have helped her once the two kids were gone. I think there was a gap there that she is relatively OK about but at times is a pain for her.

Couples change during a long marriage; they develop new needs. Perhaps this had happened?

I accept that. Maybe I didn't take all the changes into account. I'd have liked her to have had something to make her feel she was doing something worthwhile. To a certain extent her voluntary charity work fills that gap but I think it could have been something a bit more, yeah.

*

Robert and Louise are a genuinely affectionate long-term couple. Robert was aware of the inequity in their relationship, but he saw it more in terms of the fact that he 'didn't mind' about a single income or the fact that meaningful work might have been useful for Louise's personal growth after the children had left home. He did not appear to consider that such a change might have enhanced their relationship. Rather he saw the immediate cherishing benefits to him of the status quo.

At the start of a relationship, couples like Robert and Louise agree on how much financial or domestic equality they want, and for several years the relationship proceeds on those agreed lines. But when changes occur (the chance to gain qualifications, the loss of one person's income, the departure of children from the home), this can affect the partners' original ideas on equality. If those changes are not coped with satisfactorily, their commitment will be damaged. In Chapter 5 we see what happens to Robert and Louise when such a change occurs.

Some partners previously in an unequal marriage may make efforts to change this when they change partners. If they also change from a heterosexual partnership to a gay one, the move to equality may be easier.

COMMITMENT SCENE: NEW EQUALITY: BLAKE AND JIMMY

Blake, a 46-year-old Canadian, was happily married to a female student financially dependent upon him for 14 years. He nursed Jen through cancer until she died. Today he is determined on equality in his new partnership with Jimmy, a 40-year-old lawyer:

> Sometimes I wished Jen would work so I didn't have to. I want a relationship where we treat each other as equals, I don't want to get into 'this is my part, that's your part'. The reality is Jimmy and I probably won't put all our money together but what we share in common I want to make sure it's as equals. The fact we are two men working, both have incomes, is different from when I lived with my student wife.

Blake sees shared roles as significant as two incomes:

I don't want to get into a nursemaid position again. I wanted to do it for my wife. If Jimmy got AIDS or cancer I'd do it again willingly. But I don't want to caretake an emotional person or be the only one who has to do the nursing.

The 1990s: Younger marriages: 'Marriage as a relationship': Changing commitment

To many younger couples today the notion of equality under-pins commitment. Expectations held by women under 35 are fiercer, more optimistic, more uncompromising than they have ever been before. Young economically independent women are aware of their own value. They match this with keen self-asser-tion. As Natasha Walter says: 'Women are becoming more and more powerful . . . I don't believe that young women feel them-selves to be victims; rather the contrary.'[9]

They are no longer prepared to put up with marital commit-ment on male terms. They want a 'domestic democracy'.[10] They want husbands who will discuss emotional issues. When men find this impossible, young women refuse to put up with them. This has led to a series of marital breakdowns.

In December 1997, a major conference in London called 'The Chaos of Love' pivoted on these radical changes in women's public position and personal demands. The conference, arranged by the British marriage and partnership organisation One Plus One – worried by the 1997 *Social Focus on Families* report from the Office for National Statistics – looked at moves towards more egalitarian relationships. Researchers believe that women's changing ambitions and men's resistance lie behind figures show-ing that numbers marrying have halved, numbers divorcing trebled, the proportion of children born outside wedlock quadru-pled. One Plus One's director emphasised:

Women are no longer prepared to put up with relationships that don't take account of their feelings and needs and their way of wanting to address issues in the relationship . . . There is a kind of chaos in relationships and a feeling that we have to find new ways of halting the number of them breaking down.[11]

Professor John Gottman from Washington University, Seattle,

who has spent two decades studying married couples, argued that commitment was maintained where men 'had the emotional intelligence to accept the influence of wives'.[12]

He believes that the childhood socialisation of many men, which leads them to suppress their feelings, often makes them withdraw just at the point when their wives wish to make that emotional connection. The male model of traditional marriage, to which for centuries women have had to accommodate themselves, has suited men well. Modern marriage, according to the young wives interviewed, is about talking, listening, bringing in equal incomes, sharing chores. Traditionally men have not defined 'love' in that way. Researchers feel it is time for husbands to make compromises if commitment symbolised by marriage is not to be lost.

Cohabitation: Marital alternative or pre-marital phenomenon?
In both the USA and Northern Europe cohabitation rates have risen significantly. Typically, cohabitation shares many characteristics with marriage: shared residence, sexual intimacy (or the appearance of) and an economic union of the one-pot/two-pot/three-pot style. One major difference between cohabitation and marriage is that living together does *not* assume a necessary commitment to permanence at the start of a relationship. Though some cohabitees see their lifestyle as a 'trial marriage', others see it 'for the moment only'.

Although many couples choose it as an alternative to marriage, in many countries cohabitation is predominantly a premarital phenomenon. In Sweden over 90 per cent of first marriages involved couples who had already lived together. In Britain nearly 60 per cent of women who married in the late 1980s and early 1990s had lived with their partner first. Marriage and partnership research organisations estimate that by the year 2000 80 per cent of couples who marry will have first cohabited.[13] Most cohabitation in Britain is short-term and occurs among those who have never been married. However, divorced and separated people are more likely to cohabit than bachelors and spinsters.[14] Amongst couples I interviewed, highly qualified professional women chose cohabitation in order to wield economic control or to maintain a sense of autonomy.

The average duration of cohabitation before marriage is two years, but many cohabiting couples break up rather than marry. Those who do change from living together to marriage often do so when the woman becomes pregnant or soon afterwards. The myth behind this change is that what is perceived as a 'more binding commitment' will achieve a democratic revolution over child care and housework. Under-35s in this study consistently reported that this change was 'to ensure that BOTH parents contributed time with the children and shared the tasks equally'.

Writer Melissa Benn, who became a mother at 37 while happily cohabiting, in consequence decided to write an excellent book which meticulously investigates what has improved or worsened in mothers' lives.[15] She strongly believes that cohabitation 'does not merely represent a *lack* of something, moral fibre, commitment to children'[16] but can offer appropriate commitment on its own terms. She decided *not* to get married in order to improve her child-care chances:

> My own ethical system involves concepts of high fidelity and long-term loyalty. However, as I believe that these qualities are more likely to come from genuine reciprocity between partners and parents, friends, and eventually parents and children, I look to an ethically informed love to do the job rather than rules and contracts. This is why, despite twelve years of happy union (with the same person!) I am, have not been, and never will be a married woman.[17]

In the face of positive statistical shifts towards cohabitation, these 'rules and contracts' however form part of the cultural myth that marriage is a more committed situation than cohabitation, to which cohabiting couples are extremely sensitive. Several couples who felt firm in their choice of living together reported that friends 'saw us as less committed than the married ones'. It was as if cohabitees lived one experience in which they knew themselves to be satisfied but played it out against a more committed marital fantasy experience in their heads (and the heads of their peers), culled from traditional wedding symbolism in magazines, television, radio and films. Britain for example has one of the highest marriage rates in Europe, exceeded only by Portugal.[18]

Getting there: Commitment to wed

In the past when marriage was 'taken for granted', perceived as 'natural', few inducements were needed to encourage that commitment. But how do people arrive at it today?

Dr Catherine Surra, an American academic interested in how couples reach the marital stage of commitment, identified two types of relationship.[19] The first, a 'relationship-driven commitment', progressed in an orderly fashion; each partner reported regular increases in commitment. The second, an 'event-driven commitment', had commitment soaring one month, plummeting the next, rather like a roller-coaster ride.[20] I have traced similar patterns. Long-established couples like British pair Louise and Robert (Chapters 3, 5), the Americans Maurice and Dolly, (Chapters 3, 7) and French- and English-speaking Canadians Marie-Claire and Rupert (Chapters 3, 4) – all of whom were relationship-driven – saw a steady committed future as their goal and worked purposefully towards that, reporting new evidence of commitment every time we spoke.

In contrast Rose, white, British, and Bobby, black, American (Chapters 1, 6) and Americans Fifi and Ricardo (Chapters 3, 6), who reacted strongly to events in their lives, found their commitment decreased by a bad row (of which they had plenty) or increased if they had spent a happy vacation together, or had enthusiastically attended a friend's wedding. Relationship-driven couples expressed more positive feelings of commitment than couples influenced by events.

When commitment ends in divorce

Marriages do not of course ensure a lasting commitment, as we know from the significant increase in divorce rates in the USA and Europe. Almost one in three marriages will end in divorce if current trends continue.[21] European statistics show divorce had risen from 11 per cent of marriages in 1970 to 30 per cent in 1995. In Belgium and Sweden, the most divorce-prone countries, more than half their marriages fatally falter. Finland, England and Wales, and Denmark now have rates of 49, 45 and 41 per cent.[22]

UK figures for the 1990s show on average 300,000 adults and 150,000 children involved in divorce proceedings *each* year. In 1994[23] there were 158,000 divorces in England and Wales.[24] Peaks for jettisoning marital commitment nationally are at one year and twenty years of marriage.

British research shows that couples who cohabited before marriage had higher divorce rates than those who had not first cohabited.[25] Those who choose to live together often have different values from those who would never choose cohabitation. They are less religious, more liberal about the idea of divorce, and appear to have a lesser commitment to marital permanence.

In relationships heading for divorce, commitment runs out quickly. In the USA, where almost half of all marriages currently end in divorce, recent statistics confirm that the majority of those marriages last less than seven years. Long-lasting commitment is not unconnected with the age at which a couple marry and, as we have seen, how long they spend courting. Between 1980 and 1990, when the divorce rate was rising rapidly in the USA, most of those who divorced were relatively young when they married: 21 per cent were aged under 20, 37.1 per cent 20–24, 18.7 per cent 25–29, and 9.3 per cent 30–34 years of age.[26] This means that nearly 90 per cent were the optimistic under-35-year-olds.[27]

USA divorce figures have risen so rapidly that the right-wing press and the right-wing Christian Coalition, have campaigned for stricter divorce laws to return the country to a situation similar to 40 years ago when a commitment to marriage in most cases meant commitment for life.

One state, Louisiana, positive about that kind of marital commitment, has a new law which came into force in August 1997. It established two tiers of marriage: the Covenant Marriage, intended to be permanent, and the impermanent Non-Covenant Marriage.

Louisiana has allowed divorce by consent after six months. The covenant scheme means that if marriages fail, non-covenanters can divorce with minimum restrictions. However, couples who have chosen a permanent covenanted marriage cannot procure a 'no fault' divorce. One partner must prove a spouse's adultery, or desertion, or either spouse can sue for sexual or physical violence which carries with it a severe prison sentence. The other alternative for covenanters is two years' separation. Pro-covenanters feel strongly that tougher divorce laws would be better than the emotional consequences for children of broken homes.

Although Louisiana is the first state to experiment with this Covenant Divorce, other Southern states at least may follow her example.[28]

Reasons for failing commitment (which eventually leads to divorce) most often cited by couples I interviewed were firstly, communication problems; secondly, the partner's 'inability to compromise over long working hours', 'insufficient help with children', 'different attitudes to money', 'sexual anxiety' or 'sexual betrayal'.

Remarriage

In Great Britain the number of second (and subsequent) marriages has risen from 36,000 in 1971 to 60,000 in 1991. Though previously remarriage usually followed premature death, today it is more likely to follow divorce. In the last two decades, remarriages of divorced people have more than doubled.[29] More divorced men than women remarry. Less restricted in their choice of partners, they often marry younger women. This says more about their greater social freedom and the fact that they rarely have custody of their children than it says about whether or not it is easier for a man to commit to a woman who is not their peer.

That over one-third[30] of current British marriages are remarriages for one partner or both is another indication that men and women buy into the notion of marriage as an indicator of 'real commitment'. That was how Charles, 72, saw it on his third marriage.

COMMITMENT SCENE: REMARRIAGE: CHARLES AND LILLIAN

Charles's first marriage ended in 'a bitter divorce' which prevented him seeing his children. His second, where they lived together for twenty years but only married during the last five, ended in his wife's death.

Grief-stricken for five years after her death, he coped:

I wrote books, shopped, cleaned the house, I even learned to cook at a lunch club. I have little boxes which tell whether I need to buy this or that ingredient for Cod Carousel! Lillian, my third wife, says she only married me for my cheesecake! There were periods when I felt very lonely. I missed the commitment, the companionship. I wasn't looking for someone . . . in *that* sense. I was looking for companionship. I rather preferred women to men, found them easier to get on with, more sympathetic, less boring. Men talk about all those gadgets whereas women are more people. This is not a popular view, I'd be drummed out of the masculine establishment if you quote me on that!

Lillian's second marriage, which she endured for 34 years, was so intolerable that she left her husband for four years, but eventually a sense of duty forced her back:

We had nothing in common, no children, no sex life, no touching. But we were committed to a marriage so I supported him publicly. The world thought he was happily married to a smart intelligent woman. The only escape for me was dreaming of independence. I used to dream about being able to speak Italian. So gradually I took all my exams, passed, then told my husband, 'I'm off!' Of course we didn't get divorced but I shot off to Italy.

Her second husband pursued her:

He never left me alone. Once he persuaded me to go to a ball. We were each dancing with somebody else, when he ruptured his achilles tendon! I nursed him through that, then I didn't have the nerve to say, 'All right, I'm off again!'

Lillian returned to what she saw as an endless commitment, and for a further 12 years they endured a marriage of 'separate lives', her depression somewhat lifted by her work as a translator. Then illness struck again: 'He had cancer. A messy business. I nursed him for a year through till he died.'

Charles, in search of companions, joined a national arts group which took cultural visits abroad: 'It was the sort of place you meet interesting females. I liked the women I met.'

One of those women was Lillian, who had been on her own for eight years:

> I liked her sense of humour. She appreciated my jokes and I appreciated hers. She was on my wave-length, or I on hers.

They met in London, he stayed at her house in the country, a friendship evolved on trips abroad. The fact that they were forced to pay single supplements annoyed them both.

> Not only did one pay a supplement but one always had the room at the back over the garage rather than the room at the front overlooking a delightful bridge. So for that reason I thought it would be nice with a companion around, as long as there was no groping, as long as one didn't bump into each other going through the bathroom door, it would be worth £30 a night! If you've got a friendly companion what's wrong with that?
>
> *(Charles.)*

> He often said, 'It's not fair that people on their own have to pay supplements.' I thought, is he suggesting that we spend holidays together? I thought what the heck! I'm sufficiently old, it doesn't matter if he says 'No'! So one night over dinner I said, 'I have a proposition to put to you. What about us sharing a room for holidays so that we get a decent one?' He said, 'Excellent idea! But there couldn't be any sex because I still feel I'm married to Greer.' I said, 'That's fine! I'm not looking for that. It would just be nice to talk about things.' So that Christmas we did it. It felt marvellous. There wasn't one thing he did that annoyed me. He said the same. Sharing a room was wonderful . . . with twin beds, quite close . . . Not one thing went wrong. I wasn't self-conscious or shy. Not at all.
>
> *(Lillian.)*

How did the situation change from friendship into committed partnership?

Are we talking sex now? Well, I went with Lillian to Vienna on the arrangement that there should be no groping, no sex, just sharing the room, having friendly chats. It worked absolutely splendidly for two whole days! I was very pleased about this. This is splendid! I've got everything now! A very cheap holiday, a friendly companion, what more could I want? But because I am hard of hearing – and of course we had separate beds – I was lying on mine and I moved closer to her bed so I could hear what she was saying. Suddenly we found ourselves in an embrace so there you are . . . that was the beginning!

(Charles.)

It only lasted two days! How we bridged the gap between platonic and non-platonic was very funny! The beds were very close. One afternoon we decided to take a rest; we lay on our twin beds diagonally. He kept moving nearer and nearer until he bridged the gap between the two beds and just kept on talking. Eventually he was so close I thought, 'Well, what do I do with you? I've either got to get up and walk away or I've got to put my arm round you.' So I put my arm round his shoulder. It just went on from there.

(Lillian.)

Initially they decided to live together rather than remarry:

We decided not to get married because of our age . . . not really worth it.

(Lillian.)

We weren't young any more. Marriage didn't seem to offer us anything we didn't have already. We lasted two years. Then one day I was lying in bed and I thought this is a loving relationship, it would be rather nice to go ahead, to do it. So I suddenly said, 'When are we going to get married?'

(Charles.)

When he proposed I said, 'I thought we weren't getting married.' But I felt it was fine. It gave us something extra. I felt more relaxed. Before we were married, living in two places, I was never quite sure whether he really wanted me to come back up to the flat or not. I didn't like to take it for granted that he'd want me to come. He seemed to want to be with me all the time but he was still a free agent. So I thought yes, being married would be lovely. It's turned out beautiful. Incredible.

Their third marriage is warm and harmonious. They value what it has brought them:

I love him more than this idea of falling in love. It's a real bond.

(Lillian.)

I would say I love Lillian but it's not so much falling in love, it is more important than that. It is suddenly appreciating and recognising you have something here of great value. It is like a precious Ming vase. You have to insure it.

(Charles.)

The couple spend time cherishing each other:

She's very caring. For example aromatherapy. She massages my feet at night and I go straight off to sleep. We have an extraordinarily happy sex life and we hold hands and hug and touch constantly. She is a fabulous fantastic creature.

(Charles.)

Those years of being with someone who never touched me, I knew how much I needed warmth and intimacy but I put it aside. Now I look forward to going to bed every night, it's quite ridiculous! Quite lovely! I feel I've gone back fifty years! Everything that happened in my previous marriages I hope never happens in this one. We are so close it would break my heart to be separate again.

(Lillian.)

Like the Americans Dolly and Maurice, their commitment to this third marriage is rooted in remarkably similar tastes:

Professionally, being a translator she is closer to me than my previous wives. We like ballet, opera, music, literature. I will watch the kind of television she is interested in. Recently, coming back from the country, Lillian said, 'Shall I drop you off at the house to have a rest?' I said, 'No! I'd like to come with you to the shops. Keep my eye on you!' We're not living in each other's pockets, but we are terribly close. We trot about together! You've got it! Trot about!

(Charles.)

Neither of them asks questions about previous marriages. Both feel free to talk if they wish.

What does the decision to remarry give Lillian and Charles?

It is the sharing of a name for one thing. Marriage gives us the stamp of permanence. I know we felt it was permanent anyway, but this seemed nice.

(Charles.)

What have they learnt from their third marriage?

I've learnt flexibility. Tolerance. I'm infinitely more tolerant.

(Lillian.)

What you learn from marrying more than once is to think like a couple, not to think like an individual, and that's not easy to do, but unless you do it the relationship is in jeopardy.

(Charles.)

Canadian novelist Carol Shields offers an insight into a remarriage, which, like Charles' and Lillian's, occurs at a late age when individuals have to relearn to 'think like a couple'.

Charleen Forrest, heroine of Shields' novel *The Box Garden*, a poetic but incompetent woman for whom kindness is a sort of hobby, lost the remnants of her courage when her husband deserted her. Charleen's widowed mother, Mrs McNinn – frugal, anxious, judgemental, a bundle of negative echoes – displays in Charleen's view some enviable bravery when at the age of 70, with her left breast surgically removed to stop her cancer spreading, her linoleum newly waxed, her toast cut into economic triangles, she tells Charleen she is about to remarry. Charleen and her eccentric biographer sister Judith are astounded. Their timid implacable mother in her uniform of indistinguishable print house-dresses, who was married to their resigned, laconic and ill-paid father for thirty years, should now be respectably entering her twelfth year of widowhood. Instead, she is about to embark on a marital adventure with an almost total stranger. This alien creature, this 72-year-old proposed groom, met Mrs McNinn at the cancer clinic where he was on his third operation, heavily punctuated by severe asthma attacks. Is it that they have illness in common, Charleen and Judith wonder? Is that what this remarriage is about? Despite the incredulity of her two daughters, a modest (in the daughters' view frighteningly frugal) wedding takes place in the thin shrunken suburban bungalow where the girls grew up, with its 40-watt bulbs, fringed candlewick bedspreads, brown Formica table and well-scoured sink. The minister arrives, Mrs McNinn changes out of her floral house dress.

Judith and Charleen recognise that for reasons they cannot understand, Louis – the elderly asthmatic groom – actually loves and respects the parent they fear and have never been able to please.

The ceremony is performed in front of the artificial fireplace. Charleen watches her mother closely:

> My mother's voice repeating the vows is exceptionally matter-of-fact. She might be reading a recipe for roast beef hash, and curiously enough, I find her lack of dramatic emphasis reassuring and even admirable.

Louis, however, seems overcome. He dabs his eyes as he chokes on the words. Charleen wonders if this is the result of asthma rather than emotion. Charleen can see only their backs but as she observes them, suddenly for her and for Judith their mother's remarriage falls into place. It carries with it its own internal sense.

> They look rather fragile as people always do from the rear; it is after all the classic posture of retreat. Retreat from what? Age, illness, loneliness? Louis slips a ring on my mother's finger and they stand for a moment with hands joined. Two is a good number, I think, and like a chant it blocks out the remainder of

the service for me. Two is better than ten; two is better than a hundred; two is better than six; when all is said, two is better than one; when all's said, two is a good number.[31]

Throughout this study, interviewees see two as better than one. Two as a good number. People do get married and remarried, because becoming a two and staying a two is seen as a measure of commitment. In the case of remarriage of divorced people, however, that commitment may not stay the course. Recent British research shows that remarriages involving divorcees are more likely to break down than those where neither partner has been divorced.[32] I discovered from formerly divorced couples who experienced problems over commitment that unresolved issues from their previous marriages affected their current relationship. If they could not resolve those problems this time, they too would be heading for the courts.

Gay marriage and commitment ceremonies
On both sides of the Atlantic, lesbian and gay marriage is no longer seen as impossible, though in some quarters it is still viewed on a scale from 'improper' through 'outrageous' to 'sick'.

In some countries, including Scandinavia and the Netherlands, it is already a reality. In others it is now on the political agenda. The fundamental argument advanced by supporters is rooted in the idea that as the right to marry and form families is enshrined in the UN Declaration of Human Rights, the present prohibition denies people's human rights by discriminating on grounds of gender or sex.

However, for some lesbian feminists, who have long seen marriage as a significant cause of women's oppression, the idea of lesbian marriage presents a political problem.

Many lesbian feminists live purposefully 'alternative' lives (often incorporating ex-lovers or children of ex-lovers into family arrangements). Because such lifestyles challenge heterosexual marriage, some feminists feel that a legally imitative gay marital partnership could undermine any such challenge.

Celia Kitzinger, an English lesbian psychologist, robustly declared that marriage would have to change if lesbians tried it out. 'You can't simply add lesbians to institutions developed by heterosexuals and leave the institutions unchanged.'[33]

As marriage is bound up with social arrangements such as taxation, welfare benefits, immigration and inheritance, gay marriage as a 'right' could have far-reaching consequences for gay people specifically, but also for all social communities. In Sweden, for example, partners in a couple or members of a household are treated independently in relation to welfare benefits, whilst all cohabiting couples whether married or not, same-sex or opposite-sex, have the same legal rights and responsibilities.[34] In the USA by contrast, where free social benefits are almost negligible, health insurance – given to married couples on one partner's insurance – becomes a significant issue for gay couples.

In Britain the gay marriage debate has been slow to get off the ground. Parts of the Conservative Party, determined to uphold the family, still feel that support for committed gay relationships would undermine it. Some politicians like Norman Tebbitt, who jibe at 'those who advocate sodomite marriage',[35] are shocked at the idea of *both* gay partners who adopt a child being recognised as legal parents. Nevertheless, there are changes in the wind.

Marriage has long been a key to entry to Britain for a partner who is not British, but impossible for some couples either because they could not divorce or because they were same-sex. Recent changes in British immigration laws mean that over 200 gay men and lesbians are among the 35,000 unmarried couples now allowed to apply for foreign-born partners to settle in Britain. The Immigration Minister Mike O'Brien said that although the Government recognised the 'special position of marriage', the change was proposed because the policy 'we inherited for common law and same-sex couples was unsustainable and may have breached human rights laws.'[36]

A gay couple, however, must offer greater proof of commitment than a heterosexual couple. The old common-law policy requires relationships to be two years old. The new policy insists that a gay couple must show they have been living together for four years and intend to continue to live together permanently. Once in Britain, they will have to show that the relationship has subsisted for a further year before being granted settlement.

An even greater revolution regarding the rights of same-sex couples is taking place through Britain's sex discrimination laws.

Cherie Booth Q.C. has won an initial but considerable victory for her client, 29-year-old rail worker Lisa Grant, whose employers South West Trains refused to give her live-in lover Jill Percey the travel concessions available for railway workers' wives, husbands and common-law opposite-sex spouses. Michael Elmer, the Advocate-General of the European Court of Justice in Luxembourg, declared it was a breach of EU law for an employer to deny equal rights to lesbians (or male homosexuals). If the full European Court upholds his 'non-binding' opinion, it could firstly be a legal milestone for Europe's 35 million lesbians and gay men (and their employers), and secondly a substantial symbolic validation for gay partnerships and 'marriages'. If it is overturned, it is obvious that future cases will continue to keep this issue in the public eye.

In the USA, same-sex marriages have been permitted in the state of Hawaii but as other states have not yet recognised this, it has become a key constitutional issue. In advance of fully legalised gay marriage, many American gay male Christian couples have taken advantage of Gay Christian marriage ceremonies.

COMMITMENT SCENE: GAY MARRIAGE: JACK AND ROY
Jack, 36, a Los Angeles computer analyst and his partner Roy, 34, a sales director, both of them blond-haired and radiating contentment as they nostalgically flick through the video of their wedding:

> Did I always want to be in a couple? Be really committed? Yeah, this is something I've been dreaming about since I was a little kid.
>
> *(Jack.)*

After dating Roy for two years, Jack, a member of the Los Angeles Gay Christian community, suggested that they marry on Labor Day weekend. Roy's and Jack's primary motive in marrying was a shared spiritual belief:

> My definition of a couple is commitment so obviously that meant a wedding. I have always wanted to commit to someone who will share the good times and who will walk beside me during the difficult times. That is when we are vulnerable, open

and connect at a very deep level. When that spirituality is tapped it is unlike any other experience.

(Roy.)

The most important element is our shared spirituality, our shared Christian faith. As a small boy I wanted a big wedding – I'm 36 and now I've had it! I have traded the level of excitement that goes with being single and dating – I'm more the homebody; I like the sort of emotional security of a couple.

(Jack.)

Roy offered to run the video of their wedding: 'I'd like you to see it. Other than the fact it was two men getting married, it was traditional!'

Unlike traditional weddings between heterosexual couples, it raised significant issues about which some members of their families felt sufficiently comfortable to attend, but which so outraged other family members that they boycotted the event:

The only member of Jack's family who came was a cousin! Jack's grandmother intended to come but fell and broke her leg. The rest didn't come.

(Roy.)

Jack's father, who hasn't spoken to him for seven years, cannot accept his sexual orientation or his HIV status, let alone the fact that he got married:

He's an alcoholic who lambasted me the first time I went for an HIV test. 'What are you doing having sex with other men? Don't you know it's unnatural? Don't you know it's against everything God intended?' Knowing my father had cheated on my mother, I thought this is a man who is really screwed up! So no, he didn't come to the wedding. My Mom is a conservative fundamentalist Christian who loves me very much but can't deal spiritually or emotionally with homosexuality. So she didn't come. But now that my sister has vanished off the face of the earth and Mom has discovered I'm HIV positive, she's afraid she'll lose me too. So she has said: 'I don't like this relationship. I don't like your orientation, but as things haven't changed after ten years you're not planning on changing them! So I'll pray that you'll work yourself through this thing, meanwhile I want to get to know you again as a person. Maybe we can find some middle ground to have a relationship.'

Roy's family more actively supported the marriage:

My family are small-town people whose bottom line is that they want me to be happy but they don't get this! They don't understand! But they *were* at the wedding. Since then I've taken Jack home and they've decided to accept and support us.

Bearing or rearing children

Two predominant ideas attached to the institution of coupledom are firstly that coupledom is the most secure situation in which to have children, a notion which persists despite a weight of evidence which shows that children are often unsafe; and secondly that children offer strong evidence of a couple's commitment. In the words of one interviewee: 'Proper couples have children!'

Three couples of different ages and social classes illustrate this.

COMMITMENT SCENE: PROPER COUPLES HAVE CHILDREN: SADIE AND SAM

Sadie and Sam, in their early 70s and married for 50 years, wrangle good-naturedly over whether they had intended to become a couple or to have children.

'Intended? Of course you intended! I was your intended. I wanted a white wedding so you wanted a white wedding. I wanted children so you wanted children,' Sadie says firmly.

'I don't think I intended . . . as a boy . . . I was only a boy, who knows what my intentions were?' remarks Sam wonderingly.

'*I* know!' Sadie is as always decisive:

So who doesn't want to be in a couple? So what else is there? We should be so lucky. We had nookie, so later we had no nookie, he's not always so good at nookie, runs out of steam, know what I mean? But single we weren't. It's not a 'mitzvah' being single. And children, of course we wanted children, I wanted children so you wanted children, so a couple we had to be.

None of our children thank God have been single. But grandchildren we have. Four of them barmitzvahed already. A lot of 'nachas' from our children . . . And fights. All couples have fights. Fights you expect. It's normal for a marriage.[37]

Sam interrupts her flow. 'Sadie, we haven't had a fight in 15 years. We *like* each other.'

Sadie winks at me. 'So now he tells me! It takes 50 years of marriage and six grandchildren and now a reporter on couples for him to tell me he likes me!'

COMMITMENT SCENE: BABIES STRENGTHEN RELATIONSHIPS: LESLEY AND PAUL

Lesley, mother of three children, a supermarket assistant in her 40s, has been with Paul, an electrician, for 11 years and married to him for 7. She saw her upbringing as responsible for her strongly child-centred views on commitment:

> I was brought up to think I should be in a couple. My parents believed that once you got to a certain age it was time you were courting and eventually became a couple. Then you get your children. But not necessarily to get married.

Lesley's three daughters, all under 8, hang on her and vie for attention. She hugs the eldest.

> Even when I got into my 'situation' with Rosalie, I didn't feel any pressure from my parents to get married. But yes, I did do it but it was my choice. We got a home of our own, plus expecting a new baby, it all just fell into place. We became more of . . . well we were a couple before but we became more of . . . well, it did just make the relationship stronger, living together, the baby and all that.

Paul also sees children as the core of their commitment:

> At first we had an on/off relationship. I was a taxi-driver. She was young, very naïve. Everybody warned her about taxi-drivers. I played the field considerably. I decided I was getting in too fast, too quick, with Lesley . . . it started as a laugh, going

out together, then it just sort of baled on from there, it was getting too deep, too quick, so I just broke it off. Then we sort of bumped into each other and sort of carried on. We always decided should Lesley fall pregnant we would get married, make it a real commitment. In a sense it was the best thing that could happen, we would still be just going out now, but she fell pregnant so we got married. It's a family trait, her grandmother was pregnant with her mother, and her mother was pregnant with Lesley before she got married.

Rooted in bearing offspring, their commitment maintains a high focus on family life.

Our children are what count. If Lesley makes a decision I will back her up, same with me. If I make a decision she will back me up. Goes for our children, goes for us. We're committed because we've got our children, so you can tell easy we're a couple.

COMMITMENT SCENE: PROPERLY COMMITTED COUPLES LIKE STEPKIDS: EVIE AND MATT

Evie is a housewife who works part-time as a care assistant, has two sons from a previous marriage and a new husband Matt, currently unemployed.

I was brought up to look up to other people that were couples, not exactly to look down on those who weren't in them, but it was definitely normal to be in a one-to-one relationship. Mum and Dad made me think a couple was a good thing. It was stable. You were properly committed. They said . . . and I think . . . you do seem more of a couple if you've got children.

Evie, who met Matt through a newspaper dating agency, was determined that her date should like children.

In the advert I put about my hair, colour of my eyes, my likes and dislikes, and of course my children. I like music and stuff, and art, so he could take an interest or not but he had to be a family man. I got thirty-three replies but when I went out with

Matt I thought, 'Yes!' We clicked because he had that soft sort of warm personality, a caring nature, I reckoned he would care about my kids. When he said he'd move across the country to be with me and he'd take on my two kids that was it, really. That convinced me to marry him.

Evie's previous marriage had made her wary of men who felt that children infringed their freedom:

My ex, their Dad, well we grew apart not together . . . after the children . . . not attached, he wanted flashy things, spending money on them, wanting more money for himself. I wanted us to be a family, that's where the money should go. My ex wanted his own independence again, not being trapped with children. I would ask myself did he want to have those children? Yes, and in a way no. I don't think he did but I did. That's why I want me and Matt to be a proper couple, him being good with the children.

Like Lesley, Evie's focus on children as the pivot of a 'proper committed couple' stems from her own early years when, in her case, each parent had tried to control her:

I didn't have a normal childhood, I was always relying on other people's stories, I was sent away from home till I was seventeen, really insecure and unsafe. I was piggy in the middle, I was. Two people always controlling me without me having my own life. I didn't have the actual love and devotion of parents you should have if your parents are in a proper couple.

The importance of children as integral to self-definitions of 'committed couples' can be highlighted when the children leave home. Take the case of Jane. After more than 20 years' marriage to Claud when her two sons have left home she suddenly decides to divorce her husband. Jane speaks to an understanding woman friend: 'I've become a convenient single woman . . . I'm starting to find myself seated next to the divorced man at dinner parties.' Gallantly Jane asserts her new enjoyment in living alone: 'I watch films on TV in the middle of the day, and go to exhibitions, and get in touch with people I'd let slip. I can be untidy.' Her gallantry falters. 'The house feels large, though. For ages there have been four of us living there, and now there's just me.'[38]

For two decades Jane had rushed out to her full-time job as an architect, raced home to her rackety house full of clutter and clamour, loud boys and a husband yelling for her attention. She had washed and ironed, ferried the boys to and fro, given dinner parties for her colleagues and Claud's colleagues. She had played Monopoly which bored her, chess at which she always lost, overseen rages and sulks, acne and schoolwork, suffered loud records from another planet, sat evening after evening with Claud in the sudden quiet before supper, sipping gin and tonic, going to bed every night knowing that her days were so full there seemed no room left for her. She dreamt of not being in a couple, being alone with a book by the fire.

> Now there was no loud music, no sulks, no calls from a phone box at one a.m. . . . . They'd all gone, and I could do whatever I chose: my time was my own, which was what I had always missed. But I didn't know how to deal with time, so I filled it up.[39]

Jane is a fictional heroine in the novel *The Memory Game*, written under the name of Nicci French by Nicci Gerrard and Sean French who are interviewed in Chapter 9. Though Jane is a fictional woman, her difficulty with singlehood is founded in hard fact. Like many women in this study, Jane never quite sees singlehood as 'natural', after life in a couple with children, noise, constant chores, clamour and demands.

If – as Sadie and Sam, Evie and Matt, Lesley and Paul believe – commitment is intricately linked to coupledom perceived as 'natural', with offspring that strengthen that commitment, then it becomes hard for child-free couples to see their situation as valid. Couples who did not want or could not have children felt that *in the eyes of the world* their commitment was weakened.

COMMITMENT SCENE: COUPLES WITHOUT CHILDREN: LEONORA AND PHIL
Leonora, a retired nurse, is 49; Phil, also retired, is 69. They have been married 26 years.

I never wanted children. As a teenager I knew I wouldn't want them. But it wasn't heard of to be in a couple and not to want children. I had friends who thought I should see a psychiatrist about it! So when I proposed to Leonora on a foggy night, alongside the Thames, I felt I'd better say it out loud. I didn't know what she would think. She did not say much. We discussed it roughly. I wasn't quite sure what she thought for, though I was 40, she was only 20 and had grown up in a family amongst a lot of old people. She seemed to accept it. I felt if we weren't having children it wasn't fair for her to have to pump her body up with pills, so not long afterwards I had a vasectomy so that settled it. I don't like children that much. W.C Fields, the comedian, said to an American, 'How do you like children?' The American said, 'Parboiled!' That's my view exactly, but it isn't a popular one!

(Phil.)

Leonora held similar views, but had more difficulty matching them to outside expectations.

When I was born my mother had a stroke, so she always used to say, 'Never have children. Look what happened to me!' It made me feel terrible. The stroke affected her right side and her speech; she was young, in her thirties, permanently disabled. She never adjusted psychologically. I felt rejected. On the one hand she talked about how much she loved children, wanted children, implying she wanted me to have them and give her grandchildren. On the other hand she talked of the horror of giving birth, of having me. My rational self knew that was crazy, but emotionally I grew scared of having a child. I thought of the pain. I thought I might have a stroke. So I needed to find someone who didn't want children. But it didn't seem likely.

At 20, Leonora met Phil who was 20 years her senior:

We discussed it almost immediately, certainly before we got married. Phil said, 'I don't want children.' I felt some relief. But I was still stuck with that received wisdom that says everybody wants children, you are not properly committed if you don't have children or at least don't want children. When I was young I really did think that was the case. Lots of people are pressured into having children that they don't want. They feel they have to bite the bullet.

Do they have any regrets or feel in any way less committed?

I've had no regrets. People probably think us strange. We have four cats as our children, we haven't been tied down, Leonora is all my life, I've devoted my life to her, really I have. I'm quite happy to spend my life looking after her, doing things for her, sharing things with her. I couldn't feel more committed.

(Phil.)

With her fears of compulsory pregnancy allayed, ironically when she was in her thirties she felt able to change her mind:

The pressure was off me. I knew we were committed to each other without children, so I was able to think well maybe it would be nice. But Phil didn't want children. We had already decided he would have a vasectomy so off he went. Today I enjoy my friends' children. I don't look back and wish for something different. If you want to do something, do it. No point in saying 'if only'. We have been able to focus more on each other, pay more attention, listen to each other. We haven't had to deal with the fraught lives of those with small kids, but we have had to deal with people's attitude towards us as a childless couple.

For Leonora and Phil, the decision to remain childless in no way impeded their commitment to the relationship.

Sometimes commitment to a childless partnership is aided by the fact that one of them has borne if not reared a child. Such is the case of Tabitha and Gerry.

COMMITMENT SCENE: THE LOST CHILD: TABITHA AND GERRY

Gerry is 15 years older than me, married twice before, with three children, two of whom he was left to bring up. Did a good job!

There have been several points when feeling so committed to
our relationship I have thought about children, but he'd done
his bit. I helped bring up his two eldest, but I was never that
comfortable with the stepmother role. There were times when
the eldest would refer to me as his mother. It was odd – perhaps
because I had been a mother though Gerry's children never
knew that. Most people don't know. I had a baby, had it adopted
after birth. It didn't make a difference to how I felt about Gerry's
children, but it did make a difference to how I felt about being
childless in our relationship. I remember an astrologer telling
me that I wouldn't have the desire for another child. But after I
had this child I had the desire to replace – to make up for what I
had done.

(*Tabitha.*)

Tabitha, now 46, a Canadian doctor with a thriving practice,
talked about what she had done 26 years ago:

I was just 20. I was a student, just starting on my life. My
mother wanted me to have an abortion. To my mother that
made sense. I was unmarried. I told her I didn't want to marry
the baby's father. That would really be a big mistake! Friends
said just get married, then get divorced. I couldn't do that. I
had the sense even at 20 that I must pursue just one
relationship, be committed to one person. That baby's father
wouldn't do.

Though Tabitha sounds resolute now, at the time she was in
turmoil:

I felt this, I felt that. I went through conflict, I went through
denial, I had opportunities but I did not pursue them. I guess I
could not have an abortion.

At one stage Tabitha considered bringing up the child:

I did contemplate keeping the child, but I did not want to
contemplate my life as a welfare mother. I had him adopted (I
do know the baby was my son) because I didn't want to bring

up a child without a father, without a family. At that time, not being able to offer two parents and at least a comfortable lifestyle didn't seem right. I thought I was doing the best for the child.

Does Tabitha still think that?

Today I am not sure. I think I was more capable than I realised. Sure I have regrets. I've thought of making inquiries. I have registered, so that he could probably find me. But in Canada it's a matching system, and I have no faith that it works. Under Ontario law there's a registry of birth parents, and children looking for birth parents can also register, and if both do there could possibly be a match, but I'm told it takes years before they even realise they have a match. I know private investigators who could do it . . . but it is not something I have done. I would be very interested to know where he is on the one hand, but on the other hand I'd be afraid that he might have had a dreadful time. Then how would I feel?

How has this experience affected her 20 years' marriage to Gerry?

For some years after, I had a desire to make up for what I had done. But as I got older I don't think it was part of my life-plan. It may in fact have been part of my life-plan to have a child early on to fulfil a kind of biological need. I enjoyed being pregnant very much. I do feel there is a drive. It wasn't much but that drive was satisfied. We discussed having a baby in the early part of our relationship, then put it aside. Then when I was in my very late thirties, I decided to become a doctor. The decision to become a doctor was also a decision not to have a child. If I am honest about my natural disposition, it's not maternal. I am serving people as a doctor, through my mind rather than through my nurturing qualities. I think if I had not had that child, I would not have been satisfied with a relationship with Gerry without a child. I would not have felt so committed in a childless relationship, but as it is that commitment is there.

Sexual fidelity

Sexual fidelity is often an unwritten rule in a commitment contract, particularly inside a marriage.

In 1993 the proportion of British people who thought extra-
marital affairs were 'always or almost always wrong' was 83 per
cent.[40] Virtually the same proportion (86 per cent) rated being
faithful as critical to a committed marriage. Furthermore, 97 per
cent considered consistent unfaithfulness a sufficient reason for
divorce.[41]

There is a strange discrepancy however between these attitudes and people's behaviour. Adultery is common: surveys
show between a quarter and three-quarters of married couples
have affairs. However it is hard to find reliable estimates of the
frequency of adultery, because people responding to question-
naires or interviews either exaggerate their experience of adultery
or do not report it if they feel guilty for not having 'confessed' to
their partners. In this study, two women who had not told their
male partners about their affairs told me in confidence. One
woman anxiously asked me not to interview her male partner in
case the subject of 'sexual adventures' came up and my expression 'gave it away'. The other woman panicked, then revealed the
affairs to her partner:

> Fifi told me about those 'episodes' after she'd done that first
> interview. Deceit makes me very angry. To find out she'd been
> unfaithful! I was furious! But I've come to understand some of
> the reasons for it. Our relationship wasn't balanced at that point,
> she was looking somewhere else for what she couldn't find in
> me. Since she's now been honest I can't say I forgive her, but it is
> in the past and I can't hold it against her.
>
> *(Ricardo.)*

How would Ricardo have reacted if she had told him at the
time?

> Part of me says I'd rather have known so I could have made
> changes more quickly. But if she had told me, I don't know if
> we'd have worked anything out because my anger would have
> been so overwhelming.

Sexual infidelity was seen by couples I spoke to as 'highly reasonable' grounds for divorce if married, or splitting up if partnered. This bore out national attitudes. In 1990, 38 per cent of all British divorces were granted on the grounds of adultery. Men are much more likely than women to petition for divorce on grounds of their wives' adultery.[42] If you take that together with the fact that men commit adultery more often than women, in terms of marital commitment men see wives' fidelity as imperative and are less inclined to forgive lapses, whereas wives wish their husbands would be faithful but their commitment seems able to encompass affairs.

The Sexual Lifestyles Survey found that 4.5 per cent of married men and 1.9 per cent of married women reported having had more than one sexual partner in the last year.[43] The figures for cohabiting couples were higher: 15.3 per cent for men and 8.2 per cent for women. Although these figures may merely reflect the fact that more cohabitees have been together for shorter durations (so the other partner mentioned just might be their previous lover, rather than a sign of infidelity) a stronger possibility is that the figures symbolise the less committed nature of cohabitation.

Are there types of men who are more likely to be unfaithful? Are there jobs which encourage or allow for infidelity? Some surprising figures showed that professional well-educated married men like lawyers, doctors, dentists and architects are more likely to be sexually unfaithful than working- or lower-middle-class men. There is however no evidence that it is the same for women (whether married or partnered), nor for cohabiting couples. It may be that married male professionals' careers bring them into more contact with women and thus give them more opportunity for adultery. Not all professionals enjoy affairs. Charles, a retired professional, speaks up:

> Of course there are opportunities, but I certainly did not do that in my second marriage. And now? If I was in a hotel bedroom at the other end of the world, if some slinky woman came in and said, 'Have you got some coffee?' I might just be tempted, but in practical terms I would not ever go down that path. I wouldn't have to. Lillian and I have a marvellous sexual relationship.

It is unimaginable that he would be unfaithful to me. I imagine he feels the same about me. It is totally unimaginable that I should ever be unfaithful. I don't need it. An affair would be a bore and a nuisance.

(Lillian.)

The idea that sex, like cement, can act as a binding material at the start of a relationship, was voiced by many couples:

Sex can be a bonding, a way into intimacy. In the past when I have really wanted somebody passionately, I have felt bound to them emotionally in my head.

(Oriel, partner to Daphne, British.)

In our terms being faithful is part of that commitment. Once I decided I was going to be faithful to Gulliver, I had that emotional sexual direction sorted out, so then I could get on with my work. I'm a lawyer and that has to be taken seriously.

(Tess.)

Sometimes sexual fidelity which begins as a bonding material can become restrictive:

With Bob sexual fidelity is a big criteria of our couple. He told me 'If you ever have another sexual relationship, that's the end.' It makes me feel trapped because, though I do want to be in this relationship with him, I can never predict what will happen. It makes me feel controlled and constrained. I don't actually want to sleep with another man, though some days I feel that could be liberating. I just want to be released from this embargo. If I was, I am sure my commitment would be just as strong.

(Janice, 25, British; school-teacher partner to Bob, 40, British, engineer.)

Bob, however, finds Janice's uneasy acceptance of sexual faithfulness reassuring.

I've been married twice before. I'm a lot older than Janice. Both wives went off with other fellas; one told me, one didn't. We had

never made a pact, not either time. Well, you don't get bitten a
third time. So when Janice and I decided to move in together I
just laid it on the line. Let's get this straight. I want to be with
you. Not marriage, I wouldn't risk that again. But being
together in the same house, having kids if you want them. We
love each other. All I ask is that you say straight up that you
wouldn't sleep with anyone else. I couldn't bear that hurt again.
She's a wonderful girl, my Janice. She understood at once. She
has said a couple of times about it feeling a bit strict, but I know
she understands what real commitment is about.

Male couples have traditionally incorporated changing sexual
partnerships into their couple ideology but this too is changing.
When the two men do not hold the same view it can cause conflict:

Roy and I have different ideas about what it means to be in a
couple. I am very much a one-man man. I have one partner and
I have no interest in pursuing anyone outside that parameter.
Roy feels comfortable with me as his primary; but on a physical
standpoint he feels if there is someone he loves a great deal and
wants to get to an intimacy level greater than he can do by
talking through emotions, then physical intimacy is the only
way he has of getting to that deeper level. That's an area I feel I
don't want to share with anyone else. I don't want to stifle his
growth as an individual by not allowing this part of who he is to
manifest itself, but I need to be true to my own values.

(Jack.)

Roy's view was different:

If he were unfaithful in that he had a sexual experience with
someone else, that would not be that much of a jolt. If it were an
isolated incident, if he told me within a reasonable time and
didn't try to hide anything or cover up . . . that would not be a
huge deal. The greatest issue as far as unfaithfulness is
concerned is the possibility of him falling in love. Him having
sex is not as important.

What makes commitment harder?

Commitment can be affected or weakened by institutionalised sexism, racism, anti-Semitism or homophobia. Any of these can have drastic negative effects on a couple's bonds. As we saw, Roy and Jack, subjected to intense homophobia, had great need of their religious community. Here I look at the effects of racism.

COMMITMENT SCENE: THE EFFECTS OF RACISM: RITA AND BRAM
Rita, 37, a white TV researcher, and Bram, 44, a black British social worker, partners for 19 years, married for 9, have faced several crucial changes in their long relationship. The first change occurred when Rita, then 18 – who had only been involved in short relationships with white boy-friends, sanctioned by her family – met Bram at a disco:

> He picked me up. We fell passionately in love. There were no black kids at my school, so he was the first black person that I knew, that I'd ever talked to.

Rita was totally unprepared for the violent racism she, and subsequently Bram too, encountered from her white family:

> I'd arranged to go to Israel for six months. But we kept in touch by letter, then Bram came out to Greece to meet me and on our return to Britain we decided to live together. My best friend said: 'Oh my God, what's your Dad going to say?' I told my Mum Bram was black and she said: 'Your father will have a heart attack.' Ultimately I took Bram home. It was like a scene from a soap! I brought him in and my mother looked, then she turned as white as a sheet. Then she disappeared quickly upstairs. Dad was sitting in his vest. Looking back, I suppose if I'd wanted to be diplomatic I should have managed it better, because Dad felt embarrassed in his vest in front of the telly. He tried polite conversation for under two minutes, then he too went upstairs. They had the most mighty row upstairs which we could hear quite clearly. I was so upset I had to get Bram to leave. I said goodbye, then had a terrible row with Dad. He said

I was not supposed to bring a coon into his house. Not ever.

Rita's reaction was initially one of bewilderment, subsequently of resignation and anger:

> I felt shocked and surprised, because it's at that point that you realise there are things about your parents you don't like. I realised they were seriously different from what I'd thought. Dad used to tell racist jokes and I used to say: 'You don't mean that.' He'd laugh. Now with insight I realise you don't tell racist jokes unless you are racist. But I didn't see it coming. I stayed uncomfortably in their house for a month, but they would not relent. I thought there might be a little friction, but I had no idea of the depth of their feelings.

Those hostile feelings towards Bram, and by extension towards Rita as his girl-friend, never changed and had implications for their partnership. The most significant was that Rita's parents never visited them.

> So Bram and I just lived our lives . . . we chose to have mixed-race friends . . . and I lost my parents. I used to pop back to see them two or three times a year. In a sense I thought it was better than Bram being expected to sit through Sunday lunch knowing that fundamentally they hated black people. We didn't bother with all that. I made my choice and then in a sense my parents were the ones who lost, but in my book that's their own fault.

Bram's initial reaction was that they should split up. He felt it was going to become 'too much hassle'. Rita, indignant, said: 'Several times, at that point, I thought we probably would split up, but we should do it in our own good time, for our reasons, not for anybody else's.'

Bram worried that Rita was young, and was only with him in order to act out a rebellion against her parents. Rita, shocked at this suggestion, considered it seriously and also analysed the extent to which she had internalised her parents' racist views.

I decided his worries were needless. I think you only do have racist feelings about groups whom you know nothing about, like I know nothing about the Japanese. He's not part of a group. He was my boy-friend. I don't see him as black, I see him as an individual. So we tried to put the issue behind us and tried to make sure it didn't affect how were with each other.

For three years Rita gallantly did without her parents' support for her choice of partner, but was consistently perturbed by it:

I kept trying to raise it but they wouldn't talk. I wanted to square it with my father before he died but when he was very ill my mother said, 'Don't do that. He won't change his mind. It will just upset him and you.' I wish eternally I had done, because I think she was wrong. She was stronger but hid behind him. I think he would have come round – what a difference it would have made to our couple.

In the event Rita said nothing. Her father died of cancer when she was only 21. Neither of them had spoken about the issue upper-most in both their minds.

During the 5 years between her father's and her mother's deaths, Rita again attempted to discuss her position in a multi-racial couple with her mother:

My mother said: 'It's no good talking. I don't like *them*. I don't even like sitting next to *them* on buses.' She was as racist as they come. Mum's boss expressed surprise that black people could even drive a car because they were the next best thing to monkeys. That was my mother's view too. She couldn't bear the thought of her daughter being with one of 'them', of people knowing that we were together. It was hopeless so I just gave up.

The effect on Rita was to isolate her from childhood and kin. She clung more closely to Bram, invested more in their life, for he had become her whole family. Bram felt they should choose care-fully which people they mixed with:

Obviously, as a black/white couple we didn't go and live in a racist area. Among the middle class, people were more hypocritical, so they didn't openly confront us – just gave us a wide berth if it mattered to them – and we chose friends who understood.

For a decade the couple lived together, electing not to get married.

I couldn't see the point of marriage. It was not something I wanted to do. My politics and feminism meant I couldn't see the point in having a ceremony. My parents' racism meant they probably wouldn't have come to a wedding.

Bram's parents had not been married and he had lived through 'the hell for black and mixed-race kids in the Sixties'. More to satisfy Bram than Rita after 10 years' cohabiting when they decided to have children they also married:

My parents were comfortably in their graves by several years. I felt if marriage means that much to Bram then fine. He was a black bastard at school, so if he said it could give kids more trouble I just had to take his word for it. So we had a lovely day. Probably the best day of my life.

How has the change from being partners to being husband and wife affected their commitment?

Marriage itself hasn't changed anything, except that Bram has this ludicrous irritation that I haven't changed my name. As a socialist and a feminist, it hadn't occurred to me that this would be a problem for him. It is the name I work under. It is part of my identity. It is who I am.

Bram, however, felt that as part of Rita's commitment to their marriage she should want to change her name. He said it had never occurred to him that she might not.

My sense of commitment is nothing to do with it. I don't see any reason to change myself fundamentally. I do think that if you saddle on somebody else's name you are saying, 'I belong to that person.'

Bram's argument is that the name is actually Rita's father's:

> There is no real answer to that because how many generations do you want to go back? This is me and I am not substantially changing myself because I am your wife! I had no idea how much this would mean to him.

In the nine years of their marriage Bram has intermittently brought up the naming issue, but Rita has resolutely refused to give way. They reached the compromise that Rita retains her maiden name but the children bear Bram's. Slowly Bram has begun to see that commitment to their couple is not negated by separate names.

Varying levels of commitment
For some couples there is constant anxiety about whether one partner is as committed as the other, or whether they feel they can commit themselves at all:

> I don't think anything lasts, not jobs, not relationships, not love. So though I know I love her now, I simply feel too cynical to tell her what she wants to hear – that I will always love her. We have lived together for two happy years, but I have been in three previous relationships that all failed. I wish I could say 'I am committed' but I can't. It is the main issue in our partnership.
> (*Genevieve, 30, British, media consultant; partner to Heather, 24, airline stewardess.*)

Levels of commitment may vary widely in partnerships. Take the case of Pete and Jeff:

> The most difficult thing is to be honest about our level of commitment. It creates tension, because it hurts Jeff to hear me say that I'm not as committed to the relationship as he is. I am definitely not dating anyone else and I wouldn't want to. So I

am committed on that front. But he sees wedding bells happening. We'll have a house. He knows where we're going to live. I don't have that. So maybe we have incorrect perceptions about the reality of the relationship. I spend all my time writing, so my goals include a lot of space. Our biggest issue is how to communicate our different level of commitment.

After four weeks he told me he was committed. Being able to be together is most important to me. I have to learn how much he needs his own space. My main hope is that we get married, have a wonderful life together for a very long time: that's my ultimate goal. When we discussed it he would always say 'if' and I would always 'when'. Now he says 'if and when', so I can see it down the future for us. At this point I think I am much more in love with Pete than he is with me. So I'm willing to wait because I love him so much – and respect him.

(Jeff.)

Couples I interviewed all articulated a central notion that commitment was normative, validated by societal approval, substantially legitimated by children, whether one's own or adopted/fostered/step- or co-parented. Commitment was seen to be potentially long-term, was endowed culturally with high value. Religion or socialisation had led most couples to believe that being unable to maintain a long-lasting relationship indicated individual failure. If the couple was heterosexual, that failure was usually thought to be a consequence of interpersonal relationship problems. If the couple was homosexual, however, outsiders often ascribed commitment failure to the partners' homosexuality. As one man put it 'people think because we are gay we flit from affair to affair.' My research, which shows to the contrary that gay men consistently establish long-term committed relationships characterised by love, support, nurturing, mutual caring and stability, bears out evidence in other recent studies of gay male couples.[44]

Falling in love is like diving into an unknown sea. One has no idea what rocks there are ahead. Commitment is a pledge to stay there as the loved one negotiates those rocks, but other tools are needed to help him or her to come safely to shore. Commitment is a strong tool for a good relationship, but by itself it is not enough. As problems occur couples have to *communicate*, and *changes* in their lives have to be accommodated by both partners. Two things then become necessary: a great deal of *cherishing* and a great many *compromises*. The next four chapters show how this works.

NOTES

1   Hester Lacey, *Independent on Sunday*, 17 August 1997; see also Dr Marilyn Tysoe, *The Good Relationship Guide*, Piatkus, London, 1995.
2   Melissa Benn in *Madonna and Child: Towards a New Politics of Motherhood*, Jonathan Cape, London 1998, illustrates this point in considerable depth, with great clarity.
3   One Plus One: The Marriage and Partnership Research Charity.
4   Ibid.
5   Benn, *Madonna and Child*, pp. 68–72.
6   Tysoe, *The Good Relationship Guide*, Piatkus, London 1995.
7   The projection in the USA for year 2010 is that nearly a quarter of the population will never marry.
8   'Changing Marriage', Information Pack, One Plus One.
9   Natasha Walter, *The New Feminism*, Little, Brown, London, 1998, p. 15.
10 Term coined by Melissa Benn.
11 Penny Mansfield, Director of One Plus One, to Angela Neustatter, *Independent on Sunday*, 23 November 1997.
12 Professor John Gottman to Angela Neustatter, ibid, 23 November 1997.
13 One Plus One.
14 One Plus One points out that the proportion of divorcees and separated people in Britain who currently cohabit is greater than the proportion of never-married people who cohabit.
15 Benn, *Madonna and Child*, Jonathan Cape, London 1998.
16 Ibid, p. 245.
17 Ibid, p. 245.
18 The marriage rate in Great Britain was nearly halved between 1971 (68.5 per thousand) and 1991 (36.3 per thousand). Marriage statistics 1991, OPCS. One Plus One Information from charity to author, 1997.

19 Dr Catherine Surra, University of Texas, USA.

20 *Independent on Sunday*, 17 August 1997.

21 Eurostat statistics. *Independent*, September 1997.

22 By contrast Italy has low figures: fewer than one in ten marriages ends in divorce.

23 Latest year for confirmed statistics.

24 *Independent on Sunday*, 24 August 1997.

25 One Plus One, article on cohabitation and relation to divorce.

26 USA Statistics. Marriages/Divorces. Chart 148, p. 105.

27 USA Statistics. No. 148, Percentage Distribution of Marriages by Age, Sex and Previous Marital Status. These USA statistics show that there is considerably less chance of marrying the older you get: e.g. 7.8 per cent were 35 years to 44 years. Only 5 per cent were 45 years to 64 years. Only 1 per cent over 65 years.

28 Mary Dejevsky, Washington, USA. Article on divorce-proof marriages, *Independent*, 13 August 1997.

29 From 15 per cent in 1971 to 34 per cent in 1991.

30 36 per cent.

31 Carol Shields, *The Box Garden*, Fourth Estate, London, 1995, p. 209.

32 One Plus One, article on remarriage and stepfamilies.

33 Celia Kitzinger quoted in 'For Better or for Worse' by Jenny Rankin in *Trouble and Strife: The Radical Feminist Magazine*, No. 34, p. 7. This article, including an examination of lesbian marriage in New Zealand, gives a very clear explication of the pros and cons.

34 Good analysis of these policies in *Trouble and Strife*, ibid.

35 Quoted by Suzanne Moore in *Independent*, 10 October 1997.

36 *Guardian*, 11 October 1997.

37 Barmitzvah: term in the Jewish religion to denote the ceremony and celebration marking the 13th birthday of a boy who then assumes his full religious obligations.
    Mitzvah: Hebrew word meaning commandment or precept, especially one found in the Bible. It is used colloquially for a good deed.
    Nachas: Yiddish word meaning a blessing, often used about children in a family.

38 Nicci French, *The Memory Game*, Heinemann, London, 1997, pp. 36, 37.

39 Ibid, pp 37, 38.

40 One Plus One, statistics on Adultery.

41 One Plus One, Report on Adultery and BSA (British Sociological Association) Report on Adultery, 1989.

42 Women more often petition on grounds of 'unreasonable behaviour'.

43 Johnson, A., Wadsworth, J., Wellings, K., Field, J., *Sexual Attitudes and Lifestyles*, Blackwell Science Ltd., Oxford, 1994.
44 The most useful is David P. McWhirter and Andrew M. Mattison, *The Male Couple: How Relationships Develop*, Prentice-Hall Inc., Englewood Cliffs, New Jersey, 1984.

CHAPTER 4

Communication

Good communication is undoubtedly the pathway to intimacy. To allow someone access to your private dreams, your hopes, your fears is to connect at a magical level. It does away with illusion, it lets in more light. Communication between partners can either enrich that partnership or damage it.

Couples interviewed understood communication to cover connections through speaking, writing, body language and sexual closeness. Their main focus however was on language, which they saw as a consistent obstacle to relationships.

Young women particularly emphasised 'talking and listening', skills which were not high on men's lists of achievements. The 'Having It All' generation of the Madonna–Thatcher era where women's goals became work, money, power, control, self-promotion, with motherhood fitted in somewhere along the line, was not prepared to be given the silent treatment. If young men couldn't or wouldn't communicate, then subversive feisty females were prepared to look elsewhere.

Jacky, a 24-year-old Afro-Caribbean woman on a London housing estate, living with two children on benefits, said:

He goes off to work mornings. It's pretty isolated on the estate. No one lets their kids out, too dangerous. Gets you down just feeding and minding them, this week the benefit's gone so we're down to tins again! When he comes back, never says a word,

and refuses to listen. I got narky. 'You can piss off!' I said last
week. 'I've got my kids and if I want another bloke who'll
fucking talk to me there's enough round here!' He shut up after
that. Knew I was serious.

Young mothers complained the most. Nor were these confined
to single parents or those on welfare. Several middle-class mothers, partnered or married, recently unemployed, reported that
men who had paid lip service to the ideal of communicating
when they were working no longer bothered. Clary, 25, gave up
her full-time post as a political researcher to care for their two
infants. Her partner Brad still works in the Civil Service:

> We used to discuss politics, films, and our relationship
> endlessly. Now he comes in when I'm feeding the little ones,
> kisses everyone, says, 'Poor soul, you do look busy', puts a few
> toys away, then pulls out his paperwork. Sometimes he does
> omelette and microwave chips, or gets a take-out, but he never
> talks to me properly. It's as if he thinks my mind has gone for
> the season! I've told him it's harming our relationship. He said,
> 'It's just fine. Stop fretting! You never used to fret. Still, I know
> how tired you get with the kids.' He meant it reassuringly but I
> didn't feel reassured. It's hard to feel as committed as before.

Hearing a similar line – 'How can I keep up this commitment
when he[1] won't talk about what matters to me?' – in other interviews, I recognised that poor communication skills dented many
couples' *Commitment*.

Communication, the second 'C' element, is also intricately
linked to the other three Cs and the Big 'I'. I noticed it was virtually impossible to cope with *Change* when a couple were unable
openly to discuss their feelings about that change. *Compromises*
were rarely reached without numerous conversations. Sometimes
talking about their deepest feelings for their partner acted as a
more profound *Cherishing* tool than a bouquet of roses, though
those were appreciated too! As for *Interdependence*, a balance was
rarely struck between keeping an independent identity and
acting jointly as a couple without discussing where those margins
were for each partner.

Acquiring the skill of what to say, how and when to say it, can bring couples closer together, but that closeness can be resisted or prevented by misuse of communication. This can operate in several ways.

CONTROL THROUGH COMMUNICATION

The Silent Treatment

People often withhold conversations to control partners. Some use silence as a defence. When distressed, they withdraw into their shells and won't utter a word. The other person is left to guess the reason. This gives the Silent One a necessary emotional distance, but it can make the silenced partner feel rejected or confused. Other people use silence as a weapon; when angry, they punish partners with a forbidding shutdown. Victims of this tactic (for it does feel like victimisation) have no redress, no way of mending the breach. This is often a pattern set within families. It happened in my own, where my mother used silences to control us all. It takes hard work firstly not to imitate such bullying methods, secondly not to perceive all silences as threatening.

Don't finish my sentence

Others control their partners by never letting them finish a sentence. Some partners on the receiving end of this weapon become assertive enough to point it out. Others may accept it as 'just what he/she is like' but underneath feel frustrated or resentful.

You're not listening! You're giving advice!

Giving unsolicited advice to someone who merely wants you to listen to their feelings can be thoroughly irritating. The effect is to cut off the opportunity for a partner to share emotions. If they want someone to help solve their problems, they will no doubt ask. If they have had a tense or troubling experience they may merely wish to exorcise it by talking. But they need a willing audience who understands their motive. They do not want communication stampeded by the wrong response. More men than women use this device, so I deal with it in detail when discussing gender communication.

POOR COMMUNICATION

Many couples who were *not* trying to control their partners nevertheless had poor communication skills. Some kept closely guarded secrets; others felt their childhoods were 'off limits' as discussion topics; a few couples acted out their deepest emotions instead of verbalising them; several felt incapable of expressing anger; many fell into the trap of second-guessing their partners' needs rather than discovering them.

KEEPING SECRETS

I was surprised by the number of couples who confessed intimate facts about personal lives, or revelations about their relationship, which they had not told their partners. Some people had withheld for five, ten or fifteen years significant emotional information about affairs, abortions, sexual abuse, fraud, illness, adopted children, violence in their family, or their sexual orientation. Many misjudgements between couples were made on the basis of insufficient information; many rows took place because one partner, knowing no better, had expectations of the other that could not be fulfilled.

Two men who were gay had married as 'a front'. They were frightened of revealing their sexual interests to their wives. However, their dislike of heterosexual sex made their love life uneasy, their secret trips to bars and cruising places added webs of deception to their marriages.

One working-class woman had given birth at 15 and had allowed her parents to bring up her child. At 25, serving in a pub, she met a man 'above my station' whom she married. She remained scared of entrusting her architect husband with the truth.

I didn't want him to know about my rough beginnings until we had children of our own. Unfortunately my innards got tangled up in that first birth, so I can't conceive again. I daren't tell him why. The situation has got worse because he despises my real son as a 'cheeky loud-mouthed brat'. He's always slagging him off, thinking he's just my badly brought-up brother! We row a lot, I'm frightened he'll leave me, but I can't tell him the truth.

Secrets like this in an intimate relationship can be dangerous. If trust is to be established, then open communication about such vulnerable areas is imperative.

ACTING OUT

Several couples who had acute anxieties about their relationship acted them out instead of voicing them. Some, who later admitted they needed to be taken care of, acted out this need through illness, depression or eating disorders. Dramatic over-use of drugs or alcohol were other ways in which partners punished themselves and each other, while simultaneously fending off help or closeness. One woman who had twice overdosed on drugs said: 'I have to show I don't need anyone. I don't want her to get close to me.' A male alcoholic said: 'I can't help myself. I know I need help, but that's the one thing I can't say to my wife. She's disgusted with me, but she doesn't say anything either.'

Alcoholism, like drugs, suicide attempts or silence, screams out certain messages, but these may be misinterpreted. If couples can find the courage to talk directly about disturbed or depressed feelings, to articulate the needs the dramas cover, then the risk they have taken may be validated by increased closeness, a lessening of tension, even a positive change in the situation.

EXPRESSING ANGER

One of the most consistent acting-out ploys is either to displace anger with a partner on to something or someone else, or to use physical violence instead of trying to discuss angry feelings. Fear can make people invisibilise anger:

> My father had a fear of anger and so have I. I often let issues slide instead of communicating them because to do so either I would get angry or Fifi might blow up. I don't know which would scare me more!
>
> *(Ricardo, 24, USA; partner to Fifi, 25, USA.)*

Sometimes anger can be used as a replacement for the real emotion.

> When I discovered very late that Fifi had been cheating on me – worse that she'd talked about it in an interview before she talked to me – I expressed anger to her. But what I felt was sadness and grief. The anger was just a cover-up. I felt to convey my real feelings would make me too vulnerable.
>
> *(Ricardo.)*

Some couples, subjected to violence within families that do not name that violence and do not communicate, may be quite unable to express anger.

COMMUNICATION SCENE: ANGER AND VIOLENCE: DAISY AND NEVILLE
Daisy, 44, a Canadian academic, and her husband Neville were both brought up in violent households:

> My father hit me. My mother hit me. Then my father brooded before having another violent outburst and hitting me again. In order to feel safe I had to shut down a lot of passion in my life. I put my passion into academic work. For years I was not able to express anger. Even today, when my father is ill with emphysema, when we argued at Christmas he went purple with rage and if he could have made it across the room he would have pounded me to pulp. I had been, for the first time, trying to make contact with him. I'd said I still loved him, he said 'Fucking bullshit!' A white bolt of rage came from his chest into me, the hatred that I felt from him in that moment touched other childhood moments of such intense hatred that I ran out crying, screaming into the night!
>
> *(Daisy.)*

Her husband Neville, with whom she lived in a virtually celibate marriage for 11 years, grew up in a family where his father sexually abused all his sisters:

Everyone pretends his mother doesn't know about it. Neville's Mom would have constant nightmares. She screams and screams and can't wake herself up out of the horror. When I stayed there I would go and try and wake her and she'd say she dreamt about coming home and finding Neville's father in bed with other women, at which point she throws all her daughters out the house! So of course she knows! These are all pleasant people but underneath are these violent undercurrents. The same Christmas that my father raged, we went to Neville's where his sister told me every time she looks at her 4-year-old daughter, she remembers herself at that age when her father first started to abuse her. But while these terrible things are going on, nobody in Neville's family names them. Nobody names anything! Nobody appears to express anger, nobody speaks. Neville listens but he doesn't talk. When we first had a relationship he confessed that his father had done this and asked if I would still stay with him. Once he felt I would, he never spoke of it again. It kind of just disappeared. He won't talk to me.

Before meeting Neville, Daisy's relationships with several men were all violent:

At first my marriage was a relief: real kindness and no violence. But it became quite restrictive. We never fought verbally or physically; one of us would back down in order not to have a fight. We were afraid of what fights could do. If you fought it might end everything! So I never expressed my anger. Neville hardly spoke, he took fifteen minutes to answer a question. There was so much smoothness between us that it felt as if there was no one there to engage with. Issues that needed to be raised simply weren't because we were each afraid it would end in anger. Neville was never angry, but so silent and contained that I had the sense I had to tread softly, because if he ever broke open . . . what would erupt? The fact that he didn't communicate and each of us feared violence inhibited our relationship.

That relationship ended abruptly when Daisy became involved with Julian, a young gay male twelve years her junior, articulate, communicative, passionate, and willing to look at what anger meant in partnerships. After living with Julian for several years, Daisy is able to say: 'Now with Julian I have learnt how to express anger and not have it escalate to violence.'

TALKING ABOUT CHILDHOOD

As is clear from Daisy and Neville's story, many communication problems are rooted in early environments. Partners found it useful to talk about the communication patterns set up in their family or previous couple. Identifying them openly ensures that when one partner responds in a seemingly irrational way, the other partner may be able to recognise – perhaps even faster than the speaker – that she/he is responding not to the present situation but to something similar that happened in the past. Once partners have identified patterns, then it is worth discussing whether or not they want to replicate them.

SECOND-GUESSING

Second-guessing what a partner needs or means instead of checking out assumptions was one of the most common communication problems amongst couples I talked to. It stemmed from one person's unwillingness to recognise exactly who their partner was. Many people had a fantasy that their partner was either exactly like them or exactly the opposite. On those fantasies they pinned wishes and desires, often assuming that if they behaved in a specific way then that's the way their partner would (or should) behave. It is an easy trap to fall into. An example from my own experience shows how it works. I am extremely nervous about giving talks about my work, or performing in public. When I do so I feel much better if my partner is there sitting in the front row, smiling reassuringly. I feel even better if my daughter, my best friend, my aunt, my cousins, my neighbours, my workmates and pals are all there too!

When my partner was invited to write and read a short story for a large impressive writers' workshop, I simply *assumed* that she would want me to be there. It was what I would have needed, thus it must be what my partner needed. It did not cross my mind to check it out. I got the evening off work, bought a train ticket to the town where it was taking place, then phoned and told her the 'good news'. 'I'm going to be there on the night, so that's one less thing for you to worry about,' I said reassuringly.

Nothing it seemed could have given her less reassurance!

'Oh, no! Oh, no! Having you there in the audience will be dreadful! I'll be even more nervous than I am already!'

As you see, like many couples we have perfect communication!

Asking a partner honestly what they feel about an issue and what they want you to do about it seems hard, but taking the trouble to do it not only improves communication over that area, but also means people build up realistic pictures of each other.

Americans Ricardo and Fifi illustrate the dangers of second-guessing:

> We may not have communicated properly because Ricardo has inaccurate perceptions about our relationship. He is overly idealistic and optimistic.
>
> *(Fifi.)*

> We don't always communicate properly because Fifi sometimes has inaccurate perceptions of our relationship. Over and over she thinks because she feels one way that I will feel the same way.
>
> *(Ricardo.)*

I discovered two broad categories of communication problems: *Misinterpretations* and *Mistrust*.

1. Misinterpretations

This communication problem is based on earlier experiences of the two individuals, who then place different interpretations on the same facts.

One example is how people interpret silence. In my case, when my mother disapproved of me she simply stopped speaking to me. For one whole year, when I was 15, as my father said she 'put you into total silence'. I pleaded, I apologised, I cried, but nothing persuaded her to relent. We sat the three of us at breakfast, lunch and dinner, my mother never addressing a word to me, my father too nervous of her wrath to say more than 'Please pass the salt.' I crept about the house terrified of her unrelenting anger and ruthless silence.

In my partnership today, my partner is a quiet, reflective person who often feels most loving towards me during a period of silence between us. I have had to relearn that silence does not necessarily mean contempt or rejection, but that it can mean warmth, companionship and approval.

2. Mistrust

In this situation when communication breaks down, one or both partners may question the integrity, veracity, competence, or even the sanity of the other one:

> Every time we argue, because I have utterly different views, she says: 'You can't think that. It's weird! It's mad!'

> When you hear someone saying something that you don't agree with, you start arguing, then you start accusing them of having mean motives. I know I've done that on several occasions.

DIFFICULT DISCUSSION ISSUES

The men and women I talked to, whether in same-sex or opposite-sex couples, all found certain topics difficult to discuss. Consistent taboo areas were: weight, other people's children, infertility, sex, monogamy, non-monogamy, money, life-threatening illnesses and death.

Weight

A characteristic pattern is when a woman, either in partnership with a man or another woman, puts on more weight than she desires but is too embarrassed to speak about it. Sometimes the weight issue surrounded in silence gets acted out sexually:

> Emily used to have a figure like a dancer. She did jazz ballet, aerobics, keep-fit, so making love was a delight, almost an extension of her health and body kick. Then she gave up smoking, put on weight, weighed in at 140 pounds, wouldn't take her clothes off in front of me, hid from mirrors, and crept into bed in a long winceyette nightdress, saying she was cold. Our sex life virtually petered out, but she wouldn't talk about it. All she would say was that she 'no longer lived in her body'. I kept saying: 'I love you. I don't mind what size you are.' But she wouldn't respond, nor would she discuss whether there was that link between her weight and our love life. Because women are perceived as bodies I'm aware this is a problem for all of us, so I tried to be understanding, but of course sometimes I felt rejected. It would have helped if we could have talked it out.
>
> *(Sarah, in long-term partnership with Emily.)*

Weight as a crucial communication issue is not, however, confined to women. Take the case of 29-year-old Sherman, an American engineering consultant who seven years ago went through a Green Card marriage to his British girl-friend Amanda, 27.

Instead of openly discussing his problem over his weight with Amanda, Sherman used manipulative critical tactics:

> I need a lot of exercise. I was overweight when I was young and I don't want it to happen again. Amanda doesn't have that commitment to exercise, but I want her to do it. So I kept saying so, I probably abused her in that, saying: 'You're gaining weight!' Whereas in fact she'd only gained a little weight, not much to her. It was more *my* self-worry which I didn't talk about

much. I wanted to share exercising with her, I felt she *should* exercise, sort of encouraged her, controlled her, because now she exercises regularly. Maybe I didn't talk with her about it being for me. Instead I became very critical. I do abuse people mentally or verbally.

(Sherman.)

Illness

Long serious illnesses can put strains on relationships. Often the ill person is too frightened of the disease or the partner is too involved in the caring process to also talk about their relationship. This widow shows how bad it can get:

He got cancer, then *worse* things. At one point his constipation was so bad a nurse did daily enemas in his bed, he couldn't be moved. He was a very private man and tried to hide the disease from me. But one day the nurse was late, he was screaming in agony. I had to rush in and help. He was trying to shit but it had stuck. The pain was tearing him apart. I forced myself to get a teaspoon and cloth and quite literally dug it all out of him. He was frantic with distress, and as he got sicker he said he needed more time alone. We never talked about the incident. I felt like an intruder. He died without us talking. I was waiting outside the door for him to call me.

Money

'We are not very good at communicating over money' was a sentence voiced by all types of couples. Canadians Tess and Gulliver, married for 19 years, who in other areas have excellent communication, are a characteristic case.

COMMUNICATION SCENE: FINANCES: TESS AND GULLIVER

At the start we ran a farm together and had a joint account. I was the more financially dependent. Then we sold the farm, that was the end of our joint account period. I needed to have money of my own, be in control of my money.

The couple moved into separate work areas. Gulliver taught art and his sculptures began to sell; Tess moved from farming to photography, through radio work into law. Some years they lived together in one city, some years they had separate studio/apartments in different cities. They kept their own accounts, each person paid their own phone bill. For the first time in years they now live together in a jointly owned Ontario house:

> We split the gas and electricity, but I still pay the phone bill here just as I did when I paid my previous apartment phone bill. I think Gulliver should pay half. It ought to be easier to talk about; it comes up every once in a while. It's a bit of a grey area because he put more down payment on the house. In business I've learned that the clearer you are in your financial affairs, the more effective you can be in managing them. So we OUGHT to discuss it. I have commented on the phone bill issue a number of times, sardonic comments, but I'm not getting much reaction from him! Nothing happens. He doesn't offer to pay it. I haven't yet insisted. I don't know exactly how much money he's got either – whereas he knows exactly how much I earn and thinks I don't make enough. Says I ought to charge my clients more!
>
> *(Tess.)*

Gulliver admitted he did think that:

> I think we would like some more money. Take off the stresses. It would be nice if Tess could support more . . . but I know that for her being a lawyer is primarily about doing things for people. So we don't talk too much about it.

Gulliver doesn't talk 'too much' about the money he makes:

> We have separate accounts and I always have mine secret. I've always got secret amounts. Tess doesn't . . . you know . . . I don't think so. But I always have to have 500 or 600 dollars somewhere safe, often in cash, in a pocket. Just in case! If something happened to my aunt or if I see something . . . I don't

want to have to explain to Tess that I've spent 100 bucks! Not that she'd mind, but . . .

As for the phone bill? Gulliver said firmly, 'We have an account that pays all the bills. Well, most, well we're just working that out.'

Perhaps two small compromises might be useful. Gulliver could move in the direction of more openness. Tess could become a little more assertive. However, their good communication over other topics left me with a positive impression that it would finally get resolved.

Children

COMMUNICATION SCENE: CHILDREN AND CRISES: CAITLIN AND KURT

Caitlin and Kurt are both on a second marriage. Caitlin, 45, with one son and two stepchildren, has been married to Kurt, 55, for 18 years. Children have always been a traumatic issue for both Caitlin and Kurt, separately and together. Nor has this been particularly well aired. When the couple met, Caitlin had lost custody of her son Jonty from her first marriage and saw him only rarely:

I never did get custody. Rather than go to the courts and fight it out – I'd seen what that did to couples – I went to the local spiritual assembly of my religious community that is elected to take care of community governance issues. I asked them to make a decision about custody. Because my first husband was earning a lot more money than I was, because they felt when our son started school he'd need a male role model, they decided my first husband should have custody. He and I didn't talk about it. He actually lied and said their decision had been unanimous when it had been a three-four split. I had almost no access. So he had our son till he was 18. He wasn't a bad father. But it was awful for me. I went through years when people asked, 'Do you have any children? Where are they?' When they heard they assumed I was an alcoholic mother or had affairs or beat my child. I thought of appealing, then I remembered that Bible story of two women fighting over a child and Solomon saying: 'OK! To end the fight we'll split the child in half.' At which point one woman says: 'No! No! She can have the child.' Then Solomon decreed that that woman truly loved the child and gave it to her. I felt that as we were two equally reasonable parents, fighting for custody wouldn't make my child's life any better, or my ex-husband's life any better, it would only be better for me. So I made a conscious decision not to tear Jonty in half. But again I didn't talk about it with my ex-husband, and I have never talked much about it to Kurt.

Kurt's first wife initially disappeared with their two sons, but later allowed him sole support of the younger one for a short period. After that he only saw them once every 3 years. One son now visits, but he hasn't seen the other for 10 years. When the couple met, Caitlin's son Jonty was 2. At different stages her son and one of Kurt's each lived with them:

When we first married we had Benny, the younger, who was 11, for the first year. It caused a lot of friction. I worked full-time, did all the household work. Kurt studied. I'm a strong believer in children sharing chores. So Benny's job was to wash the dishes after tea. I was the one who had to nag when he didn't do it. Benny would play us off against each other. There was a point at which I felt I would have to . . . not divorce Kurt, but go and live in another house so that he and Benny could do their thing. That was really hard, and we didn't talk enough about it. Fortunately, after two years his mother asked for him back and he only came for holidays after that.

We had very different notions of child-rearing. Caitlin has a far more authoritarian approach than I do. I think it important to give children a clear idea what the perimeters of good living are but not to impose heavy punishments. I discovered that one of the best ways to destroy a relationship is to try and impose your own notions of child-rearing on another person. It doesn't work! Talking about it didn't get us anywhere. Benny was a little fella, so one difficulty was not what he did do wrong but what he didn't do right or he got done in a half-hearted fashion. Then

Caitlin would throw all sorts of . . . well . . . distress . . . difficult for both of us. It was a difficult issue to talk about. She liked Benny as a person but she was quite relieved when he went back to live with his mother.

Caitlin's son Jonty arrived when he was 18:

When my son finished high school, he decided he wanted to come and live with me and Kurt. I had hurt so badly all those years, and now he was coming. I was really excited. Of course there was a resentment on Jonty's part. He didn't understand that a marriage can reach a point where people can get out. He just doesn't get it! He thinks if he had children he'd never get divorced. But he didn't say it in a cruel way to me. There were no other barriers between us. It was as though we'd never been apart.

Jonty's lengthy visit, however, did erect barriers between Kurt and Caitlin which were not resolved by talking:

When Jonty was little, he'd visit and I got on well with him. But when he came to stay he was withdrawn, very sullen, I found it hard to have someone living in the house who didn't communicate on any level. Not rude, not unpleasant, just withdrawn. I tried to talk to him, but when nothing happened I gave up on it. Perhaps I didn't talk enough at the time to Caitlin. The real issue was that he would not share household chores and Caitlin was prepared to pay him to do them. In North America it gets done all the time, but I am totally opposed to payment for work done in the home, so we discussed it and he didn't get paid.

The underlying issue of how to deal with stepchildren, and the remarkably similar presenting problem of sharing household chores, remained insufficiently debated during periods of crisis. In both cases crises were invisibilised rather than resolved by the children's departure.

Early in their marriage, Caitlin and Kurt had made a decision not have children together. Such a resolution, even if openly discussed at the beginning, may become unexpectedly painful for one or both partners so that afterwards it is scarcely referred to. When children are already a complex issue, communication may be harder. Caitlin admitted she was frightened of repeating her first marital experiences:

> I had felt so isolated having one child I couldn't face that again. I couldn't take the risk of that kind of loneliness. So I just decided no more children, then didn't raise the subject again. I don't know if it would have been like that?

Kurt remains more uneasy with their decision, more aware of communication lapses:

> We talked at length when younger, but we were students, it would have been extremely difficult then, so we decided not to because we already had children. I think there is a part of both of us that would like to have children together but then in talking about it early, seeing what we were aspiring to do with our lives, we felt, we still feel, that the time required to really raise children simply wasn't there. Sometimes I'm glad of it but sometimes not so glad . . . I am still a bit ambivalent. For me, there is an idealised notion that part of being a husband also implies being a father. So yes, I still feel ambivalent and I assume Caitlin does, though we haven't talked about it much in the past and now don't talk about it very often.

Sex

Sex is often a taboo subject which couples shrink from discussing. Lillian's behaviour during her second marriage was typical. Her second husband prematurely ejaculated all the time, but they never spoke about it:

> He couldn't do it and he couldn't talk about it. I'm sure he felt quite twisted up, he must have done. But there was absolute total silence round the subject. He didn't like the light on; I like the light. He snored dreadfully. We tried a few times the first year, then we had separate rooms for the next 33 years. In all

that time we gave the outside world the impression we were lovers but we never once discussed it.

COMMUNICATION SCENE: SEX AND TALK: DAISY AND JULIAN

Julian and Daisy became partners after her 11-year marriage to Neville broke up. Sex for both of them had been a problematic area. Daisy's childhood set a pattern.

> In my childhood sex was secretive. My Dad had a weird relation around sexuality. You couldn't leave a doll undressed in front of him! If you came downstairs in flannel pyjamas, he'd scream at you, 'Get upstairs! Get a housecoat on! You're indecent!' Your body was such a temptation to him! There was always this charge in the air. If you watched television and they started to kiss he'd change channels. So you got scared to watch TV in case something sexual came up. Pretty weird effect on us!

Her marriage to Neville was by choice almost devoid of sex.

> Neville was more like a brother. Shortly after we were together all physical passion stopped. Every two or three months I would figure having sex was something I ought to do, but it was hardly there. I could predict the way he would move around my body. He might have an orgasm, but there was no sense of actually letting go. So then a part of me removed myself because I didn't want to let go either. I never went to that place of vulnerability. I made a trade-off, but I knew I was missing something. I felt there was something wrong with me that I couldn't feel passionate for a man who was kind and good. Occasionally I'd work at it, light candles, make a wonderful dinner, put a rug on the floor, make this space, but it was never reciprocated. I decided I'd rather read! So we ended with a celibate marriage. But we never discussed it.
>
> *(Daisy.)*

Julian, 31, who became Daisy's lover during the last few months of her marriage, came from a cold anti-sensual family:

> My Dad's a chronic alcoholic. He didn't beat Mom but there was

no affection. They never hugged or kissed. I was never touched physically by my Dad at all whatsoever – never! The only memory I have of being near my Dad was at four when he put me on a bicycle with training wheels and held it from the back while I pedalled. My Mom, no, neither. Occasionally she'd write 'love' in an abstract way on Christmas cards. I live now with a real sense of deprivation around physical expression or caring. I have no history of physical contact so it's important.

When Julian was 17 he became involved with Barry, a much older middle-class man who taught at the local university. He tutored Julian in everything from sociology to making love:

Barry encouraged me, taught me middle-class values, showed me restaurants. I'd never seen fresh tomatoes, mushrooms, garlic, olives . . . dinner blew my mind! It was like having a parent, being rescued, but he told me he'd fallen in love with me. He tried to hug and kiss me, rub me over. What I wanted was to be protected, or was it parented, to be helped out of my restricted life, to be touched. I didn't feel very attracted to him but I cared about and loved him. When he said if we didn't have sex he wasn't sure we should have a friendship, then I did. For six years I had sex to avoid falling back into my family and into hopelessness. I didn't want to be cast out. But I didn't talk about that to him. The 'Educating Rita' syndrome helped me effect a belief in my gayness. At the beginning there were caresses, then it became more and more raunchy sex. I had multiple lovers, mainly men, a few women, I thought of myself as gay. I hadn't learned how to talk about what I wanted from sex with another man. Barry said what he wanted. I didn't talk that much.

Julian moved to Toronto, became a serious gay political activist, then met Daisy and Neville:

The fact that I was gay opened the possibility to Daisy of a friendship with me. She was a very fierce feminist and didn't have anything to do with any men except her husband.

Daisy had begun to think about lesbian relationships and leaving

Neville for a woman, but when she met Julian she was drawn to him:

> He was our gay male friend which felt safe. We went to a gay film festival. Strangely, I had a sense of him sexually sitting beside me. We had long talks which I found attractive. In one talk at his place he said he found me attractive. I let the remark sit there. Then he touched my feet. They were alive, in the most erotic way. I reached out and touched his neck, apparently an erotic place for him. I thought this is dangerous. I said, 'I'd better get home.' We hugged each other with our coats on so we were safe, enough big layers, except it was the hug I had been longing for. It was the hug that connected body, mind and spirit. Oh God, how I'd longed to have that kind of connection with someone! He walked me up the street and we kissed each other, just a little kiss, like all those clichés about lightning. It was like electricity.

The electric energy remained and the long good talks continued. Daisy told Neville:

> I told him before I got down the road too far. I could have turned back. Neville was a limp noodle. He didn't talk. He didn't fight for me or our marriage. Though Neville hadn't ever wanted sex, the crunch for him came when I went to bed with Julian. But we hardly talked about that either. Maybe if we had we might not have broken up.

To the astonishment of Julian's gay male friends they became partners.

> I knew Julian was gay but it didn't matter about labels, the energy was there. I loved the fluidness of people categorised as 'gay'. I'd been attracted to women, I have passionate relationships with women, I pick men who are usually somewhat effeminate. So I could explore that desire. I'd been attracted by androgyny, by fluid sexuality. I had to stretch boundaries around how I conceived sexual relations. We broke out of the traditional notion of a couple, and I broke out of my

prison of silence and could talk about sex. Neville had always been emotionally absent, and I was being pulled by this other place. The aliveness, energy, passion. I discovered joy in my BODY! All the talk flooded in, it was as if one communication channel had released another.

(Daisy.)

Though I hadn't discussed my sexual feelings much with Barry . . . I was always afraid of upsetting him . . . I do have attractions that go for women or men. I fell deeply in love with Daisy, but it could have been a man if he had been similar. I could have had a wonderful relationship with a man like Daisy who talked and talked and opened everything up. My identity had been created around being a gay activist. When I fell for Daisy, I had to reinvent myself sexually and be prepared to talk about that reinvention. I was scared I would be going back, scared I would lose my sense of country.

Julian and Daisy now talk freely about their sexual relationship:

We discuss the huge benefits of bisexuality for both of us. I don't have to be macho. I know there is more to sex than penetration. My sense of desire is fluid. Between us there is more flowing of the masculine/feminine.

(Julian.)

COMMUNICATION SCENE: SEXUAL AFFAIRS: RUPERT AND MARIE-CLAIRE

Affairs can be danger zones for communication. Rupert's and Marie-Claire's British and French cultures gave them different attitudes towards sexual expression and communication:

I am much more physically demonstrative than Rupert.

(Marie-Claire.)

I come from a non-demonstrative culture. So I don't always respond sufficiently.

(Rupert.)

During their 32-year marriage, both of them had affairs but did not talk about them at the time:

> We didn't talk about or decide to have a monogamous marriage, but I assumed we would. Then time will tell . . . in fact we've both had other relationships. Being open about them was a tricky issue. If it is talked about beforehand and we agree then it's much easier to accept than if it's not talked about and then you discover it, it's like an attack on the person. That's the way it felt for both of us at different times when we found out that we had other relationships.
>
> *(Marie-Claire.)*

Rupert talked briefly about the affair he had had 15 years ago:

> It was during the period when we were both readjusting to the children getting older. It was experimental on my part and it created a great deal of fuss and tension.

Rupert had an initial difficulty communicating with Marie-Claire:

> I couldn't talk about the affair at the start. I couldn't talk while . . . within a few days . . . no, not immediately, but pretty much through it. I think we have talked about it and resolved it. I don't expect it to happen again, but if it did I should talk immediately.

The couple asserted that their relationship with each other had always been central, that outside affairs were subsidiary. Insufficient communication, however, had hindered this focus. Marie-Claire felt that if they had talked in advance then it would have felt more 'allowable':

> If your partner is aware and in agreement, then maybe one can allow the extremes – the rediscovery of sex – on a temporary basis, because I think one will come back to the ability. But without that knowledge I felt a sense of betrayal. If it was to happen again it needs to be dealt with beforehand so there is no

betrayal, so it can be accepted without being hurt. Perhaps you almost have to develop a friendship with that third party.

Their sexual relationship has changed over the years, but Rupert does not see the change as a consequence of his affair:

Sex has changed in frequency, it's probably less of an issue for both of us. I think it has changed not as a function of that affair, but just simply as a function of age. Also a feeling of being more comfortable with each other.

Rupert was less comfortable talking about his affair than about other issues:

I'm a sort of guarded person. I'm guarded by nature and I'm guarded by my profession. In my work as an academic I do interviews too! You might have probed a bit more ... I can't say what you should have asked, but sexual activity, like money, represents a vehicle for disputes. It represents a vehicle for problems of power and imbalance in relationships which maybe I just touched on in my answers.

COMMUNICATION SCENE: SEX AND SILENCE: CAITLIN AND KURT
Sex has been a tricky issue for Kurt and Caitlin for many years, and communication regarding it even trickier:

Caitlin is more physically demonstrative, more affectionate than I am. Especially after my first marriage I keep a physical distance from people, I didn't want to get close. But genital sex is more important to me than to her. I think that's perfectly normal in male-female sex relations. It goes in waves; some years I need it a lot, she doesn't. Those are the times when I feel successful, when life goes wonderfully, that's probably a male thing! Other times it goes into a trough, I'd rather have a decent lunch! At the start we had some real old rows! Well, not rows, some little disagreements. Before marriage she seemed to want a lot of sex, after marriage that changed. Her interpretation (or recollection) is that my behaviour changed. In other words I became more aggressive after we married. Yes, it's changed very much, I expect we haven't talked enough, perhaps change in this sense is almost normal when people have been married a long time.

(Kurt.)

Caitlin has a very precise memory of a number of discussions:

Sex is more important to Kurt than to me, because within this marriage I've gone through years and years of doing the equivalent of two jobs to keep the family going. So I'm tired all the time. But it isn't the easiest subject to talk about. In the first year we were married, I was more interested in genital sex. Then I lost interest, partly through being tired, but partly because what I wanted from sex – that I haven't been able to get across to Kurt – is more of that touchy-feely stuff. Not quite the hugging that goes on when you're going by each other on a daily basis but more of . . . though I hate the word . . . foreplay. I've spent years where I have *regularly* brought up in conversation the issue of: 'I need a different entrance if we are going to have genital sex. Either we don't focus on genital sex so much or we change the way in which we start on the path to it.' I've met with a defensive reaction. Periodically Kurt has said, 'Oh so you want me to look at a textbook and follow this that and the other?' I have said, 'No, that's not what I mean. I have been telling you about different places where I'd like to be touched and in what way or for how long.' I don't know how else to get through what I want. Because if I don't say anything, then it is not going to change and I am not going to want genital sex. But if I do say something, then it seems as if I am being critical and demanding or offering a textbook.

There have been periods when it has reached a blaming situation that I don't like. It's not healthy, it is destructive. So then I go through another long period when I don't say anything. I have tried many different ways of bringing it up; now I can't find any more ways. So communication has come to a halt. I have given up being able to improve that aspect.

One of the consequences of this breakdown in communication

is that Caitlin had an affair. She did eventually tell Kurt, but not until it was long over:

I hope I wouldn't have another affair. I didn't feel able to talk about it for years. It was part-way through this marriage. I took karate lessons and became involved with my instructor. It sounds horribly cliché-ish but it lasted several years. I grew out or drifted out of the relationship. I never said a word. Kurt knew nothing about it. I take responsibility for living a lie. I worry as a member of the Baha'i faith because we are told within the Bahia's writings that if we are unfaithful in marriage that hinders the development of our spiritual limbs which we need to get around in the next life. So what kind of relationship can I have with Kurt in the next dimension, the life after this life, as a result of my own behaviour in this one?

While Caitlin was dealing with these anxieties, Kurt suddenly announced that he had become infatuated with a woman he'd met on a summer course who was 20 years younger than him:

He said he was in love with her. He had never expected such a thing to happen; he had always been disparaging about married men attracted to younger women. But he was obviously right out of control. He felt really bad, said he didn't want to leave me, but was torn and didn't know what to do. I said first I wasn't going to stand in his way. He had to do what he felt he had to do. But if he was going to have a physical relationship with her I needed to go and live somewhere else. The second thing was I told him I had had an affair, because otherwise it would have been even more dishonest to let this man agonise over feeling he was betraying me and allowing me to take the high moral ground. It felt only appropriate to say: 'Don't feel guilty because . . .' It wasn't too hard because I had hated not saying it before.

Kurt's memories were reflective:

I guess when a man turns 50 things go bad. I really fell for a girl but nothing ever happened. I made a decision for a long time that nothing would happen then I told Caitlin because it was a little burden on me. In this society you are supposed to love only one person, to live with only one person, it is probably one of our biggest myths. When I told her as it turned out, I didn't know, but she had been having an ongoing four-year affair. I had no idea.

How did Caitlin's secret affair and her silence around it make Kurt feel?

That's the strange thing. It made me feel vain. Even now. She must have been feeling very lonely, really missing the caring. So in a sense I don't blame her, I have never blamed her, even today. I guess I'm not jealous in that sense. I didn't feel betrayed or untrusted. Sometimes I think when people slip into those situations there is something they need in their lives. I couldn't give Caitlin everything she needed and wanted. I was up to my eyeballs doing my Ph.D. One neglects one's partner, one becomes too single-minded. At times like that I don't communicate much. I tend to shut things and people out.

Kurt's understanding of his contribution to their communication lapses allowed him to resolve his own potential affair:

I didn't know about Caitlin's affair when I told her about the young woman. It all came at the same time. It was a bit of a rough spot. I thought what happened to me only happened in the movies. I had already recognised my relationship with Caitlin was very important. But you know how it is, most men of my age fall for young women. But really, what would I do with a young woman? I mean honestly, other than drag her off to bed?

Kurt did not drag the young woman off to bed. He talked to her instead. Told her his wife had given him 'the green light' but he was thinking things over. The young woman wrote to Caitlin:

She got cold feet! She was afraid that if I was somebody understanding enough not to lose my temper, not to be upset, then maybe there was sufficient in our marriage to last, which she didn't want to screw up. She seemed a reasonable human being. So she backed off. It took Kurt some time to recover, he kept phoning her. Meanwhile I felt just horrible. I kept turning hot and cold, waiting for him to decide. My feeling was 'go ahead and do what you have to do!' But Kurt never did follow it up physically. I had a sense of embarrassment because I didn't think that person was appropriate: she didn't have much education, she was young, though she gave him something he needed emotionally. I couldn't tell him that either. I didn't feel resentful, nor angry, and I don't have jealousy in me.

Was Caitlin more distressed at having had an affair herself or at not having told Kurt earlier?

Today I'm not angry at myself for that affair, though I feel morally it was wrong. But a couple can never fulfil all each other's needs. I do wish I'd communicated earlier. I hope there won't be another affair. There may be somebody in the future who will set all kinds of sexual bells ringing but I hope I'll be a lot firmer with myself and not follow them up. But if I did sense that happening I *would* talk to Kurt about it. Maybe I need to get through to him over the sexuality issue. I've lost hope in that direction . . . but maybe I do need to bring it up and talk about it again.

GENDER SOCIALISATION EFFECT ON COMMUNICATION

All couples have communication problems but there are specific problems related to gender socialisation which affect gay male couples and heterosexual couples.

Gender Issues

1. *For gay male couples*
There is a communication issue for all gay couples which relates to the secrecy surrounding much of their lives. For those who have long lived in the closet, who have dissembled and defended

in order to protect their privacy, it may be especially hard to be open even with each other. Gay men in a partnership face the specific issue of male conditioning which fails to teach males how to express, exchange or communicate feelings. In a heterosexual couple there is a woman to bear the body of the emotional work of communication. In a gay male couple, they must struggle along as best they might.

> It is often said that men don't communicate, which is only partly true. Men can communicate very well about certain things, like their jobs, sports, and the state of the world. But this isn't what is meant by those who fault men; they say men don't talk about their feelings and hopes and problems. That is generally true . . .[2]

Writer Bernie Zilbergeld, quoted above, emphasised this in his book *Male Sexuality*. It was true amongst gay men I interviewed, many of whom failed to discuss the most important relationship issues. Larry and Hugh spoke for many:

> We preferred doing stuff together rather than bringing stuff up. He wasn't a guy for talking, me neither. But it got bad when I wanted to get physical with a guy I'd met at the athletics ground. I'd sorta assumed Hugh and I were OK about that, we'd never mentioned monogamy. I did think I'd just tell Hugh that I wanted to sleep with this guy. He freaked out. Total freakout! Said he thought we were an item! We were but we just hadn't ever talked.

2. For heterosexuals

Heterosexual couples discovered that men and women use conversation differently, having different goals, they have different styles and different methods. In general terms men are more competitive and women more co-operative. Men's identity comes from achievements and competence, women's primarily through nurturance and relationships. Men need ego-boosting and appreciation. Women need understanding and respect. Women complain that men don't listen, or that they offer solutions instead of validating their emotions. Men complain that women try to change them in order to increase their self-growth, but that it feels like control. Women need to talk about stress, while men usually withdraw to find an answer.

In this study women revealed that the more they were cherished the easier it was to communicate, whereas men said if they didn't feel 'adequately needed' (and admired) they found it hard to communicate. Communication breakdowns occurred in couples when men and women offered each other the type of talk they each needed rather than the type the opposite sex required. Women wished men would behave towards them as they behave towards everyone. Men like Rex Harrison in *My Fair Lady* sang out: 'Why can't a woman be more like a man?' and assumed that women will want what they want.

As we live in a male-dominated society, language is posited on what males want and how males think. Gender socialisation which makes male dominance seem reasonable, even 'natural', is predicated on such ideas as the male representing the positive while the female necessarily represents the negative or the idea of male-as-norm and female as aberrant. Language is one of the crucial factors in this construction of reality. Words are not neutral. The meaning of words is dependent on the ways they are used in society. Our language and hence our communication reflects the values of our particular culture.

Feminist theorists – including Dale Spender, Deborah Cameron, Robin Lakoff, Deborah Tannen, Mary Daly, Shirley Ardener, Betty Lou Dubois, Toril Moi, Carol Gilligan and Sheila Rowbotham – see language as an index of patriarchal attitudes; an indicator of inequalities in men and women's sexual and social roles; a tool which helps implement and maintain our male-defined culture; a determining factor in reflecting thought and influencing thought; or a weapon which diminishes the range of women's thoughts, alienates or silences them.[3]

In this study women refused to be silenced and were highly articulate about the problems they found in communicating with men or the way they felt about sexist language that excluded or put them down. Women who value talking more than men do were not afraid to say so. Sometimes men found that challenging:

> If we have a conflict our way of communicating is that Marie-Claire brings it up and tries to discuss it. I withdraw and mull;

she confronts conflict in conversation, she sees it as valuable. I avoid it. She will tackle any communication head on, I'll retreat.

(Rupert.)

Men and women have different goals
Men admitted they had different goals in conversation. They feel rivalrous and combative:

> Men are always competing in conversation even if it's their best friend. They try to score, to win, there's a gaming analogy which women don't have. If you go into the theory of games, the philosophy of games, it's a masculine thing. I play chess and over a chess board I am obviously competitive. If I am looking at the supermarket and deciding which queue to join, I may feel competitive, but I do not feel that when I am talking to Lillian my wife. If I did it wouldn't work.
>
> *(Charles.)*

Men and women have different conversational styles
Several men described 'female language' as different from their own:

> Women on their own talk about themselves and talk it in narrative form, whereas men tend to take subjects and treat it as if it is a sort of essay.
>
> *(Harry.)*

> It's difficult to know what to communicate or how to communicate. Men often get the words wrong. I wonder if that is because they don't touch enough? I had these friends, she was English married to a Frenchman. They each spoke each other's language perfectly. One day she was on her knees in front of the stove because the cakes had just burnt. Her husband came through the door of the kitchen, saw her distress, and said, 'How did that happen?' It was the ultimate insult, the distancing of himself as a male problem-solving machine. So he was looking for efficiency and avoiding difficulties. His wife was looking for comfort, support and some feeling. I think that's the basic difference between men and women which is often not really understood.
>
> *(Charles.)*

In order to understand each other better, several couples including Louise and Robert used feminist language books to help them:

> We read Deborah Tannen's books which explain how the sexes use conversation differently – men to provide answers or solve problems, women to express emotions. One day in the garden I said, 'I'm not sure what I should do about this.' Robert immediately told me what to do when what I wanted was to explore my feelings, express my thoughts. I raised my eyebrows and he immediately said, 'Oh dear! I've just Deborah Tannened, haven't I?'

Robert acknowledges the usefulness of that book:

> Deborah Tannen's book about the way men and women communicate differently has been a fascinating reminder of what can happen between us. Louise will say, 'I'm quite anxious about X.' She wants me to acknowledge her anxiety. But I problem-solve. I say, 'Well, why don't you do this? Or you could do that!' My job includes helping couples and managers in disputes to problem-solve, preferably to look at six options, so I go into that! Since I read the book I know Louise wants me to say, 'How awful! I can see you'd be worried about that!' Then leave it at that.

Hello Mister Fixit

Robert was not the only man to problem-solve instead of empathising. Many men feel that if their partner is in trouble then their job is to fix it. Some enjoy solving problems. Some may be used to giving advice by the nature of their jobs. Few recognise that what may be needed is merely a listening ear or some sympathetic words. If one person needs to talk about their feelings, it is not helpful for the other person to say, 'Now it is obvious. This is what you need to do.'

Three different women arrived home to their partners in an agitated state. The first woman's employer had decided on a reshuffle of the office which effectively demoted her. The second woman's mother – who had broken her leg, and who intensely disliked the woman's male partner – decided to come and stay with them for a six-week period. The third woman's daughter had been violently attacked by her boy-friend. In all three cases the women wanted to say how they felt, express their disturbance and accept words of understanding and comfort.

The three men responded thus:

> Dreadful! It's obvious you need to sort out that work issue first by confronting your boss, then by talking to that woman who will now be your superior. I'll make you an agenda of what to say and the different stages of negotiation.

> As we only have one bedroom and the put-you-up, your mother must be made to see it's not on! I'll draft a reasonable letter, then you copy it out. A good second tactic would be to suggest a ten-day stay once she knows the limits.

> Now don't worry about her. I'll get straight over there, sort out the police, get new locks on the door, and tackle the rest tomorrow morning. Just ring and tell her I'm on my way.

Women want partners who will empathise with what they are going through. Men need to learn that.

Men don't allow women conversational space/Men make criticisms
In couple conversations men talked about themselves, monopolised conversations, made more judgements than women did. Women did what has been termed 'conversational shitwork', found out about other people, made reassuring noises, helped along conversations:

> If we are out with friends, or new people, I am more likely to ask questions and get information from them, Kurt is more likely to monopolise the conversation. It's to do with our different socialisations. I want to discover things about people; I don't want Kurt to go on about what he is doing. When he does, then that becomes a lost opportunity for me. But I do have to sit back and recognise that people love Kurt for his enthusiasm, which is why he talks and talks about his projects! Sometimes I

too love him for it, but other times I get frustrated. Do I speak up then? Sometimes I do, sometimes I don't. We have so many discussions and arguments about all Dale Spender's work on men taking over conversations, men interrupting. Because Kurt is Austrian, if we are in a group he will say: 'This is a cultural thing they use in Europe! They all speak louder, they all speak over each other!' I'll say: 'No, I'm sorry, in this case it's just outright rudeness, just wanting to monopolise the conversation. You're just using culture as an excuse!' Initially we hurt each other when we had these discussions. Now we've reached a degree of understanding and tolerance for each other's viewpoint.

(Caitlin.)

I've also learned that when Louise and I both have things to talk about we must be sensitive to giving each other time. She's a superb listener, someone I can always off-load on to. I have had to learn to be more responsive to her.

(Robert.)

Men do tend to criticise more than women do. If I criticise Amanda too heavily, if I put her down rather than offering constructive criticism, she tells me pretty much as soon as it happens! Then I back off! I get the message, I realise she's upset about it. Now it isn't hard for me to hear her or to discuss it.

(Sherman, American.)

Men don't listen

That men do not listen was the most consistent female complaint:

I was a very active feminist when I met Gulliver, so that certainly established principles. The first principle was that I should be treated as an equal, respected as an equal, and listened to and be empowered in the same respect. It was around the three-year mark, maybe 1979, when we had our first crisis over my autonomy and our first communication break-down. I had to assert myself. He wasn't listening to me; we were not communicating properly. He was crab-like, he wouldn't deal with things straight. If the relationship was going to progress we had to get past that. I had to get away from him, withdraw. I told him that I needed him to listen to me. I told him exactly what I needed, then I withdrew but with the intention of making the relationship work. I wouldn't respond to any manipulation or any of his tantrums! I withdrew sexually as well as mentally. I went on strike! It drove him crazy! He was highly motivated sexually, but he was also highly motivated to bring me close to him again. The only way he could do that was to listen! So he did.

(Tess.)

Particular issues on which men and women cannot agree

The most confrontational issues are sexism, feminism, pornography, child care and division of labour.

Sexism

COMMUNICATION SCENE: SEXISM ON THE STREET: MARDY AND WILL
Mardy is an assertive young feminist:

I was in a toxic relationship before I married Will. I learned that I never have to accept a person who does not value me, who does not uphold my values! Coming from a woman's college, you know that we can run the world! So Will would have a hard time being sexist. Generally he isn't, as he has a strong mother whom he respects. I saw by the way he treated his Mum how he would treat me and that was acceptable.

Mardy and Will are a couple who have made an agreement to deal face to face in conversation with issues that bother one or both of them. They have done it on numerous difficult occasions; the most recent was when suddenly Will's behaviour became unacceptable to Mardy:

He looks at other people, other women, on the street. Because we are so close to each other I can read his mind. He is actually ogling them. I confronted it. I told him it was unacceptable. It was a very uncomfortable argument. I said: 'This makes me unhappy, stop it!' He looked at me and said, 'Golly! You know what, this behaviour is very adolescent.' But it was also sexist.

Initially Will resisted making any further compromise. He felt that American society in particular condoned the way men look at women on the streets, and that it didn't merit a behaviour change. Mardy disagreed:

> I pointed out that I don't feel compelled to look at other men. I was finally very honest and said his behaviour was more than making me uncomfortable, it was making me crazy! He has now said it is something he will look at. That's as far as we have got. A very tough discussion.

Feminism

COMMUNICATION SCENE: MEN AND FEMINISM: KURT AND CAITLIN

> Because we live in a really sexist world, as women you are socialised to have low self-esteem, to doubt your opinions, all that stuff. Because a male partner has been socialised too he tends to do things that undermine women's self-confidence, without really being aware. This sometimes happens with Kurt or he goes through men being discriminated against when it comes to job advertisements and hiring. He feels men work hard to get their Ph.D.s as well as women so he gets annoyed when in a department it's clear they're only going to hire women because they're just so out of whack in terms of gender balance but they're not honest enough to put in the ad 'Men, don't bother to apply!' So we have ding-dongs and arguments about feminism. If I lived with a black man or woman who were trying to get across racist stuff to me, on the one hand I'd want to learn because I'd want to change my behaviour but at the same time I'd feel defensive. But it becomes onerous for the person who's a member of the oppressed group to be framing stuff in a way that someone from the oppressing group can hear without going through guilt and defensiveness. I encourage Kurt to tell me when he feels resentful. I'm trying to become more diplomatic at least in my work, so that I can be heard!
>
> *(Caitlin.)*

Caitlin is a very strong feminist. Sometimes that has caused strains. But we have worked through them by talking. There was a period when this was like a feminist campus! It sounded as if all men at all times were out to oppress women! I've done enough reading and I know that there are different strains in feminism and I have done some work on this but it can become very, very wearing. There was a period when everyone talked about coercive sexual relations. Almost by definition they were akin to rape and oppression. It doesn't enhance a relationship! I found that hard to deal with or to talk about. I said to her: 'Caitlin, look, I know I'm male, I am a man, but I cannot be held personally responsible for everything men as a group do! There are certain things I must work on and change but I am not taking responsibility for everything that all men in all history have ever done!' You know, we worked through that one! I think what a lot of feminists only dimly realise is that the generalisations they make of man are much the mirror-image of the kind of generalisations men have made about women. So the dialogue between men and women may be cut off. But Caitlin and I have tried to dialogue. Despite the difficulties it has caused, I've learned a lot from her.

While I daily do my battles for feminism out there in the community and at school, I can't be fighting all the time! So there are periods when I've got to shut up. Curiously the situation often changes then. Maybe I'm then able to frame things in a more constructive way that Kurt can hear.

(Caitlin.)

Some men do not find feminism threatening as a subject. Rupert, 55, is one:

Marie-Claire belongs to a Women's Group with whom she talks in a different way from her talks with me. It is something I totally support; I've never seen it as a threat. It has been positive for her, given her self-understanding, and has probably been helpful for me. She's become more political; she'll go on marches she wouldn't have gone on before. Feminism gives her a way to articulate and have language to describe aspects of our relationship that are common to lots of men/women. That's been important for me too. I've seen feminism as a growing awareness that is as important for men in relationships as it is for women.

Marie-Claire's view is similar:

> In practical terms I am a feminist, but not a loud feminist! But
> belonging to a women's group is important, very much so. It has
> given me a sense of self, a reason to be, showed me what a
> woman is all about, sharing and support, all this energy flows.
> On these issues I go fast though not long, whereas Rupert goes
> slow but long. So you have the hare and the tortoise!

Pornography

The Americans Mortimer and Naomi have very different views on pornography. Naomi has a 'gut reaction' against it. 'Most feminists have that though they may disagree over what should be done about pornography.'

Mortimer does not feel the same way:

> I have a different approach towards pornography. I can
> encompass violence in a film as long as it is not gratuitous. It
> probably comes down to linguistics. We finally got to the point
> where we realised it was one of those clashes which discussion
> hasn't solved.

Division of Labour

COMMUNICATION SCENE: HOUSEHOLD TASKS: RUPERT AND MARIE-CLAIRE

Until recently most men had expectations that women would take the greater share of household tasks. Rupert explains:

> When Marie-Claire and I first married, it was a normal
> assumption for me that she would be at home, that she would
> do more. We both worked, but when she was at home she did
> most of the cooking as a routine matter. But when guests came I
> did the weekend cooking.

Marie-Claire recalls their early years more tartly:

I knew early that I would have to make quite a few decisions. All practical issues were not of interest to Rupert. He prefers more abstract things, so I would be more on the concrete. We would have to divide like that. When the children were small I did all the cleaning, organising, planning school things, gardening, anything down-to-earth was my task. I do what I have to do! Did I resent it? Oh yeah! Wives can become frustrated and it will come out in anger.

Recently there have been changes which Marie-Claire willingly acknowledges:

Then he certainly didn't do the cooking. I mean I did twenty years of cooking so now he can do twenty years of cooking! Now he cooks for pleasure.

The change began when Marie-Claire went off to work on an Indian reservation:

We'd been married twenty years then. I was gone from Sunday night for five days a week for four years. We had a commuting relationship with no problems. I had a new sense of independence where for several days I was my own person.

When Marie-Claire developed her career, went away to teach on a reservation, this clearly produced a significant change. I was at home with the children during the week, performed all . . . well, most of the parental functions. She came back weekends, looked after the laundry, we probably both spent time cleaning but after that I routinely did home cooking. As her career evolved, we both worked hard and both have a sense of equity. I have developed a real sense of fairness, would not expect her to do more than I do.

When there were problems they always tried to communicate, but Marie-Claire admitted:

We don't communicate well. If I am too abrupt, hyper, demanding, too imperative, all the things I can be, then Rupert moves backwards so the communication is not good. The more I advance, the more he moves backwards. Then I have to move back so he can advance, then we can communicate. It really is work and in the heat of the situation sometimes you lose that sight!

COMMUNICATION SCENE: LABOUR DIVISION: CAITLIN AND KURT

For a number of years most of our arguments have been round the division of labour in the home. Rows happen no matter how you express yourself. If you are rational, then you can't be upset enough. You may not be taken seriously. If you're crying, then you're being irrational. Because I know those dynamics I've been able to talk about the impossibility of bringing these things up, so to some extent it doesn't go on nearly as much today. But there was a breaking point when I was going back to University to finish my Ph.D., when I'd be away from home for ten days. I'd say to Kurt: 'When I come back, can you just clean the toilet and spend an hour before I get home tidying up, doing some chores? I would really appreciate that.' But every time I would arrive, nothing would have been done, it would be just horrible. After all I wasn't just studying for a Ph.D., I was coming home to keep a full-time job going as well! One night I said: 'Look I can't take this any more. I don't like coming back to a dirty house. I don't like having to nag. It then looks as if I'm the one at fault. I think I want out! I'll stay married but I'll go and live in a different house!' Kurt was shocked. 'Would you leave me over such a small thing?' Then I had him! I said, 'If it's such a small thing, why can't you do it for me?' From then on he did. He finally got it! But I don't like having to stay on my feet and play those mind games.

Can one always talk things through?

Couples debated the issue of whether one can always improve a relationship by talking things through or whether some issues are better left alone:

Daisy always feels passionate and meaningful about her life. Mainly I don't. That can make me angry. She is very independent and competent. I am more dependent, so I can get angry at her competence. It isn't always useful to express that anger but I think you can *learn* to talk about an issue like anger. Both Daisy and I are trying to do that.

(Julian.)

Sometimes communication can be taken too far. We both tend to process too much and endlessly analyse. It can go on far too long. We used to think we had to communicate in order to find a resolution at once. But we have learned that the resolution doesn't have to happen right now.

(Daisy.)

Caitlin feels strongly that the best way to sort out difficulties is to talk. I believe eventually they sort themselves out in the course of time, or one just learns to accept that some may not be resolved. So I am perhaps less inclined to talk.

(Kurt.)

Naomi thinks if you can talk about things it is de facto a solution. But often it isn't! One of the discussions we have had from day one is that words don't solve everything. That there are always sub-texts that are going on and that while you think a resolution is taking place, it's just a verbal resolution. Some things lie deeper. Some problems can't be talked out because there isn't a kind of rational solution.

(Mortimer.)

I always had the idea that we should talk everything out but I've come round to Mortimer's view that there's a limit to what you can talk out and that the real resolution may not be through talking. I used to think a resolution was something we both agreed on; now I think as long as the other person has become more conscious of a new viewpoint, then over time it works itself out. Also there are some differences that don't get talked out, worked out or resolved but one accepts that.

(Naomi.)

There are some difficulties that I now accept that we shall never

resolve by talking. Yes. The difference between what I want
done and what I get!

(*Marie-Claire.*)

Although direct clear communication is a skill worth learning, it
is essential not to confuse it with feeling forced to talk about everything all the time with your partner. There are days when even the
best partner drives one insane. It is a poor idea to share your irritable feeling that being alone on a desert island must be better than
this! Intelligent selective communication can sometimes be the
answer. Communication may conflict with an equally important
right to privacy. Everyone in a partnership has a right to keep certain personal thoughts and feelings to themselves, or to dwell
quietly on them until a later date when it may be more appropriate
to express them. Sometimes a speech uttered in rage or haste may
be deeply regretted but cannot be forgotten. Verbal communication
requires good judgement and the recognition that it is not the only
way to connect. Non-verbal communication is equally important.

Communication does not always have to be verbal: physical connections

Communication of course is never merely verbal. Body language,
sexual closeness and cherishing contact have a major part to play
in effective connections. Some couples feel their communication
is more psychic than verbal:

We have incredible communication, and a lot of it isn't through
talking. We have bodily communication and a spiritual and
psychic communication. We even know what the other will say
next, or we think the same thing at the same moment. We talk
all the time, but the best way we communicate is psychically.
Tess's sister, who she was incredibly close to, was dying of
cancer. One night Tess and I woke up simultaneously; we both
knew in that second that she had died. I looked at Tess and she
said, 'Yes'; then we went back to sleep. But we *knew*. The next
day we found out she had died at that time.

(*Gulliver.*)

I'm such a wordy person that sometimes to swap words for other ways of communicating is restful. Just touching Julian's back gets me soothed. Body comfort after all those words is a benefit.

(Daisy.)

There's talk. There's lots of talk. Then there's no-talk. The talk is good but the no-talk, which usually happens in bed, is better!

(Katy.)

Nice work if you can get it!

NOTES

1 Sometimes the pronoun was 'she', but rarely. In general it was women who complained about insufficient communication from men or from other women.

2 Bernie Zilbergeld, *Male Sexuality*, cited in Eric Marcus, *The Male Couple's Guide*, Harper Perennial, 1988, p. 26.

3 Excellent research in this area from: Dale Spender, *Man Made Language*, Routledge & Kegan Paul, London, 1980; Deborah Cameron, *Feminism and Linguistic Theory*, Macmillan, London, 1985; Deborah Tannen, *You Just Don't Understand: Women and Men in Conversation*, Virago, London, 1991; Rosalind Coward and John Ellis, *Language and Materialism*, Routledge & Kegan Paul, London, 1977; Carol Gilligan, *In a Different Voice*, Harvard University Press, Cambridge, Mass., 1982, 1993; Tillie Olsen, *Silences*, Virago, London, 1965; Mary Vetterling-Braggin (ed.), *Sexist Language*, Littlefield, Adams and Co., 1981; Betty Lou Dubois and Isobel Crouch, 'The Question of Tag-Questions in Women's Speech' in *Language in Society* 4, 1976; Cheris Kramarae, *Women and Men Speaking*, Newbury House, 1981; Robin Lakoff, *Language and Women's Place*, Harper and Row, 1975; Joanna Russ, *How to Suppress Women's Writing*, The Women's Press, 1984; Toril Moi, *Sexual/Textual Politics*, Methuen, London, 1985; Shirley Ardener, *Perceiving Women*, Dent, 1975; Mary Daly, *Gyn/Ecology: the Metaethics of Radical Feminism*, Beacon Press, Boston, 1978; Barrie Thorne and Nancy Henley (eds.), *Language and Sex: Difference and Dominance*, Newbury House, Rowley, Mass., 1975.

CHAPTER 5

Coping with Change

Many of us believe, or hope, that our relationships are static. We
cling on to a memory of how our partner was when we first met;
how sympathetic, understanding, interesting in themselves, interested in us, they appeared; how the relationship seemed to flow
effortlessly. There was a magical psychic energy. Where did it
go? How did those very virtues which attracted us to somebody
suddenly appear as irritants?

Somewhere, secretly, we probably know that we ourselves are
changing all the time, therefore this may also be happening to
our partner, but it is harder to admit. What we suddenly see as
'wrong' with the partner who once could do no wrong may not
be wrong at all, it may merely be that a change has happened. It
could have taken place internally in one person's head, or in
both heads (new ambitions, a wish to travel, a desire for children), or externally in one person's life (a job has changed, a
serious illness has occurred, an affair has sprung up, parents
have died, an ex-lover has come to live in the same street), or in
the life of the couple (they have fostered a child, they have won
the lottery, they have gone bankrupt). Inside the couple each
person may be trying to deal with that change. Or *not* deal with
it.

Many of us strongly resist change. We will do anything rather
than confront it. Instead of trying to deal with changes in the

current relationship or changes in themselves, some people find a temporary solution by changing partners. The problem with that decision is that when similar changes occur in the new relationship, the change-resistant person is forced to move on again. And again . . . and again.

All relationships change, just as we ourselves change. This does not have to be threatening to the partnership, but to cope with change requires skills rather than mere intuition.

Changes fall into two categories: the first is changes over which a couple has little or no control or choice. These include retirement, illness, disability, AIDS, depression, death, bereavement and some kinds of financial changes. The second is changes over which one partner or the couple has some control or choice. These include the advent of children (their own or other people's), a new need for personal space, new jobs, houses or locations, new studies, interests or new friendships, new sexual habits, or sexual affairs when previously the couple had practised monogamy, and new sexual orientation from heterosexual to homosexual or the reverse. I have dealt in detail only with those changes that occurred frequently in the study.

A major change over which couples do not have any control is the onset of illness or disease. When this occurred to a formerly healthy partner, particularly one on whom the other depended, it threw their lives temporarily (sometimes permanently) into confusion:

> One of the hidden reasons for his attraction to me was his strength and physical confidence. He used to boast about never having a day's illness. I'd always been a bit weak and seedy, succumbing to any old bug, so depending on him was important. I guess I have a frail spirit too; I like being protected. Suddenly my husband had an incapacitating back injury. He has had three operations, was off work for months, now he will have to take early retirement. He walks on sticks and is in constant pain. He looks to me for practical and emotional support. I just don't seem up to it! When I'm not with him I spend a lot of time crying.

If one partner already had a recognised disease and was then required to minister to 'the healthy one', this could compound their difficulties:

> When I met Angela I had had multiple sclerosis for fifteen years. That year I was in a wheelchair. She was a professional rock climber, afraid of nothing. I couldn't believe she wanted to live with me, the wimp of the year. But we sorted a house, got it reorganised for my disability, and with her understanding and encouragement I seemed to take on some of her strength. I have been in remission twice, though back in the wheelchair a few times. I felt as long as she was around I could stick it out. Then on a climbing holiday she had a terrible accident. She fell hundreds of feet. Maybe thousands, I'm no good at figures! She's still in hospital, with so many breakages they say she is lucky to be alive. They don't know if she will be able to walk. My mind can't take it in. I know I have to be the strong one and I want to be. I love her so much. But the truth is that I am terrified.

The worldwide advent of the HIV virus which leads to Acquired Immune Deficiency Syndrome (AIDS) is a social change over which people have no control that has had implications for many couples. When a partner – either before entering a relationship or within an established couple – becomes HIV-positive, that change must be dealt with throughout the remainder of their partnership.

Couples are at increasing risk from this particular change, as we can tell from the latest figures which show nearly 20 million people worldwide are HIV-positive. In the UK alone, at least 21,718 people have contracted HIV; of these 9,025 have developed AIDS and over 6,000 have died.[1] Although in Europe and the USA the majority affected at present are gay and bisexual men, globally today three out of four HIV infections are through heterosexual transmission, and a third of those affected globally are women.[2] This means that AIDS can happen to anyone – women, men, children, heterosexual, homosexual, black or white. AIDS, initially presented as a gay disease, can and does affect straight as well as gay couples. However, as more gay men in couples were affected by this change than straight men or women in this particular study, I have used as a case study a gay male couple.

SCENE CHANGE: BECOMING HIV POSITIVE: PETE AND JEFF
Pete, 31, was diagnosed HIV-positive in Los Angeles in 1985 when he was only 20:

> I have a rare blood group so I was donating plasma for $80 a week. That's how they found out. I got the result the day Rock Hudson died and I thought, 'That's it. I'm going to die!'

For years Pete lived with this idea of death, which had significant effects on his personality and also on his relationship with Jeff. After the diagnosis initially Pete 'went wild' sexually, then he became very religious, joined a gay Christian church and became celibate: 'I became a loner. I was celibate for 12 years, so long that I didn't even consider I'd ever have a relationship.'

When he met Jeff at a gay Christian bible study group and started dating, the couple had to take into account these changed circumstances.

> I needed a lot of space and solitude to think about being HIV as well as to write. Jeff isn't much of a one for solitude. That's one issue. The other is sex. Most gay men go in for that traditional stuff. You meet a guy, you barely know each other's names, you wham-bang hump in the sack, then later you find out maybe you want to date them. We have done it differently. Partly it's the bag of religious issues I'm sorting out, but partly it is being HIV. My health status and fear has made me wary of sexual intimacy.

What is Jeff's response to this situation?

> I know that his health status means he has been alone for a long time. I want to support him over his health so I'll be right here. But I get insecure in case one day he'll just need to be by himself.

> Jeff is entirely supportive that we don't have sex yet. He knows I am nervous that I might somehow transmit to him. You hear all

these rumours. We think we know how it is transmitted, but maybe we don't. It might be easier than they say. When you're there with someone you care about you put up another barrier. It's curtailed our sexual intimacy.

This curtailment has had a decided effect on Jeff's view of their partnership. Previously he had begun relationships in the classic gay male way of sex before emotional intimacy:

It has changed my perception of where sex should fit in. Of course I want it, but I fell in love with Pete after three days and I'm still falling in love with him all the time. I feel absolutely committed so I am patient.

Do they miss genital sex?

There are times when I feel I'm going crazy without sex. Definitely times when I can't bear it. In my neighbourhood there's a health club, all men, a window facing the street; you're popping down the sidewalk and there's a gorgeous guy lifting weights and you think, 'What am I DOING?' So I go do a lot of masturbation before I next see Jeff!

Jeff's view was positive:

I love being together, cuddling, holding each other. I love to kiss him, love to hug him, love to have his arms around me. What Pete is dealing with is very hard. I don't think I even know what he is going through. At this point in the relationship I am much stronger. It has made me come a long way since we started dating after bible study.

Jeff feels their shared religion is helping them deal with Pete's HIV status:

We both feel things happen for a reason, that God brought us together and that God is giving us strength. We enjoy going to church on Sundays, worshipping together, there's a section where we have the Passing of the Peace where we give each other a kiss and a hug in church which feels comfortable. We pray together at meals, and at night before bed we'll hold hands and pray. The other night Pete thanked me for helping him through this and said I'd become his best friend through my care. I am often frightened about what if he dies, but I believe God will continue to lead and guide us.

After years of anxiety, a second change has suddenly occurred which the couple must now come to terms with. Pete's doctors have forecast that there is a slight possibility that because of new drugs Pete might live out the rest of his natural life:

I have very good T-cells and I am taking this new cocktail of protease-inhibitors and AZT which can sometimes make the virus 'disappear' or go underground. I have lived believing I am going to die for years, now there is this strange change in my head that perhaps I am not yet due to die. I don't know how to deal with it just in case it isn't true.

Neither partner felt capable of talking about the shock of moving from a probable death verdict to a probable life verdict – the news was too recent, the implications too complex – but they did want to raise one possible consequence of the new medical evidence which may make them reconsider their health-imposed celibacy. Jeff was characteristically optimistic:

Even though we haven't been intimate yet, we might be, that's the good part, all that good stuff is still to come.

Pete was more cautious:

I'm not sure about sex because I can never be really sure about my health. Also I have other issues, internalised homophobia, around it. But certainly for us it feels like there is still something good left, this whole area of intimacy that is untouched. We've got a present under the tree left to unwrap! I'm already having a very nice meal and I still have dessert to look forward to.

*

Pete and Jeff were forced to cope with a change over which they had no control. The following four couples have confronted changes over which one or both of them have had some control. When only one partner either initiates change or takes control of a changed situation, there is a difficult power imbalance. We can see this in the problems faced by Louise when Robert unilaterally decided to move away from home to study; by Denise when Olwen took up Buddhism because she needed more psychological space; by Hope when Geoffrey, who had sworn himself to sexual fidelity, had a raunchy affair; and by Daphne when Oriel decided she no longer wanted sex.

New studies, jobs or interests, if taken up passionately by one partner, can often result in the other partner feeling left behind or left out. Notions of 'streaking ahead of me', 'feeling excluded', 'no longer wanted on journey' were expressed by many couples. Louise felt this change to be particularly painful.

SCENE CHANGE: THE NEW STUDIES: LOUISE AND ROBERT

Louise (now 53) and Robert (now 57), married for 35 years, who met when Louise was 17, were quite timid as teenagers. They clung to each other as if to a rock, determined to make as stable a life as possible, without any untoward changes other than bringing up a family which they both felt would enrich their relationship, and in Robert's case making the requisite changes to earn enough money to keep them in quiet comfort. Louise in particular needed a secure base. They planned a monogamous, cosy lifestyle in which neither was expected by the other to rock the boat.

Today Robert is a senior lecturer, and known as a high-flying academic. Louise, as we saw in Chapter 3, is a home-maker, with no academic qualifications and occasional anxieties about not having had a career. But when their romance began, it was Louise who was the clever one:

> At 17 I was really very bright. I'd gone off to a rather good grammar school. I should have gone on to university except money grew tight at home, so I opted out at 15. My stepfather and mother gave me no encouragement. They'd say, 'It's a bit of a waste of time really.' Or they'd say, 'You're getting above yourself, my girl!'

By contrast with Louise's excellent school, young Robert had been pushed into 'an appalling secondary modern' where, Louise said, he had been 'well and truly brainwashed into believing he was thick.' As Robert says:

I had a very, very bleak education. I left school with no O-levels, I wasn't even conscious of having taken an 11-plus, let alone failing it. I was left feeling stupid.

Louise decided to restore Robert's self-esteem:

I swear I didn't push him, but I did give him confidence, help and encouragement to start taking exams. He really took off!

Marrying Louise and suddenly feeling good about what I might be able to do got me thinking: 'Maybe I'm not so stupid after all. If only I had an opportunity to prove it.'

He proved it with a series of O-levels, then further examination successes.

Louise's positive approach to her husband allowed them both to enjoy his successes, but it drained her own resources:

Now after all these years I realise that in doing so I constantly put myself down. All the time I'd say, 'You can do that. I can't do that.' I watched him go from strength to strength, taking exams which I never took. His work friends' wives were invariably married to a teacher or a social worker, while I sat on the sidelines. Having a well-paid nurturing job, teaching or nursing, appealed to me, but I had enormous hang-ups about being totally unqualified. If they gave degrees for basic common sense I'd have the lot. Today my own motivation to study has gone. There is a bit of frustration because I'll never know what I might have done.

What Louise did do was to enjoy her children when young, then foster babies for a decade while she volunteered to work for meals-on-wheels.

Despite Louise's frustration, their coupledom remained warm

and affectionate until what they each described to me as 'The Crisis' of 1979. Although this crisis, which followed a major change in their lives, had occurred 18 years previously, both of them recalled it in minute detail.

> Robert was 40. He suddenly decided he would leave home, leave the family, go away to university in another town to do his Master's degree. Before that if changes had occurred, if we had had minor hiccups then one would have the hiccup and one would be supportive. Not that time; we both hit hiccups at the same moment.

The hiccups for Louise were changes she had never anticipated and had no way of coping with.

> I saw too many changes: going away to university and getting a degree was a little bit more than I had expected. He was very naughty, he didn't discuss it with me beforehand; he didn't ask how I would feel about it. Given that Robert had always been one of the most considerate and kind people in the world, it seemed out of character. He just joked about it being a good thing. When I said, 'What's in it for me?' he'd say, 'Well, a very contented husband!' Up till then he'd believed that that was a fair joke. The fact that I became incredibly insecure made it not a joke to me. I resented it. So I was insecure about where he was going, or even that he was going at all. We had always lived in one house together. He had never been away before. Now he would be staying away at the university in a different town three nights a week. He was going beyond me intellectually and academically.

For Robert, the chance of this degree was the fulfilment of his secret wish.

> It was like a validation. But I underestimated the threat it might pose to Louise in terms of how I might change. I didn't voice any of that.

Their lack of communication in the face of such a big change was the most destructive aspect of their relationship at the time.

Today Louise acknowledges how Robert must have felt:

He had vocational qualifications, but it wasn't like going to university. He must have felt insecure and pressured because he had never been academic. But he didn't appear to understand how hard it was for me. He was involved in a small encounter-type group of close-knit students. He wanted so much to be part of this group that I felt excluded.

For Robert that exclusive group was a source of excitement:

They were brilliant people. It was a hot-house atmosphere. When I did come home after four days away, I'd go on and on about it and not take too much interest in what it had been like for Louise. I'd had to persuade my boss to second me, so all my energy was going into achieving the goals. I guess I didn't ask much about what it might mean to Louise. She got very distressed in the early months about the business of 'Who was I with?' Then there were tensions of how you get back together after a break. I was excited about new things and new people. She couldn't have a picture of that. Huge difficulties.

Neither of them voiced their fears nor shared their feelings:

I hadn't learned how to say what I felt then. I assumed we would somehow be OK. But to use one of Robert's words, we had a good bit of disequilibrium that year. It was a new experience for us because we both hit insecurity at once, so we were not able to look after one another. I was sad and resentful. Like my mother, I grew up believing everything was my fault, that's women for you!

What were Louise's fears?

I truly don't believe I was threatened in terms of other women. That honestly wasn't it. It was as if there was a brick wall round him, his studying and his group which I wasn't part of. When I was at my most unhappy he might phone from time to time, but I didn't particularly want to talk to him, I was too cross.

How did Louise's anger and distress affect their children?

They both noticed but they didn't talk about it. Once when Simon was 15, it was Robert's birthday and I remember coming up myself a bit sharp. I said sarcastically, 'I expect Dad's having a good time down the pub!' Young Simon said, 'And why shouldn't he?' so that put me in my place. I realised if there were sides to be taken they would take Dad's. Simon was right. Why shouldn't Robert enjoy himself? But you know . . . After that I was careful not to involve the children.

When there is tension within a couple, sometimes friends can be a major strength:

Robert and I are not very good at having friends which I think is a great tragedy, but he can't see why it matters. He has lots of work colleagues and I have two or three close girl-friends.

Unfortunately, during the year of 'Crisis '79' Louise's friends did not offer her sufficient support:

I was disappointed in them. I talked to two friends, one of whom thought I was being unreasonable. The other just said, 'Oh well, all men are selfish!' That wasn't much help. Another man friend, who was also close to Robert, said, 'You've got a streak of immaturity in you, Louise!' I would have said insecurity, not immaturity. If it happened today it would be different, I have better friends now.

Very slowly the situation improved. Robert decided to invite Louise down to the college:

It helped a lot when she met everyone and joined us for a week. But there were periods when she still got distressed. I got panicky about how her distress might lose me the programme; I might lose the course. I began to feel that if her distress went on I might have to give up.

Even though Robert's concern appeared to be more about losing his place on the course than improving their relationship, he did make big efforts to improve the partnership and thus save his ambitions:

We began finally to do a lot of talking. I began to understand how she felt. I tried to reassure her that I was not going to become intellectually out of her grasp or find anyone else socially. What happened to us I've seen happen to couples. But Louise's anxiety was something deeper about how it might change me. Would I become a different person? Would I have different aspirations that would affect us as a couple? In fact, though I became more confident, and more job opportunities opened up, I did not change fundamentally.

Louise's view is more straightforward:

Robert realised the course wasn't the be-all and end-all that he thought it was. He did benefit from having his Master's degree, and that meant a lot to both of us. Gradually we got back together again.

Strong commitment and belated but honest communication on both sides, together with Robert's acknowledgement of the difficult changes Louise had had to cope with and the compromises she had made, ensured the growth of their coupledom.

Did they feel that the crisis which developed from that changed situation had taught them anything beneficial?

Absolutely. It was a painful year, the only year that I ever worried our relationship might not last. But it was only one year in 35, and our commitment and affection somehow saw us through. I've asked myself many times whether it was a good thing it happened. I don't know. But there was growth. It wouldn't arise today because since then I have learned to say if

I'm not happy. I would say so and it wouldn't happen. Robert
has learned that he didn't handle it well, so we both learned
from it.

Robert accepts Louise's assessment:

I think I managed it badly at the time. I think it's a good
outcome but it was a very difficult period for us. It was like the
relationship that never was. The other woman that never was. It
was the affair that never was. Because it was an affair with a
college and a group of people, so it was a big test for us.

Initially Robert and Louise did not cope particularly well with
the change: their lack of adequate communication was their
biggest stumbling-block. Their problems were intensified by the
fact that only one of them had instigated the change and had
control over it. Nor was Robert willing to relinquish that control.
Through an affectionate perseverance, the couple did however
learn some very fruitful lessons.

Like Robert and Louise, Olwen and Denise are a close-knit
Proximity Couple who faced a change for which only one of them
was responsible. They had better communication skills than
Robert and Louise, which ultimately aided their adaptation to
the changes.

SCENE CHANGE: NEED FOR SPACE AND SOLITUDE: OLWEN AND DENISE
Olwen, a 35-year-old counsellor, and Denise, a 38-year-old
teacher, have lived in 'placid contentment, doing different jobs
but sharing friends, holidays and hobbies' for 8 years. A change
occurred when Olwen became heavily involved with a Buddhist
group:

Our life had become almost too interconnected. We did
everything except work together. I needed to get away, find
some solitude, so I went on a Buddhist retreat. It changed
everything. I met other Buddhist women whom I wanted to
continue seeing. Seven of us formed a group and we meet
regularly to meditate and discuss spiritual ideas. Denise has

become very upset. She was fine about me wanting a small
shrine in the house but she doesn't want to come in and
meditate with me. Strangely I wanted to share this part of it
with her, because we were so used to doing things together. I
said to her, 'Like the Buddha says, come in and see.' She tried
but it made her angry, restless, very uncomfortable. On holiday I
took my Buddhist books to share bits with her but we ended up
flouncing into the sea and arguing.

For Denise the issue is not about spirituality or the value of meditation but about her fear that Buddhism will take her partner too
far away. She felt threatened by something Olwen was involved
in that she was not and didn't want to be. It was painful for her to
confess this to Olwen. She did not want to be that sort of possessive person.

Unlike Robert and Louise, however, Denise and Olwen –
despite their individual anxieties about where discussion could
lead – decided to thrash out their feelings over the change as
soon as possible. Denise's fear was that Olwen was becoming
part of a small close-knit women's community who all talked a
different language.

When we both managed to be open, I realised that Denise thinks
I'm getting into some weird sect with secret rites that excludes
her. More than that, Denise is aware that several women
involved in the Friends of the Western Buddhist Order have
decided for the sake of their spiritual development to live
autonomously and celibately, or live in little groups. She is
afraid I will move out of my partnership with her.

Denise admitted that particular anxiety and Olwen recognised
how realistic her anxieties were:

Because I lived for years on my own, because I value
solitude . . . I loved not having to be accountable to anyone, to
be able to work through the night or make myself a cup of tea at
2 a.m. . . . and because we have had this intense togetherness
relationship, I could imagine that happening though it isn't
what I want. So maybe Denise has picked up on that.

Denise admitted first to me, later to Olwen, that she found it hard to understand the need for solitude. She was someone who did not need to be on her own. She said she needed company, approval, people, and always a special person around. She became discomfited when that person was not around.

After much discussion the couple saw that the Buddhist issue, though real in itself, also had implications for other hidden issues in their partnership. They became more aware of Olwen's hitherto repressed need for 'joyous solitude' (and her subsequent resentment over not being able to express it) and Denise's conflicting need for close companionship:

> We have always had tension around sleeping together. I sometimes need to sleep by myself. It wasn't about sex, it was about space. Denise would get distressed or feel rejected. First I wanted to console her; then I felt angry, bloody angry. We would usually end up sleeping together. It all came out in the discussion over Buddhism. That change to a new faith was probably another means of my getting the space I want.

Months of discussion have now resulted in three decisions. Denise is taking a greater interest in Buddhism which Olwen wishes to share with her. They have decided to sleep half the week in their double bed, but during the other half one partner will sleep downstairs on the sofa-bed. Their third decision is that each partner will have a separate study space where retreat, meditation or mere idleness can take place uninterrupted.

Now in their eighth year together, the system has worked well for the last two years. Denise feels more relaxed and believes the problem has been solved. She can see when Olwen has had too much 'people overload'. At times like that she says to her partner, 'I think you should plan to go away.' On other occasions Denise herself goes away.

As for the original change: the issue of Buddhism, that too has been quietly accommodated within their lives. Denise does not envisage becoming a Buddhist but no longer finds Olwen's spiritual involvement threatening.

Despite the pervasive imagery of sex in the media, despite the barrage of good-sex advice given in magazines and manuals, despite the few lone voices which point out sagely that sex does not have to be a couple's biggest issue . . . for some couples sex still remains an area of conflict, hard to discuss and, should it escalate into 'a problem', harder still to resolve.

One reason for this is that making love is a form of contact which leaves people emotionally vulnerable. To be let down or betrayed over a sexual matter strikes at one's most defenceless self. Feelings of rejection, danger and insecurity often follow.

This study threw up a plethora of sexual changes from which I have chosen to look in detail at the case of Geoffrey and Hope which illustrates a change from monogamy to infidelity, and that of Oriel and Daphne, which illustrates a change in sexual habits. In both cases, as with Olwen and Denise and Louise and Robert, one partner initially controlled the situation.

SCENE CHANGE: SEXUAL INFIDELITY: GEOFFREY AND HOPE

Geoffrey, 44, a successful British barrister, has been married to Hope, 54, for fifteen years. When they met he was 29, a bright aspiring lawyer living in the area where Hope, 10 years his senior, was a widow with inherited wealth who owned the neighbouring country house to one of Geoffrey's university friends.

Hope is realistic about their marriage:

> Though I was a lot older, we were intellectually compatible from
> the start. Loads in common, sparked off each other. We grew
> very fond very quickly. I had been widowed early, at 35, and
> was still submerged in grief. I needed some light in my life and
> suddenly there was Geoffrey, full of fun. Full of ambition too! I
> soon recognised that. I was aware I was an ideal wife for a
> barrister: Oxford First, social connections, bit of a nest-egg,
> uncle a well-known judge, and utterly reliable. I always hope he
> didn't want me solely for those assets. Anyway we fell
> delightfully in love and married.

Hope made only two stipulations: she wanted two children before she grew too old to have them safely, and she demanded sexual fidelity.

He wasn't that keen on children, maybe he saw them hampering my background work for him, but he agreed. Anyway we had sufficient money to have a nanny. He was fine about monogamy. Always said he couldn't desire anyone else with me around. I felt utterly secure. After the birth of our boys I felt I had everything I needed. I put my energies into Geoffrey's career and I loved it, though as the boys grew older I felt divided.

Geoffrey's view of their early years is not dissimilar:

I couldn't get Hope out of my mind. I was young and impressionable, I hadn't met anyone like her. I came from a poor background. Worked my way through a decent university, though not Oxbridge. Here was this cool, elegant, mature woman, always a little mysterious and terribly sad. She was like a sonnet. I wanted to make her happy so I invented silly adventures, outings to Blackpool to see the vulgar lights, tacky excursions on a canal boat that leaked, nights at sleazy London pubs, everything her kind wouldn't be seen dead in. She cheered up! Underneath the sadness she had a great sense of humour. I found her entertaining, stimulating, I learned a lot. Her education was better than mine. I knew we were going to be a great team. I had the drive, the competitiveness, she had the pull. Of course it helped that she was rich and knew everyone who mattered in legal circles!

What did Geoffrey feel about Hope's commitment contract?

Kids, um, I wasn't keen on that. Bit of a kid myself at that time. My mother died when I was eight. Maybe that's why I went for Hope, older woman stuff. I gave in about the kids, but I was frightened I'd lose her attention. At the beginning of course I wanted to be faithful. Who wouldn't with a catch like Hope?

Having caught Hope, sired two sons, begun to climb the legal ladder, with Hope's continuous help, very fast, Geoffrey's enthusiasm for monogamy waned:

I never stopped loving her. I love her today, she'll tell you that!

But in her mid-forties, always attending to the boys (ridiculous really, we had a nanny and a cleaning woman), she didn't seem so sexy. More like this well-dressed rather bossy mother. Not just the boys' mother but mine too. She was invaluable, no doubt about that. I couldn't have managed any of my life without her, but she just didn't turn me on. The worst bit was I felt angry with the boys. I felt like they were my bloody rivals!

Hope's understanding of that period matches her husband's:

I knew he was withdrawing. I suddenly began to feel that bit older while he looked just the same, the bright young man in Chambers. He was surrounded by other bright young men and women, clerks, secretaries and researchers. He came home less often. I had bought us an apartment in London where he began to stay overnight. If I phoned, often Ellen, his secretary, would answer. I knew and yet I didn't know. I felt so unsure of myself that I began to baby up the boys, which was bad for them, and get a bit needy with Geoffrey which he hated. He liked me strong, cool, amusing and in charge. I didn't feel amusing. I did some things I regret. I used my money and power to dictate what we should do. He almost literally wrenched away from me and was strange, short-tempered with the boys. The more I nagged about fatherhood, the less he paid me attention in bed.

Despite their psychic understanding of each other and their respective needs the couple were unable to communicate and their sexual relationship deteriorated.

The crisis occurred when Hope decided to take her sons and go to Paris for a week:

I needed time to think and a new environment. We parted affectionately. I almost cried. I knew underneath we loved each other, but everything was obstructing us.

On her third day in Paris Hope phoned home. Geoffrey answered the call and was his old charming, witty self:

Suddenly I recognised what was happening; his voice had that sexual ring to it. He used endearments like he used to, but I knew with total clarity that they were not for me.

Hope left her sons with a friend and flew back:

I didn't phone from the airport. He should have been in London but instinct told me he was in the country. I drove there without stopping. I saw his secretary's bright red car in our driveway. I had paid for that! Geoffrey had convinced me last Christmas that we should buy Ellen a new motor. I kicked it as I walked past! Highly uncharacteristic.

Inside the house Hope hesitated. The noises from the master bedroom upstairs were not quite what she had expected:

Ellen was certainly upstairs. Her Laura Ashley dress was on the sitting-room floor. Her tights were trailing the staircase. I heard music, but there were several voices crying out and thumps. My heart was thundering. I thought I might have a stroke with fear! We had an interconnecting door between our bedroom and our second sitting-room. I walked in that way. They didn't hear me. She was lying on the sofa facing the bed and away from me. She wore black frilly pants, nothing else, and her hand was down there between her legs. You know, masturbating. Geoffrey was on the bed. I don't know how to tell you. One of his researchers, a young pansy type, was lying there, well, was lying on his back under Geoffrey, his cock in Geoffrey's mouth, while another young man whom I'd never seen . . . Oh God! It was dreadful, he was half on top of Geoffrey and well, you can imagine what they were doing. I was standing inside the connecting door. It was like a scene from hell! This was my husband, this debauched person. The girl saw me first and screamed my name. Geoffrey rolled over and if ever I saw fear in someone's eyes it was then. He shouted 'Out!' Just that word 'out'. Like he owned or controlled them. They got out and I went and locked myself in the children's bedroom.

Geoffrey reluctantly tried to explain what had happened:

I had never done anything with boys before. Shit! I'm not a queer! I'd had an affair for a bit with Ellen but it was never serious, never important. Just a bit of fun, an experiment, anything with someone young to make me feel I was a man. Ellen knew it was just nothing. Everyone knew how I loved Hope. It was awful, the worst thing that's ever happened. Hope wouldn't talk to me for more than a month. She didn't want explanations. She asked me to move to London to the apartment while she decided what to do. I was terrified. I knew my career could be ruined, our marriage was in shreds. Christ knows what she told our sons. It was when I started thinking about our boys that I realised my feelings about them had had something to do with using my male researcher and his boy-friend. I paid them, you know! I had to pay them a lot more to shut up! I was shit-scared, but I knew I did love Hope even if she were to leave me.

Geoffrey's state of fear and confusion led him to seek professional advice.

I've never had any time for those counsellor types, but I was in such an anxiety state that I went to one to try and talk about letting those young men in on the scene. Why the hell did I do that? I tell you the one thing I am not is a pansy! This counsellor type was a good bloke. He helped me see that I was fucking them in some weird symbolic way to get back at my sons for taking up Hope's life. He told me not to try and see Hope, that she would need space, but to write an honest letter to her. What a mess, what a mess!

Geoffrey's action in seeking advice and following it allowed Hope time to consider how damaged she felt and whether there was any way they could repair their relationship. Geoffrey found other jobs for his secretary and researcher. Hope and her family kept the news out of the press. She said nothing to her children. After three months, she too consulted a marriage guidance counsellor.

I realised that my fears about ageing, my domineering ways that came from my reliance on my own financial independence and my resentment of his lack of proper fathering to our children directly clashed with his fears and anxieties. Geoffrey wrote several honest letters to me and I replied. But I couldn't get that nightmare scene out of my mind. I felt as if he had raped me publicly. I never wanted him to touch me again. At the same time I knew that if we wanted to try again at our marriage, and at one level I did want to, if we didn't ever make love what would stop him turning elsewhere?

Geoffrey's recollection is of 'terrible shame' and the feeling that he 'would have done anything to set it right'. What he did was to stay in London, ostensibly on business, make formal friendly trips to see his sons, attempt to pay them considerably more attention, and to talk to Hope, without ever touching her, whenever she was prepared to communicate. After six months they were spending some of each week together but in separate bedrooms:

> We tried to hold on to the good things we had left. It can never be the same again but after a year first we had a new bedroom decorated and then we decided we would have a shot at continuing our marriage, so we made a big move to a new house. Anything to lose those memories.

The dramatic change from sexual fidelity to (as far as Hope was concerned) betrayal and disloyalty cut to the heart of their marriage. The psychological damage was considerable and today their physical relationship is uneasy, and episodes of resentment can still spring up.

They have however made a joint decision to communicate over the issues that they find difficult and to reinstate the ideal of sexual fidelity. 'There is no way I'd go through that again or make her go through it,' Geoffrey asserted stoutly.

Hope as usual is pragmatic:

> He won't do it again. Or anything like it. That isn't one of my worries. But I shall always wonder if it is fear of the consequences constraining him rather than my sexual attractiveness.

More robustly Hope added:

> There have always been solid virtues in our marriage. They are
> still there; those are what we concentrate on nowadays. Anyway
> you can't keep up the heat of an emotion when it's several years
> after the episode; things change, even in your head, and you just
> have to get on.

In coping with such a traumatic change, what Hope discovered
was the need to take back some of the control that Geoffrey had
been exercising. What they both learned about themselves and
about the need for continuous communication, even through a
traumatic situation, allowed them to inch forward cautiously in
their partnership.

The case of Oriel and Daphne bears some similarities to that of
Hope and Geoffrey. Change is again located in the vulnerable
area of sex. Change is again instituted and controlled by one partner forcing the other to respond as well as to cope with the
change.

SCENE CHANGE: NEW SEXUAL HABITS: ORIEL AND DAPHNE

Oriel, 42, a British acupuncturist, and Daphne, 41, a college head
of department, partners for seven years whose previous relationships had been highly sexualised, followed the same pattern
when they first got together, but after two years, Oriel decided
she did not want much if any sexual activity in her partnership:

> Sex has never been important, but before this relationship I
> always thought it should be. That's because I lost my virginity
> young, went to a big mixed comprehensive where sex was 'in'
> and lived wildly through the Sixties and Seventies where sex
> was the big thing. Often I did it with men and with women
> when I didn't want to. I used to like the chase, the lead-up, but
> then, oh no.

Oriel read the magazines of the time which confirmed her feeling that sex should be a key part of a good relationship:

Terrible pressure from women's magazines and the media, mainly aimed at heterosexual women, made me feel insecure. But even inside the lesbian community we've absorbed that ideology. We all feel pressured to have sex. I felt it was impossible to live in this society and not feel inadequate if I didn't have sex. So I did!

The relationship immediately preceding her partnership with Daphne was one of 'complete lust':

It was very passionate, loads of genital sex, really lusty, it felt like basic animal lust, but for me it wasn't emotionally intimate. I knew that wasn't a person I would choose to live with. Then while I was doing all that, I met Daphne. Immediately I felt drawn to her, but it wasn't sexual. I felt as if I'd found a new friend. She was a bit of a soulmate. I spent 18 months trying to understand why it felt so deep yet it wasn't the sex. I kept breaking up and restarting my current lusty relationship and wondering about Daphne. Should I stay in a relationship that was passionate but not close emotionally, or move out of that and be with Daphne about whom I didn't feel sexy? Eventually I broke up and began a serious relationship with Daphne. We started it as a sexual relationship. I almost felt I had to have the sex in it, even if I didn't feel that sexy about her.

The pervasive ideology that 'good' relationships must be rooted in a 'good' sexual life led both Daphne and Oriel to believe that 'regular sex' should be an integral part of their partnership. For about two years they operated their couple in that way. Daphne reported that she enjoyed it and felt reassured by it. Oriel's report was more complex :

In fact the sex was fine although what I felt was that as we had both been very sexual before we were both good performers. But I did not feel as if having sex with Daphne was as important as my soulmate feelings. So hell, I was confused. Then the big change occurred.

To achieve the change Oriel desired from constant genital

sexual activity to as little as possible needed open honest discussion but neither partner initially communicated:

> We didn't talk about it at first. I just didn't initiate any sex. So it was my action or lack of it. At one time I thought I'd just gone off sex for a bit. So we accepted that as a phase I was going through, though we still didn't talk much. Then I was in therapy where it came up as part of a discussion about my fear of intimacy. I shared that with Daphne, which meant we could talk more openly.

Daphne's initial reaction was of great distress. She felt in some way to blame for what she saw as 'a flaw' in their partnership. Oriel was well aware of her partner's feelings of deep disturbance and rejection:

> At first Daphne still felt very sexual and was upset. She felt rejected. But when I said how it's a relief to be in a relationship for the first time in my life where I don't feel under pressure to have sex, she began to understand. Now she has come round. I don't know whether 'come round' is a good term, but she says that she doesn't feel that sexual – not in that genital way – very often either. Partly it's our work. We are so busy! We joke about it and say with our levels of work it would be hard to find a place for sex! But when I say we don't do it, what I mean is we don't have genital sex but we have all the rest. That's what makes it feel so good. It is so loving and tactile.

After seven years together what is their relationship like at present?

> Now we hardly ever have any genital sex. It feels like a big relief to me. It doesn't seem to bother Daphne now. Occasionally we will do it but it doesn't seem high on the agenda. We have lots of cuddles and kisses, I would say we have a lot of non-genital sex, also a lot of talking, being close, warm, touching each other. Daphne says she feels we have such a tactile close relationship that she feels loved all the time.

Oriel and Daphne's experience is not unusual amongst lesbian couples:

It is probably because in a lesbian relationship you get to emotional intimacy quicker and on a different level than you do in heterosexual relations which means genital sex becomes less important. I have always felt that sex can be a vehicle into emotional intimacy, a bonding. But once I have the intimacy, sex feels less significant.

Oriel and Daphne have weathered this change well, but what if one of them suddenly decided they would like more sexual activity, perhaps with a third person?

We have talked about that and agreed that if either of us has a sexual relationship with anybody we just don't want to know about it. If it was just pure lust and a good experience, then it wouldn't harm us. If it was a terribly significant event, then we would have to talk it through. You don't know how you are going to feel until it happens. I would hate such a thing to take me back to that place of feeling inadequate. I might understand, but I would prefer not to know. We both feel so content at present that it does not seem like a threat.

Daphne's view was rooted in her commitment to Oriel. She said that she could not imagine wanting to sleep with anyone else other than Oriel.

The key strengths which enabled Daphne to cope with a change she had not expected and which deeply affected her were her persistent communication skills, her patience in being prepared to hear Oriel out, and her solid commitment to the relationship. Oriel also possessed a talent for open analysis of feelings. Moreover, her decision to cherish Daphne in every possible way apart from genital sex meant that her love could not be doubted.

Oriel and Daphne like the previous couples struggled to cope with a change over which they had some control but which was brought about by one of them.

In the changed situations faced by Bram and Rita, who become parents after ten years together without children, and by Jacob and Natasha, who suddenly have to cope with financial, employment and even possible relocation changes, *both* partners are able to exercise some control.

SCENE CHANGE: ADVENT OF CHILDREN: RITA AND BRAM

The change to parenthood for many couples is the most difficult they will ever have to encounter. The 'idea' of having children is very different from the actuality. Rita and Bram were united in their belief that, 'Having children is the biggest change we could have imagined. Our lives have utterly changed.' What they had not imagined were the unforeseen practical problems and the lack of shared outlook which can put pressure on even a stable relationship. In addition for this couple, whose multi-racial partnership was severely tested by racism (Chapter 3), this alteration in their domestic situation was particularly profound because added to the challenges of a change to parenthood was the fact that their kids were of mixed race.

Having dealt with the racism of Rita's family for a decade now they had to consider how to deal with potential racism towards their children. They agreed that they did not want the children to grow up in a totally white environment 'so that it seemed as if their father was somehow odd'; thus initially at Bram's suggestion they lived in the multi-cultural area of East London. Against Bram's wishes they then moved to a more suburban, predominantly white area near the river, where Rita thought the education was better.

Bram had compromised over the move. Rita in return carefully checked out the schools.

> Although our new place is quite a white environment, the
> school has a large catchment area from other multi-cultural
> places. I went to the nursery school and literally counted up the
> black kids who would be in my daughter's class. Each time I go
> to assembly I do a head count. There are five faces that are black
> and ten more of different racial mixture, so the school ethos is
> OK.

*

During the early years of parenthood they tried to make race descriptive rather than political.

> Our conversations with the kids are purely observational. We talk in descriptive terms. When Janey says to me, 'I look like you, Mummy', I am careful to say, 'Your skin is darker than mine but your eyes are the same colour.'
>
> We don't contradict what the children say. We let them observe. We don't talk about black and white; we talk about shades. We try to deal with race in very exact literal terms. We say a certain friend has a dark skin like Daddy, or another friend is brown. You try telling a kid that somebody whose skin is brown is 'black' when they've just learnt their colours.
>
> *(Rita.)*

Bram is afraid that 'someday soon somebody will say to our daughter that her Dad's a coon and then we will have to deal with it.' Rita worries that the children will have 'the hard time' meted out to her husband. She is however more optimistic than he is:

> I'm more prepared and less fearful than I was. With kids, there are so many other things that are more important or as important. Like somebody thinks she's stupid or pulls a face at her. For a child it's only in that order of things. To say your Dad's a coon is probably in the same order as to say your Mum's fat or a ninny. It's not a big deal yet.

So far, the change in Rita and Bram's social life through parenthood is more of a problem to them than potential harm to their children through racist attitudes. The couple used to spend their evenings wandering through London seeing bands and films. Now they feel they should be at home with the children. They could afford babysitters but they do not choose to. For Rita at least it is partly the cost but also her feeling as a working parent that 'the least I can do is to be there in the evenings. I think that should go for both of us.'

Bram does not put a high focus on 'doing things' with the

children. As long as he is 'around' and they are 'around' he feels this is satisfactory. Rita disagrees:

> Social workers have a great amount of preparation and as he is monumentally disorganised that drives me to distraction as he faffs about pretending to work instead of paying the family attention.

Rita wants them to meet this change in a particular way:

> I feel strongly we should deal with it as a family. In common with a lot of men, he hasn't quite come round to the idea that being a family and having kids means being selfless. He puts space and time for himself first, to do whatever he wants to do, go for a walk, swim, watch television. We cannot ignore the change to being parents. We must deal with it together.

A central problem is that though both parents work outside the home, the couple do not share child care equally. Bram appears content to mind the children during part of the weekend, which Rita feels is insufficient: 'He thinks if he looks after the kids for a couple of hours on a Saturday it is a big deal!'

Rita, who wishes to control the situation, has tried to resolve it by doing more than her share of child-care chores but constantly encouraging Bram to join in pleasurable family outings:

> I want us to do things as a family. But what happens is that on a Sunday I organise something with friends who have kids to take them all out, then he doesn't come. Just occasionally I manage to get him to come out.

The weekend before the first interview was an example of the effects this change to parenthood is having. Rita booked and paid for tickets to a children's concert at the Royal Festival Hall. Bram agreed to go and expressed enthusiasm. But five minutes before the couple were due to leave for the concert hall, Bram said to Rita that he had work to do and would not be able to go.

Rita's response was fiery but firm:

I said to him: 'At £7 a ticket you're bloody well coming!' So he did. But what is sad is that it is not his main priority to spend time with the kids. He'll talk about it, he'll think he does, he'll pay lip-service to it, he'll worry about the fact the kids aren't doing this or that, but basically it's all down to me. I think it should be much more shared.

Rita, aware that she was 'running him down', was nevertheless firm in her belief that Bram's attitude was thoughtless rather than malicious: 'I think it is selfish but I don't think it is intentional.' Her willingness to concede this point makes it easier for Bram to negotiate with her.

Their problem over this change stems partly from the way they had previously conducted their child-free leisure time. Having very different interests, they had in the past pursued them separately. Rita was happiest curled up on a sofa with a novel. Bram was content watching many hours of television or 'wandering about alone, poking in skips'.

I was a solitary excluder getting on with my books. Bram was a bumbler. Watching anything on the box just to relax.

(*Rita.*)

The psychological change to parenthood feels sufficient to Bram but Rita wants them to make a second practical change to joint communal activities. Bram finds this harder than she does:

We try to talk through the issue. Sometimes it gets somewhere. We sit down and agree that we must do more things together. It may work for a bit, then there's always some reason why it doesn't.

Both Bram and Rita accept that the only way they can deal successfully with this change is to continue to try to communicate without 'becoming angry, sarcastic or cynical'.

What works to their advantage is their history of mutual support. Bram is appreciative that Rita remained loyal to him during her parents' antagonism. Rita is grateful for Bram's allegiance during her father's illness and death. As partners, they share a

definition of 'a couple' which is closely tied into their understanding of the word 'love'. Bram and Rita said that love means
'not being able to care about anybody else'. Thus despite the very
real problems which they are currently encountering, they have
not considered giving up on the relationship:

> In the past when I have been really pissed off with him, we have
> discussed separating and I have thought about it. But love
> means that ultimately I'm not able to say, 'Well, actually I don't
> care what you do, because I do. No matter how angry I am, how
> upset I get, I wouldn't actually want to leave him.'

Like Rita, Bram has a concept of 'love' composed of romance
and friendship which he hopes will enable them to cope with
changes. 'We don't give each other flowers or sort of kiss and
cuddle or give each other love tokens.' Yet having said that,
Bram recently bought Rita a wooden heart. Their daughter
asked them if that was romantic and Bram decided it was. The
couple said they could go months when they were at war, then
they had a truce, then went through a 'lovey dovey' phase.
Each saw the other as his or her best friend. Rita felt romance
lay in the fact that they saw:

> the best in each other and don't want to denigrate the other
> even though we drive each other mad. I can still see the good
> things about him, that's romantic, if you can still see something
> good about somebody after twenty years.

In their willingness to see good points in each other, and their
decision not to assume that mistakes, even constant mistakes, are
malevolently intentional, Bram and Rita show an ability to cope
with change.

The way couples handle financial change is often symbolic of the
way partners feel about each other. When one person's income is
raised or lowered, a couple may need to develop new skills to
surmount the change and ensure it doesn't develop into a crisis.
When one partner loses a job or is offered promotion to a new

one, further psychological problems can arise. If that job offer for
one partner is for a position half-way across the globe, the
couple's domestic stability could be shaken. If all three of those
possible changes occur to the same couple within a brief period of
time anything can happen. Natasha and Jacob's narrative sets
the scene and illustrates the delicate balancing that is needed in
the face of triple changes.

SCENE CHANGES: JOB AND FINANCE: NATASHA AND JACOB
For 15 years Natasha and Jacob each earned a high salary that
was about equal. Financial independence was an important element in their coupledom:

> We have had two separate accounts from which we feed a joint
> account for household bills. We tried to split things equally.

The first change was when Natasha made a highly successful
career move to become a tax administrator: 'I suddenly overtook
Jacob's income. I earned about £55,000, probably twice what he
earned.'
At that point Jacob's work in computer research satisfied him.
This meant he was able to deal positively with Natasha's changed
(and superior) financial status. They both agreed that his lower
pay did not negatively affect their emotional relationship:

> It never became an issue. Jacob was wonderful. He wasn't
> bothered by how much I earned and was supportive of how
> well my new career was working out. He's the most 'new man
> person' I know in a genuinely internalised sort of way! I haven't
> had to reconstruct him!

However, within a short time Jacob's job became more mundane and he grew daily more dissatisfied. There was a decided
imbalance not only in the partners' salaries but also in their job-
fulfilment reactions. When Jacob's work showed no signs of
improving at 50 he decided to take voluntary redundancy which
meant a very significant drop in his income:

> Although we were not going to be poor, the issue was that for

the first time in our relationship one of us will be to a large extent financially dependent on the other.

The couple, who over other issues – such as whether or not to have children – have found communication difficult, this time talked at length about the implications of this financial change.

They reported that they found money easy to discuss because they put the same value on it: that of security. Natasha was the more worried, even though her income had not been cut:

> I personally couldn't cope with a high level of financial insecurity. My attitude to money is sort of learned behaviour. Money was always a huge issue in my parents' relationship. My mother never had any money of her own. She was very generous, very extravagant. I'm extravagant, sometimes ludicrously so. Now I'm well off, if I go for dinner with my friends I might pick up the tab for everyone because I earn more than most of them and I remember what it was like not to have much money.

Jacob is considerably more cautious than Natasha so she is always entirely straightforward with him, particularly since his income has been drastically lowered:

> My mother was always concealing money things from my father. I have to admit I've even done that. I've never told Jacob exactly how much I spend on clothes, so I wouldn't do so now. I tell him part of the story. But whereas my mother was in financial pickles, my extravagances have been within my income, but things will be different now that Jacob isn't earning. Now it will be my income that supports us.

The change has come to the couple at the point when they say they have been 'thinking ahead, knowing we want to be comfortable in our old age. So it is a worry.'

After months of dealing with this second change and its consequent anxieties, a third change occurred when Jacob, Australian by birth, was suddenly offered a computer consultancy in

Australia. He decided to take it for eighteen months in the hope that it would become permanent and that Natasha would agree to join him.

This time Natasha is finding the change hard to bear:

> He has been away nine months. They have offered him a permanency. He wants to take it. It has been hard for me on my own in England, though I have visited a lot. I don't know if I want to leave England. I've not rushed to be at his side! I've not stood by my man! There are some possibilities for me to work out there, but career-wise it would mean almost starting again. It is a huge issue. He wants to live out there but only if I am there.

How Natasha deals with this change has been further complicated by the fact that the head of her tax organisation is about to retire and Natasha as his deputy is a prime candidate for his post:

> Jacob and I are in limbo. We simply do not yet know how to deal with this most recent change. We have talked long-distance by phone. We have to reach a compromise. If he gives up Australia he will return to financial dependence on me. If I go out, I have to start my career again. Yet we cannot indefinitely keep our couple going across the globe.

After Natasha had successfully completed the first two job interviews for the new position, she and Jacob agreed on a compromise:

> If I get this job, Jacob will come home. I shall then earn a great deal of money, so we shall be in a financial position to look at more options. Jacob will certainly be able to return to Australia for projects or short-term contracts for maybe three or four months at a time. That would be manageable. What isn't manageable is being apart full-time. If I don't get the job I shan't want to stay in the organisation, so that will probably give me the kick up the arse I need to say, 'OK, I'll try Australia. I have nothing to lose!' These changes have certainly brought us to a major crossroads.

The delicate balancing needed by Natasha and Jacob to cope with the series of changes, all of them unexpected, none of them easy, relied a great deal on their commitment to each other and their talents for negotiation. The way this couple negotiated their proposed compromise in the light of these several changes was not based on superficially logical or 'fair' factors such as the fact that Jacob's new job opportunity occurred many months before Natasha's possible promotion was envisaged. It was based rather on the individual capacities of each partner to cope with fear of financial insecurity, willingness to rebuild a career, and need for intimate companionship.

I have looked at several key changes that confronted couples in this study which could confront couples anywhere. How couples dealt with change themselves and the different responses they made to each other's feelings often made the difference between the survival of their coupledom or its breakdown. Alongside an ability to accept change and adjust to it went the other significant components: a need for honest communication, a sense of deep commitment, and a great deal of cherishing during the process. Though a couple's first commitment was useful, it proved insufficient on its own to see a partnership through complex changes. The partnership needed ongoing maintenance such as renewal of trust, or repetition of key discussions. Changes involved constant negotiation, adjustment and above all flexibility.

Most couples had learned, sometimes painfully, the challenge of first acknowledging the need for a change, then accepting some personal responsibility. Where they marginalised their partner's conflict over making a change or accepting one, or where they tried to gloss over the whole issue, their relationship faltered. Where they communicated openly and tried to deal with change as a couple, while taking into account their individual needs, their respect for each other and their trust in the partnership increased. Change was seen ultimately as valuable. It refreshed tired partnerships. Couples who deal well with change felt they certainly would not stagnate.

What most couples found was that hot on the heels of a major change came some kind of compromise. I shall deal with that issue in the next chapter.

NOTES

1 Figures to March 1994.
2 According to WHO, the global picture in 1993 showed that of the more than 13 million men, women and children infected with HIV, about a third were women, most of whom contracted the virus through heterosexual intercourse.

CHAPTER 6

Compromise

Couples in this study found compromise to be the most challenging of the five critical 'C' elements.

Most couples paid at least lip-service to *Commitment*; they reported a strong belief in the importance of *Communication* or were saddened by its lack; they acknowledged the enjoyment of *Cherishing* each other; they were able to speak out when they felt insufficiently cherished; and they were realistic about *Coping with Change* (though few found it easy). However, for many couples the sticking point was *Compromise* because it involved them in giving up individual control.

The word 'compromise' is rooted in two notions: firstly the idea of each person giving up something and receiving less than they asked for; secondly, the idea that one may be exposed to danger or suspicion. Couples indeed rarely wanted to settle for less than they thought they could get. Some acted with suspicion towards the other member of what was supposed to be their home team. Many couples wanted to hang on to their own views, finding it difficult to be flexible.

Some shoals on which couples floundered were serious. Issues relating to outside sexual activity fell into this category. Mistresses of 'family men' in many cases felt that their existence as part of a live-out couple was always a compromise as their lover invariably spent Christmas, Thanksgiving, the New Year and anniversaries with wives and children. In some cases the compromise for the mistress was that her role in the couple was a secret:

> I'd lived with him 15 years in our city apartment and he only went home to his wife and kids at weekends, though of course they took vacations. In our eyes *we* were the couple! The compromise I made all those years was to agree he shouldn't tell his wife. We had our friends in the city, they had theirs upstate. When he died suddenly on a boat, it was the family who took over the funeral arrangements. It was terrible. I couldn't go to the funeral. My grief . . . it was as if my grief had no context. After all those years, he had become theirs. *She* was the widow and I felt I wasn't entitled to mourn!
>
> *(Janet, 41, New York.)*

When I talked to wives of husbands with mistresses, where the situation was openly acknowledged, some reported that it was *they* not the mistresses who made the concessions:

> I'd known about her for years. I could never think of her as 'his mistress'. That would have given her a role. I knew he had to do it and I was never prepared to leave him over it. But many times it was unbearable. Whenever I needed him for a little something to do with the girls' schools or someone being sick, if it was his 'night away' (that's what we called it) I felt I couldn't phone him. We started our marriage with honour. Philip was an honourable man. These last 10 years he feels he has been honouring two commitments. I feel our marriage is a terrible compromise.
>
> *(Gillian, 48, British.)*

Occasionally the system works agreeably and both wife and mistress find workable negotiations:

> I was on my second marriage but it was going badly. We didn't sleep together, we didn't make love, well I didn't like the way he did it . . . he suffered from premature ejaculation and he trembled . . . so I didn't want him to. We had no children, little in common, so I took up Italian. I even dreamed in Italian. I took

my exams and then told him I was off to Italy. When I got there I started a very strong relationship with a married man who had eight children. He was amazing but very dictatorial, like a little Mussolini. Things went wrong in his marriage and one by one his children revolted. They kept secrets from him. One Christmas he learned quite by accident that he was a grandfather. He was terribly upset, so he moved in unasked with me. One day his wife came to see me, to set things straight. She was very upset, but she was still very much his friend and I really liked her. Gradually we seemed to approach each other and realise that in some way I was fulfilling some position within their relationship. We each made compromises and to my amazement it worked well. We became good friends.

(Lillian, 73, British.)

That such compromises can work out is shown by the fact that though the 'Little Mussolini' died, Lillian and his wife have remained good friends.

The change from a couple to a threesome was not merely a marital issue, as it also occurred in cohabiting heterosexual relationships and in lesbian partnerships. In this study, despite the many compromises made in order to maintain such situations, amongst couples containing women there was a high level of dissatisfaction.

Gay male couples who participated in this research had considerably less difficulty in adapting to the presence of a continuous third person or making suitable compromises. Although many gay men establish stable long-term committed partnerships that focus on monogamy, the expectation of outside sexual activity is still the rule for male couples. David McWhirter and Andrew Mattison, who conducted a survey of male couples in 1984, reported that not only was sexual exclusivity not an ongoing expectation but some male couples found that outside sexual contacts contributed to the stability and longevity of relationships.[1] Where a male couple in my research took on a third person, McWhirter and Mattison's finding held true. However, the increase in the spread of AIDS and subsequent anxieties meant not only a practical decrease in outside sexual activity but also a psychological compromise on the part of the men to look at fidelity in a way they had not previously been socialised to do.

Whether the issues were seen as threatening or frivolous, all couples talked about how difficult it was to give up their own view. Often they expressed a tearing need for control over what in retrospect turned out to be quite trivial matters, such as silly arguments about different holiday locations or whether or not to have the central heating on or the window open in the bedroom. What couples frequently discovered was that beneath their initial inability to compromise over small areas lay deeper issues with which they had not dealt.

Although some issues were lighthearted and amusing – as in the problems over compromise faced by the New York couple Nancy and Saul who held divergent interests in films, or the Texas couple Mardy and Will who had conflicting views on how they expressed affection – the need for one partner to assert 'their way' as the 'right way' of handling issues was still a strong component.

Saul, 40, who worked part-time as a waiter, part-time as a masseur, liked what Nancy scornfully called 'brash crap Hollywood blockbusters, the kind you have to be brain dead to sit through!' Nancy, a 43-year-old university neuro-scientist, liked what Saul termed 'smalltime arty-farty movies that no normal person can understand!'

Nancy said Saul's taste needed uplifting, so Saul agreed to try out her kind of culture. For eight weeks she dragged him to complex low-budget artistic hand-held Film-Noir movies, sometimes followed by an intense 'therapeutic discussion'. After watching 32 such films, and listening to 16 hours of film buff analyses, in darkened halls without popcorn or adverts, in desperation Saul said weakly, 'Please, please, let's go to a movie somebody other than your university crew has heard of!' Nancy burst into laughter, which enabled a serious discussion to take place.

The issue however was less simple than it appeared. In a later discussion Nancy admitted that though she had married Saul (who had been her masseur) because he was 'gentle, sensitive, not macho, not driven by intellectual work' after 3 years the way other people viewed Saul's work as a masseur and waiter disturbed her. In the eyes of her university friends he was seen as poorly paid, effeminate and anti-intellectual. By attempting to 'educate' him culturally, she was in fact trying to conceal her anxieties and refurbish his image:

> I still loved who he was underneath, but I was rattled by how he appeared to the top-level scientists I work with. I've learned that innuendos aren't important. The next time someone at work makes a bad joke about Saul's terrible taste, I shall confront them there and then!

The couple decided on a compromise which meant they saw a few favourite films together, taking turns to choose the genre, but they spent most cinema outings with their own friends. Even more productive to their relationship was their recognition that beneath a superficial difference in cultured tastes lay a social class issue which had to be dealt with.

Will, a 34-year-old architect living in Texas, and his Filipina wife Mardy, also 34, who is the marketing manager for the family firm, have been married 14 years, during which time their only consistent difference of outlook is over the way they express affection.

'Will likes to snuggle. I don't.'

Will agreed that he did indeed. For him snuggling was a joyous overflowing of sexual expression, but he was aware that Mardy was 'not a touchy-feely person':

> I certainly am not. That is not the way I show my love. Will also thinks sex is much more important than I do. There are times when to his chagrin I have said I don't want to make love, that I am not comfortable right now or that if I am writing (the one thing I do independently outside our family's architectural work), I need to be free to be celibate.

Initially Will equated 'snuggly behaviour' with emotional commitment and wished to impose his way of expressing it on Mardy. Over the years he has decided that his reading of the situation was mistaken. He now feels their relationship offers such substantial rewards in terms of affectionate companionship that he is prepared to compromise. He regards Mardy as his 'friend' as well as his sexual partner. Mardy feels even more strongly that 'he is my friend first'. Their joint view is that some friends snuggle, some do not, and that no particular form of behaviour is better than any other.

Talking to both these couples about what had been small but niggling compromises, which nevertheless hid the issue of which partner was in control, I was struck by their warmth and sense of humour. Couples who found it harder to compromise were those who saw relinquishing any form of control as stressful or threatening.

Gay couples found their most consistent combative compromise occurred in situations where only one partner was 'out' to family or employers. In both heterosexual and gay partnerships, the most contested areas were child-rearing, sex, housework, tidiness, educational or social class inequalities, and most particularly money. Not only were expert skills of negotiation needed, but so was enormous good-will on both sides.

In a society where women still earn substantially less than men, women often find they are compromising over how the money is spent. In this study many women who were low earners or no-earners did not feel they had 'personal money'. Instead they saw it as 'household money', whereas men in this study rarely had difficulty over the concept of 'personal money'.

Some couples can talk honestly about what money means to them in their relationship, what their inhibitions are, what frightens them about the other person's money methods, but other couples fear to raise the subject. It can become the last taboo in a partnership. Income disparities, though a challenge if they result from a sudden change (as we saw in Chapter 5), are often easier to deal with than opposing styles of money management. If one partner links extravagant spending with a philosophy of 'live today for tomorrow you may die', while the other believes in 'cautious spending and rainy day saving', merging monies may produce tension unless compromises are discussed and reached in advance.

Financial styles are often linked either to parental influences or to social class background. Two people may have had widely divergent upbringings. In one person's home money may have been freely used for pub outings, films, videos, or package holidays, whereas in the other person's home money may have been carefully allotted for charities, books, further or higher education. For these partnerships to work effectively several compromises have to be negotiated.

In this research, both in the USA and Great Britain, a high percentage of couples had opposing styles of money management which were accompanied by educational inequities, cultural or race differences and a clash of social class environments. I have chosen three couples to illustrate some of the problems and solutions. Franny and Tom are a white middle-class/working-class British couple; Bobby and Rose are a black American working-class and white British middle-class couple; Fifi and Ricardo are a white middle-class/working-class Irish–American and Italian–American couple from Los Angeles.

A COMPROMISING SCENE: MONEY AND CLASS: FRANNY AND TOM
Franny is a 48-year-old British school-teacher with two adult children, formerly married for twenty years to a composer:

> Just the kind of man you would think would be right for me. He was musical, clever, middle-class, been to university, similar politics, interests. On paper we looked the ideal couple! But we weren't. We lived apart for many years after I couldn't stand the affairs.

For years, still legally married, she managed as a single parent with very little social life. For the last 5 years she has cohabited with Tom, a 46-year-old construction worker whose childhood was spent first in a children's home, then in and out of care, who truanted from school, was sent to an approved school, and left without any qualifications.

Tom and Franny, who like Nancy and Saul came from different social classes, saw themselves as an 'unlikely couple' who met in an unlikely way.

When her divorce finally came through, Franny decided to take 'a girlie-midlife-womanly break to a friend's flat in Corfu'. On her fifth day there she met Tom, who was serving cocktails behind a bar:

He started to chat me up! I was behaving irresponsibly with a great feeling of abandonment. So my friend and I ended up going on an island tour in his jeep.

Franny's first impression of Tom was far from good:

He was like a bit of rough! He was absolutely not the kind of man I'd ever dream of having a relationship with. But in my inebriated state I started flirting. Maybe after years of marital misery and single-parent responsibility, I was rediscovering my flirtatious femininity. Having felt for years I was not God's gift to womanhood, I realised I could still pull a bloke. Of course he responded. Lots of chat-up lines, some charisma, but just like a building worker who'd wolf-whistle you in London.

Franny's assessment was accurate. Before Tom left London for Corfu because he was 'fed up with England', he had been a building worker in London, and cheerily admits to wolf-whistles:

Before Franny I was that kinda person. Liked a laugh, pretty restless, if anything got on my nerves I'd say 'stuff this' and go! I'd been on my own some years since my marriage broke up. I was working the bar, happy-go-lucky, just didn't give a damn!

Tom's initial view of Franny was more generous than hers of him:

She was pretty attractive, slimmer than now (it's the good lifestyle I've given her!), yeah, pretty attractive! She was wearing an off-the-shoulder-type top, no bra and flashing her boobs all over the place! One girl on the trip said, 'Cor blimey! That woman's a bloody tart, an Essex bird!' Well, I didn't think Franny was! In Corfu you see all sorts, I could judge where they came from, council housing estates, middle classes, the upper middle. I knew where she was from with that accent. It didn't put me off though. Asked her out for a drink an' that.

Did 'an' that' signal an affair?
Franny responded readily:

I was incredibly irresponsible. Untypically so. I did everything I'd never done before, and wouldn't ever recommend my children do. I had unprotected sex with a man I didn't know, whose medical history I had no knowledge of, whom I believed I should never meet again!

Tom was extremely reticent, protective about Franny's reputation:

Hum, did we sleep together? Um, pass. Do I have to answer that question? Did Fran answer it? Oh, well, if she said it, yes we did. I'm like that at work, never one to discuss personal things. Never said, 'I had sex with the Missus last night' or 'Picked this girl up and we had a bonk.' Don't normally discuss it. The important thing about Franny was she was this interesting person, I felt relaxed with her, us being different class and stuff didn't matter.

Franny said it did matter to her:

He did seem more caring and sensitive than I'd thought, but we were from different worlds. I gave him my English phone number, but I never expected to hear from him.

However, after flying home, as she walked in the back door to be greeted by her son, daughter and ex-husband, the phone rang and her son repeated with incredulity: 'It's a Tom from Corfu!' Tom wanted Franny to know that he did not consider it a mere holiday romance and that he intended to follow up his call with a series of letters:

Hardest thing I done. Writing letters is a strain like forms. I can't do anything where I've got to sit and write!

Franny was confused:

I wanted to slam the door on the experience. But I was unsure. I couldn't believe what I'd done. Who was it who had behaved that way? I described him to everyone as a fat balding man with tattoos up his arms who'd lost a fight and couldn't write articulate letters. I can't believe how snobby I was. The best thing he's taught me is not to be snobby, though that lesson . . . all our lessons have been at a price. We have had to make a lot of compromises to stay together.

His letters touched Franny, who began to respond:

He was clearly more interested in me than I was in him, but after twenty years of a loveless marriage, my self-esteem kicked as low as it could go, the fact that he seemed to care and would try to express his feelings gobsmacked me.

When Tom flew to England for his mother's 60th birthday, Franny met him in Hull. 'I wanted to have a very good look at him and see how I felt.' She met his family, his ex-wife, even his son whom Tom hadn't seen for years:

I realised we were extremes. His family were like border-line criminals, just on the right side of the law. That weekend was symbolic of our life together from then onwards in that it was extreme. We each had to compromise, make allowances. We had a celebration with his family in a rugby club with a rough comedy act that I didn't find funny. Smoky, beer-swilling, crude jokes, women dressed in clothes I wouldn't have been seen dead in. It sounds snobby again, but it was just so crude! I said what I felt about it too! I don't think he understood about the jokes, and he was understandably defensive about his family. But he did understand my concerns about 'Could we work as a couple when we come from such different backgrounds and have such different interests? What kind of compromises would we have to make?'

Tom was prepared to please Franny.

I tried to get an understanding of how her mind worked. She started showing me more points to life. She likes to go to the theatre, watch plays, or the cinema. I've tried those with her. Cinema-wise no problems! Mind you, not the ballet! Once I

quite surprised her when I said if she couldn't get anyone to go
down the opera I'd go. Her fear was I'd fall asleep!

Franny began to relax:

We did things that were more 'me': walks in country parks, pub
lunches, quiet talks. Tom managed to flip comfortably from one
world to another.

Tom said he had no trouble in adaptation.

Once I had a sales and marketing manager's job, so I learned to
deal with all brackets. If I was mixing with bloody Princess Di
and her people, I'd behave in the manner required. If I was
dealing with the local head-bangers from the estate, same again!

Franny however found 'flipping worlds' difficult.

I managed his world by putting my professional hat on as if I
was working with a group of people who didn't hold the same
attitudes and values as I did.

The couple, whose feelings of affection were becoming stronger,
decided to persevere.
    Like many of her friends, Franny's children were suspicious of
the relationship, but eventually Franny flew with them to Corfu:

At first they found me a slight shock. The tattoos, no posh
accent what they're used to, two teeth I pulled out myself, fights
an' everything, but we got on OK.

                                                          (Tom.)

A positive factor in the children's relationship with Tom was his
genuine interest in Franny's son's football-playing: 'I'd kick the
football which his own father never did. He was well into music
stuff.'
    Franny decided to pay for Tom to fly to England regularly,
where they continued to compromise over class and cultural
styles:

If I wanted to look round museums and cathedrals, he would sit in the car outside and wait patiently for me.

She liked 'em! I was happy to take her and happy to wait. Takes all sorts.

It would have been preferable to have Tom share that, but it was a very good compromise.

She even come a little downmarket, started watching my kinda telly programmes. She didn't always laugh but she curled up on the sofa and watched.

Tom wanted Franny to 'up sticks and come out to Corfu' and help him run a bar. Franny refused. She had become frightened by his lack of finance and his irresponsibility with any money he made:

I was suspicious. I wrote him a powerful letter which upset him, saying how come a 42-year-old man can have no material possessions, no house, no car, a life that is lived hand-to-mouth? How could you have got to this stage and have nothing?

After months of a commuting relationship, with Franny footing all the plane fares and 'bailing Tom out' several times, Tom decided to 'up sticks' himself and return permanently to England, again at Franny's expense:

I wanted him to come, but I knew money was the issue. I resented having my destiny set out as a provider. He promised to find himself a flat, but ultimately he settled into my house.

Tom has dealt very caringly with Franny's children:

One of the best things about him has been his sensitivity towards their feelings. He has not tried to push in, just let it evolve. He will cry for them, he would kill for them undoubtedly. He really loves them. I'm not sure they know that, but I find it incredibly moving.

Her friends still tell her: 'You could do better,' but Franny herself has blossomed under Tom's affection.

> I function better as part of a couple. I'm never going to have it
> all, and what I've got in comparison with what I had is brilliant,
> loving and affectionate. He meets my emotional needs. I feel
> loved almost unconditionally. That's the best bit; it allows me to
> feel confident and grow as a person. It is a real foundation, like a
> tree in good soil. He is my really good soil. He nurtures me in a
> way that allows me to grow and develop.

Tom too has changed:

> In the olden days I'd have been happy out boozing with the
> lads. Now I'll curl up with her and watch telly, and there's
> always alcohol in the house!

Today, despite a warm and loving relationship, their main
compromise is still over money:

> I earn at least £22,000 a year, while Tom's wage varies from
> £3.55 to £5 an hour for construction work. We have separate
> accounts. He is supposed to pay me a third of the bills, even a
> third of the mortgage; it happens more than it doesn't happen,
> but as he is not always in work often it cannot happen. I have
> paid off all his credit card debts, his car loan, the lot. Money is
> still a disaster area with us because he gambles and I get angry
> and resentful.

The disaster which brought them to crisis point came two years
ago when Tom took out a £2,000 loan, which Franny guaranteed,
to attempt a business venture. The venture never took off, but
Tom assured Franny the money was securely in his bank account:

> A few weeks later we went out with the kids for a pizza. Tom
> stopped in the street and said he needed to draw out some cash.
> He went to the hole in the wall, then showed me his balance. It
> was less than £20! It should have been well over £2,000. 'What
> have you done with it?' I screamed. 'Oh,' he said, 'it's just gone!'

It was madness! The kids were waiting for their pizza! I was shrieking in the street! 'What do you mean it's all gone?'

They went to the pizza parlour. Franny could hardly swallow: 'Tom tried to make a joke about it. Nobody laughed. That day I thought we might have to split up.'

Instead of separating, they talked more openly and more seriously than at any previous time:

> We had to change his easy-come-easy-go attitude to money. If he gets angry at a job, he just walks out and may pick up another one a week later. Meanwhile I am working hard! There are many times in my job when I'd like to say, 'Fuck this! It's too bloody hard.' But I can't walk out. I have too many responsibilities. I pay the mortgage and the standing orders, while he feels he has the choice to come and go.

Franny gave Tom an ultimatum:

> He had to pay me more regularly and I said, 'If you ever, EVER do anything like that again, you cannot live with me, you cannot share the house. If you lived up the road we might still see each other, but we cannot carry on if you do crazy things with money.'

Tom said he took it very seriously.

> That was a time when I might have spit the dummy out or thrown the teddy out of the pram. The old me would 'ave gone storming out, but I'm not going to jack it in. I wouldn't like to lose this relationship. I'm making changes. I'm paying Franny regular. I'd even be happy to have all my money paid into her account if that's what she wanted. We've both tried to compromise. Possibly Fran gives more towards myself than I've given towards her. So I'll make an effort.

Their joint efforts are paying off. Tom has a better-paid job. Their friends have learned to accept them as a couple. They argue less. Franny is more relaxed. Even pragmatic:

It still seems that it will begin and end with me as the provider and traditionally men have been providers. But where is it written in tablets of stone? If I lived with another woman and she earned less than me, would that matter? Money still rears its ugly head, but it's the price I'm paying for the good bits that clearly outweigh it. As the years have gone by it has become easier because we're more a settled couple, so we help each other out. I no longer feel so used or exploited.

Only one issue remains over which so far no compromise has been attempted. Tom would like to marry Franny:

We've got the ups and downs of marriage without the piece of gold and the scrap of paper. If she wanted to, I'd get married to her tomorrow.

Two years ago Tom proposed. Franny, feeling romantic, accepted. Then, waking up in a cold sweat, told him she could not go through with it:

I was hurt, but I did then and still do understand the reasons why she said 'No'. It wasn't secure enough financially. Haven't asked her again. Why waste me breath?

It was a terrible thing to do to Tom. I hadn't acknowledged how hurt he was. Maybe now I've reached a point where I could, but I don't. I think we are as committed to keep working at this relationship without that piece of paper.

The house is still in Franny's name, and her will ensures that it goes to her children. But on her death, if Tom is still alive her life insurance goes to him: 'That way he can buy himself a little flat so he won't be homeless.'

Tom says that if the house was in joint names it would make the relationship 'that bit more secure, it would give added security to both parties', but he understands Franny's viewpoint. 'This house is her bit of security.'

Talking to them separately and later together, I saw clearly that because the compromises have been made willingly and thoughtfully, it is they (and not the house) who have gradually become each other's security.

A COMPROMISING SCENE: RACE, MONEY, CULTURE, CLASS: ROSE AND BOBBY

Bobby, the 39-year-old black American sales executive from Chicago, and her Intimate Commuter partner Rose, a 36-year-old white British writer living in Los Angeles (Chapter 1), have fought and loved their way through a relationship fraught with difficulties over similar central issues of financial asymmetry and class and educational inequalities, with in their case the added element of racial difference. They are approaching them in a very different manner from Tom and Franny.

Bobby earns about $150,000 a year. This is more than five times Rose's salary of $27,000 with a take-home pay of $1,500 dollars a month, which in Los Angeles only allows her to live 'like a student and buy clothes from thrift stores'. Yet Rose comes from a comfortable, secure, well-educated British family, while Bobby's childhood was impoverished and depressing:

> I'm from a poor black Michigan family, so like my money shows I've succeeded. I've sure proved I'm accepted by American society.

Any reminder of economy or thrift, the values with which Rose was raised and of which she approves, takes Bobby back to a childhood she despises.

Bobby feels that Rose has never confronted real poverty such as she experienced as a child and which, like Scarlett O'Hara, she has fiercely vowed never to see again:

> We had like nothing! There's a real attitude here towards black kids. I saw it as a young black Catholic who believed in God and knew I was put on this earth to do something. Their attitude tries to stop me. Making money shows I did it. They don't feel if you're black you can make money or get anywhere. I felt it when I was starting out in sales and management. I guess it's pretty amazing for a black person from where I come from to own their own home, to have a

wealthy job, to be in management, so there's all that crap. People still make a snap judgement when they see me before they even hear me speak. I hate that judging me by the colour of my skin. They go, 'Snap, yeah, she probably doesn't work', or 'Snap, yeah, she's just a no-good black person', or they snap into something negative. Whatever it is, it's going to be negative! Like: 'What is SHE doing here?' Right off the bat! Excuse me, I belong here just as much as anybody! That's who I am. I've always had to fight for who I am from the jump start. So I've fought through that. My money shows that!

A major obstacle is the different way they look at what money means. Bobby enjoys the luxury of expensive hotels and first-class travel, a luxury she never imagined as a child. Rose's preoccupation with the welfare of other less developed countries leads her in an opposite direction:

I know that the money we are spending on a hotel could pay for the education of a child in Malawi for a year. Guilty English things like that keep cropping up! I'm from the impoverished English middle class who get a kick out of bargains, and insist their children have second-hand clothes from Oxfam. I'm a Scrooge in that I will cut every single corner to save money. I hunt the second-hand bookshops and use libraries. I cry if I get a parking ticket.

Bobby admits how different their tastes are, but would rather pay for Rose to enjoy what she herself enjoys than compromise and try some of Rose's more economical pleasures:

I guess I make a lotta money. But I feel responsible about it. I'm totally happy to share what I have with Rose. I like nice hotel rooms whereas Rose doesn't care what it's like because for her cheapness in one area always affords her something she wants in another. If we use my money we can have the best.

Rose feels that Bobby has to control what is 'the best' in their partnership:

I had a dream I'd meet an Englishwoman from a similar background who wanted to go back-packing round the world. I was about to leave the States, return home to track down this Englishwoman in a cottage with roses over the door, when I fell for Bobby who hates back-packing, and gets no thrill out of sleeping on beaches. It horrifies her!

Initially my compromise was to suggest the Motel 6 chain, around 30 dollars a night for a nice clean bed. But Bobby would rather eat her own liver than stay in Motel 6! It has to be five-star luxury. You order room service as if you'd never boiled an egg! I've been to Dallas twice, Houston twice, but I've never been outside hotel rooms in either city. As she's happy to pay for hotels, the compromise is more in my mind than on my purse. On each trip I give her the money I would have spent had I travelled in a way I could afford. She feels fine. I am slightly unsure.

Their different cultures mean that even when Rose compromises over hotel rooms, once inside they face another obstacle: a conflict over opposed television viewing habits:

I was raised in England to pick out good TV programmes but never to watch on a sunny day. When we went to Dallas it was a hot summer's day, just right for a walk. She was exhausted and said she wanted to stay indoors with the air-conditioning and the TV on. I wanted to please her, so in we stayed. The TV was on for 11 hours. She channel-surfed, flicking backwards and forwards never watching anything properly. We actually had sex while she did that!

After much discussion, Bobby agreed to compromise at Thanksgiving by joining Rose at a back-packers' lodge. But even on this trip they had disputes about their different styles of behaviour. Bobby is orderly, tidy, punctual and almost fanatical about time. Rose, often late, is sometimes imprecise.

Rose persuaded Bobby to go on a short hike up a mountain where the view from the top was splendid. Tired and fretful, Bobby asked how much longer would it take. Rose said, 'About fifteen more minutes.' Exactly thirteen minutes later, Bobby said she would walk for two more minutes. At precisely fifteen minutes she sat down on a rock and refused to move. Bobby explained how an apparently trivial issue concealed a more significant one:

> I was angry. Rose never understands about time. Seven o'clock for Rose means somewhere between seven and seven-thirty. That is absolutely not acceptable to me. My previous relationship broke up over my ex-partner always being late. It drove me nuts! At home when Rose is late I just say, 'Honey, I gotta go! I'm walking outa that door! I got the car keys!' Then she gets it together. Later we talk about it. The good thing is we can talk about everything, even the bits we disagree on. But here we were on a mountain. We hadn't reached the top in time; it wasn't part of the deal.

Bobby admits that control is crucial to her in any relationship, and that compromises do not come easily:

> It's true I always wanted to control. I was sexually abused as a child for years, then I was doing drugs, cocaine . . . yeah, so there's an issue of what I need in order for me to feel like it's OK.

> Bobby has such rigid rules. There's a lot more slack to me than there is in her. She kept I saying, 'This isn't part of our deal! How dare you drag me up this mountain when we haven't reached that view!' as if we had a written contract. I felt she might sue me if we went one minute over the fifteen. It was a terrible thing. I seemed to have set a bargain, or an agreement, with her.

At the time, Rose pacified Bobby and finally persuaded her to walk a few more minutes:

> In just two minutes I got her to the top to an amazing vista of a hundred miles where she almost cried at the beauty.

But the conflict has had lasting repercussions for both of them.

At present they live on different sides of the USA, with an expensive commuter timetable. Bobby sees as a solution the relocation of one of them and the merging of their monies and lives:

> I have this long-term plan. I want to make enough so that Rose and I can bring up a family in comfort. I can't have children; I had endometriosis, and a hysterectomy at 29, and a bunch'a stuff. But I want children with Rose. She wants to be a writer so we need a big space for kids and writing and a nanny, because we'll both work. I can have a mortgage up to 300,000 dollars today and more tomorrow. I'm the one earning, so sure we'll live off my income. When Rose starts selling screenplays, then we'll merge our two incomes.

Rose believes their problems might increase if they merged money:

> Bobby trades in her new car every three months. She fills up a shopping trolley with luxuries she doesn't need. Tiny tacky details drive her demented. In hotel rooms, if there is no soap she has a screaming fit at the concierge. If Bobby was spending *my* money in that way, there would be a real problem. If I suddenly earned good money as a writer, I simply couldn't indulge myself, I should spend money on my family and buy books.

Rose believes that many of their conflicts come from feeling 'foreigners' to one another. It is harder to compromise when your behaviour patterns are rooted in different cultural standards:

> We can't take anything for granted, from how you brush your teeth to what TV programmes you watched as a child. It is a constant battle to compromise, to see her point of view, to change and fit in with her ways. But they are not just her individual ways, they are American ways, part of a materialistic culture I am not at ease with.
>
> That we each feel foreign to the other is an issue from the moment we get up until we go to bed. The only place it's not an issue is in bed! But outside bed, every minute something has to

be debated. She will comment on the coffee I buy or how I brew it. If I pick up a T-shirt that I'd worn the day before and sniff the armpits before I put it on again, she almost faints. To an American that is disgusting. They can't believe we wear a T-shirt twice even if it is totally clean. I believe they've been brainwashed by Lever Brothers soap manufacturers. They really think we smell!

A major issue over which they have learned to compromise, like Franny and Tom, is rooted in their educational and cultural socialisation:

Though Bobby reads a lot she dropped out of college and is not educated. This means she knows a lot about social skills and street wisdom but nothing about Cubism or Sartre. If I talk about a life well lived or the importance of being true to yourself, I must take care not to link it to literature. She knows a lot about football, but I'd rather watch paint dry!

Generally Bobby, like Tom, prefers to let Rose go to museums or galleries on her own. Unlike Franny, who was relaxed about following her own pursuits, Rose wants to share her preferences with her partner. Thus when they went to Paris, Bobby agreed to compromise and accompany Rose to the Louvre. It became the scene of another row:

I got annoyed with people taking photos of the Mona Lisa. They do it with flash and eventually they'll fade the painting. In a hundred years we'll be looking at a white canvas. I hate their greed, wanting their own special little 2″ by 4″ Polaroid snapshot rather than pay the Louvre for a beautiful print. I ranted on, but Bobby thought I was crazy. So we screamed and shouted at each other.

Rose was patronising people like me. How dare she put herself up on a pedestal just because she is educated and privileged? I told her, I don't have the education to know that flash photos ruin paintings, so you're patronising me when you patronise them!

Rose acknowledged that they needed to respect each other's separate areas of expertise and not put each other down. But for her this involves a big compromise:

> I have accepted I cannot be fully myself. Initially I saw us reading the script of *Pygmalion* with me as Professor Higgins! Now I know I have to adapt to the gaps in her education yet not patronise her. I need to learn from her what she can teach me. But it's much harder work than being with someone with whom you take things for granted.

After several months of hard work on both sides, there have been some improvements:

> Rose used to . . . like . . . teach me, but now, yeah, she more tells me. I could listen to her for years! She's amazing all the things she knows! She told me the history of England in four days! I loved her for it.

There are two areas the couple have in common over which there are no battles. They have a passionate sexual relationship – they both insist they make love many more hours than they squabble – and they both despise singlehood. Being in a couple is desperately important to both of them. However, these two factors may not be sufficient to keep them together.

Rose has big doubts:

> To be together I have to get a permanent Green Card to live in the States for ever and pay the penalty of barely seeing my family and friends or she has to suffer the same in England. Our sex life is wild and passionate, but the climb over the other obstacles may be too hard.

Bobby is more optimistic :

> When I was in rehab from cocaine, we learned the *how* principle. It means Honesty, Openness and Willingness. I think that's what Rose and I need: openness about our differences, honesty about our feelings and willingness to compromise. She understands

my driving need to get things done, like I have to control it all. I
understand her need to write and have time and space and be
very English. If I wasn't in a couple I'd never have to
compromise, but I am and it is a joy. I have to accept the kind of
person that I now include in my sphere.

If the couple can indeed apply sufficient honesty, openness and
willingness, and become more flexible – or at least less resentful –
over their compromises than they are at present, their partnership
stands a chance of becoming more mentally healthy. But critical
differences over American–English lifestyles at present impede
them in ways which are more serious than were felt by the British
pair Tom and Franny or the American pair Fifi and Ricardo,
whose narrative shows that a different outcome can result from a
parallel situation.

A COMPROMISING SCENE: EDUCATION AND MONEY: FIFI AND RICARDO

Fifi, dressed in open-toed sandals and dungarees, like the
Grateful Dead fan she admits she is, looks like a Nineties Los
Angeles version of a hippy and plays up to her looks. She is,
however, a clever graduate student of a university film school
where she also holds a good post as an administrative assistant.
Ricardo, 24, is thoughtful and hesitant, olive-skinned, with a shy
smile, less talkative than Fifi, and works as a cook. Their partnership is quarrelsome, vibrant and affectionate:

> Both of us are temperamental and quite capable of hitting each
> other, though so far we have kept that in check.
>
> *(Fifi.)*

Ricardo's job as a trainee chef is across the road from the university building that houses Fifi's office:

> Sometimes it bothers me when I'm working across the street
> cooking that I am working thirteen hours a day standing all day,
> and Fifi can work her seven-hour office day sitting on her rump.
> I'm angry because she can't understand why I am so tired. I
> want her to understand the different energy it takes do our

different jobs. I'm always going to have to deal with that fatigue, because men are expected still, which is a shame, to do more physical work than women. Women are now in the military, so they should get the same shit jobs we do! This is a hell of a compromise!

Their unequal earning power is partly rooted in the couple's unequal qualifications:

A big part of our problem is that Fifi is much more formally educated. My father was an athletic director in New York, and always pushed education down my throat to the point where I didn't want anything to do with it. I left school early, been living on my own since 16, so I'm more worldly educated than her. But when I go for a decent job and they realise the highest education I had was twelfth grade they don't want to know.

Ricardo feels these inequalities also disadvantage their shared social life, where again he feels he compromises:

I'm new here in LA, so I haven't many friends yet. These education differences cause us problems when we get together with her friends who are spoilt little rich kids. They don't respect the amount of work it takes to make it outside the sheltered school life. They've never been evicted, they've never been on welfare, they've never experienced hardships. If you're in school, it's easier to have plastic relationships because you don't have to depend on them. They're all graduate students at posh schools who turn up their noses when they hear that I've never been to college. I'm uncomfortable, but they are her friends so of course I go along.

On the domestic front, they make small compromises attended by short, hot flare-ups and long, warm make-ups.
Ricardo does considerably more of the cooking and cleaning:

Fifi is a slob! So tidiness is sure an issue. I don't mind cleaning when I need a good release. If I'm frustrated I'll clean the whole house. When I'm angry I'll clean three houses. But I do get frustrated because I know I am the only one who does it!

He does not however have the same attitude towards the two tasks. Cooking he regards more as an act of cherishing than a compromise:

The cooking I don't mind. Fifi can't cook, and being able to do it for her brings me joy. I hate cooking for a living, but I love doing her a really nice dinner and have her say what a wonderful cook I am, and maybe draw a bath for afterwards just to get that beautiful look in her eyes.

Fifi, guilt-free, is delighted with what she sees as mere minor compromises on Ricardo's part:

I don't care about housework. I guess he does. He definitely knows how to cook, whereas I don't even know how to cook cereal for breakfast. So he takes control of the small things, the details, like where I put my glasses, and I take control of the larger things, the deep philosophies, the academic stuff, and deep financial situations. Quite honestly I wish he was a bigger person, more financially stable.

It is the major compromises relating to finance which produce the greatest tension:

Our most consistent arguments are about money, my irresponsibility, the fact I don't earn enough to support both of us. If I could change anything about our couple, it would be our unequal financial status. That's where the compromises come in. We live together and have a joint account, but my compromise is that I let her have control of the money. I guess Fifi compromises by putting much more in.

Fifi is not at ease with the joint account, despite her control of it.

Budgeting has got way too mixed up. Neither of us knows whose money is whose. It usually ends up being my money. It had seemed an easy solution, but it has caused way too many headaches. I firmly believe a couple should have separate accounts. I need respect for the work I've done and the position I'm in, and if I'm not getting it on a joint account then a separate account could symbolise that. The fact that I earn more than he does is an issue. We did go through a cycle where he was earning more than I did, and that felt comfortable to both of us. Maybe because in some way we are old-fashioned and believe that to a certain extent the man should make more than the woman. Because I think they *can*, then if they *can* then they should.

Whether or not Ricardo *can*, at present he does not:

Sometimes I think, 'I can't believe she's making that much more than me!' But we don't fight over our different job earnings. We fight over worse things, like that I have a real hard time saving and I often lie to get myself out of situations which would reflect badly on me for my choices with money.

The choice Ricardo makes which causes Fifi most distress is to spend a great deal of money on sex calls:

He had this real problem. He was making substantial long 1-900 number calls[2] compulsively, never less than 45 cents a minute. He couldn't stop. It just got sickly dysfunctional. I felt he needed therapy, I was sure it would help. I also said that I'd be prepared to break up over this issue.

In addition to the issue of wasting money, Fifi feels they fight over the psychological issues which involve her in an unequal amount of responsibility:

One thing I look for in a couple is financial stability. That is as important to me as love, or having a laugh, or spontaneity. If one partner doesn't live up to their responsibilities, it feels like you're carrying their emotional as well as financial baggage. I had hoped somebody might have carried some of my baggage. Sometimes it's the bills, sometimes it's his lack of ambition. I would hope he would be more ambitious and want to make me less of his mother and more of his partner. Right now I'm his mother! It wasn't something I wanted so I have had to compromise over that, but the longer I've spent with him the more I seem to have become his mother.

The problem was intensified because they lived together in a small space:

I want to stay in this relationship but not live together till he is more sorted out. When I live with him I have to be the nag, and he has to call me the bitch. He feels threatened, so he has to be the slacker. That's the kind of roles we play and toss around. The more times you are called something, the more you are unable to change, the more you take on that role. We need to be away from that, so that we can inspire each other rather than strike each other down and resent our compromises.

Does she want to give up on the partnership?

No. I am stuck with the idea of unconditional love, that you can't really run away because you have made a certain commitment, that's what makes me angry.

Fifi decided that the way for her to compromise less might be for the couple to have counselling. Ricardo agreed:

We went into couples therapy because of the money issue. It did make me start fessing up about every money mistake I've made, which was so hard to do. But once you start facing up to it, it tends to get easier. The pit in your stomach goes away when you face the music.

After months of wrangling and heated discussions about their individual compromises, Fifi decided to try to encourage Ricardo to begin studying, and the couple decided temporarily to live separately. The separate spaces helped their situation:

Ricardo got a taste of financial independence. He still has money worries but it gave us a clearer understanding. Once we were living apart, we started the pillow shuffle back and forth every single day because we really wanted to be together. We were paying twice the rent and it ended up causing us more stress. I wanted to urge him on to study. I could do that more easily if I was with him.

After several months, the couple have moved back together.

The fact is I am going to worry about him no matter what, because I love him. He can move two thousand miles away and if he's hard up I'm going to send him money. When we were apart I realised Ricardo is this knight in shining armour who goes out to battle and I'm his princess, and he leaves me and we make love the night before he goes off to fight his battle and he leaves his sword behind. Well, that's ridiculous. Who's going to let someone they love walk out into battle without their sword? So here I am back with him chasing after him with his sword. But I don't resent it as much as I did because you know what – he jumped out of bed when I got back and started studying and he has got into college. Things are going to get more equal!

Ricardo, who has just started a basic course at college, though frightened is also more optimistic:

I am terrified, I haven't been to school since seventeen. It's the hugest step I've ever taken. But I want to better myself. I think despite our arguments, being in this couple with Fifi has inspired me to better myself, and that's probably the biggest benefit. She's not like my Dad, she didn't push me. She's shown me through her actions how to make things happen and how to change myself. I've become more responsible since I'm with her.

Part of his new sense of responsibility has been to take on two part-time catering jobs while studying so that he can contribute towards the rent and expenses. The couple's verdict when I last spoke to them was:

Though most of the financial burden is still on me, I see the desire and the passion and the work ethic coming through and that's enough for me!

(Fifi.)

The relationship has sometimes driven me fucking crazy but no, it hasn't been detrimental.

(Ricardo.)

Like Hope and Geoffrey (Chapter 5) this couple were prepared to seek outside help over their most confrontational issue. They felt they benefited sufficiently to address other problems in the relationship more calmly. They were fortunate in that their intense commitment to each other was stronger than their need to exercise control. This allowed them to share some of that control and compromise effectively.

As we saw in the case of Bram and Rita (Chapter 5), the change to parenthood can cause tension and disturbance to a formerly secure couple. Even those couples who enjoy having children feel that their life as 'a fun couple' is badly compromised.

A COMPROMISING SCENE: CHILDREN AND WORK: SIMON AND KIMBERLY
Simon, 45, an American film producer, and his wife Kimberly, 43, a screen-writer, have a 9-year-old son and twins of 4:

The biggest shift is when you become a parent. You've gained a new part of your identity because you've joined the great group of parents. But you've lost the independence of your personal identity.

Simon's attitude to parenthood and the compromises it brings is positive but thoughtful:

Children bring you a lot of joy, that kinda sense of building a family. The parental side has benefits, but it feels overwhelming; the general exhaustion level is high. Though having kids brings you together it kinda also separates you from the couple you were, that tight intimacy you used to have. It makes you focus less on your partner because you end up focusing on your children. That's a pretty big compromise! The responsibility of having kids kinda creates this transitional thing where in terms of the romantic part of being a couple, it's a pretty big bucket of water!

The other compromise Simon feels they make is over leisure time:

> You need time with your kids. A lot of time. That doesn't give Kimberly and me the time we used to take to go out and be frivolous. I feel strongly we need to remember the fun, frivolous side of our couple, so I say let's have a 'gate' night to ourselves each week. Let's go out on our own.

They have succeeded, and Kimberly reports that it has 'replenished and refreshed' their relationship: 'We are such great companions. We're in the same business and he's really someone to share things with.'

She does however feel that the compromise *she* makes is spending more time with their children than he does, because he works long hours at the studio while she writes at home:

> He is so work-oriented that it dominates his thinking. He is work-driven, like his father who was a doctor. I wish it didn't occupy so much of his mental space. I need to speak up about it.

Eventually Kimberly did speak up, and the pair discussed compromises. Simon found it easier to negotiate over practical matters:

> I changed diapers and got in on the bottle action when she wasn't breast-feeding, but now they're older it's true I'm working harder. Having the twins made me feel like I should work harder, longer hours, but I recognise Kimberly ends up doing more. We're kinda working on that.

Their biggest argument echoes Rita and Bram's.

We don't have many fights, but I guess we have the same fight over and over. I work too hard and I don't spend enough time with the family. We sat and talked it around, and when I realised that I only spend 20 per cent of my waking time with the family – well, I have to translate that into some action. Take more time to be with them.

Kimberly describes their couple as 'very well suited', and in terms of their ease in attempting compromises that will ensure parenthood enriches their relationship, they are indeed well suited. Kimberly was content to give Simon time to effect an adjustment to his working life: 'Simon is always willing to say he is sorry and to try and change.' Simon himself was trying to understand his own work compulsions.

In Simon and Kimberly's case, though having children produced some problems it was fundamentally a source of joy. If one partner does not want children but has to take on responsibility for their partner's children, this – as in the case of Frankie and Dilys – involves a much deeper level of compromise.

A COMPROMISING SCENE: OTHER PEOPLE'S CHILDREN: FRANKIE AND DILYS
Dilys, 42, Irish, formerly married for 18 years, lives with her son John, nearly 20, and daughter Jancy, aged 21. Dilys also takes part-time regular care of Teddy, the 8-year-old from a previous partnership. Dilys is now in her third year of a long-term Intimate Commuter Couple with Frankie, 10 years her junior, who lives half the week with Dilys and her children and the other half at home with her parents. Dilys is a social worker, Frankie a children's officer.

Despite working professionally with children, Frankie never wanted either to bear or to parent them:

I didn't want to feel responsible for years and years for somebody else. I didn't feel I could give what I think children should be given, that feeling that they are most important for 16, 18, or 21 years.

For Dilys, motherhood is her most important role:

I wanted children, so they are extraordinarily important. I wanted to be an effective parent. I think Frankie recognises that she doesn't come first: I told her from the beginning that she never will. It will be different when they've left home. Then Frankie will take up most of my time, most of my head space, but my children will always be a part of me. I'm never going to get away from that.

Initially Frankie was distressed that in Dilys's eyes she was not the most significant person. However, because she agreed with Dilys about the necessity for making children feel emotionally central, she was prepared to compromise over spending most of their shared life with them:

I made an effort when I realised Dilys *did* want me around and this was to be a long-term relationship. I had to take on board the children, but it has become our biggest issue. If we are going to have an argument the children would get in there somewhere. I never said I would substitute-parent them, but I have shared responsibility with Dilys.

How does this work in practice?
For Dilys it is an emotional co-operation:

I can talk easily to Frankie about issues relating to the children's emotional states. She knows how to relate to them.

For Frankie it is largely practical:

I contribute money to the household and stuff for the kids. With the elder ones I advise on things I know about. Help Jancy with CVs and job applications; try to get John to open up, talk to me. I play games with Teddy and help with homework. Having Teddy (who is only 8) at weekends means there's no lying in, nothing spontaneous. It all revolves round him. Even though I only live there half the week, I take an equal share in cleaning and running the house.

Frankie is rigidly organised and orderly, and feels Dilys's

house should be similarly organised. Taking the matter into her own efficient hands, she set to work:

> Frankie's degree of organisation is fantastic. She cleans our house, keeps it nice. Pulls stuff out of our cupboards, puts it into boxes, replaces it neatly. She has sorted the kitchen out. She regularly encourages me to clear my wardrobe, get rid of clothes I don't wear. She tidies the garden, cleans out all the sheds. She'll get all her clothes ready the night before, plan our washing, her baths, tell me that when she has time off she will polish everyone's shoes! That's the last thing I'd want to do on a day off! She contributes a considerable amount (as well as enormous financial generosity) so I'm sure she does feel like, 'Well, I clean it – it had damn well better be partly mine!'

Alongside Dilys's genuine appreciation runs a thread of irritation:

> Sometimes her organisation drives me mad! I come from a large family in Ireland, with few timetables, no absolute set times, an easier relaxed life. I've been used to doing it my way!

The conflicts between 'my way' and 'her way' have become the issue, which best illustrates their individual need to control personal space. It is also the issue over which Frankie feels she has had to make further compromises. For the 'my way/her way' conflict reached a point of high tension over the children's participation or lack of it. Frankie has very high standards of behaviour for children, and in her view Dilys's offspring fall far short:

> It's fine for Teddy to be dependent, but when I first arrived there John was 16 and Jancy was 18, but they were almost as dependent as Teddy. They let Dilys do near enough everything for them. I felt they could do much more in the house. They didn't show enough respect – hardly acknowledged – the fact she worked full-time. I thought John's behaviour was real rubbish! He did nothing! Surely it was time for them to give her some pay-back for her 20 years working for them?

In making her strong views known, Frankie believed she was acting considerately in her partner's interests:

I thought I was supporting Dilys. I wanted them to understand that, yes, your Mum does certain things, protects you, works hard, but it would be nice if you ever once made her a cup of tea, or took her up something in bed. I thought Dilys would be pleased. But she wasn't! It made her feel she could never have a relationship with someone because she had these kids who would always be a problem.

Dilys felt defensive about what she initially saw as Frankie's attacks, but realised there was some truth and sense in them:

She works very hard in our house so I do feel the kids should clear up to a degree after themselves, but I wouldn't have a big argument about it. I see what upsets her. They come in, leave their stuff where they dump it, use everything in the bathroom like shampoo, soap, they think it's theirs to share. They'll sit and eat meals but rarely cook, put their dishes in the kitchen but forget to wash up. Pay something like £30 a week for their keep, but not consider that may cover only their food. I do have reservations about all that, but don't feel it's important enough to lose sleep over!

The couple report that they have had to recognise there are needs on both sides:

We have different expectations around children, and Frankie's never lived with them. I feel they should be given special treatment because they're younger. Frankie is an adult who works with children, understands the issues, should make more allowances. I want them to do it differently, but I want Frankie to understand what it's like to be a parent. How can you if you've not been one?

Frankie reasonably points out that there are many ways of being a parent; she is suggesting one way. From the outside, it is clear that what Dilys initially wanted was a partner who not only understood her way of being a parent but also allowed the joint household to be controlled by that method.

As the couple have excellent communication skills, they decided on serious discussions about possible compromises:

> Dilys asked me to make allowances. I tried. She said in return she would sit down and talk to them about cleaning the house, cooking, shopping, sharing things out more. Dilys said we should lead by example but she did take on board my ideas.

Frankie suggested the house should be divided into cleaning areas and all four adults should play a part. Dilys, Frankie and Jancy cleaned diligently. Not so John:

> I hate to admit this, but we gave him the easiest, the stairs. Then he said the dust would affect his asthma so he'd do the sitting-room, but he never touched it! When Teddy came he broke things and made a mess. So it was down to the women cleaning!

At home with her own parents, Frankie in fact does very few chores. With characteristic honesty she admitted:

> I'm very hypocritical really, because my Mum does everything for me even now. I've tried to stop her but it doesn't work. I've really had to think that one out too! But I like order and tidiness and a place run properly.

Frankie and Dilys were acute enough to recognise that they both enjoyed their own kind of order, were both used to running their own lives, were both used to control, some of which they would need to relinquish.

> Having had to advise and guide the children, it sometimes makes me parent Frankie too, probably because she's ten years younger. I think I'm a better parent than a good lover or partner! I have to keep remembering I'm not a parent to this person. It is a complementary relationship, so I must ease up, not control everything, share.

I've had to learn to ease off more with Dilys's children. They saw me doing my share so it's starting to work out. I'd like us four adults to be like equals.

How do Dilys's children view Frankie, the newcomer to their home?

I haven't a clue what John feels about me underneath. He probably doesn't dislike me because I've never told him what to do. If I can't be this warm nurturing person, I'm certainly not going to be this person who tells him what to do. He'd really dislike that! He doesn't see me as a friend, more as his mother's partner. But yeah, I think he likes me. Jancy probably likes me some of the time, but sometimes she thinks I'm around too much and take too much time off her Mum.

(Frankie.)

According to Dilys, Frankie's perceptions are correct:

John does like her. She's very good to him, though she has been quite negative in the past because he takes advantage. If he wasn't my son I could probably be very negative about him too! As it is, I feel like I'm always defending my children. Jancy really likes Frankie. She's happy that I am happy. But she has bouts of, 'Mum, you never spend any time with me.'

In an attempt to remedy this situation, Dilys compromises over the time she would like to spend with Frankie and makes a special time for Jancy:

I've made arrangements to do something with Jancy. Then she's not there to do it. She's gone her own way. She's off! Typical!

The compromises and communication over the changes have been ongoing for three years. The couple feel matters have changed and improved during this period:

I keep my mouth shut more than I did. I've adapted more. I see the situation resolving when Dilys's children leave. Meanwhile it has improved a lot. I haven't changed my attitude towards children, but they have changed for the better and I think my input made that happen. I do care about the kids and what they do, but I wouldn't be upset if they moved out.

In the past I was constantly struggling, battling against them all, always feeling like a piggy in the middle. Not now. Frankie is very good with communication. She always wants to talk about things, so it has got better over time. I've learned to give up a bit of control and share my space. We have both grown up through the relationship. Grown up and grown.

One compromise that Frankie asked of Dilys was that she would tell her son directly about their lesbian relationship, to which Dilys agreed:

As soon as I started my relationship with Frankie, I said I needed to talk to him. He said, 'I already know what you're going to say!' I said it anyway. He said, 'OK' and scuttled off! Typical.

Dilys had already told her daughter that she was gay, but Frankie is anxious that Jancy is still a trifle homophobic.

She worries it will reflect on her. But she now tells her friends, and her loyalty to Dilys means she won't stand for any homophobia from them about her Mum.

Ironically, Frankie's own loyalty to Dilys has not extended to telling *her* parents directly that Dilys is her partner, which has resulted in another conflict. Though Frankie came out as a lesbian to her family when she was 18, the shock to them was so great that she never referred to it again. Subsequently she has been utterly discreet about her private life.

My Mum thought my sexuality would cause me problems with everybody else in my family. She's probably right, I'd get hassle, so I've never gone on about it. She worries about me, so I've left it alone. Though my parents know about my sexuality and though they like Dilys, they don't treat her like they treat my brothers' and sisters' partners. There's a big difference. My parents treat Dilys at the level of some of my friends, which upsets her. I am upset too that she's seen on the same level as other people.

Dilys does not feel hostile towards Frankie's parents but the situation causes her increasing concern:

Sometimes people aren't sure how to treat a gay relationship. They are not sure what they are supposed to do. It may mean us having to teach Frankie's parents or Frankie having to teach them. I shall have to be different in that I involve myself more in their lives. I don't pop in unexpectedly, I don't make myself at home when I'm there. To do that immediately would be unacceptable, but perhaps gradually.

Frankie, being a planner, of course has a plan:

My plan is to sit down with my parents at a meal and bring it into the conversation casually. Ten years ago when I decided to tell them about my sexuality, they were watching telly. I marched in, switched the telly off and made an announcement. I did it in a way that sounded like I thought it was negative. I don't want that to happen again; I don't want our relationship to sound negative.

Dilys, as a parent, understands how Frankie's parents felt:

They were frightened more than angry. They wanted only good things for their children. They didn't know how to cope, how to deal with it. It was difficult for them.

Though they have taken Teddy round for tea, and Jancy sometimes phone's Frankie's Mum, at present Frankie's parents have very little involvement with Dilys's children:

They've devoted their lives to bringing up their children, they idolise their grandchildren but they ignore mine. That's because Frankie so far hasn't seen her parents in connection with me; I have been something separate. She has always been seen as a single person with no children of her own, so this is quite new for her and for them.

Frankie believes her disclosure plan could change her parents' attitude:

Dilys is my partner, and as she has these children they're part of our family now.

In Dilys's view:

Frankie is part of my family but my children are not part of hers, which is difficult. People have said to me, 'Oh, Frankie's parents are in effect your children's step-grandparents' and it hadn't even occurred to me. But they are. And they idolise her sister's and brother's children! In a heterosexual relationship their treatment of my children would not be heard of. My children would be a big part, either positively or negatively, but they would be considered.

Frankie found the idea of her Mum and Dad as step-grand-parents almost too difficult to consider:

I'm not saying Mum should see them as step-grandchildren, because I'm not sure that would work out. However, they will have to know that I'm planning my life round this woman. Therefore Teddy, John and Jancy are important to me. If it's family events, Dilys must be seen, must be asked. It may not be an issue for me but it certainly is an issue for her. Dilys will not be settled until I do it!

Frankie has assured Dilys that she will make that compromise, though by the end of the research she still hadn't done it. Dilys, however, had great faith in Frankie's loyalty to her:

I trust her *absolutely*. When she says she will do something she is totally reliable. She is very sensitive to her mother's feelings, but because she recognises it causes difficulties for me she will get round to it.

*

The two issues highlighted by Dilys and Frankie's narrative – firstly, whether or how to compromise over bearing children or adapting to someone else's; and secondly whether or how to compromise over revealing a couple's sexual orientation – occurred a great many times in this research. Daphne and Oriel (whom we met in Chapter 5) had as complex a struggle with gay confrontation as did Dilys and Frankie but ultimately met with more success. Whereas Oriel had been out to her family as a lesbian for twenty years, Daphne's family had no idea of her sexual orientation and Daphne, nervous about their reaction, refused to tell them for three years. When she finally managed it her fears about her mother's reaction of hysteria and hostility were justified. A further two years of alienation ensued. Eventually Daphne's parents made one visit to the couple but felt unable to maintain good relations with them. Daphne and Oriel are still working on the problem. Nanette and Jonathan fought over the child issue but Nanette unlike Frankie refused to compromise.

NO COMPROMISE SCENE: I WON'T HAVE KIDS: NANETTE AND JONATHAN

Jonathan and Nanette were married for 21 years, during which period Jonathan consistently wanted a family while Nanette was bitterly opposed to it:

> Jonathan very much wanted to have children. It's been a sort of issue for years. Not having children was entirely my choice. I never felt the slightest interest in having them; I come from a big family and it put me off.

Her mother's life had a decided effect on Nanette's refusal to compromise:

> My mother was wonderful, a very traditional kind of mother, always at home, always putting us, the five children, and Dad first. She was the one who nurtured and cared, and I think it stifled her. Not that she ever said so; she never seemed anything other than completely satisfied by all this nurturing of children. She was a talented woman, and I think she could have done other things like I have. She always encouraged my career; I couldn't have had this career with five children.

Nanette's determination not to have children was based, as was Frankie's, on her fear of other people's dependence on her.

> I don't like dependence. I couldn't bear the thought of people being dependent on me. Jonathan and I are fairly independent. We depend on each other for emotional support, but we are not clingy. I don't want someone who clings and depends. I don't even look after house-plants! It's that sort of feeling, not wanting the responsibility. I suppose it's rather a selfish attitude. Jonathan's sadness did make me feel guilty, but it didn't make me feel so guilty that I had to do something I didn't want to do.

Jonathan and Nanette both regret that they did not spend more time communicating their conflicting points of view. Jonathan said they did not thrash it out, merely drifted. Nanette said: 'We didn't talk endlessly about it at all. We should have done.'

Two years ago Jonathan started exploring certain issues in his personal life, at which point the 'baby thing' came up again and then they talked. Nanette felt that the issue became more urgent as she got older: 'Obviously now I wouldn't contemplate it, so I think it has sort of gone. Gone by default. Gone past.'

Has the problem genuinely been resolved, or has it merely gone under the surface? What effects has it had on their relationship?

> I think he's given up wanting them now because I don't want them, but it has been very difficult for him.
>
> *(Nanette.)*

Jonathan told Nanette that, despite his initial sadness, the fact that two years ago they finally talked about it has been useful for their relationship. He is still sad, but both partners feel they have come to terms with it by simply accepting the fact that they are not parents.

Jonathan is clear that by compromising his loss is that of a fatherhood that might have increased his happiness but would not have increased Nanette's. He felt if Nanette was unhappy their relationship could not thrive.

Nanette admits to gaining 'selfish things like being able to do what I like, not having to consider anyone except Jonathan, not having to put myself last, which is what I observed my mother do.' She does not feel the relationship has necessarily gained, 'because everybody I know who has children feels it has enriched their relationship. Nobody I know regrets having children.'

In this couple's case their commitment to each other was not in doubt, but the issue was of such significance to one partner that compromise seemed impossible. Where they admitted they fell down was in not giving the matter sufficient communication until it was virtually too late, at which point a decision was made by default.

When faced with the necessity to adapt and adjust, couples in this study made several discoveries. The first was that if they were well intentioned then it became easier to negotiate new terms with their partners. These well-motivated couples said that where it 'mattered intensely to the other person', ultimately they were willing to do things differently. The second useful discovery was that allotting blame to a partner was rarely constructive, whereas admitting one's own faults or mistakes often led quickly to a compromise. The third discovery was that it is easier to modify behaviour patterns than it is to alter attitudes or change personality. Thus compromises based on adjusted habits or behaviour were usually effected speedily and worked well.

In a no-compromise situation like that between Nanette and Jonathan (over the issue of having children), where one partner seems incapable of bending or meeting the other one half-way, it is sometimes possible for the less rigid partner to make changes in herself or himself in order to accommodate what at first had seemed impossible.

NOTES

1   David P. McWhirter and Andrew M. Mattison, *The Male Couple: How Relationships Develop*, Prentice-Hall, Inc., Englewood Cliffs, New Jersey, 1984, p. 5.
2   1-900 numbers are in this instance US sex chat-lines.

CHAPTER 7

Cherishing

WHAT IS CHERISHING?

An ideal couple is like lichen. That's because lichen is an alga and a fungus which live together and give each other mutual support. Lichen flourishes under adverse conditions because it cherishes and is cherished. The worst kind of couple would be one with a host and a parasite, where one would feed off the other and do harm. The best kind of couple would operate symbiosis like lichen.

(Nancy, 43, scientist, New York.)

The notion that satisfactory coupledom is rooted in symbiosis, where each partner supports the other, is also the view of Dolly, the 75-year-old former Hollywood screen-writer, who for 54 years has had an affectionate and humorous marriage to 76-year-old Maurice:

I guess the best kind of couple are two people who have a symbiotic relationship in which somebody really understands you as well as you feel you understand yourself, or close to that. My feeling is that I understand him, and that you each treat the other with understanding.

Most women and men in this study identified this emotional

protection or *cherishing* as the key to the intimate caretaking which characterised the most successful (often long-lasting) couple relationships.

Cherishing includes the lichenose idea of mutual support:[1] the feeling that your partner is on the same side as you; and the belief that your partner is also your good friend. Integral to the notion of cherishing are several aims: to boost the relationship, to mutually enhance it, and not to say anything you might later regret.

In this society women have been socialised to cherish other people, to boost the egos of men in particular, and the expectation of both men and women is that within partnerships women will continue to do the nurturing.

For male-female relationships to work fruitfully, men as well as women need to acquire cherishing skills:

> Cherishing means choosing never to take his affection, his love or his being here for granted.
>
> *(Nancy.)*

Never assuming a partner knew she or he was loved; never forgetting to take the time to tell him or her; always protecting each other's interests as well as one's own; were three decisions central to the concept of cherishing, taken and carried out by couples who saw themselves as fulfilled within their relationships.

This theory of mutual cherishing which accepts that partners crucially depend on each other for emotional nurturance – as well as maintaining a sturdy autonomy – is, as we saw earlier, at variance with some contemporary viewpoints that attach a higher status to individual separation as the path to maturity. There are, however, some key researchers in the field – including Carol Gilligan, Janet Reibstein, Robert Sternberg, Michael Barnes and John Gottman – who, while using different terms, value the idea of cherishing which at its best implies a regard and respect for the partner, does not attempt to undermine him or her, offers encouragement, validation and concrete help and allows for a partner's vulnerability.[2]

Whether a relationship moves forward productively, stagnates to a standstill or, worse still, topples backwards, destroying the couple in its wake, is strongly influenced by how each partner interprets the other's behaviour. There are often two choices about how to behave: one being *conflict-promoting behaviour* which is unlikely to produce an improvement either in that particular situation or in the couple's general interaction, the other choice being *cherishing behaviour* calculated to improve the immediate situation and enhance the relationship.

Rarely, however, is the more mentally healthy course of action easy to carry out. But it becomes easier if each action is part of a system of cherishing set up and consistently carried out by both partners. This system means that within a couple, each partner does what is necessary to ensure that the other flourishes and grows.

HOW DOES ONE CHERISH?

As with Elizabeth Barrett Browning's love, there are many ways that couples can count to actively cherish someone.[3] The protective tools most often mentioned by interviewees were sexual, sensual or physical cherishing, verbal cherishing, empathetic listening, and keeping in touch by letter or telephone. Laughter and sharing jokes were seen as useful; as was acting as if partners were on the same side, behaving as a supportive friend, celebrating anniversaries or special occasions, keeping up rituals and giving gifts. Two cherishing methods seen as integral to a good relationship were helping the partner in countless practical ways and stopping arguments at an early stage, or where possible not provoking rows.

Sensual, Sexual, Physical Cherishing

Intimate touching, body massage, stroking the partner's body, hugging, holding hands, were the most common examples of the physical manifestations of affection shown by couples in this study which were found to be valuable in improving a relationship:

> We have this huge bath. John draws me a bath if we both come home from work stressed or done-in. Then he throws bubbles in

and when the foam reaches the top he dives in behind me, sits cradling my buttocks and rubs me gently all over my body. He takes his time, that's what feels good about it. Sunday mornings, we have breakfast in bed, then we have our weekend special with the Jacuzzi. His touch makes me feel he cares about me as a person.

(Ginnie.)

There are days when I get back from a board meeting. A really dumb one! They've all been really dumb! A drink isn't enough, I need a whole lot of restoring. Ginnie gets me undressed, then does the whole massage bit. It's a real work-over for my body, yet I don't feel like laying her.

(John.)

There are considerable gender differences over sensual and sexual cherishing. Women in this study found physical cherishing, that was either not genitally focused or did not lead to lovemaking, easier than men. One reason is that, as research has shown, men initially discover sex as desire, generally through masturbation or erotic images of women that are today considered oppressive. Only later do men learn to build affection and love into sexual expression. For many men genital sex was still seen as in some sense 'superior' to other forms of sensual or sexual intimacy, which were perceived as a lead-up to intercourse. As one male theatre aficionado put it: 'Shopping and Fucking, that's what the difference is! The low-level stuff is shopping. Women are better than guys at that!'

Women, by contrast, more typically see love and sex linked and have to learn to separate them. Their early sexual fantasies are more often relationship-oriented than are men's, which allows them to use all forms of sexual expression freely as cherishing tools.

Claudia was typical of many women accustomed to slipping from sexual to sensual expression. Her partner Mark was less used to it:

I was wild for the guy! I'd strip him soon as eyeball him! We couldn't get enough of being laid. All round the apartment.

Anywhere. We'd race round naked, dripping. He'd smear his semen everywhere. Like it was his power! I loved that guy! Later I'd want to stroke him, you know, just stroke and stroke, 'I wanna tell you I care,' I'd say as I stroked him. But he didn't get it; he always thought I was trying to rouse him. One day he'll get it!

> *(Claudia, 25, salesgirl, Canadian; partner to Mark, 30,*
> *horticulturalist, Canadian.)*

Generally, heterosexual men were more aware than Mark of their partner's need for non-genital cherishing (even when they didn't carry it out), because women's desire for physical cherishing is openly acknowledged and expressed.

Gulliver, a 62-year-old sculptor married to Tess, a Canadian lawyer, points to differences between sex and sensual cherishing:

> I don't think women ever want sex as much as men want sex but Tess and I have always had a loving, touching, sexy relationship. It has been much wider than genital sex. It is mystical more than anything else. It is when two-ness becomes one-ness, a mystical thing, a joining. I am more into sexual yoga where you're joining and moving up the chakras simultaneously. Tess is more down to earth. But the actual embracing is as important to her as to me. It is a marriage in the alchemic sense. You're not whole until you've got a partner in that mystical sense of the union of two-ness.

As women's desire for non-genital cherishing is seen in our society as more acceptable and appropriate than men's desire, Gulliver's open acknowledgement of his desire was atypical. In the past, for the same reasons, two men in a relationship found sensual cherishing less easy to accommodate than a man and a woman. However, the increased visibility of gay male couples and the new openness which allows them to express their actual needs – as opposed to those scripted for them – means that this situation is gradually changing.

In this culture men are socialised to value space and be

independent. Certainly not to care for each other. Gay men grow up needing connection because they don't have it. They are not connected with society, so they desperately need connection and caring. Ultimately gay men value space less and can begin to care for each other.

One of the best things he has done for me is to tell me that I have a soft heart, which I was always knocked down for as a kid. Boys can't grow up soft! He nurtures me and enjoys it and enjoys my nurturing him. I have looked for someone who does not belittle that part of who I am. It has always been an important part to me, but men are taught to scorn it.

In some cases bisexual men learn from their heterosexual experiences:

Men don't learn how to cherish each other or how to be romantic with each other. I was fortunate in the sense that I loved a girl in high school and was able to experience a lot of healthy good dating. I got to know what it was like to please somebody else without sacrificing my identity. I learned how to be romantic, how to nurture. There were a lot of things in my heterosexual dating experiences that I was able to transfer over to my gay dating experiences.

In my previous affair with a woman, she was perfectly accepting of my need to be looked after. I think she liked it! For the most part men don't tend to be able to hold on to or grasp or nurture that kind of softness, tenderness, what my partner calls my 'faffiness'. He is the first person who has not only accepted and nurtured me but has wanted to make sure that part of me grew. It was one of the things that made me fall in love with him.

Some men in same-sex partnerships feel that their early erotic training is both a help and a hindrance:

Guys definitely learn about lust! Fooling around with guys, yeah! So when you do want to translate it into something else again, you know how. But you don't get any hints on holding each other stuff. But kissing, hugging, just holding the guy or giving him a massage, that makes you feel plenty good too.

As men in a heterosexual society are taught to take active sexual roles, the discovery that they might enjoy less genitally focused gestures or a more passive protective engagement can come as a surprise. A married male couple discuss their different perspectives on active cherishing:

> Before we got married I was better at actively doing good for him. Being passive, accepting, was hard. I was a bit unsure when he touched the soft part of my heart, as he calls it. Now I let him reach in and either recognise it and nurture it or encourage it to come out and express itself creatively or emotionally. In our marriage that kind of cherishing has helped me grow as a person and enriched our relationship.

The intrusion of AIDS into couples' lives has in many cases allowed men to make changes in their stereotypical love styles:

> Men are expected to be emotionally tough. Because Ben is HIV-positive, which if I could change anything I would change in a heartbeat, it has allowed us to care for each other in ways we might not otherwise have tried. It has enriched our relationship. Ben's HIV status has meant that I have become more compassionate, more able to be in touch with my own feelings.

> I think I was pretty macho, but the shock of finding him HIV-positive has let my personal awareness grow in this couple. I realise how selfish I am at heart. . . . nothing like being in a couple to realise that . . . I've grown in my ability to care for another human being. That's been exciting.

Several men felt that because they had been socialised to strive for equality, this had a positive effect on the cherishing neces-sary in a two-man relationship:

> Maybe because we are both men we both feel responsible for making this intimate side work. Both of us need to take the

initiative to be affectionate with one another. I feel I
concentrate more on affection and Martin concentrates more
on sex.

Women who change from a heterosexual to a lesbian orientation notice critical differences in sexual cherishing. Kath, a
34-year-old Irish psychiatric nurse whose first long-term couple
was with a man, and whose second was with a woman, describes
some of the differences gender makes initially to the start of a
love affair and later to the consistent use of sexual cherishing.

SEXUAL CHERISHING SCENE: KATH AND FERN
For 5 years Kath was involved in an affectionate common-law
marriage with Al, a steel worker:

The sex was very good. We seemed committed, but there was
always a question mark in my mind. Although the commitment
was there I always felt it was going to go, that it would be taken
away. Although the sex seemed fine, Al and I were drifters who
didn't communicate enough, drifted apart a little. Maybe we
didn't take care enough of each other physically.

Then Fern, a young actress, was brought into the hospital ward
on which Kath was working:

We got on really well. When Fern left we stayed friends; both Al
and I saw a lot of her. I connected with Fern in a way I hadn't
with anyone, not even Al. I had an intense emotional reaction.
She'd got into my head in the sense that she grabbed my
imagination, stimulated my intellect, there was a need to be
with that person. Sex with Al didn't stay good when I was
feeling those things. I felt guilty all the time, I wanted to be with
her when I should have been with him. When Fern went on tour
I missed her desperately. I felt I wanted to physically look after
her. When she returned one night we were all watching a movie
on the telly. Fern fell asleep. I looked at her and thought 'I really
want to kiss you!' Of course I didn't. It was like the cliché of the
year. My heart did flip over. I didn't kiss her! No way! I started
to question what was going on in my head or my guts. It *was* in

my head, it *was* in my heart. None of this was like known. I'm
an Irish Protestant. Upbringing. Anything like *that* was sort of
'Thou Shalt Not!'

Kath decided to continue living with Al. For several months
she hoped fervently that she could hold on to both relationships:

I went on living with Al and for a while we went through the
motions. Living in the same flat. Sleeping in the same bed. I
was deluding myself I could have the best of both worlds.
Fern and I phoned and saw each other all the time. Then one
night during a four-hour phone conversation while Al was
asleep, she just simply said, 'I'm in love with you.' There it
was: the declaration had been made. There was this pregnant
pause. It presented huge problems for me. Here was this
person saying these words while my partner was asleep in the
bed. Yet they were words I wanted to hear. If I'd been reckless
I would have gone round to her right away. But I'm not
reckless! I didn't say what I felt. I tried to be adult and mature
and suggest we talk about it. I said calmly, 'What do you want
to do about it?'

What they did about it was that eventually they become
lovers:

Al took it horribly badly; he was upset in an upset way, not an
angry way, he just crumbled. He spent a lot of time crying over
the next few weeks. I wanted somebody else to come and tell me
exactly what to do so that nobody got hurt and everybody got
what they wanted! But once I'd slept with Fern that was the end
of sleeping with Al in any sense, not only sex. In a relationship I
feel very tactile. I want to touch the person I'm in love with. I
want to feel their nearness, their body against me. So I felt I had
to give up those caring things with Al.

After months of traumatic discussions, Al and Kath split up,
but Kath has managed to retain a close friendship with Al whom
she sees regularly most weeks. Today Fern and Kath live together
in a committed partnership in which sensual cherishing as well as

(and separate from) lovemaking plays a significant part which for Kath has certain important differences from the mutual cherishing that she enjoyed with Al:

> My physical closeness to Fern is different from the sexual
> intimacy with Al in much more than the obvious ways. It feels
> more natural, it feels more comforting, more loving, it feels like I
> have arrived. Physically it feels like coming home. A good fuck
> is really good and I enjoy it, but we are much more into the
> whole loving, cherishing sensual thing. I can't separate the
> hugging, kissing, stroking, embracing, all of that.

Verbal Cherishing

Verbal acts of cherishing include praising partners, telling them how talented they are or how beautiful they look, using phrases which will raise their self-esteem and avoiding words that belittle, patronise or show contempt.

Most of us like to hear words of encouragement, comfort or support, but often we fail to say them to the person with whom we are most intimate. Most of us enjoy being thanked when we have done something thoughtful, yet many of us fail to express our gratitude for kind acts carried out within a partnership. Verbal cherishing enables a relationship to flower; it allows someone to feel special, valued and appreciated.

Maurice, the former Hollywood motion-picture executive, describes his marriage to Dolly as 'half a century of conversational devotion'.

> It is a total partnership in which we have had a conversation for
> fifty-four years. That's the basis of the marriage. Total
> communication – always, whether we are alone or with other
> people. We tell each other that the main thing is our good
> companionship. That's the first important thing. The second is
> that you never say 'to hell with it'. Thirdly, it is important you
> keep up the conversation between you. You like each other, and
> what creates that liking is respect. You're honest with each other,
> you know everything you need to know about what concerns
> the two of you. Then you tell those things the other person

needs to know. Dolly happens to be a terrific person and I'll tell her so. That's what it comes down to, this ongoing conversation for more than fifty years.

Dolly holds a similar viewpoint:

One of our major benefits is the talking. You have someone to talk to, to exchange views with, someone whose shoulder you can cry on as well as someone who will enjoy the things you enjoy. If you meet two people, I think you can tell by the nature of their conversation how well they get on.

Maurice elaborates on how from their first meeting they felt able to verbally cherish each other:

I met her when we were 22 or 23, I was very attracted to her, and there was nothing then about her which irritated me, so I told her. All these years later, I can't think of anything that irritates me about her. I'm telling you and I'd tell her. I was attracted to Dolly because she was smart and very attractive. She is practical, she asks lots of good questions. She is just an easy person. That's what it really comes down to. Good-looking and very smart. She still is. And I tell her. I would say to her that those things are still there.

Dolly has always returned this verbal cherishing because she appreciated her husband's talents:

He was very handsome and I love good-looking people! He was very smart and I love smart people. . . . he knows that! We really did see eye to eye; we had similar political views, social attitudes, cultural attitudes – they were attractive to me and I would say so. I know he likes the way I talk and the way I care for him.

Verbal cherishing is a gift many of us are happy to receive, yet it is a gift we often fail to bestow because, according to the couples interviewed, it often feels 'soppy', 'kinda dumb' or 'too much like hard work'.

One interviewee admitted:

> It wasn't easy at first, but taking time to compliment or hug the
> other person with words has become important. She started it
> but now we both do it.
>
> *(Vince, New York, engaged to Anne, London.)*

Some men find certain cherishing phrases particularly difficult to verbalise:

> I used to question falling in love. I used to question whether
> what exactly happens at the time is just hormones going crazy.
> For myself, I don't like it very much because I prefer a certain
> degree of predictability in my life! Now I feel more relaxed
> about it and can sometimes talk about it. Though to say you've
> fallen in love to your partner – well, it's a phrase that's over-
> used, and for men it is very hard to say, 'I love you.' For many
> men it just isn't done, it is really hard. But yes, it can happen,
> it has happened to me, so now I will sometimes say it to her.
>
> *(Kurt, 55, partner to Caitlin, 45, Canada.)*

Researchers into marital and couple behaviour, as well as relationship counsellors, show that positive verbal affirmation is a
prime ingredient in successful partnerships.[4] In this study, couples who saw themselves as happy, when interviewed separately
said 5–10 times more positive things than negative things about
their relationship. These were also the partners who reported that
in their couple interaction they aimed to say positive words to
each other whenever possible. When criticism was needed, they
attempted to make it constructive:

> When I teach screen-writing workshops, I always find
> something positive in the student's work to talk about before I
> bring in the criticism. I always tell them they must create a safe
> place, a secure harbour, because they are all feeling vulnerable.
> I've tried to do that in my relationship with Bernie, though it is
> harder in a deeply personal one-to-one.
>
> *(Cynthia, British, screen-writer.)*

*

The other guideline adhered to by couples who expressed a reasonable level of satisfaction with their relationship was not to moan about partnership difficulties to friends or family. Instead, they analysed exactly what felt distressing or irritating, then set aside an uninterruptible time to discuss it with their partner.

Sometimes a partner believes that 'by now' the other person knows that they are loved. The truth is that often they don't. Couples struggling in relationships were those who made assumptions about their partner. Couples who satisfactorily accommodated each other did *not* assume, but made efforts to find out what partners were feeling or thinking.

Several couples who related well reported that they kept hold of the memories of particularly fine times. Then when there were rough times, they wove those memories into a conversation that had started to go badly which otherwise might have turned into a row.

I have tried out this particular tactic in my own couple. Six years ago in a hotel room in Rhodes, my partner and I had a fiery row (about solitude and space) which escalated so suddenly that we were forced to separate for half the night – one of us storming angrily about the bedroom, the other in nightshirt and bare feet sitting stonily on the marble stairs in the hall outside, a prey to curious glances from other, merrier guests. That row ended about three in the morning when we decided to make up, go out to the Old City in Rhodes, have a delicious Greek meal and try to talk about our feelings.

Four years later in England a similar issue resurfaced. Before the argument reached silly proportions I managed to say, 'We'd better not separate for the night, like we did in Rhodes, because there are no delicious all-night Greek restaurants here in Cambridge!'

The memory of that otherwise joyous holiday worked to remind us of the mainly good times we have together and of how necessary genuine communication is. We did not storm about on that second occasion, but sensibly decided that as we were too fraught to discuss inflammatory issues calmly, we should set aside a time for talking a few days later.

Couples who can use the *memory-cherishing method* capitalise on the goodwill in a relationship and defuse what could be a tense situation.

Empathetic Listening

Listening is as important as communicating. Couples who cherished each other through attentive listening reassured their partner that he or she was being listened to by making encouraging sounds or nodding. Later, they acknowledged what the other person had said by checking the information to ensure they had heard it correctly.

Several couples who had benefited from couples counselling used a Cherishing-Communication exercise which helped to improve their discussions. The couple would spend about twenty minutes with each other, with no one else present. They sat on a sofa or in armchairs placed near to each other, then each partner in turn talked for ten minutes while the other partner did not interrupt but listened with total attention. The attentive focus helped to establish intimacy.

On the agenda for that *Cherishing-Communication exercise* would be any issue the couple had found difficult to confront or discuss. It could be one partner's habit of leaving a new set of dirty dishes around the sink just after the other person has washed up. Or it could be the other partner's unpunctuality which seems to worsen when the occasion is important, such as a wedding, a funeral, a school meeting or a visit to a difficult relative.

Each person had to remember that their aim was *not* to point out what is wrong with their partner but to express honestly how they felt about their partner's actions. To facilitate this aim certain phrases were allowed, certain phrases were disallowed:

> When Steve talked he tried not to use confrontational phrases
> such as 'You always' or 'You never'. We decided he should
> consistently use self-defining or cherishing phrases such as 'I
> feel' (upset/angry hurt etc.) or 'I think you will understand
> when I tell you that I feel . . .' It certainly wasn't easy for him,
> and I had an even harder job when I did it! But it began to work.
> We really started to listen to each other.
>
> *(Susan, married to Steve.)*

The underlying aim of this exercise was that the distressed

partner was not out to repair the other person's irritating behaviour (though that may be a positive outcome) but to listen attentively to what the other had to say about their feelings in order that the problem could be solved *together*.

In this study, several couples who made use of this technique on a single occasion decided to build it in to their relationship on a regular basis.

Two of my interviewees, Christopher Spence and Nancy Kline (interviewed in Chapter 9), jointly wrote a pamphlet called *At Least A Hundred Principles of Love*. The principles – which addressed the art of loving ourselves, establishing close relationships with another person and leadership in the world – used the notion of cherishing throughout. In relation to verbal cherishing, Principle 8 suggested:

> Each of us needs at least one relationship in which we exchange a minimum of fifteen minutes every day for listening to each other. We need time to talk about what has been good or difficult, about the progress we have made towards our goals and about the next steps in our lives.[5]

Principle 28 suggested:

> Set up equal time to listen to each other without interruption. The art of asking questions is an essential component of effective loving.[6]

Nancy Kline and Christopher Spence try to follow these cherishing guidelines in their own relationship in which democratic verbal participation is critical:

> My having an equal say in and co-decision-making about whatever we do is important to us. We have a policy that if one of us wants a change we propose it and the other has to agree. It's sort of like the Quakers, that the status quo is the status quo until you both agree to change it.
>
> *(Nancy Kline, 51, American.)*

They both believe you cannot understand an issue until you can

talk about it and, more crucially, listen to the other person's interpretation:

> We talk and we listen all the time about everything. We don't let
> issues slide, or maybe for one day.
>
> *(Christopher Spence, 53, British.)*

> Once I start talking with him and feel I am listened to, I always
> feel I understand it even better. A good example is when I first
> came here from America to be with Christopher permanently
> and had to establish my identity in this country through my
> own work as a leadership consultant and a writer. Some people
> assumed I would be doing work with Christopher for the
> Lighthouse, so we had to talk it through and listen carefully to
> each other. It was a bit of a crossroads.
>
> *(Nancy Kline.)*

In establishing herself in England, Nancy faced another crossroads when Christopher retired from active daily work at the
London Lighthouse. This too needed the application of the talk-
and-listen cherishing principle:

> Although I have a constant vigilance about any form of sexism,
> so that I don't fall into the expectation that he will be better than
> I am because he's male, during the last seven months since his
> retirement this new issue cropped up. He was at home and I
> was surprised to find him doing not all but almost all the
> household things and the cooking. For a time it made me feel
> unsure, it made me start to question – surprisingly, I really
> surprised myself – whether that meant I wasn't a woman. I had
> never realised that there would be that much deep-seated
> expectation that part of my womanhood was defined by my
> role.

The couple spent several hours discussing the issue and utilis-
ing the cherishing tool of empathetic listening:

> Your feeling about me managing the house and all the domestic
> work – you were relieved when we talked about it – through

talking about it you came to some clarity about what was the real issue.

(Christopher Spence.)

It took a little bit of doing to get over that, but now I'm more relaxed about it. He's a brilliant cook. He's always been a good cook but the fact that I am not less of a woman because of it is the point!

(Nancy Kline.)

The other point is that it is a kind of daily occurrence for us to discover we understand an issue because we have talked about it.

(Christopher Spence.)

Keeping in touch

This is particularly important for Intimate Commuter couples who live some distance from each other, or for Proximity Model couples who travel regularly. Kurt and Caitlin, University professors in Canada, both travel as part of their jobs. Kurt emphasises the importance of long-distance communication:

I have just been away on sabbatical for three months, and I called Caitlin every day. We were going to try to save on telephone charges, just call twice a week, but in the three months I only missed two days because I was in the wilds with no phone box. I had to phone because I really wanted to know how she was, how she was doing, I missed her, wanted her with me, but it was not a possible situation.

Maurice and Dolly, like Kurt and Caitlin, have lived as a close-knit Proximity Model couple most of their married life. On one of the few occasions, in their 40s, when Maurice was away on a movie-making trip, letters became essential:

I went off to Montreal to make a movie. Then I travelled to New York every six weeks; it was hard for us to be away from each other. We had constant letters back and forth and telephone calls. She would come and visit as much as possible. We could not have managed without it.

Because we have had similar careers we understand what each other's work means; so when Maurice went off to make a movie, though I didn't like his being away I could understand that he *had* to and I accommodated that. We kept in touch all the time. Lots and lots of telephone calls. At least twice daily. More I should think! People should have the chance to be apart, it's good for them, but they also should keep in touch.

Kath, the Irish nurse and Fern, the actress who was often on tour, built the cherishing tool of letter-writing into their partnership from the start:

Whenever she was away, before we lived together, I wrote to her. Twice a day sometimes. Though I often twist myself on telephones I phoned constantly, which surprised me. With other friends the contact could be six months between speaking to someone, but I couldn't be blasé about this. I needed to speak to her, I needed to hear her.

(Kath.)

My relationship with Kath began to change when I went on tour in the States. Travelling for nine weeks with people I'd never met was really hard. But Kath, who was still living with Al, wrote to me constantly. Sometimes twice a day. That was just amazing because no one's *ever* done that for me. My parents used to write once a week when I was away at school. That was it! It is a really big issue for me that someone takes the time to write. I felt cared for in a way I never had before.

Fern did not in fact write back.

I'm not much of a letter-writer so I didn't write back, but I phoned. My phone bill was £958! That is over £100 a week. Even though we now live together, when I am away on tours Kath still writes. She never lets me feel out of touch. I feel loved, cared for, respected. Things that I've never felt from another person.

Is Fern unusual in her appreciation of the hand-written word? In the era of modern technology, have letters become outmoded?

He sends me the occasional e-mail or fax, but it doesn't feel like I'm being well looked after. If he would just post me a pretty card, something like that. Or even a silly sloppy note.
(Anne, 28, British secretary; fiancée to Vince, 36, New York radio presenter.)

Some couples understand this need and act on it:

I send him little cards and notes every once in a while. I sent him a thank-you card and put an autumn leaf in with it. Little things like that is what I love to do.
(Roy, Los Angeles.)

Mardy and Will are a married couple seldom away from each other, either at work or at home, yet they constantly check in with each other.

We have agreed that what we mean by care is that we care about what the other is doing, saying, or feeling *at all times*. So Will would check in during the day, even though we both work for the family architectural firm in the mornings, before I go and pick up the kids. We are interested in each other's opinions, we are interested in sharing ideas. We are not apart for more than three or four hours but we check in with each other at least twice in that time, certainly before he comes home in the evening. We have been doing this for years. Will's parents do the same. They work together with us, and they have been working alongside each other for 35 years. My parents do it too. It's back to the family of origin, it is what we all expect of each other.

Some people however do not feel cherished by constant checks or missives, instead they feel taken over. Bernadette, a quiet archaeologist, is one. Her partner Cynthia, with whom she lived for a decade together with their two sons and two daughters, is a screen-writer in the British film industry who used to leave Bernadette notes and drawings all over their house. Several months after they had with sadness agreed to separate, they decided to discuss the issues that had driven them apart, to see if they still had a workable future. Listen to them debating the issue of cherishing through letters:

Bernadette: You felt you were nurturing me with those bloody notes. I felt it was a tactic you used for not staying under the carpet. You wanted to be visible in my life. The notes and letters syndrome were a part of that. There were notes and bits of film everywhere, those bloody notes! I rue the day I bought you stick-on post-it notes. There they were staking a claim. I felt they were stuck on my forehead.

Cynthia: I never knew that. I just wanted us to be constantly in touch. I am a screen-writer, so I write. It is the first thing I think of. I was away such a lot. I thought it was a warming thing to do. I wanted you to feel cared for. I didn't know it made you feel claustrophobic and . . .

Bernadette: Invaded! Yes, it did!

Cynthia was both a giver and a receiver, who would have enjoyed being the recipient of her own style of cherishing. What she failed to realise was that by imposing her own style on her partner she was failing to take into account their very different personalities and needs. Where the couple had run into trouble was that over this issue and others they had failed to communicate their conflicting feelings adequately at the time:

If there was any sign of a row threatening, I just wanted to bury my head in the duvet and hope it would go away.

(Cynthia.)

We had so much on, with bringing up four kids, with all their problems, that we didn't get round to talking about a lot of what mattered to us. We are talking more now we live apart than we did in nearly 10 years living together.

(Bernadette.)

That couple's experience illustrates how some aspects of cherishing are not welcomed by everyone, and that communication remains an essential tool for working out relationships.

Using laughter . . . Sharing jokes

For many couples, laughter is a cherishing tool that can stave off rows.

Michael Holroyd, the biographer, and his novelist wife Margaret Drabble (interviewed in Chapter 9) use laughter as an argument-preventer:

> At the end of a day when things have gone a bit wrong or something's been very hard, we laugh a lot about it. That sort of shared laughter dissolves difficulties or things that might irritate one, as on work trips together. When things simply go wrong, we tend to laugh them away at the end of a day, and that is very nice. I don't say we long for things to go wrong so that we can have a good laugh, but it is a safety-net.

Other interviewees used laughter for similar reasons. Ricardo, a cook, and his partner Fifi (Chapter 6) see laughter as the way out of their bickering, which is usually about finances:

> Laughter helps us. We laugh at ourselves and our families. Sometimes it is the only thing that gets us through.
>
> *(Ricardo.)*

> He gives me laughs during stressful times. Laughter is the most important benefit of our couple. Ricardo and I can laugh at anything except about money. When we are out with other people we'll exchange looks because we are laughing at the same things underneath.
>
> *(Fifi.)*

One couple felt laughter was so important that they incorporated it into their wedding vows:

> We wrote our own wedding vows and as I am a very serious

person, far too serious for my own good – a very intense
person – one of the vows is that we promise to embrace the
child in each other and help him to play. Jack is better able to
play than I am, so I have given him permission to help me play
and he's good at it, he makes me laugh a lot!

(Roy.)

Some partners with dark childhoods see laughter as the key
feature of a cherishing relationship:

Julian makes me laugh, but more than that he even thinks I have
a sense of humour. I never had that because there was no
laughter in our family. Nobody laughed. My childhood had no
laughter in it. Laughing is a benefit. Before Julian and I became
lovers, when I was still married to Neville, and Julian was just
our gay male friend who had come for a Christmas meal, he
made me laugh at the way I was so controlling in the kitchen.
Neville noticed him teasing me and when everyone had left he
said, 'Julian teases you in a way I don't seem able to. He can
take you up on things you are serious about. He can make you
laugh. I can't. You and Julian would make a really good couple!'

Daisy was startled, since she had never thought of Julian in
that way.

I was shocked, kind of confused, like what did he mean? Julian
was into gay politics; he was my gay college friend. He was only
31, 13 years younger than me. Kind of not really a real man. But
yes, he made me laugh and feel cherished.

That laughter, that cherishing, was the start of an unusual relationship between Daisy and Julian which culminated in Daisy
leaving her husband and Julian breaking with his gay male world
to be with her.

Act as if you are on the same side

Being on the same side does not mean that couples need to share
the same viewpoint on every topic. It means that a couple feels

that together they enhance each other.

Many couples whose children included step-children or co-parented children said that when some or all of the children tried to divide them as a couple, the importance of a united stand could not be over-estimated.

Another common situation where feeling your partner was on your side was genuinely helpful was when one person was having difficulty at work and was in great need of support at home. If the problem was about the threat of redundancy, a career change, a possible resignation or a colleague's unfair promotion, a partner might be able to offer practical help such as composing a difficult letter (as long as they were not 'problem-solving') or writing a list of advantages and disadvantages for each situation. Cherishing reinforcement could be done by validating a partner's emotions, such as anger or excitement, or by expressing similar sentiments such as, 'I'd have done the same thing in your shoes,' or, 'I can see the way your boss behaved was very manipulative,' or, 'I am not surprised you got angry.'

Sometimes acting as if you are on your partner's side can be achieved by offering advice, but only when it is asked for. A point many couples made was that when a situation calls for advice, it is essential to make that advice constructive:

> I remembered how I would feel if he criticised me harshly so even when my husband's being a prat, but desperately needs helpful hints, I soft-pedal!

There were partners who used constant criticism in the guise of advice as a weapon against their lover or spouse, only to discover that in terms of effective results for their partnership it was the antithesis of cherishing.

Being a supportive friend

Friendship was rated high amongst the cherishing techniques used by interviewees.

Maurice identified friendship as a core element in the mutual cherishing between himself and Dolly from the time they first met on a blind date:

People like us who are good friends, who have been married for
ever, are not the same as kids who are just feeling each other
out. I consider the fact that we're friends to be the main thing.
That conversation I described before, which has lasted all these
years, that being together, doing things together, comes out of
friendship.

To Maurice, this thread of friendly support runs so deep that it is
like a limb:

She is my right arm. But I don't worry about my right arm. I
trust her totally. I don't ask about my right arm or how my right
arm is feeling or how I feel about my right arm. That's the way I
feel about being married to Dolly.

Acts of supportive friendship amongst couples I interviewed
included offers of time or skills, making phone calls on behalf of
a partner, writing difficult business letters, helping with a CV,
cooking something special, cleaning the car or taking care of
the children so that the other person could work or visit someone.

Fifty-three-year-old Marie-Claire, a Frenchwoman living in
Canada, who has known 55-year-old Rupert, a Canadian resident, for 40 years and has been married to him for 32, said that
her definition of what being a wife meant relied heavily on
friendship, support and protection:

A wife means a friend, a support, the person you want to spend
quality time with, pleasurable time. That wife would be a
supportive friend.

Marie-Claire, who met Rupert when she was only 13, felt she
was his friend from the start:

I certainly didn't fall in love! (She laughed very loudly at such
an idea.) Absolutely no I didn't . . . Falling in love is when
people just let go and get excited. Just not the kind of thing that
happens to me! Even as a very young girl I would have looked
at the trustworthiness of the person, the reliability of the person,

the understanding, the protecting. I was looking for being a friend and having a friend before anything else. That friend would be ready to cherish and support me. The trait of character of that friend would be complementary to the one I had. From when I was 13 until I was 21, Rupert and I had that time to be friends, to make that support, to make that protection. After that we looked at other possibilities, then we married.

Gifts, Treats, Rituals, Celebrations

The gifts can be material in order to mark an occasion or to remind the other person how much you care for them; or they can be gifts of time or effort.

Dolly was typical of many couples who enjoyed talking about birthdays and celebrations:

> The occasional flower or box of candy doesn't hurt! Nor remembering birthdays and anniversaries. Romance means the same to both Maurice and me. It is about extra thoughtfulness, isn't it?

Gulliver, the 62-year-old sculptor, believes the courtship of a wife becomes more important when a marriage has lasted over twenty years:

> We are in love, we tell each other we are in love, and I must say I court her. I bring Tess breakfast in bed, buy her things; she likes being courted, taken out, given treats, though not necessarily expensive things. If anything, she might forget my birthday but I don't forget hers. I used to fear she'd leave me, but after twenty years it gets to be unlikely. I now feel secure in this relationship, but I don't want to take it for granted. That's why the courting bit is important. The last thing Tess would like is being taken for granted!

In this study men in couples with men were just as romantic as men in couples with women:

> We are both romantic schmucks! We celebrate every anniversary

every opportunity we have! We celebrate the day we met, the day we decided to commit, the day of our wedding! We go out to dinner. We spend real time together. I enjoy cherishing him with rituals and over any anniversary.

(Jack, American.)

Some rituals may seem pedestrian to outsiders but have great meaning to the couple:

Ritual and ceremony is more important to Caitlin than to me, but yes, we do have certain pre-set repeated behaviours that we enjoy. Yes, we are quite ritualistic in our behaviour. Every morning we have a cup of tea out there on the deck overlooking the garden. It happens before we go to work or depart for separate ways. I don't like to miss it. As I say, I like a bit of predictability in my life, so that maybe is why we are ritualistic.

(Kurt, Canada.)

Some regular and rewarding rituals may be deeply missed if the partner dies:

For years, every night when I arrived home from work Donald would be there ready to pour me a campari and soda. He bought the bottle, he did the pouring. After he died I didn't have any inclination to go out and buy alcohol. Every night when I turn the key in the door, it is one of the small things I miss.

(Deirdre, 85, British.)

Practical Cherishing

Practical cherishing is what many of us think of as 'love as maintenance'. The poet U.A. Fanthorpe describes this kind of cherishing in her poem 'Atlas'. She delineates the cherishing element as that:

Which checks the insurance, and doesn't forget
The milkman; which remembers to plant bulbs;

Which answers letters; which knows the way
The money goes; which deals with dentists

And Road Fund Tax and meeting trains,
And postcards to the lonely; which upholds

The permanently ricketty elaborate
Structures of living; which is Atlas.

And maintenance is the sensible side of love,
Which knows what time and weather are doing
To my brickwork; insulates my faulty wiring;
Laughs at my dryrotten jokes; remembers
My need for gloss and grouting; which keeps
My suspect edifice upright in air,
As Atlas did the sky.[7]

In my own intimate couple relationships, I have been fortunate in being practically cherished many times. Small significant actions stand out just as much as expensive gestures, though inevitably I recall those also.

One unforgettable cherishing memory occurred twenty years ago in the late 1970s on my then partner's birthday. She suggested that prior to the birthday lunch arranged for her, we should drive to a sheepskin factory where she wanted to purchase herself a winter jacket. I agreed and we had a delightful drive to a country village through snow-covered landscape. I watched her trying on jacket after jacket and made helpful comments. Then she asked me to try on several so that she could get a better look. The weather was freezing and in those days, because my income from writing was negligible, I had no winter coat, and suffered dreadfully from the cold, so I snuggled cheerfully into whatever she pulled off the rack. Finally she chose the most beautiful, paid some exorbitant price, and headed us back to the car. I was about to drive off when she placed the parcel into my hands and said, 'Happy Unbirthday!'

Earlier than that, during the 1960s, when I was in hospital for many months, very sick and pregnant with my now 31-year-old daughter, my second husband flew to Amsterdam. He returned to the hospital twenty-four hours later bearing a bouquet of fresh red tulips. Being a musician he played his way into the ward, outside visiting hours, to the strains of 'Tulips from Amsterdam'! Every hospital rule had been infringed, but the nurses like the patient were enchanted.

Today, in the late 1990s, it is practical and emotional acts of cherishing which are the heart of my current long-term partnership, and are its most visible element. One day I was ill, but insisted on spending hours going from house to house in my neighbourhood, delivering Labour Party posters and canvassing for the Party. I fell home, too weak even to boil an egg. My partner drove 60 miles from her house to mine, with a gastronomic meals-on-wheels in her tiny red car. On another occasion after her departure I noticed all my jewellery had vanished. A few days later the partner and the jewels returned:

They were incredibly tarnished. You couldn't possibly wear silver rings or necklaces in that state. I've spent many hours polishing them. They're fine now!

The most recent act of cherishing is one of those good deeds that quite literally shines in the night. I have a strange habit of getting up several times a night and cleaning my teeth. In my own house, knowing exactly where brush and paste are, I can do this without opening my eyes. In someone else's house I have to wake up and generally become irritable. We went to stay at a very tidy friend's home. They kept all toothbrushes in a mug on the bathroom windowsill. This meant that if dutiful visitors followed suit (which we did), there would be no way of finding one's own toothbrush in the middle of the night without first waking up and putting on the light. Imagine my surprise when I groped my way to the bathroom to discover that my thoughtful partner had caringly removed my brush and paste from the mug and placed it on the sink ready for my use.

Couples I interviewed all had similar anecdotes to tell:

She has better headed paper than I do, so she writes references whenever I or my children need them.

She helped me mark thirty-six exam papers when I was stricken with flu.

In our relationship love is the practical cherishing. On a day-to-day basis it is whatever we do that benefits the other person. Sometimes it is romantic, but most of the time it is practical. I vacuum his apartment, he fills up my car with petrol.

My partner is a wonderful gardener and he doesn't restrict his efforts to his own garden. He always makes me half-a-dozen hanging baskets in the summer, and plants up several bowls of hyacinths and crocuses for me in the autumn. I try and do my bit by mowing his lawn when I'm round at his place.

She interrupted her own work to cycle round and spend several hours repairing my fax machine. It saved me an £80 mechanic's call-out charge.

There are lots of opportunities to care for one another in practical ways . . . everything from doing the dishes or making the dinner when the other person is tired. I like to think of practical day-to-day things that will show him I love him. Not just show him but tangibly care for him.

The last time I had a cold my fiancée posted me two tiny plastic bottles, one containing whisky, the other brandy, and in the same parcel was a jar of honey and a bag of lemons.

PRACTICAL CHERISHING SCENE: GULLIVER AND TESS

Gulliver has been married three times, has three sons by his first two wives, and each marriage reflects the same practical cherishing pattern. He has enjoyed nurturing his wives by doing the majority of the child care, the housework and the cooking:

In my first marriage in Britain, which lasted 10 years, right from the start I always did the housework, looked after the kids and the cooking. My first wife didn't have any concept of housework, whereas I have to have a tidy space. When we split, our two children were 11 and 6 and I took them on and eventually moved to Canada and took care of them. I was a single father long before it was fashionable. People think I did well, all that caring. But you never do well as a parent. I don't think I did that well. But being a single man with two kids is very attractive to women (it's not like the other way round); they think you must be nice if you've got kids, they think you'll be nice to them too, so I had lots of girl-friends. I liked talking to the girl-friends about the kids rather than about art. Sometimes art talk gets boring! But the ladies never did any of the nurturing or cooking. There don't seem to be ladies that do these things anywhere!

Gulliver's second wife didn't stay around long enough to cook:

She was my girl-friend for eighteen months, and I looked after her too. Then she needed a Green Card to come with me to the States. So we married, she got pregnant, we split up, she went off with an American painter. I didn't see that son from the time he was six months old until he searched and found me when he was 16. That was one child I did not look after.

Tess, a lawyer, his third wife, like her predecessors also abhors the domestic arts:

I never had those skills as a kid. I was totally lacking in home-making skills. Gulliver does much more of the house-cleaning than I do. He certainly does most of the cooking; he doesn't like me cooking. He likes looking after me in those ways, and I like being looked after.

On this subject the couple are in absolute agreement:

Tess doesn't like cooking or cleaning. She can do it if she wants, but she doesn't. She doesn't see her environment as being untidy, as I do. Her mind is highly organised, that's why she's such a good lawyer, but she's so disorganised in other ways that at first it drove me crazy. She loses things, she's late, and there are pieces of paper everywhere. I first met her 20 years ago at an arts brunch and discovered she was a marvellous photographer. We had art in common. I had to see her again.

Tess had already viewed an exhibition of Gulliver's sculptures, and felt she knew the artist intimately before she had met the man. She too wanted them to meet again.

When Gulliver, a man with an extraordinary gastronomic repertoire, wants to impress a woman, he invites her to a home-cooked meal:

> I invited Tess for twelve till one for lunch. I cooked something special. As I was giving up at four-thirty she burst in and said: 'Am I a bit late?' She had lost something on the way. It was quintessentially Tess, being late and losing something. Strangely, despite that we became real close friends, but we didn't become lovers for some weeks. Then it developed and developed, and 20 years later it is still developing. We have lived together and run a smallholding, we have lived apart in separate apartments in different Canadian cities, but always I have tried to create a home for her directly I get there. Even when she and I were living in different spaces to me doing that, making the nest, feeding her, is very important.

During those 20 years, in a variety of nests, some at opposite ends of Canada, Gulliver has cherished Tess in every practical way:

> I can do the whole housework, then Tess can rush in with an excited plan and it can look like between fifteen people have landed! But I don't worry any more. I like to get up and cook her breakfast. She still loses things once every two days and I'm really good at finding things. So I think now that when she loses something she knows that I'll find it and it gives her a nice sense of: 'Oh, he must be caring because he is busy finding my keys!'

Gulliver's primary cherishing, however, is still in the field of culinary delights:

> I never think she is eating properly. When we lived apart and

commuted, I felt she would stay at work and eat junk food.
Now we are living together in our new house I like to make her
a different menu every night. It makes her feel good, gives her
that bit extra; I think I'm sensitive to that, and I think she is
sensitive to me too.

Gulliver's artistic sense has transformed their current home
into a wild extravaganza of colours, sculptures, abstract paintings
and vivid pottery:

She lets me look after the house, she never worries how I
decorate the rooms, she never cares where I put anything. By
now I'd find it difficult to live with someone who wanted to
know where I put things or who said, 'No, don't put it there, put
it here!' It would be weird. I wouldn't like that!

Tess is deeply appreciative of the constant cordon bleu cooking, but is also realistic:

I know people think that it's unusual to have a man doing
most of the looking after, the tidying, the nurturing, but it is
not unusual amongst male painters and sculptors because they
tend to be home and they like to control their space. So that's
part of what Gulliver is doing too! But the consequence for me
is wonderful. I have to say Gulliver really is 'good wife
material' as well as 'good husband material'. When you talk
about empathy in relationships, they require the same
qualities.

Gulliver interrupted one of his interviews with me in order to
prepare for Tess's homecoming:

People say to us, 'Oh, we thought you two just got together
because you're always so lovey and dovey!' I think that's really
nice! We have to stop now, sorry, because she'll be home soon
and I have to decide what to cook her for supper. I didn't make
that pizza in the fridge so we won't have that. I think maybe rice
with shrimps and a new sauce . . .

Not provoking rows and knowing when to stop rows

Spiteful remarks or exaggerated blaming can be very hurtful and hard to forget. Couples decided that knowing when to stop a row if one took place is crucial. Two useful suggestions for mending discord were firstly, ceasing before the argument gets out of control and secondly, if anger was at its height, temporarily changing the subject or going to separate places. This is a good way to cool the temperature and give each other the physical and mental space necessary for recovery.

Sentences that can lower a heated temperature included: 'I know this isn't just my problem, it is our problem'; or, 'I know how hard it is for you'; or, 'I am trying to understand your viewpoint and I'm sure you are trying to understand mine.'

Even if partners don't and aren't, it is still worth saying, because it can produce a very helpful response which then allows for the issue to be more calmly discussed.

PARTICULAR SITUATIONS THAT CALL FOR CHERISHING

Obviously there are particular situations, such as illness, bereavement or other emotional traumas, that call for extra cherishing; and there are particular men and women whose personalities are such that they respond sensitively and patiently to such predicaments. Stephen is one.

PRACTICAL CHERISHING SCENES: STEPHEN AND EDIE: STEPHEN AND ARABELLA
Stephen, who is a parish priest, is a person whose sympathetic nurturing resources were called upon for almost the whole of his 28-year marriage to his first wife Edie:

> It was only 6 years after we married that she developed multiple sclerosis. She had it for 24 years, and for the last twelve she was chairbound. So yes, I had to care for her all the time. Obviously I see a marriage as a pastoral relationship in the sense of caring for your wife, but with Edie – yes, she did need constant practical care, although she never gave me the idea that she was

poorly. She was tremendous. In her capacity as a person she was very strong, a very strong person. She never gave the impression of dependency, not even in a wheelchair, not even in those last hard six months.

Stephen's second wife Arabella, an artist, had never met Edie but admires what she knows about her from Stephen and from all the villagers:

Stephen adored her. He cared for her and nursed her for years. Everybody in the parish adored her. There's a dedication in the church to her. There's a plaque near the community centre which I go past when I go to the shops, that gave me some difficulty in the early months. She was such a strong person and gave so much; she was obviously a very remarkable woman. I think perhaps one thing that has happened since I've been around is that Stephen maybe has blossomed more . . .

As Edie's strength deserted her, as she became progressively weaker, as her sight failed, as she deteriorated from being chair-bound to finally becoming bed-bound, both she and Stephen put an even greater trust in their faith, which he sees as the basis of his cherishing:

As she became increasingly helpless, she showed great courage, great sense of spirit, which came from a great faith and great trust. She had faith and trust for her life and its living and its outcome. Even when she was very ill, she was a partner with me in the work of the church and of the community. She had her own place in the life of the church and the village. She would get into that electric chair and she'd whizz off down the road to the school or to someone's home. It was *her* part, her own *independent* part.

Stephen felt that it was Edie's amazing independence which helped him to support and cherish her for nearly 30 years without patronising her. As she became sicker, it became even more important that he continued to recognise her autonomous spirit:

The way I was with Edie wasn't sort of obsessive, nothing like that, but just by nature of being a carer. There was a sense of her dependence, but it didn't encroach on her personality. I planned a routine because routine does help in a situation of disability, but at the same time as recognising that disability I was always conscious of how much Edie achieved within the limited scope she had. I would want to understand cherishing in the way that you view the life and the work, and cherishing supports that. Edie and I supported each other, and that's a form of cherishing.

When Edie died, Stephen spent many long, painful months attempting to deal with his grief:

I worked and worked over the grief situation. I'd say I got the T-shirt for that! But grief is important, it is useful. You don't get over it, but you come through and start again.

Stephen felt the discipline and order he had enjoyed with his first wife helped to stabilise him after her death:

That routine I had with Edie helped me in a situation of bereavement. But I didn't keep up the routines after Edie died because the important thing was to let Edie go. As I would put it, to give her back to God, which I did fairly early on. I didn't rush it, but He helped me to do this, because as Edie was dying I said to her: 'Are you going to give me a box of ashes? What am I going to do with them?' It was wonderful that I could speak to her like that. She said to me: 'Holy Island. Scatter them on the sea on the outgoing tide because the outgoing tide is going out and away and that is how I want you to remember me.'

Stephen together with their son and daughter took Edie's ashes and scattered them on the outgoing tide at Holy Island:

It felt right because she was going out, going back in a sense to the Creator. It wasn't easy. It isn't easy. I like talking about it because it does help to talk. I was kind of OK for a year after her death then I became severely depressed. In that second year everything seemed to take hold of all my energy. I had clinical depression at first. Nothing lifted it at first.

Practical help, and some much-needed cherishing, came Stephen's way when one of his parishioners – Arabella, whom he would eventually marry – called him out late one night because she too had suffered a death, in her case that of a close friend.

What started as a pastoral relationship soon changed into real friendship. Arabella drove me down to my sister's on the other side of England. Going there was part of the treatment for my depression. Arabella and I talked all the way, and it was great. Arabella was a good part of my coming out of that depression.

Arabella saw a man who helped her with her own grief, a man who through their growing affection thrived on her support. What did Stephen see?

I saw a person who wanted to discover a new life, who wanted to discover God. She was living as I would put it by God's grace and I wanted to be part of that.

The challenge for Arabella, who has a full-time career as an artist as well as carrying out much of the work of a vicar's wife, is that she has had to face following in the footsteps of a remarkable woman:

I have not tried to follow in her footsteps. I've made a bit of a bolshie statement that way. I couldn't possibly try and emulate her could I? I've absolutely no desire to. I just couldn't begin to. I simply had to make sure that everybody understood I was an artist and I was different. Edie was extraordinary: she was always providing and baking and arranging and doing. I just don't do any of that. I've made sure that everybody around the village knows that I don't cook. It is not quite true but it is what I say. If I'm known not to cook, I can't possibly be asked to bake!

Stephen openly acknowledges the problem of how parishioners might view his new wife:

> Arabella says she doesn't make a good vicar's wife but I think she does. She is very good with people. Obviously people compare how Edie and Arabella relate to the churches and what they do. I'm not saying they are right, but they are human and it will be said. But painting is Arabella's great gift . . . she has been an artist longer than she has been my wife! I would want to be there to support her in that, just as she supports me in my commitment to being a priest. Cherishing comes in there very importantly, that you see each other as being supportive.

The personal challenge for Stephen has been to move from one long-established couple to a newer and radically different couple:

> The challenge for me is letting go of the previous relationship. I've done it but I find still sort of reverberates. You've dealt with something but you still have to deal with it. You know it is OK but you still have to handle it. The grief doesn't stop but it gets better as you get into the new life.

Stephen still treasures a large framed photograph of Edie:

> When I married Edie I wrote on the bottom of the photo: 'This one God gave to me.' Then when I married Arabella, I added the word 'first' to the inscription so that it read: 'This one God gave to me first.' Because I believe God gave Arabella to me second. I do believe that. I'd want to believe that to be true of our partnership for life.

The practical and emotional cherishing strengths of this man Stephen were extraordinary, and the case extreme. But even in a couple's more mundane, less perilous situations, cheerful and patient cherishing and consistent practical support can renew the life force of a partnership.

NOT WANTING TO CHERISH A PARTNER

Most people want to be cherished, but not everyone wishes to do the cherishing or feels able to do so. Some people are fulfilled by caring for others, offering them attention, but others resent it.

Women in particular feel that nurturing is part of their stereotypical role and see it as an inbuilt obligation that not all of them want to carry out: 'I'm not the maternal type, but that is what he/she expects me to be' was a refrain I heard many times:

I nurture the kids. Now, even though he doesn't live with me, he wants bloody nurturing! As a strong feminist, I think fuck that! I know all those messages in my head. All that stuff about the angel in the house. I don't want to listen to those messages. I want to be free.

(Single mother in Intimate Commuter couple.)

When your partner is ill every day, every single day, you just can't keep being that kind of person. Sometimes in desperation I suggest he goes for a short walk to get through the pain barrier, just so that I can get my own head in order. That cherishing, all that attention, it takes so much time and energy.

(Married woman with husband who has multiple sclerosis.)

She gets depressed. I suppose it's the job. It's not that she says anything but she looks kind of sad. There are times when I not only don't want verbal claims on me, but I don't want *any* claims on me.

(Woman in Proximity Model lesbian partnership.)

I know what is expected of me, but I don't want someone sitting in a puddle in his armchair clutching his hernia bag.

(Gay male with older male partner in Proximity Model relationship.)

I believe in the obligation of partnership that says we should cherish one another. But in practice I can only meet this intermittently. My definition of a saint is one who can meet it all the time.

(Artist married to a clergyman.)

WHEN A PARTNER FEELS UNCHERISHED

Lack of cherishing can become a major irritation within a partnership. Those who felt taken for granted had plenty of examples.

Not only is he untidy, coming home dumping his bag in the kitchen which he knows I will have to move immediately, throwing clothes all over the bathroom and bedroom floor – but he expects me to pick them up, look after him, cherish him.
(Woman in Proximity Model partnership.)

Every time I talk about a problem at work, he tries to find a solution. That's not what I want, I need empathy. When I discuss what has gone wrong with the kids, he starts throwing around advice. I don't want that either. To feel understood and looked after, I want him to listen on my wavelength.
(Woman in Intimate Commuter couple.)

Nobody can do everything right, but ever since I was made redundant and took on that part-time job for a contract cleaning firm, she nags and criticises. It's hard to feel she cares about you when it's nag-nag, criticise-criticise all the time!
(Husband in Proximity Model marriage.)

If someone always tells you if they are popping out to get a paper or go for a walk, it does make you feel cherished, that you count in their lives. He's quite capable of going out without saying he's going, even leaving the front door wide open. He doesn't think what impact that will have on me or the family. I yell downstairs to him, or talk to him, thinking he is in the living room, and will find out he's gone without even saying. In itself it is petty, but it irritates the hell out of me, and things like that are cumulative. I feel as if I am not worth saying goodbye to. I mention it and he says I am nagging. Over time I have accepted that is how he is, although it does irritate me.
(Married woman in Proximity Model couple.)

This particular situation was echoed in the lives of many couples who felt strongly about the necessity of not leaving the house without saying goodbye. Mardy and Will, the Texas couple who check in constantly with each other, have made it a point of principle:

> Early on in our marriage Will told me a story that stuck. When his parents were newly married, his father went out of the door to get cigarettes and didn't check in with his mother. He did not say, 'I'm going out to get cigarettes'; he just walked out! When he came back twenty minutes later Will's mother let him have it! Tongue lashing! So Will and I said to each other we will never ever not share in that way, even something as small as 'I am going round the corner.' Because if you just walk out, that assumes the relationship is secondary to what you are popping out for – in that case the desire to give in to cigarettes. With us the relationship has to come first!

NOT WANTING TO BE CHERISHED

Cherishing is not always a mutual act. In some partnerships, one partner consistently nurtures while the other more often receives. Where this is satisfactory to both people, as in the case of Tess and Gulliver, the relationship works well. In several cases, however, the active cherishers said they would enjoy some return of nurturing. In a few cases, one partner felt unable to receive any form of cherishing whether it was a gift, a supportive message, or a special home-cooked meal.

> I can't cope with being given anything. I don't mind whether it costs a lot or it's nothing at all. It makes me feel trapped, like I want to run away. I get quite shaky when Patrick my fiancé arrives with some massive gift. He is always trying to shower me with stuff. Do me good deeds, you know? Treats, flowers, the whole bit! I don't know whether that's because he's twenty years older, wants to look after me, but I can't take it. It's hard to tell him though.
> *(Tracy, 20, British hairdresser; engaged to Patrick, 40, Canadian garage owner.)*

After two interviews, Tracy did discuss it with Patrick, who had admitted he had felt hurt. A few months before their wedding, the couple went for pre-marital counselling. During the sessions, Tracey discovered that their significant age difference often led her to equate Patrick with her father who had sexually abused her as a child while lavishing upon her presents, luxury trips and the appearance of generous caring:

> We kinda got it sorted now. I kinda hold back, which is hard because I love to look after her. But now she is making moves in that direction towards me.
>
> *(Patrick.)*

Sometimes not wanting to be cherished is part of a fierce desire to be independent at all costs and an anxiety about having one's autonomous self taken over. The ability to preserve useful acts of cherishing whilst respecting the partner's sense of self, requires a delicate footing on a high wire that can all too easily throw a couple off balance. The fine line between independence and dependence will be analysed in the next chapter.

NOTES

1. Lichenose; the adjective can also be spelt 'lichenous'. *Collins English Dictionary*, William Collins, 1979.
2. Janet Reibstein, *Love Life: How To Make Your Relationship Work*, Fourth Estate, London, 1997; Carol Gilligan, *In a Different Voice*, Harvard University Press, Cambridge, Massachusetts, 1982; John Gottman, *Why Marriages Succeed or Fail*, Simon and Schuster, New York, 1994; Robert Sternberg and Michael Barnes (eds.), *The Psychology of Love*, Yale University Press, New Haven, 1988.
3. Elizabeth Barrett Browning, Sonnet XLIII, 'Sonnets from the Portuguese', in *The Poetical Works of E. Barrett Browning*, Oxford Complete Edition, Henry Frowde, London, New York, Toronto, 1906, p. 327. The first lines run:
   'How do I love thee?
   Let me count the ways'
4. One Plus One: Marriage and Partnership Research Charity; P. Blumstein and P. Schwartz, *American Couples*, Pocket Books, New York, 1983; Frank Fincham, Professor of Psychology at the

University of Wales, Cardiff, and Professor John Gottman, cited in *Good Housekeeping*, November 1997; Janet Reibstein, *Love Life: How to Make Your Relationship Work*, Fourth Estate, London, 1997; Maggie Scarf, *Intimate Partners*, Century, London, 1987; Dr Jack Dominian, *Marriage and the Definitive Guide to What Makes A Marriage Work*, Heinemann, London, 1995; B. Berzon and R. Leighton, *Positively Gay*, Celestial Arts, Millbrae, Los Angeles, 1979; S.M. Campbell, *The Couple's Journey: Intimacy as a Path to Wholeness*, Impact Publishers, San Luis Obispo, 1980.

5   Nancy Kline and Christopher Spence, *At Least A Hundred Principles of Love*, LLMS Ltd, London, 1993, p. 7.

6   Ibid, p. 10.

7   'Atlas', U.A. Fanthorpe, *Safe as Houses, Poems*. Peterloo Poets, (UK), Story Line Press (Oregon, USA), 1995, p. 6.

CHAPTER 8

Interdependence

Beryl Bainbridge's magnificent novel *Every Man for Himself*, about the fictionalised events played out by a group of passengers, some grasping, some gracious, on board the *Titanic* during the last four fraught days of its doomed maiden voyage, offers an acute insight into how couples (or would-be couples) behave under extreme stress. Is it 'Every (wo)Man for (her)Himself', or do couples stick together as the chips (and the boat) go down?

Mr and Mrs Straus, an elderly pair, are consistently seen as extremely dependent on each other:

> We both watched the snail-like progress of Mr and Mrs Straus through the doorway. As usual they were arm in arm. The way they leaned together it seemed that if either one let go the other would lose balance. I couldn't be sure whether I found this touching or disturbing. Such dependence was surely dangerous. If one of them got detached, what then?[1]

As the unsinkable vessel started to sink, the chief saloon steward hurried a scared procession towards the far-too-few lifeboats, 'slowed down by the stately progress of Mr and Mrs Straus, linked as always'.[2] Officers bellowed, 'Women and children first.' Most women obeyed but Mrs Straus, being led to a window, stopped and said, 'I'm not going without Mr Straus.' She was dragged a few further steps, then broke free and stumbled to the old man's side. 'We shall stay together, old dear,' she said. 'As we have lived, so will we die.'[3]

Is such mutual dependence touching? Or disturbing? In what ways can it become dangerous?

Many couples felt that genuine *interdependence*, getting the balance right between individual autonomy and connection as a couple, was tricky. For some it proved more challenging to maintain personal identity within a partnership than to make compromises or to cope with change. They were uneasy about what they saw as blurred lines between commitment to their couple and allegiance to themselves. Strategies were needed.

STRATEGIES FOR STAYING INDEPENDENT YET CONNECTED

Couples who found interdependence easiest were those who felt secure as individuals. Helpful strategies for individual security included having had a period of singlehood or celibacy before entering a new partnership, having a separate space in a joint house, having equally visible careers or jobs, maintaining independent friendships, pursuing some independent leisure interests, being a strong feminist, being discreet about marital status, and having some money to call one's own:

> Having your own salary helps you feel independent at home when things are good, and the possibility of being economically separate gives you the freedom to go if things get bad. When I left my first marriage, the first thing my husband did was to tell the bank – without telling me – to switch our joint account to a single account in his name! That was my first sense of feminism! I phoned the bank and complained: 'How could you possibly do this without my consent?' In those days they could, I was just a wife.
>
> *(Caitlin, 45, Welsh New Zealander.)*

Singlehood before entering partnership

A long learning period alone prior to a relationship was seen as highly productive:

Having lived on your own can teach you to be centred and happy in yourself, which makes for a *healthy* couple. Since the AIDS epidemic hit I've seen many gay men go into relationships because they're afraid of being alone. They become dependent, they hope this other person will help solve their problems. It might be bliss for two months but it's a nightmare afterwards. Whereas those who'd taken time to develop themselves had a greater understanding of who they were. They tended towards healthier longer-lasting relationships. They depended equally on each other yet were independent because they didn't have to prove anything.

(*Jack, American, married to Roy.*)

Celibacy before entering partnership

I was celibate as well as single for ten years. Because of the pressure to be in a couple or have sex at first I felt an outsider, but when I shook that off I felt I was growing internally. I learned to feel good about my body and to understand my own psychological needs. Now, though we have fights in my new relationship, that strength makes me clearer about dependency issues.

(*Sue, partner to Stella.*)

Concealing marital status

Married couples felt they had a harder time preserving independence than those who cohabited. 'Once we married, friends saw us as husband and wife, not as individuals,' was a frequent comment.

Some saw concealment of the 'married' label as a necessary strategy.

Naomi, 50, and Mortimer, 56, who married in the 'hippy San Francisco late Sixties' when most of their peers resolutely refrained, purposefully avoided telling anyone. Thirty years later, Sherman, 29, American, and Amanda, 27, British, who went through a Green Card marriage so that Amanda could stay in the States, were similarly discreet.

INTERDEPENDENT SCENE: ARE WE MARRIED? NAOMI AND MORTIMER

The Americans Naomi and Mortimer talked round a lunch-table oblivious of the tape recorder:

Naomi: We didn't tell anyone! Friends said later, 'We must have been really horrible if you couldn't tell us you'd gotten married.' But in 1969/70 in San Francisco in our sub-culture between the Women's Movement and the Left, there was a strong feeling of opposition to traditional marriage. We felt if people knew we got married they'd see us differently! We'd be seen in traditional roles like men expected to be bread-winners, women to be submissive. There wasn't an alternative way to be married then.

Having lived together for 2 years, what made them get married?

Mortimer: (*laughing*) Naomi's mother!

Naomi: My mother was very ill so it was actually my father! He called to say how Mom was doing after her open-heart surgery. He said, 'She's really depressed. She doesn't feel she has much to live for but if you got married she'd feel happy. It would be something to cheer her on!' Where my parents lived on the East Coast, people didn't just live together. My mother had already said: 'I feel obliged to say for my unborn grandchildren that you should marry because they'll be seen as those horrible outcasts'; so we'd already thought we might get married if I got pregnant. So I put my hand over the phone and called to Mortimer: 'Do you care if we marry like before I'm pregnant?' He said: 'I don't care!' So I told my father: 'OK!'

Mortimer: If you're not politically keen on the idea of marriage, then you decide to get married, you certainly aren't gonna have a big Jewish wedding or tell anyone! So we didn't. We just got a priest friend who used to stand on picket lines with us to sign a marriage licence.

Naomi: Then I got worried about my independence. So we had to go through this feminist rap against marriage, how I was never gonna take Mortimer's name, how we had to *both* raise the kids. The priest had called in his secretary as a witness so we told him, 'You mustn't tell anybody. You must swear her to secrecy.' But we did tell Mom who was pleased. We were so against what happens in regular marriages that we were scared of what people would think if they knew. I didn't wear a ring, I've always called Mort my partner, not my husband. When we came to Britain, if people asked if we were married we decided to say, 'No, only legally.'

Naomi and Mortimer felt that two issues about dependency within marriage were entwined in the label they refused publicly to adopt:

Naomi: My biggest fear was I didn't want to be a suburban housewife. Mortimer didn't want to be the sole or even the main breadwinner. Lots of women can't respect a man who doesn't make much money, or doesn't make more money than them, but for me that's never mattered.

It mattered more to Mortimer.

Mortimer: It's important in any relationship that one person doesn't make the money. If one is the absolute breadwinner there's always a sense of power. This world expects men to earn the living and provide for the woman and yeah, I expect that myself at times. Those kind of social expectations work their way down. When we're feeling absolutely impoverished I feel more guilty than Naomi does. But Naomi has been pretty good. She's never laid any kinda major trips on me!

Naomi: I refused to be stuck at home with our first child while he went out to work. It worked out OK because he preferred to write at home and mind our daughter. So we lived first in an alternative commune in San Francisco where men did a bunch of child care. By the time we had our son, we worked jointly as puppeteers.

Mortimer: The interesting thing about puppetry is that it's a real Victorian art in which you do everything from script-writing, designing, making clothes, building props, to performing the characters. If you can actually work together with somebody

like that over a couple of years, then you've worked out a hel-
luva lot of personal things. We began to understand each
other's humour. We learned to be tolerant of each other's
peculiarities. We respected the idea that people must live
together as individuals as well as a couple. We have intellectual independencies. So we tried not to make demands on
each other to view things the same way. To do that people's
hearts must be on the right side.

Naomi: For the next 30 years we did most projects jointly. Some
years Mort studied while I taught. Some the reverse. We've
shared work-places; when we first got a computer we shared
computer time. Whoever wasn't on the computer minded the
kids. Mostly we job-shared. Even today with the kids grown
up we job-share a lectureship in London three days a week,
the other four days we write at home

Mortimer: When we work, often on the same course, there are
sometimes difficulties because people aren't used to couples being work partners. Some people who've worked with
us a long time don't know we're married. We tried not to
base our lives around the project of bringing up children. We
have maintained separate identities because we also each
had intellectual outlets. We have many separate friends who
all view us as individuals. We don't get together with couples.

Has the achievement of an interdependent marriage been more
difficult for one partner?

Naomi: The pressure of trying to be creative, often without much
money, while society gives you rules has been harder for
Mort. The expectation is that a man should have more of
whatever time or space is going. He has had to be willing to
give up some of that power which society saw him as having.
Against some odds we stuck to a shared vision. Shared
values. Equality.

The periods when mutual support was hardest was when one
partner was having success with their writing but the other
wasn't.

Naomi: One time Mort was being published easily, often, and I was struggling. That was hard.

Mortimer: It was a problem when I had book after book and Naomi wasn't getting published. The real difficulties we've had have manifested themselves there. Initially Naomi never conceived of herself as a writer so part of her always felt a kinda insecurity that I didn't feel. I've been writing since I was a kid. Writing was very important to me. In the beginning I was helpful to her. I'd read her stuff. But the more experienced she got, the more of a real writer she became, then it was difficult to give her a critique. It became harder too for her to critique my stuff, especially when her second book was rejected. At that point you wish desperately you weren't writers at the same time! She'd had so many rejections she kept hoping things would get published any minute now, and that's when it's hard to be congratulatory of the other person. It was hard for us! I was in that nice period when anything you're gonna write is gonna be accepted, you're in a state of grace for a limited period, but you don't recognise it as a limited period when you're in it!

Their difficulties increased when Mortimer was forced to recognise that temporarily their situations were reversed. Increasingly he found it harder to get published, while for Naomi it became easier.

Naomi: It's a bit more difficult to be in a position where the woman is doing better than the man. There hasn't been much jealousy. What's worse is when you're both down. When one is up, maybe the other might wish they were doing better but at least the up person can be supportive. If you both get nothing but rejections, there's no support.

Mortimer: What saved us was our broader understanding of the publishing industry and how writers and artists are forced into those relationships.

Their shared religious and cultural background has helped their interdependence.

Naomi: We're both very physical, feely,-touchy Jewish–Americans which gives us a nice sense of intimacy. I'm happily monogamous because not being so takes up too much time and energy that I'd rather put to something creative. We're not religious but we're culturally Jewish, so that's important. We share that common culture. We're both Ashkenazi, both come from Eastern Europe where despite the general subservience-of-women ideology, there was also an acceptance of certain women going out and earning money if their men were bright and studying in 'shul'.[4] This meant I had a context where women could work independently outside the family.

Mortimer: Being Jewish has influenced our relationship, which I wouldn't have said 20 years ago. Within Jewish culture stability is in raising families and staying together. If you come from a tradition where families split up, then it doesn't seem so shocking, but we don't. The shadows of forgotten ancestors hover around.

Naomi: That's right. Our expectation is to stay together. When both of us got angry we said, 'Do you wanna split up?' 'No.' 'All right then, we'd better do some more to make it work.' We've affected each other's viewpoints and offered each other a supportive environment.

Though their children have Mortimer's surname, Naomi doesn't:

Naomi: I never changed my name, not even on my passport. With different names many people still don't know we're married, which helps our independence. But interestingly, where we teach in the same college they do know we're married, yet I feel independent because I don't feel I'm in a traditional subservient relationship. I do know we're not gonna break up with each other! We've never used the label 'marriage', but we've worked at a partnership to make it equal. We've had conflict but we've worked it out because we wanted it to work. Having a family has been important and the chemistry between us has always been good.

Mortimer: The ingredient that has kept us interdependent and got us to this point is the element of surprise! So many people we knew got married *with* the expectation that they would last for ever, then they broke up, but we came together with the expectation that it would last just as long as it lasted! We always joke about the Long Weeekend that lasted thirty years!

INTERDEPENDENT SCENE: DON'T CALL US HUSBAND AND WIFE: AMANDA AND SHERMAN

Sherman, 29, an American engineering consultant, and Amanda, 27, a British health administrator, married for five years, had never planned or intended that kind of coupledom. They both saw marriage as an obstacle to interdependence:

We didn't feel we needed to get married to have a commitment. I didn't want to have kids at the time, and I didn't think that made a difference anyway. My mother did! I didn't see any religious need. I saw a legal need at times for things like tax purposes. In the US it's always better financially to be married. Once we married, my car insurance went way down! As soon as you're married they think you're so stable you won't wreck your car! But apart from that we didn't need it. I'm sure we'd still be together, but we probably wouldn't have got married if we hadn't been forced into it. Amanda came out to the States for a visit and she just didn't leave, so we decided that we wouldn't get married if it was at all possible.

At the start of my first week's visit, Sherman said something like, 'If we have any hope that this is going to last on a practical basis, we're going to have to get married!' So it was kinda raised but we didn't like it! I felt it made you less independent. We had tried living on two different continents but it was too hard. We wanted to be together all the time. But both of us were politically opposed to marriage. So it was a hurdle! I went home to England, back to the US for a week, then things got more serious. So I decided what the hell, I've got nothing to lose. I'm just going to go over there! I packed everything up and arrived with one suitcase, £500, no job, no friends, had only met his family for one evening, and had no inclination to marry! We lived together for six months, but I couldn't get work; I needed a Green Card. I applied for an extension to my visa but I got a notice telling me I had thirty days to leave the country. Time was

running out. Neither one of us said, 'Will you marry me?' but
the pressure was that we were going to have to do that while we
were still opposed to it. Marriage was Establishment. It was
very 'old hat'. It's bad for women. We felt people treated you
differently. Women particularly are treated like possessions.
Neither of us agreed with that.

Despite their objections, four days before Amanda's visa ran
out they took the decision to marry secretly.

We didn't even tell my mother who I'm close to. Not Sherman's
parents. Not his friends. Nobody!

No, we didn't tell anyone we were going to do it. If you tell one
you've gotta tell everybody. When Amanda was told she had to
be out like within a week, as we wanted to stay together we
knew the only way was to be married. In Connecticut it's real
easy, you don't need a witness, just a Justice of the Peace and a
licence. It only took five minutes.

When the Justice of the Peace came to our apartment Sherman
was wearing his boxer shorts, I was wearing an old T-shirt and
sweatpants. It took thirty seconds to get married!

We worried what people would think.

(Sherman.)

We did! It was scary because though rationally I knew it
wouldn't change the way we felt about each other, it was going
against our belief system.

(Amanda.)

According to them both, their marriage *has* made differences to
people's perceptions of them:

I called my mother in England after it happened. She was very
happy, she cried. She would have liked a big traditional
wedding but she was sensible. We didn't tell anyone else for six
months. Sherman finally told his Dad, but asked him not to tell

the family. But on Christmas Day at the dinner-table he suddenly said: 'I've got something to announce: Sherman and Amanda got married!' I thought: 'Oh God! Don't do this!' There was total silence, then his aunt said: 'Why did you go and do that?' I thought: 'You cow! You didn't have to say that!' But then everyone did start to treat us differently. Society does. Conservative people see it as we've grown up, we're being sensible. Or, 'Well now it's real.' They see us as having more of a commitment. They look on us as a unit so we have to guard our independence. The most challenging thing is to be separate as well as together. To still have separate friends. To still *do things* with your friends. To still have a separate identity. We don't wear rings, and it's taken me 5 years to say the phrase, 'My husband'. One disadvantage with marriage is that some people always ask you out as a couple. If I don't know the husband or wife of a friend, I purposely ask just the friend to do something! We've found we have had to make up new rules for our marriage and not go by the Establishment's rules.

(Amanda.)

Marriage has made definite differences. Things I don't like. People look at you differently if you say 'This is my mate' than if you introduce that person as a wife. When we moved from Connecticut to Texas, people either saw you as having a girl-friend or as married. If you had a girl-friend, you had the potential to be single. If you were married, you didn't. People may not invite you out somewhere late because they figure you gotta get home. They even try and ask you out together.

After several years, they now feel more pragmatic about their marriage connection and have established autonomous identities:

As an individual I wanted to make sure I could pursue my own career, do whatever I wanted to do. But I wanted to let Amanda do that as well. I don't want her to feel there's any reason why she shouldn't do whatever she wants to do. And because we needed to do both those things together, co-ordinating those two things can be hard. There can be clashes of time or travel. We *are* tied; sometimes I'd like to have a career where I travelled more, but then I wouldn't be able to see Amanda as much. At first there was a lot of balancing, but now we just get on with living.

We struggle to maintain our independence but also enjoy our marriage. We have separate hobbies. Sherman belongs to a car club. He loves listening to live music, he enjoys CDs and records with his friends. I can gossip and be more emotional with my women friends. I can talk about more personal things which, though Sherman listens to, I can tell he's not interested in! He feels like my best friend. We have a special connection, an inter-connectedness as a couple. We want to share things, but also think of our ideas and opinions as being separate. We don't try to change each other's views. It feels OK to do things separately and I have every intention of continuing that. But I'll still know that he's the one!

Working together: harm or help?

Some partners (more often women within heterosexual couples) felt that their professional autonomy would be damaged if work associates knew they were in partnerships. This seemed to matter most if their partner had a similar career or worked in the same company.

One British and Australian couple who worked in the same British university department kept their Intimate Commuter rela-tionship secret from office colleagues for eleven years until they moved to Canada where, despite again working in the same uni-versity department, they suddenly bought a joint house, had children and proudly disclosed their coupledom to everyone:

At the British university where Roland and I both worked, women scientists had a hard time proving their worth. Because he was more established than I was, if senior colleagues had known that Roland and I were a couple my research would not have been taken as seriously. That would then have affected our partnership. My identity was at stake. So we hid our relationship publicly. We would even go to conferences abroad and sleep in separate bedrooms so that no one suspected. It was a relief when we moved to Canada. Here we work in the same department, but it's much more democratic than England, I have tenure now, and we can afford to be open.

(Kay, scientist, British partner to Roland, scientist. Both Canadian residents.)

Several couples, openly 'coupled', have worked profitably together without Kay and Roland's anxieties:

When we first got jobs in the same department, there was a degree of fear whether it would work out. At work, would we feel we had to back each other up on everything? At home, would we end up fighting because we saw each other a lot? None of that has happened. We have independent identities in our department, even though we tend to agree on ideological issues. Seeing each other all day at home has been quite delightful. I don't think you either have to see yourself as part of a couple or see yourself as independent. I don't like that either/or idea, I don't want to have it dichotomised that way. I am independent in that I have my own mind and opinions, but at the same time who I am to a degree is the commitment that Kurt and I have to each other. It has helped form who I am and what I have to offer to the world. That is because it is a degree of security to come home to.

(Caitlin.)

I never had any fears about working in the same department because I know Caitlin to be independent-minded. She's her own person, as I am. That we see a lot of each other is not a problem at all. I like it. How many people have an opportunity to talk about work to their partner who understands? Not only about the work but the sharing of gossip and laughter. Caitlin is a highly independent person, never clingy or dependent, and because of that we have disagreements. Yet that is the very thing I like. It means that when Caitlin disapproves of my professional aspirations it makes me look at my own life, and often not pursue them if they were likely to harm our couple. I trust her judgement.

(Kurt.)

We met at work. Kimberly was the director of acquisitions for a major movie company and I was a reader, so I actually worked for her! Today I produce films, run a production company, she writes screenplays but we interact. I read her stuff and discuss with her what she wants to do and advise various choices. Because we both do artistic work, we know the personal anxiety not just about stress or mechanics but of 'Are you doing what you really wanna be doing?' We depend on each other to understand that, but we do independent work. From the start, working in the same industry has given us benefits of security, advice and the support of someone you trust. A general sense of well-being. There's a lot of independence, but you always feel there could be more!

(Simon, 45, American film producer; married 13 years to Kimberly, 43, American screen-writer.)

There's some dependence because before we married I worked as a book editor then did well in the film industry, always supported myself. But after we married and I had a baby, Simon did so well that it allowed me to do what I wanted and write. But our couple also gives me the benefits of interdependence. It allows me to be on my own when I want, but Simon's a great companion to share stuff with. As for being in the same business I understand what he goes through. He's a real help with my writing. Since the kids, I just can't imagine what it must be like not having someone to partner them with. There's no tension about child-rearing, we seem to flow with that. Because I have to take care of three kids, he seems to take more care of me. I guess we're interdependent but not always equal; he relies on me for his emotional needs, whereas I have female friends for some needs. The only thing that ever makes me angry is that he is so work-driven that sometimes I cannot get his attention. The kids could call, 'Daddy! Daddy!' five times before he hears! But I can express that anger because I can be myself. I have preserved my identity. If what I've wanted to do has created conflict, I've seen that we resolve it without giving up what I wanted. Other people see us as a couple, a family, but our long-time friends see each of us as individuals.

Maintaining separate friendships

Maintaining some separate friends and interests were the two methods most couples mentioned:

> Preserving our identity is important for us both, but a little more for me. We work hard at maintaining our individual friendships. Jack and I are friends in a very significant way, but it's different because of the romantic element. We both feel we need that other part, the 'just friends' part of those outside our couple. The need for variety of personality and interaction. I'm a 'people person', so there's no way Jack could meet all my relational needs. Also, a good friend gives me someone to talk to about my relationship with Jack. We make sure we get time alone separate from one another. We have our own projects. As we didn't get married till we were 34 and 36, we've each had a long time being our own person. That's not going to go away!
>
> *(Roy.)*

> We are very clear about making sure we maintain contacts with other people that are good for us. While we were dating, before we committed to one another, there was one night each week designated as 'Others' Night'. This was the night when technically we could each go out with other people. We might do activities with a group which you wouldn't normally do because of your relationship. We would hang out with friends, have dinner with one particular person, not feel you had to take your partner along. Though now we don't have a formalised night out, we still encourage each other to do independent stuff. Roy was involved in an ex-gay group, and he still works with people from that. It gives him a chance to be who he is, or to expand, then he can come back from that experience and bring what he learned into our relationship.
>
> *(Jack.)*

Keeping in touch with her own friends has always been vital to Violet, now on a third marriage to Walter:

I have more friends than Walter. They are not run-of-the-mill people: most are artists, poets, or interested in ley lines!

Violet sees a 'best friend' as someone who knows more about you in certain ways than even a partner, which helps to preserve individual identity:

My best friend and I have been through a lot together. I've seen her through everything that went wrong. The worst time was when she needed an abortion, in those days when abortions were fairly dodgy. They gave what they called a sponge and left her to it. So I had the job of clearing that up and disposing of the baby. I went to Hyde Park and put it in one of the wastepaper bins there. I wasn't really conscious of the implications. If I'd been caught with this little parcel, getting rid of it, it could have been awkward. When I look back, I realise we've never mentioned it ever since. I've never told anyone. Neither of us has. But I think that made a big, big bond. We don't talk about the intimate things she knows about my life either. But our extraordinary history is what makes our friendship special and different from my couple with Walter.

DANGERS TO INTERDEPENDENCE

There are dangers to establishing interdependence when one partner overshadows the other professionally or personally, or when one partner tries to control the relationship.

A person who is seen to be successful professionally may keep reminding their less successful lover how important his or her career is, and how it needs to be given priority within their partnership.

One may have a job perceived as 'more interesting' or 'glamorous'. Kath, the Irish nurse, sometimes felt that people were over-awed by Fern's career as an actress and rather ignored her own profession. Similarly, Bernadette the archaeologist felt that friends were more interested in Cynthia's latest film script than they were in her latest dig. 'Sometimes the joke, "Found any precious coins, Bernie, or is it still old bones?" wore pretty thin!'

One partner might be a higher wage-earner who far too frequently reminds the lower-income partner of their unequal financial status.

One partner might be more dominant, speaking more, holding the floor, commanding attention, while the other person lurks in the shadows, seen as part of that couple but not as a strong individual.

There can be dangers when one partner is considerably younger than the other. This can lead to a mother-child or father-child relationship in which there is too much dependence from one partner and too much protection from another.

INTERDEPENDENCE SCENE: I'M YOUNGER THAN YOU ARE: TAKE CARE OF ME: DAISY AND JULIAN

Julian at 31 is 12 years younger than Daisy and feels dependent:

> As the eldest of seven I very quickly, very young, became able, competent, old and responsible. Julian s desire to be mothered meant he was attracted to that kind of confidence.

> I'm not as accomplished as Daisy. She's been at it longer. She's been around the emotional loops longer, been able to establish herself longer. There are ways I don't feel I've caught up. I like being with people who are older; Barry, my previous lover, was older than me, so that's been an issue around age. With Daisy the up side is that she's very competent, incredibly intelligent, and successful. I'm drawn to that. The down side is that I have this part of me which wants to be taken care of and rescued, so I get hooked into: 'Here's a confident person: Daisy's been a pseudo-mother of seven, so she can take care of me in a whole bunch of ways!' In the past I didn't live with Barry, I took care of myself, but despite that now I'm with Daisy all this dependency stuff comes out!

> There's been a struggle throughout our relationship about his incredible need. Sometimes I laugh and say, 'You'll cure me of this if it kills me!' It isn't just a pattern with *him*, it has been a pattern in all my friendships. I would become the listener for

people, the strong one, the one people called with problems. So no one played with me. No one laughed with me. There was power in it for me too. I became the big sister/controller. I began to think most people were not as able as me, or that Julian wasn't as competent because he wasn't as old or hadn't been through as much. It was the Big Sister thing of never thinking anybody was as big as I was or could carry as much! I felt quite ashamed of how controlling I was! When I refused to play that part with Julian, it was much better for both of us. Much as he wanted it, he knew it was debilitating. An example is that I've always been the successful academic person, so he would invest in my doing that rather than doing it himself. He would push me to get ahead in my career in a way that was really about his desire for security or having an income. I'm not as invested in those things as he is. So if he pushed me to succeed, I could then look after that need of his. I've now refused that role and he must take it up for himself.

Julian described how the change between them occurred:

At the start I sank into a place where emotionally I wanted her to rescue me and she was happy to play the rescuer part, but now she's done her own psychotherapy work she wants to change that. She doesn't always want to be the person who caretakes. I lose the capacity to be adult in myself and divest it on to Daisy but now she doesn't want me hanging on to her! She wants a more equal relationship, someone who can engage with her. She wants *me* to provide emotional support. I want it, but I don't know quite how to do it. I wanna be a big person in the world – be able to make my own way, feel good about myself – but I still have this incredible need to be taken care of. I am working in a dynamic with Daisy to try and develop that capacity. I now try to nurture myself, give myself a bath, try to be an adult in the world.

Julian has an investment in the situation *not* changing but for the health of our partnership it has to change! Individually I also have to stop focusing on my relations with others as opposed to myself. Because we live together it is a constant struggle. I have been helped by starting to write, which has given me a passionate relationship with myself. It felt like the most revolutionary thing for me as a woman. But it means I am less available to other people.

INTERDEPENDENT SCENE: GIVE ME MORE SPACE! PETE AND JEFF

Jeff, tall, slim and fit, looks younger than his 48 years. His eyes light up when he talks about Pete, with whom he would enjoy spending 'every minute of the day'. Pete, 31, looks like a chocolate-coloured labrador, with dark straggly hair and big brown eyes. But despite his almost cuddly appearance Pete, a part-time writer, can be distant or aloof. He loves Jeff, but needs long spells on his own. If he fails to achieve this, his skin reddens with stress. He needs considerably more psychic space than Jeff either needs or allows, thus autonomy is their most consistent conflict:

I was not in any relationship for almost a decade so I'm a very independent person. What makes me angry is feeling misunderstood, feeling there are expectations put on me which I can't meet. My level of commitment is less than Jeff's, so when he wants to spend all his time with me that makes me angry.

(Pete.)

Part of their problem lies in Jeff's history. Before Jeff and Pete became involved, Jeff had a long, highly dependent relationship with another man:

It lasted seven and a half years. I became co-dependent on him and he on me. What started out good became bad. I was real clingy. I was trying always to be with that person. He was unhappy and I smothered him. Then he verbally and mentally abused me.

(Jeff.)

Jeff's romantic history means he gives everything to a relationship and keeps getting sucked into this dependence. I'm a loner. I could go two weeks without seeing the person, but that isn't healthy either.

(Pete.)

Jeff understands Pete's needs but cannot always meet them. Sometimes when he tries, Pete – anxious on his part to please Jeff – fails to express his needs until a crisis point is reached:

> There was a big blow-up when I'd been with Pete and other family members for a whole week's vacation. He was suffocating! I'd told him if he wanted me to leave after spending a few days with him, he should tell me. Well, he didn't do that. After his family left, he asked me to go to a show with him and some friends. I found it not tasteful, said so, left, and he blew up. Whether it was that he'd been embarrassed in front of his friends, or whether he was trying to please me by asking me to go along or perhaps he was just suffocating because he needed space. It took us four nights on the phone, both of us hurting deeply, to discuss it. Talking through it did make the relationship better. I realise I've got to let him have his own space because of the work he does. That's a problem, because I want always to be with him.
>
> *(Jeff.)*

The couple live in separate apartments to allow greater independence:

> Because we live separately sometimes I sit at home by myself knowing Pete's out somewhere, wondering what he's doing, how late he's going to come home. It's part of my insecurity. But when he comes home and calls me then everything is OK.

Even separate residences do not allow Pete sufficient autonomy:

> When we lived two hours' drive apart, if I went out to a party mid-week I would feel oddly guilty as if somehow he should be there. If it was up to him we'd move in together tomorrow. So he has moved nearer to LA, only fifteen minutes. As it is I feel sometimes I have to justify why I don't want to get together or if I'm doing something with friends.

Pete's close social circle recently held a pre-wedding party for a group member:

I wanted to go to it without Jeff. I really wanted to do something without him. But initially I didn't communicate clearly. I told him about the party. He knew and liked the people, and they him, so he said, 'OK, I'll come with you!' Immediately I said, 'OK. That's fine!' Then I went away and thought about it and wondered, 'Why did I do that? Surely it's OK for me to go to a party without him. We've been together all this time, and it's OK to have a life of my own!'

(Pete.)

The reason Pete gave for behaving like that was the same reason other couples offered for over-'couply' behaviour:

I guess I fell into this bad fantasy that if you're in a relationship you do everything together. I've had enough straight role models of friends who pair up, then you never hear from them again or if you do get to do something with them you end up doing it with their partner. We've had such big conflicts in this area that I hope my relationship with Jeff doesn't become like that.

On this occasion there was a successful outcome:

Jeff phoned me the next day and said, 'I've thought about it. I'm really sorry. I just sort of invited myself.' I said: 'Oh, I should have spoken up more about it!' Then I actually told him I would rather go by myself. That I hadn't been totally honest with him. That I was ready to have him attend the party when in fact I didn't want him there. I should have said: 'Jeff, this is a party I need to go to by myself. It doesn't mean I don't want to be with you. It's just important for me.' As I didn't, I gave up a little bit of myself. That's always the tendency in a relationship. You can't be 100 per cent loving *and* truthful. You have to be on guard about losing the truth, shaving things or agreeing with things you don't approve of.

The men are working very hard at this difference between their needs and styles:

With Pete I've had to learn not to smother, to give space, not to be co-dependent. To let him do some things he has to do himself, even though I love doing them for him. I've had to pull back and say, 'Hey! I can do that for myself, he can do that for himself!'

Jeff is forcing me to come out of my shell and do things together. Conversely, I'm forcing him to be less dependent. I'm not sure whether my work or my relationship is more central to my life, or whether it has to be one or the other. When I was alone, wanting to date, I thought that having a relationship would be central. Now I'm in one I'm not so sure. It is definitely important but being a writer that's important too. So I am trying to find that balance.

During the progress of this research, Pete and Jeff struggled with this issue. Pete felt he needed more space, not less. After the last interview, the couple agreed to separate temporarily in order to work on their independent needs.

INTERDEPENDENT SCENE: OVER-DEPENDENCY: CYNTHIA AND BERNADETTE

Cynthia, a screen-writer, and Bernadette, an archaeologist, had lived together in Britain with Cynthia's two sons and Bernadette's two daughters for a decade. When they met, Cynthia was an alcoholic who had temporarily lost custody of her two small boys. After Bernadette had helped her recover both her health and her children, Cynthia began to have considerable success in the film industry. Though deeply in love, they had stopped communicating over the issues which divided them. Cynthia buried herself and her distress in her work. Bernadette, feeling that Cynthia liked the security of their coupledom but had stopped paying her attention, turned her own attention to another woman. By the time this inconsequential affair was finished and the couple realised it had merely been a symptom of their communication breakdown they had sold their house and were living separately. They decided to use the Couple interviews to analyse where they had gone wrong and to see if their relationship could be reworked.

They saw interdependence as a central issue, because for ten years they had lived intricately intertwined lives bonded by interests in women's politics, social issues, literature, film, dance, music, food, walking, and of course their teenage children.

Bernadette: I want to explore how our relationship was almost right but *wasn't* quite right. Not getting the balance between dependence and independence was one element that made it go wrong. Those first few years we were very dependent on each other. We went everywhere together. We had joint friends.

Cynthia: At first we didn't even have people round . . . we wanted to be together. . . . we were utterly . . .

Bernie: (*laughing*) Utterly! We were so used to doing things together that I remember once you said that you were going down the town on your own on your bike. I felt really bereft! Now it seems absolutely ridiculous that I should feel like that.

Cyn: (*laughing*) Where was I going? What was I doing?

Bernie: Just round the town on a Saturday afternoon, nothing spectacular. Do you remember when we used to go to Sainsbury's sometimes I'd say to you: 'I'll do it on my own, I can do it on my own' but you insisted that you came too!

Cyn: Yes, I wanted to come.

Bernie: (*sternly*) Now don't let's get over-romantic about Sainsbury's! I can remember many a battle when you used to grab all those expensive big bottles of shampoo and I used to shout at you: 'Those aren't household things! They're your own things!' Do you remember the battle of the baskets?

Cyn: (*quietly*) I do! I do! I remember it all.

Bernie: What does that say about us? I was really longing to go to Sainsbury's on my own and get it over with. But you interpreted that as a slight.

Cyn: I interpreted it as that you could run that household without me!

Bernie: (*reflectively*) Do you think I have that effect on people? Make them feel irrelevant?

Cyn: (*quietly but firmly*) Yes, I think you do.

Bernie: Do it all myself?

Cyn: Yes.

Bernie: Wonderwoman?

Cyn: Yes.

Bernie: One-woman band?

Cyn: Yes.

Bernie: No one else needed on voyage?

Cyn: No, I think people are needed on voyage but not to run it. Crew! I think you like crew!

Bernie: (*half laughing, half appalled*) Crew! Did that affect how I dealt with independence? Did it make us think it was a good thing to have had that we'll-go-everywhere-together-like-Siamese-twins?

Cyn: Was that really bad?

Bernie: Not all that healthy. I don't think it was very good for growing.

Cyn: Did it make people see us as a couple?

Bernie: Oh yes, absolutely. Absolutely! We both liked people seeing us as a couple but was there any element for you that you wanted to be seen *with me* as well? To be shown at my Mum's? So that you would be seen as a proper part of my life?

Cyn: Yes. At the beginning definitely. That was all to do with 'don't put me under the carpet'.

Bernie: You would be one of the hardest people to put under a carpet! I don't think it is totally a good thing that people began to see us *only* as a couple, not as two independent people. We had that house, those children, we were like an institution.

Cyn: But it was obviously what we wanted to do.

Bernie: Did it stunt us? I think it might have done.

Cyn: How did it stunt you?

Bernie: I felt a sense of loss if you went down the town on your own, but on the other hand I can remember thinking I would like to go down the town on *my* own. I can remember feeling exactly the same two things at more or less the same time. Or perhaps you want the other person to be dependent on you but you don't want to be dependent on them!

Cyn: Why does one want someone dependent on us? Why did you?

Bernie: Perhaps it makes you feel necessary.

Cyn: Yes, it was rather nice.

Bernie: But in the last 3 years you must have wanted to break away a bit because it was you who instigated doing some things on your own – badminton, going on cycling trips, camera classes, more and more film stuff. I never remember going to an evening class on my own.

Cyn: I was dependent on you while I was growing more healthy, after I came off alcohol. I read something about how if someone rescues you it has a lifelong effect. That's a kind of dependence, isn't it?

Bernie: Do you feel some kind of resentment that I helped get you off drink? You must have resented me surely, because it made you less independent?

Cyn: No! I never have. No, not ever! It was hard, but it has brought me nothing but good. I am clear that I felt no resentment. But I do feel some special relationship with you because of it. You have an access to me that other people don't have. It has had a kind of interdependence effect. A special access to each other. It seems to make me feel more exposed to you.

Bernie: Well, I think you did resent me, because I had to control or curtail some of your activities. You used to shout and rave when I persuaded you not to drive at all while you were coming off. You shouted about 'Bernie's house' and 'Bernie's car' and 'Bernie's bed'. Remember the battles over the car? 'Let me drive your car.'

Cyn: You said that I couldn't drive it, not because I was a recovering alcoholic but because it was *your* car. For you there were things that were yours but nevertheless there was 'us'. You did seem to have it both ways. Early on there didn't seem to be 'me'. I was upset camping in your house with my two boys, everyone squashing up, because I felt I didn't have anything very visible of my own. As you said about me later, I needed to put my geography around me, to make myself feel I existed independently. It improved when I was off drink and we bought a house together.

Bernie: I don't often think back to that. It doesn't seem relevant any more.

Cyn: I just wondered if it explained our mutual dependence?

Bernie: No! I think people are always struggling for an equilibrium. I don't actually think we got it right. We didn't do enough things in our own right. We have so much in common outside of work pursuits. The effect was that we were hardly out of each other's company for several years. For a time it made us unable to relate to other people.

Cyn: (laughing) Well, we struck out! We separated! We split up! We related to other people! You found a new person. I found more film work. We've been living independent lives!

Bernie: (thoughtfully) But here we are back talking about what went wrong . . . We must have something to offer each other. Maybe it is a sort of dependency on each other. *(laughs)*

Cyn: (seriously) We had things like caring and growth, strength and challenge.

Bernie: (laughing wildly) Strength and challenge! Challenge and strength! Yes, all those things. But it *is* curious that we are talking again.

Cyn: You mean having foraged out and found other lives, here we are! How does it make you feel? Do you find it bothering?

Bernie: Yes!

Cyn: Why?

Bernie: (pause, sighs deeply) Because I thought we had sorted things out. *(coughs, splutters) my* throat cancer is coming on!

Cyn: (laughing) Keep going!

Bernie: Shut up! You are thoroughly enjoying every second of it. Don't glower at me either. *(coughs)* I can't speak now.

Cyn: (coughs uproariously) Maybe you find mutual dependence more bothering than I do!

Bernie: (seriously) Yes maybe I do.

Cyn: Maybe you have to keep proving you are independent, maybe you have to keep showing that you don't need anyone that much!

Bernie: (quietly) Maybe.

Cyn: Maybe you actually resent doing these interviews, even though you agreed to it as much as I did.

Bernie: Yes, perhaps on some level I do. I rather like it when I am here. But I do always need to have my own independent space and I will make it somehow no matter what! Whatever part of my life I have been in, I've always wanted to *(long pause)* keep a measure of independence. *(sighs)*

Cyn: (bitterly) At the cost to no matter whom.

Bernie: I like to think out things for myself. I don't like to think that other people are thinking them out for me. I do like my own space. It was a big mistake to have our bedroom also as your work-room. God, you couldn't get away from the film, the celluloid, the visuals, the audios, the screens, big screens, small screens, there was always a bloody screen blinking away! And notes! The notes just cascaded off the walls! Bits of paper everywhere!

Cyn: (quietly and depressed) It was my work-room. *(pause, then staunchly)* Well, we can learn from that. We need independent spaces.

Bernie: Yes. *(pause)* Those are my complaints. Have you got any complaints?

Cyn: (sadly) No.

Bernie: (crossly) Oh stop it, Cyn! For God's sake have a complaint!

Cyn: I'd rather make a suggestion about having more separate activities. You had one interest of your own that kept you independent.

Bernie: Yes, gardening.

Cyn: I had my film scripts.

Bernie: Yes, you had films and writing! Maybe that's part of it for you. Whereas I feel strongly that independence/dependence is a dilemma, you don't seem to feel it.

Cyn: I think scriptwriting gives me considerable independence. It sounds pretentious but I feel writing is who I am.

Bernie: Quite a luxury then, isn't it? There aren't many people who can spend their working lives doing something that gives them themselves to such an extent!

Cyn: Perhaps that is why I don't cavil so much about a need for independence. Curiously, during this period of interviews when we've begun to talk about our relationship, I haven't been able to write a decent script. These discussions about dependence/independence have got in the way.

Bernie: If you have scriptwriting, what do I have? Should I go away for weekends on my own or with other people?

Cyn: Perhaps that would be constructive.

Bernie: But I never did that. Every weekend we used to spend together.

Cyn: It was lovely! *(sees Bernie looking cynical)* Whoops! Sorry!

Bernie: (crossly) If you are going to keep saying that all the time . . .

Cyn: (ironically) It was awful!

Bernie: (laughs)

Cyn: (ironically) It was really dreary! *(seriously)* But are you saying that you think that it is a bad idea?

Bernie: No, but we should accept people *do* go off at weekends. In our relationship that element was missing. In the last few years you used to go away to make films but I just stayed.

Cyn: Not like you and that new lover you took up with!

Bernie: (ignoring sarcasm) That's true. Since we split up, at first I found it hard in my relationship with Selina that she took it as part and parcel that she should go away alone for weekends. She went to see a joint friend and I found myself thinking, 'I ought to go too'; then I realised that it's not on! Because if she and I had trooped off together like you and I did, then we would have had this corporate nature with other people. At first with Selina I tried not to mind. Then I got used to it. Nothing awful happened. But it would have been quite dramatic if you and I had done something like that.

Cyn: Yes. It would have been. I did occasionally have a drink with Kay, but I always had it after our film class. That was because I knew it would make you feel funny if I had a drink with her on a normal evening which I might have spent with you. Sometimes Kay and I would say to you, 'Come and have a drink with us.' I would have felt really funny if we hadn't asked you.

Bernie: Yes, you see you always feel you must ask the other person. Then they can refuse. I think that is bad. It meant we were using tactics when there was no need. Did you feel guilty that you were going to see Kay?

Cyn: Yes, yes.

Bernie: But you shouldn't have done. We never talked about it. You never said, 'Would you feel really bad if I go off and have a drink with Kay?'

Cyn: No, I didn't.

Bernie: (critically) We always pussy-footed around it or tried to find ways of accommodating it. It's not healthy not asking, not talking.

Cyn: (very upset, shouting) The only way I can go on with this exploring is if I can see a goal, like changing things so we can have a new future together. I can't do it any other way. I have taken this on in that spirit. Haven't you?

Bernie: (pause) Mmm.

Cyn: That is what it is about, isn't it? It is about how can we improve things? Yes?

Bernie: It doesn't have to be about that. I think it is valuable in itself to look at the issue of dependency.

Cyn: You mean academically?

Long pause.

Bernie: It is . . .

Cyn: Finish your sentence!

Bernie: (angry) Don't tell me to finish my sentence! *(pause)* It is valuable in itself because no matter what happens, *no matter what happens*, we shall have learned something! We had all the misery and sadness when our relationship finished, but we didn't really know what had happened. Did we? We just thought, 'Oh dear' or 'Bad luck' or something.

Cyn is too upset to continue the discussion.

Bernie: (exasperated) What? What *is* the matter? You're sitting there quivering!

Cyn pulls herself together.

Cyn: Right.

Bernie: (shouting) I want to know! I want to know! I want to know what it was, where it went wrong. Don't *you* want to know? *(infuriated)* You don't, do you! You just think, 'Oh well, oh dear!'

Cyn: I do. I want to know.

Bernie: You don't! You just want to have a means to an end. If it is going to lead to X or Y, then it is a good thing but if it is not going to lead there then you are not interested.

Cyn: That is a bit hard!

Bernie: Well, this does seem to be what you are saying . . . you seem to be saying that these interviews have no value unless there is an end for us. You've got to have a goal. For you there has got to be a reward at the end. But, Cyn, we are not in grooves rolling on to something. We are trying to find out what is true in our relationship.

Cyn: Or what works.

Bernie: Yes, what works. And what doesn't work.

Cyn: (airily) OK!

Bernie: You sit there with a sort of sickly smile on your face making out everything was so lovely, and *(shouting)* a lot of it was bloody horrible! You are still clinging on to some golden picture. That it was all lovely, and all we have to do is to get back together and it will all be lovely again. But there were many things that went wrong.

Cyn: (quietly) I know!

Bernie: (shouting) Wrong!

Cyn: (more quietly) I know. I thought that was what we were trying to do, work out what was wrong.

Bernie: Part of the effect of taking part in these interviews is bound to throw up all these things. Maybe we'll remember things that make you think: 'My God!'

Cyn: You mean: why would I want to do *that* again?

Bernie: (chuckling) Exactly! I m not saying that is it overall. Part of it is that it's too easy to tidy away all the grot.

Cyn: (dourly) Yes, I know it's true. Part of me agrees with you and part of me thinks, 'Well, shit! I was managing very nicely after we broke up and now this!'

Bernie: No you weren't!

Cyn: Yes, I was! I was managing jolly nicely!

Bernie: No you weren't! You said yourself it didn't feel quite right.

Cyn: Right? It was bloody comfortable! I wasn't in tears half the time!

Bernie: You aren't in tears half the time now.

Cyn: Every time we talk about these things I am! *(pause)* As well as being very excited when we talk. But I am saying that part of me agrees with what you are saying, and part of me thinks that if you think our life was so awful and you are now happy, just stay away!

Bernie: (refusing to rise to gibes) I want to continue trying to find out what happened, though I am beginning to feel this is mostly an imbalance problem. This matter of independence and dependence seems to be mostly *my* problem, but I want to continue to think about it.

The two women, who had already discussed painful areas of their relationship including communication, compromise and their children, *did* continue their analysis of interdependence until Bernadette broke off the interviews and discussions. They did not restart their live-in partnership, but managed with barely a break to renegotiate and sustain a close intimate friendship. They both said they learned a great deal from the interviews on interdependence.

INTERDEPENDENT SUCCESS STORIES

Couples agreed that establishing interdependence was 'very hard work'. Kurt spoke for many:

It's hard work because every day I have to question my motives, question whether in fact our relationship has that balance, is getting better, stays the same or is slipping. I think it's hard work for Caitlin too because perhaps we're too sensitive to each other's needs and moods so that's not easy.

Yet several couples subjected to the same elements that others saw as dangerous to their interdependence – such as tightly connected lives, similar friendships, similar interests, careers in the same industry – nevertheless managed to achieve strong bonds as a couple and confident personal autonomy. Maurice and Dolly, married 54 years, report.

INTERDEPENDENT SCENE: HOW IT WORKS: MAURICE AND DOLLY

We have always been couply. ALWAYS been that for 54 years! That's what we are. We are a close co-operation, a ghetto. But we are independent people.

(Maurice.)

He really is a lot of my strength. I know he is there for me all the time. That's true for him about me as well. We are dependent on each other for different things, but it is not dysfunctional. We are not leaning on each other because of our weaknesses. We are leaning on each other to give each other strength.

(Dolly.)

This strength comes from a unified viewpoint which allows each of them a free spirit. They see that balance as the clue to the way they have sustained their first love and found increasing joy in each other's company.

They both feel their successful marital interdependence rests on what was, for their period, advanced social and political attitudes. They see as the most significant feature Dolly's separate career for 50 years ago it was rare for mothers to have high-powered, high-paid careers:

Dolly has always worked. Today for women to work and have small children is normal, but at the time she did it it wasn't mainstream, not even in the motion-picture industry. People used to give me a nudge and say: 'What's the matter, Maurice? Can't you support your wife?' Still she landed a nice job, so she could work at home. I stood up to the people, I would sneer at them.

Outside her marriage, Dolly's full-time career wasn't always seen as approvable.

My field – writing, later films – was all men. Male literary agents, male publishers, editors. I was unusual. I used to have criticism from women who worked hard as housewives, who really dedicated themselves to their children. Men in the industry would come up to Maurice and say: 'Why do you let your wife work? You don't need the money, so why do that? Why do you *let* her?' Which is a great line! But for my independence in our marriage, I needed to work.

How did Dolly find the strength to resist these outside pressures?

I got the strength through Maurice's recognition that I loved working, did not like being a housewife, but was able to accommodate my kids.

Her strong feminist attitudes have added strength to her marriage:

I think Dolly was one of your earliest feminists that ever lived! She made herself independent, she was expressing herself. I thought that was very good.

At the university where she teaches screen-writing, Dolly is outspoken about women's rights. In Writing Division faculty meetings where are gathered sixty men and four women she will remark openly on the discrepancy. One of her conversation-stoppers when welcoming new men to Hollywood, in a circle where other women reflect male egos, flirt or listen, is to discuss the tough time women have in Hollywood. Maurice feels that feminist issues have positively informed their marriage:

Dolly knows about the unequal time women have had. When I think of my parents' marriage, I would say ours is far more equal. My mother, born an American, in those days had a very traditional marriage. The husband was literally the boss. She was a housewife.

Although their closest friends are shared, they also have individual attachments:

Our close friends are those we're both attached to, but there are certain people I've met at work that I'm much closer to. He has made friends with people I don't care about much. I think a couple should have the chance to spend time apart. Absolutely! So we have other interests. Until recently he was a keen tennis-player. Loved to play every weekend. I loved his going off Saturday and Sunday mornings!

We have both grown within our couple. I've seen many changes in my own personality. I have had to fight to grow and

develop – but only within myself, not within our marriage. I feel
I can be totally myself in this relationship. I'm not sure there is
any way that being in this couple has been harmful or
detrimental to me! If there is, I don't see it!

(*Dolly.*)

We are together yet independent. We have never had a crisis
where we said, 'Let's break it up!' Over 54 years I don't seem
ever to have worried that it might not last. Never! My attitude is
we are a couple. Maybe I have no imagination but no, really, the
idea of breaking up – I can't imagine that.

(*Maurice.*)

Most couples had some difficulties over interdependence.
Those couples who saw themselves in some way as creative were
particularly conscious of the need for self-preservation, solitude,
space and individual autonomy. In the next chapter, several well-
known creative couples discuss their partnerships in the light of
the Five Cs and the Big I.

NOTES

1 Beryl Bainbridge, *Every Man for Himself*, Duckworth, 1996; Abacus,
   1997, p. 160.
2 Bainbridge, p. 184.
3 Bainbridge, p. 186.
4 Synagogue.

CHAPTER 9

Creative Couples

Creativity is often described as a uniquely talented individual's struggle for artistic fulfilment. That struggle is usually seen as solitary. Yet set against this prevailing belief that art in all its forms is produced by solitary individuals is our society's dominant social structure: the pair, the partnership, the couple. Conflicting ideologies no less. Opposing frameworks which can challenge partnerships between two creative people.

A further complicating element can be the notion (often put about by artists themselves) that what creative people of any sex need is 'a wife'! Do two creative partners then wive each other? Some *may* wive and cherish. Some may enrich each other's creativity. Others, however – like writers Ernest Hemingway and Martha Gellhorn, Zelda and Scott Fitzgerald, and actress Claire Bloom and her third husband writer Philip Roth – allow problems of competitiveness and collaborative conflict to add two further Cs to the other five.

Can one creative person help establish the conditions necessary for their intimate partner's artistic productions without sacrificing their own or without damaging or invisibilising the domestic side of the partnership?

Exploring the differences and difficulties arising from gender, sexuality, age, race and class amongst couples who have a shared creative context dramatically highlights the issues of commitment, communication, cherishing, coping with change, compromise and most particularly interdependence.

Early biographers saw one partner, often the woman, as the shadow or imitator of the 'great man'. Domestic support for an artist's work was generally viewed as an obligatory female system even if that female was herself an artist. Despite the endless complexities of intimate partnerships, gender stereotyping has meant that the traditional patterns have been those of 'male genius and female absence'.[1] An acute case in point was Picasso and his creatively invisibilised mistress Françoise Gilot.

Recently those earlier stereotypes have been partially dismantled as biographers have asked radical questions about the *reciprocal* influence of artist-couples such as painter Georgia O'Keeffe and photographer Alfred Stieglitz, painters Vanessa Bell and Duncan Grant, artist Dora Carrington and critic-biographer Lytton Strachey, painter, dancer and writer Zelda Fitzgerald and her novelist husband F. Scott Fitzgerald, and writers Simone de Beauvoir and Jean-Paul Sartre, Virginia Woolf and Vita Sackville-West, Lillian Hellman and Dashiel Hammett and Anais Nin and Henry Miller.[2] Creative partnerships now appear far more complex, fluid and equitable than they were once presented.

In our own time theatrical and literary couples live partnerships subjected to media glare. Sexual or domestic issues preoccupy magazine and newspaper feature desks even more than the artistic talents of ballet dancers Lisa Pavane and Greg Horsman, writers Rose Tremain and Richard Holmes, actor Antony Sher and director Gregory Doran, and from film stage and television Ruthie Henshall and John Gordon Sinclair, Hugh Grant and Liz Hurley, Prunella Scales and Timothy West, D.H. Pennebaker and Chris Hegedus.

Pennebaker, now 72, chronicled the Sixties counterculture with a series of legendary cinéma vérité documentaries directed by his wife Chris Hegedus. Later they moved into the field of rock, making *Don't Look Back* about Bob Dylan's 1965 tour and *Monterey Pop* which offered extraordinary footage of Janis Joplin, Ravi Shankar and Jimi Hendrix. More recently they collaborated on the Oscar-nominated *War Rooms*, a behind-the-scenes epic of Bill Clinton's first presidential campaign.

'Making films together is a real act of faith,' Pennebaker said. For his wife it was trust as well as faith:

It can be gruelling . . . it can be very isolating. But to experience it with someone you really trust makes it very worthwhile.[3]

(*Chris Hegedus.*)

Trust is also the keynote for creative coupledom between Antony Sher, the 48-year-old white South African actor, painter, novelist and his partner of ten years theatre director Gregory Doran. Together the couple wrote *Woza Shakespeare!*, the story of their triumphant South African production of *Titus Andronicus*, their first collaborative theatrical venture. In the book there is a vivid description of Sher's reaction to his father's death. While rehearsing the critical scene in *Andronicus* where Titus the father is forced to confront his dead sons' heads, Sher relived his own father's death.

Doran said, 'It was not until months after (his) death that I saw Tony cry for his father, crumpling at the waist, reaching out to clutch me, gulping with sobs. That's what Titus does now. I recognise it.' Sher's view of that scene is: 'I realise I have never trusted a director enough to risk completely opening myself up before.'[4]

Despite their trust – a key theme in conversations with all creative couples – one risk they hadn't worked out in advance was the danger of intensive work together on stage followed by passionate reworking at home. At one point their discussions grew so fierce that they escalated into a real-life drama with flying crockery.

In their most recent successful collaboration, where Doran directs Sher in the title role of *Cyrano de Bergerac*, they decided not to discuss the professional intricacies of the play at home but to allow a greater distance and space.[5]

Sher and Doran are not unusual in needing space both from shared work projects and from each other. Domestic arrangements of successful creative people have often included, whether by necessity or choice, a degree of separation, distance and an imaginative balance of dependence with independence. The distance or privacy may be instigated intellectually and emotionally within one geographical location, or it may be achieved by physical distance and separate residences.

Novelist Rose Tremain, 53, divorced twice, now living creatively with biographer Richard Holmes, shares her house with him in Norfolk and spends part of the time in his London flat. In Norfolk they are companionable but separate:

> We're perfect company and work at opposite ends of the house.
> We both work rather long hours. Mine are about 10.30 a.m. until
> 7 p.m. I then do half an hour's yoga before coming down to
> cook our evening meal, which I love. Richard comes down at
> about 8 p.m. We give each other a great deal of space, which is
> so important for a writer.[6]

Greg Horsman and Lisa Pavane, senior principal dancers with the English National Ballet, pointed to the extraordinary intimacy that comes from a couple who work together but they also emphasised the difficulties of two artistic temperaments in a single unit, and the possible consequences of clashing ambitions. They too felt strongly space was necessary to stabilise the relationship:

> Dancers' marriages are notorious for falling apart, so we were
> terrified at first . . . There were ego problems. What if one
> became more successful than the other – would each hold the
> other one back?
>
> *(Greg Horsman.)*[7]

Occasionally their heated dance discussions at work spilled over to the home front:

> We've learned almost without discussing it to build in times
> away from each other.
>
> *(Lisa Pavane.)*

Woody Allen, a self-confessed workaholic, ensured that his recent marriage to Soon-Yi Previn included a formal agreement on her part that she would retain her own apartment whilst Allen continued to maintain his in Central Park to which she had strictly limited visiting rights. In their case, the decision was unilateral and the element of power unmistakable.

Some creative couples make genuinely democratic decisions about interdependence and commitment in order to enhance their professional conditions and private lives. Novelist Margaret Drabble and biographer Michael Holroyd offer an imaginative example.

CREATIVE COUPLE SCENE: MARGARET DRABBLE AND MICHAEL HOLROYD
Before Margaret Drabble and Michael Holroyd married in 1982, they had known each other a decade. Michael, now 62, had been engrossed in writing a biography of Bernard Shaw; Margaret, 58, had been writing novels, editing the *Oxford Companion to English Literature* and writing a biography of Angus Wilson:

> We were part of a community of writers and would meet as colleagues at the Society of Authors or other places. It changed the day I had lunch near the British Museum with a Shavian vegetarian. Maggie happened to be at another table. She saw this pathetic sight of me eating with this Shavian vegetarian and thought: 'This has gone too far!' She rang me up that evening and said would I be a 'spare man' at her dinner party. So we went from a long friendship into a short, intense courtship. Christopher Hampton the playwright had a première of a play out on the West Coast, so we decided to go out. We had a curious honeymoon which took place in Hollywood *before* our wedding. It was like *Alice Through the Looking Glass*. We got the sequence of events wrong! So when we returned in 1982 we had to go through the formality of a marriage by a formidable woman dressed in black with a bunch of keys for wedlock, in the Chelsea Register Office. Because I hadn't had much practice in marriage, I suddenly realised that you need to have a best man or woman. I suggested to this formidable woman that since the Register Office was next to the Public Library I could go into the romantic fiction shelves and pluck someone reading romantic fiction who would be only too pleased to go from one building to the next! She was not amused by this so eventually we got Beryl Bainbridge as best man!
>
> *(Michael.)*

Michael had never married and Margaret, after one try, had said late: 'Marriage is a dangerous, dangerous relationship, full of potential destruction of personality. People aren't meant to be together 24 hours a day.'[8] So why did they decide to wed?

We wanted to continue our relationship but while we weren't ever recognised quite as a couple, or people didn't know, there was always a doubt in people's minds. It's amazing how people *don't* know things unless you broadcast them through a megaphone or bullhorn which we are not inclined to do. Though gregarious we are also private, elusive characters. Also if you phoned up or got in touch with the other person there was a slight effort . . . Were you intruding? It wasn't on automatic pilot. We both felt that marriage would make assumptions easier. There'd be less walking uphill.

(Michael.)

The first time I got married in 1960 to Clive (Swift) was because living together was not something my mother would have approved of! So getting married was the real breaking the link with home. We lived together for about seven years. After we split up we still saw each other because of the three children Adam, Rebeccca and Joseph. After my divorce, for 22 years I lived initially with my children, most of the time with no permanent adult. Deciding to marry Michael was partly because he had never been married so it seemed an adventurous thing to do. Partly too because Michael said it didn't matter if it didn't work out. He didn't take it heavily, so I didn't either. He said: 'If we discover it's not a good idea, what does it matter? We're hurting nobody but ourselves!' When you're young marriage is all or nothing. That feeling of terrible failure. I thought Michael's attitude was excellent. If it went wrong we wouldn't blame ourselves or think it was the end of the world, yet it's a commitment to get married at all. It meant building a long-lasting relationship; we just tackled it in a different way. To make any kind of permanent statement is a commitment, that sense of 'everything's failed if it goes wrong' is an unnecessary burden. We feel there *is* a commitment and you will work at that commitment but if something unforeseen happens then you change.

Did that commitment hinge on a belief in monogamy or an open marriage policy?

I started life shy and lonely. When the Sixties came everything opened up. You could take girls to dinner and they'd pay half! That was a wonderful time for me. I caught up, had a very good time. My education has come through women, not through school. Had I not had those twenty years of fun I would have felt different but I entered with marriage a completely different place because everything had evened up. I was not in my first youth. It's not the marriage of a 21-year-old, alas! So I felt this didn't really apply in any serious way any longer.

(Michael.)

I think we would believe in an open marriage . . . but I also at my age find monogamy the easiest thing in the world to stick with! I would not have done when I was younger, but there are certain marriages for certain ages. It also has to do with the emotion and energy that goes into your writing. Monogamy is easier. You know where you are; the rest of your life is on an even keel. But having said that, in that area of one's life the most amazing and terrible things happen to people and I don't think people should ever be blamed when they do happen. I wouldn't blame the other person. I imagine Michael would say exactly the same, that something completely knocks you off your balance then don't blame anybody. Just say life is . . . it's hard.

Once married, Drabble and Holroyd successfully conducted marital life from separate houses for thirteen years from 1982:

We didn't feel we had to live together. Michael said, 'We don't have to change life very much. We don't have to uproot ourselves, live in the same house, do everything differently. We just don't do all that.' It was reassuring.

(Margaret.)

'Live together' is a curious phrase. If we were not married people would have said: 'Do you know they're living together?' Once we married they said: 'Do you know they're not living together!' Really it was that we both worked at home. Maggie had teenagers who spent time at her house, plus an assistant to help her over the *Oxford Companion*, so there was hardly room for me as well! I had Bernard Shaw, well you know what he's like! He took up the whole house. At that stage I hadn't bought the top flat in my house so neither place was big enough to have a home and two offices with separate libraries where you would not hear the other person tearing his or her hair out in anguish or exhilaration! Maggie's house wasn't an easy place for me to work, having no area I identified as my work-place. Most people live apart in one sense: their work is apart, so we decided to have these two places twenty minutes apart with the cleverest route in between. I would go to dinner there in the evening during the week, she would come here at weekends. Because she was more in charge of meals, it meant she kept two households with a number of forks, knives and spoons. Perhaps the travelling suited me better than Maggie but the system worked well for more than a decade. It was risky getting married because I had no practice and Maggie had been married before but it hadn't worked out. But we thought it would be riskier putting ourselves and our work in one place.

I didn't want to live with Michael in the same house, my children hadn't quite left home. I didn't particularly want Michael to come and live in *my* family house. He would have found that quite stressful. I would have found it stressful too . . . irritating having to sweep the children out of the way. The children get on terribly well with Michael, partly because they've kept their distance and he's never interfered. Whereas if you live under the same roof and someone's making a mess of the bathroom, then somebody's got to say: 'Don't do that!' So we completely avoided the issue by not living under the same roof. My house was completely full of the *Oxford Companion to English Literature*, so there were also very good work reasons. Our nights together changed every week in terms of – this sounds very Hampstead – where we were having dinner. The benefit was space and solitude. The difficulties were forgetting at which end of the journey you'd left what you were about to change into. Michael had no cooking equipment so gradually I brought bits of gadgetry or bought things but I never cooked anything satisfactorily here. At my place it was all under control.

Were there moments when one person felt sad or emotional and needed their partner nearer at hand?

Um . . . no. I was *so* used to being on my own, if anything it was the other way! If I'm sad or reflective I want to be on my own. Having said that, I've remembered one time a bus drove into me and I bumped my car. I did ring Michael up and he did come over and spend the night with me because I was upset. I wailed: 'Look I feel terrible! I've done this incredibly stupid thing!' He said, 'Do you want me to come over?' I wailed: 'Yes!' He drove straight over, which wasn't a night we'd planned to spend together.

Travelling together became a joy:

Very often married people who are what I call 'married alive' need holidays apart in order to have a holiday! We had holidays together. We share travel, share laughter, and that enriches the joint experience; we come back with more things to share.

(Michael.)

We enjoy seeing new places, finding ourselves in peculiar hotels, meeting odd people. We are brilliant travel companions: we're totally punctual; we never miss aeroplanes, but if we do we have exactly the same degree of anxiety about it. We don't leave things to the last moment. We double-check. We occasionally get it wrong, but we don't ever blame each other. Michael's never angry. He's irritable, fusses, is fussy about being pedantic which is why travelling is good because he gets it right. I can get irritated with him worrying three days in advance about where to park the car, but I do it myself!

Loyalty and trust are keynotes of their partnership and may involve compromise:

Maggie is the loyalest of people, and loyalty and priority are central to us. When two things might clash I give Maggie priority. It doesn't mean to say that no other interest exists but she has priority. It may be more difficult for her because she has more family so there may be countercalls but I don't think either of us are too possessive. If Maggie is not back at three o'clock when she said and doesn't come in till five, I'm not worried sick. She is an adult, extremely capable of looking after herself. She trusts *me* to come back on my feet! So we are not anxious about every breath taken by the other. Which doesn't mean to say that there's no care or interest, but we have a sense of security.

Being a good couple rests on loyalty, not undermining the other person. My mother was terribly undermining. Always complaining about my father – I never wanted to do that. A certain kind of fidelity is necessary, being loyal and faithful to the person that you believe the person to be, not betraying them by concealing things. Fidelity is not being double-faced, being straight. If you have to give up certain things for that, then that's fine. You might have to give up going to certain parties or seeing people that are too irritating for the other person.

(Margaret.)

To avoid irritations, the couple who share some friends also retain separate ones:

Probably some of my friends Michael finds too boring or too wild! I see them on other occasions. It's quite unusual for two people to like one wild or eccentric peculiar person, so couple friends are more moderate. We have many couple friends which, as someone pointed out, means they have to go through two lots of vetting to be acceptable. They're doubly vetted.

(Margaret.)

In the last year of their separate residences, Michael encountered a serious health crisis:

I was walking back from a party with Maggie and I cracked a joke. There was a loud report in my back. Suddenly I couldn't walk. I insisted on going back to *my* house because I didn't want to disturb her. The doctor discovered I'd slipped a disc, so I couldn't go with her to Spain to deliver a paper. I said to her: 'You've really got to go. We can't both not go.' So she went. In her absence I got much worse. When she got back she had to get me straight to hospital. I felt as I'd lived alone so long I should have been able to deal with this crisis, but I couldn't move, I was alone, it was very bad, I was very pleased to see her back. Although I worry about illness, particularly death (I'm Vice President of the Euthanasia Society), generally we are neither of us very good at looking after ill people. Any symptoms of illness we do not encourage in the other. She certainly wouldn't encourage it in me!

That physical crisis was terrible. I had to go off to Spain to give both my lecture and his lecture; when I returned he was in bed, immovable! I had to get a stretcher. It was absolutely dreadful! I was terribly worried about him and his rationality about it was hard to cope with. I don't think I responded terribly well. I just shoved him in hospital. Maybe I did the right thing, I just don't know. I had to take a certain amount of responsibility for him which I'd never had to do before.

After 13 years as Intimate Commuters they risked a single residence:

The children all had their own flats, houses, none of them needed to come home so much. This house was too small, too dark for him to come here. I'd been in Hampstead long enough; I was bored with it. The same shops, the same faces, the same good manners, the same people. In terms of material, I'd been there quite long enough. There's all sorts of fascinating stuff here in Ladbroke Grove. It's new territory to explore. It was also a feeling that we'd been married quite a long time and it wasn't going to be a disaster. Obviously it was still a risk but Michael said if it didn't work we could just go back again or get a flat. He's a great one for saying: 'If it doesn't work, alter it!' Other people feel such a sense of failure if things don't work. He doesn't feel that. I find it reassuring whenever he says pragmatically, 'It's not a failure. It's just that you didn't like it. Let's do something else.'

Maggie got sick of her house, which had been a family house but the children had flown the nest – she was beginning to rattle around. When she had finished the Angus Wilson biography and was left with 40 boxes of papers she felt it was like a shell that had been used. It seemed sensible for us to be here when I got the whole house and could afford to do it up.

Today they have moved from a creative semi-detachment to an imaginative use of space, flexibility, and graceful tolerant affection within a shared home. Sharing and prioritising is at the root of their definition of a couple:

A couple must mean they have a shared social life. They don't necessarily have to live together. Do people still share bank accounts? I suppose they do but we do not. We have completely separate finances and we're in the fortunate position of forever trying to press the other person to let us pay for things. That's because we're very lucky. Michael is amazingly generous. When I first got to know him before we took a plane flight he said: 'You keep both tickets. If you lose one, never mind, because I don't want my ticket if you lose yours!' It's a very nice attitude which he always has about money. I always try to pay the bills. We do share finances in the sense that we are forever snatching things from each other and saying: 'Let me pay that one!' I appreciate that that is partly because we have enough to go round.

Sharing beds is seen as more important than sharing bank accounts:

A couple probably have a shared bed or share a bed somewhere, or have an ability to share a bed, or have shared a bed in the past. I think a shared ability to sleep under the same roof and occasionally in the same bed is being part of a couple. In this house Michael and I have separate bathrooms but we share a bedroom.

In fact they share two bedrooms, a winter one upstairs and a summer one in the basement with French windows to the garden where they often eat. The top half of the house is divided from the bottom so that each partner can have separate studies, telephones and bathrooms for which they have commissioned fantasy scenes from artist Manou Shama-Levy. Michael's bathroom is cool blue.

Mine is a wonderful ox-blood red where I can have wonderful red baths, which was Michael's idea for me.

There are two floors between our offices. We have separate libraries, though we can go up and down and pinch books. Maggie cannot hear me in my despair which I live with in my green room. I cannot hear her at all, as she lives with her exhilaration in a yellow room. There is a red room between us. Colours are more important than I ever thought they would be. I decided that we should have bold colours in each room, Maggie decided the exact colour. We have a warm red room, a blue room which I've got the pictures in. Yellow has become a favourite of mine because it is sunlight and sand. It has worked!

I've learned to like yellow too. Though I still like red and he doesn't so much, he likes blue and green and I don't so much.

Margaret's orderly spacious study with her books neatly arranged, computers whirring, overlooks the garden and has its own kitchen. Michael's study, messy and interesting, books piled on every surface, has an original Dora Carrington fireplace. Bronze busts of Augustus John, Lytton Strachey and Bernard Shaw gaze down seriously from three mantlepieces throughout the house, reminding visitors of Michael Holroyd's achievements. Unlike his wife, Michael works with pen and paper:

The technological revolution took place as I was a third of the way through Bernard Shaw. Do I stop now in mid-flow and change my system, put things on disc? I decided to go on. The book took me 15 years. I had hoped of course to produce a literary masterpiece. What I emerged as was a new illiterate in the world of technology.

I've learned to use a computer, and I wrote *Angus Wilson* on it. But I don't compose fiction it; I use an old manual. I had always worked in a certain amount of chaos. When I first met Michael I had the photocopier in the bedroom which he didn't approve of! He said you shouldn't sleep with your photocopier! Whereas he used to go back to bed in his dressing-gown and work in bed! I would never do that! I always want to get up, get on with the day! I feel if you don't get the day started it will be frittered away. As I don't know how my writing is going to work out, I like to be utterly alone for three or four days so that nobody knows that I chickened out after an hour or two. I don't want to be condemned because I said I was going to work for three hours!

We work in different ways. When I go into the yellow room, Maggie's office, I am appalled at the terrible mess, the conglomeration . . . it's like a technological slum! She has the latest machines that sing out to her, buttons you press, I'm appalled by them. She's on the cutting edge in my view of modernity! In my study everything has its eccentric place. Could be on the floor, piled up against walls, never reaches the ceiling. When she comes into my neat green study she exclaims with horror at the terrible mess! I cannot understand what she is talking about!

As writers, their different working methods have to be accommodated.

I need cumulative concentration. Quietness. An 'exclusion zone'. It's not that one is unsympathetic to anybody else, certainly not unsympathetic to Maggie working, or she unsympathetic to me, we're both interested in the other person's work, but there is no way you can involve another person in the creative or re-creative process. You have to do it yourself. There's a temptation if you're close to somebody sympathetic to say: 'Look I've got this terrible problem'; then you speak the problem away into thin air and you don't work it on paper. There's no short cut. That sort of temptation is not assistance! I don't feel the need to discuss my work but if things go wrong what I need is somebody to say: 'Let's go out and see a film, let's go away for the weekend.' I want someone to raise my morale rather than to solve my problems on a page!

(*Michael.*)

I don't *need* someone to discuss my work with, but we do do it. Sometimes it's fun. I've got quite a lot of ideas from Michael, who is an ideas person. I can point to actual sections in a novel that I got directly from something he said. One piece I put in was about Bernard Shaw and the founding of the LSE.[9]

The common floor of their house includes a crimson drawing room, blue and silver dining room, kitchen and bedroom. A major change in their life is sharing breakfast:

We have breakfast together, which we never have had before. I rather like it and Maggie humours me to that extent. I make the toast, the complicated operation, and the coffee. I mean it's not easy!

It seemed strange to be having a proper bit of toast. Ah! That *is* new! I'd never bother by myself. But I know it's a good move. We've evolved a routine. We read our post together, then go our separate ways just after nine.

(*Margaret.*)

A useful tool in their bid for privacy is a pair of handbells:

We both have a bell, so we're like Pavlovian creatures. What we do is to ring it before we come upstairs or go downstairs so that people are aware. When you are together you must also respect people's privacy. You want two lives which overlap, but one doesn't have to eclipse the other. One still has a door to shut.

(*Michael.*)

Our little bells mean there is no invasion of territory. We're not good on the intercom, so I will come half-way up and ring a bell. He'll say 'Hello', then I'll say, 'Have you anything for the post?'

One small cherishing act is their insistence on communicating before they leave the house.

> We always say if we're going out because it's terrible not to say that you're about to leave, then they start looking for you. So we always let each other know where we're going.
>
> *(Margaret.)*

Cherishing, as long as it isn't 'sentimental', Michael's bête noire, is seen as important:

> Michael is good at buying little delicacies, paying attention, at turning on hot water, making hot-water bottles, thinking ahead, making things comfortable and cosy, ensuring if I've been away that everything is nice when I return, making sure that one feels welcomed home.

Both of them admit that it is sometimes hard for a writer to cherish someone when they are immersed in their work:

> It is hard. That's why one has to separate off. Writers understand the kind of concentration and attention that one is giving at a certain patch better than other people would. Both of us understand that and can make allowances.
>
> *(Margaret.)*

Communication is central to their coupledom:

> Men generally don't let on about their feelings but Michael is good at talking about his. He will admit to fears of ageing or death.

> We have different methods of discussing something. Maggie uses free association. A fault of mine is that I can stay too pedantically at a point and say: 'But that's not what we were talking about five minutes ago!' She would say: 'Well, for goodness sake, these things have got to flow!' All I would have scored was a logical point! We can talk about most things. If I think she has a neurosis about something I would not introduce

that subject willy-nilly. If she felt I was vulnerable, she would not I think introduce that. We have awarenesses that people have days which are difficult and we don't wish to make them more difficult. We talk to resolve differences but we don't agree on everything. There's some point in discussing but after a certain amount you are really saying: 'Would you please change who you are.' There's no reason why one should! One weakness in communication is I am not able to get angry. I tend to make my anger mock anger and dissipate it in a little bit of opera. My cowardice is avoiding direct rows when perhaps I should take them on. I'm getting better. I look forward to an old age where I'm very grumpy indeed! But on the whole I don't like rows. Maggie's family enjoy a good row and it clears the air. She's rather good at it!

I can get angry. I enjoy getting angry with my daughter, and Michael can't understand that Becky and I enjoy shouting! I now tend to repress a quick hostile response because Michael obviates the need for it but it's so natural in me I have to do it to other people instead. Like my daughter!

They agree there were risks in Margaret moving into Ladbroke Grove:

Would she find an area where she was happy working? The answer to that is about 75 per cent yes, 25 per cent no. She would prefer to work at a novel in the country but that was the case anyway. We have internal clocks that are slightly different. Maggie would like to be up earlier. I would like to stay up later. We compromise. But then I can always come to the bedroom later. She doesn't mind that, though I notice that I don't do it.

They have a cleaner, share some household tasks, but it is still Margaret who cooks:

I lived alone for years and kept alive perfectly well, but am not a cook, therefore the burden falls largely on her. I'm in charge of the wine, I can lay the table, cut bread, make toast, I have small efficiencies. I'm pretty good at washing-up. I buy things and take Maggie out to dinner to give her a break.

I still find risky the idea that I feel guilty if I don't cook supper. It's true he can't cook. On his own he'd just have an egg or a banana. He doesn't mind eggs. I think more about it than he does! During my work day I'll think about what to make for supper. On my own, I wouldn't have that thought. It's annoying that he doesn't like spaghetti as much as I do. He might be irritable if I gave him pasta every night, whereas I could live off it for a week. I *can* say to Michael: 'Get your own!' but I don't ever say it, I just do something different. I get out of it by saying I've a lot of work to do, then go off to Somerset and just do it!

In Somerset is their country house which was originally Margaret's:

It is a safety-valve. I'd had a place there before, then we bought a new one in '89. I go there by myself more; he comes at weekends. I write my fiction there, I wrote the last four novels in Somerset. In London people can't resist ringing you up to see what you're up to. My daughter will ring four times a day! I'm pleased but it's annoying when you're trying to work. In Somerset I have a garden shed, like Bernard Shaw, with no telephone, a long way from the house so I go down there and nobody can get me.

I haven't had a place of work there so I can't do primary work but I do secondary work, read proofs, read books, make notes. Nothing in Somerset is exclusively mine but we've now added on a room so it may turn out to be my place of dreaming and work where I can look at the clouds, for light is becoming even more important to me. That pattern where you are not together 52 weeks, 365 days, is good. It is very nice that we are apart sometimes. If one of us is in Somerset, we will ring and always send each other postcards. We follow instincts and hope they are like compasses which point in the right direction. I think we would not have married unless we felt our instincts complemented each other's. If Maggie wants to go down to

Somerset one day or another day, that seems to me fine. The only thing I would say is I would like to know in advance and she wants me to know. I think the house in Somerset is our safeguard for any risks we took about changing our method of marriage. It is our safe house!

Growing older has made Michael wish to spend more time with his wife:

There is a change in my life. I am, as I just manage to remember, in my sixties. I have done three books which have taken fifteen years and twelve years each. I cannot run that race any more. So as I have to change gear I am working more here. Perhaps it is a comfort as things draw in to be together more of the time. There's a tendency for me sometimes to get self-obsessed. My work is an elixir of self-forgetfulness and self-development, travelling into other people's lives. If I don't do that so much, it's good to have someone here because you get into *their* life a little.

To avoid stress in case the living-together operation does not work out, they have decided never to see it in terms of success and failure:

Had it not worked I would not have felt it was a terrible failure of me and my house in a personal way. Everything is an experiment. If it works, that's good, if it doesn't, you learn from it then do something else. It could also be that this works for ten, twelve or thirteen years; then when we're older, if it's not what we want we'll change again. Commitment doesn't mean to say no to change. It means quite the opposite. It means when things change you have to find the best track. You just hope your best self comes into play. I don't think we have any sense of rivalry, nor do we count the number of times we each did something the other wanted last week. None of that occurs.

(Michael.)

Do people perceive them differently now that they live in one residence?

I think that we are less interesting!

(Michael.)

CREATIVE COUPLE SCENE: DAVINA AND LARRY BELLING

Davina and Larry Belling who have lived much of their domestic and professional life in a city not known for long-term stable relationships, have a 30-year partnership sometimes affectionately called 'the longest marriage in show business'.

After residing in Los Angeles for many years, today the couple are temporarily resident in London where Davina, co-founder of Film and General Investments, co-produces films with her business partner Clive Parsons, while Larry, currently UK representative for the largest reference library on the Internet, also writes for BBC Radio 4.

Davina, British, 56, a bubbling articulate doctor's daughter from Bournemouth, worked for several years on Broadway financing and casting plays such as Richard Burton's *Hamlet*, and the Royal Shakespeare Company's production of Pinter's *The Homecoming*. Today she is a highly successful film producer whose first film was the challenging X-rated *Inserts* which featured Richard Dreyfuss and Bob Hoskins, followed swiftly by a string of widely acclaimed movies including the musical *Breaking Glass* with Hazel O'Connor, the sensitive small budget award-winning *Gregory's Girl*, *Other People's Money*, starring Danny DeVito and Gregory Peck, the controversial films *Scum* and *Britannia Hospital* and the Royal Command Performance film *True Blue*.

She first met Larry Belling, a 58-year-old quiet, witty Californian, in the Sixties when they both worked in the New York theatre for Broadway impresario Alex Cohen; Larry as a theatrical publicist, Davina as Cohen's second-in-command.

Relationships are influenced by the context in which you've met. So because Larry met me in a situation where I was a key person for him and his associates, there was a certain aura of power around me. It was a small world but a key world to him. That makes a huge difference in terms of respect; when you meet somebody in that position then you form a different relationship with them which is in some sense carried through life. Respect is what I feel for him too.

Davina has always been a highly focused creative artist, pushing ahead dynamically in one area for more than twenty years. By contrast, Larry, multi-talented, easier-going, interested in artistic byways as well as highways, moved gracefully from theatrical to film publicity, tried his hand at writing children's books, became a writer–producer first of radio commercials in the UK, then of TV commercials in the States. His TV production company won several major advertising awards. Only recently has he turned his artistic skills to the successful world of computers.

There have been key periods when Davina – who has consistently maintained the higher public profile – has also been the major wage-earner, whilst Larry engaged, in one art form or another, received considerably less than his talents merited:

It's true that I have more often been the one with the higher profile, sometimes with more money, and usually it's OK. I've always encouraged Larry to go in whatever creative direction interested him. He's certainly always encouraged me. Just sometimes it's difficult if you're married to what is easiest described as a Renaissance Man who has almost too much imagination, too much creativity. There's a great danger with those people of not being focused on any one thing long enough to establish themselves, so it's very easy to flounder unless you happen to hit success. I used to say: 'It's fine when you're 25, it's a lot less charming and endearing when you're 38!' Larry has always been prepared to make financial sacrifices for his art which I admire. But the pragmatic side of me – which is why I could never be married to a late-blooming genius – feels if someone isn't succeeding when they're making sacrifices then change direction. I'd say: 'You gotta do something else! You gotta do something sensible!' As long as genius was blooming that's fine. There's a family joke that if something didn't work materially I would say to Larry: 'You should go to plumbing school!' Part of me was serious because I looked around and successful people were in service industries. Fifty per cent of them were highly educated, had had lives in advertising or the media but had fallen on hard times. Material success matters to me but only in terms of having choice. Not possessions. Just freedom. The more money you have, the more freedom you have. But we've always dealt well with all our financial situations. If Larry didn't sell a book he quickly wrote commercials. Though we have separate business accounts we've always had a joint personal account, never had this business of you take care of the utilities, I'll take care of clothes.

We always make a point of encouraging each other in all our ventures, we have always wished for each other's success. But sometimes one person's stability, their financial position, how well they do, is a challenge. I had some great years in the early Eighties where I made a lotta money and we were able to buy a house, build on a second storey, do all that stuff. But for many years I didn't do very well. There were years that were pretty crappy because if you're creative you go from feast to famine back up, back down again! Davina did carry our relationship for a year . . . for some years. Maybe there were a couple when I wasn't earning anything when she paid the mortgage but on the other hand I've always managed our money in such a way that I've provided for our future. Even when I wasn't earning I provided for our years ahead through good management of our assets. You always have conflicts when money isn't coming in, but I never felt I should be doing something different. I felt it would all come round! I'm a great optimist! There were times when I said: 'Shit! Why didn't I learn a real trade when I was young? Like be a lawyer.' Then it became too late to do that. During those fallow times when the advertising business wasn't coming in, Davina said: 'Why don't you go be a plumber? Why don't you go to carpentry school?' I just didn't have the knees to be a plumber! Then there was a reversal in the early Eighties when I had solid accounts with Columbia Pictures and Universal Pictures, when I earned more than Davina but that didn't create any problems! We are both thrifty so money has never been an issue. We've always written cheques on the same account, don't keep our monies separate. It's not 'hers' and 'mine'. We have a Living Trust which has all our money. That way, if you die you don't have to go through probate. So if I get run over by a bus Davina's not gonna have to incur an enormous amount of legal costs to transfer the assets of the Trust to her.

That they have avoided stress over their finances says a great deal for their underlying harmony, which is in marked contrast to their blatantly different personalities:

I am highly organised and have an ability to be charmingly bossy. I can motivate people to do things they don't always want to do at a price they don't always want to agree to! I have initiative and a sense that there's no such word as 'No' or no such phrase as 'It can't be done!' Larry isn't like that at all.

Does this make for any difficulties on the domestic front?

No, because I can behave differently at home. At work my partner Clive is as strong as I am, which leads to competition. When you're in an equal situation and you are temperamentally different it involves survival. Both Clive and I go for survival. There's something at stake each is always trying to enforce. Larry unlike Clive is not competitive. Larry is one of the few people I know who is not controlling. It has to do with having great self-esteem so he's never been my rival. He doesn't see himself challenged by my activities; in fact he takes great pride in my success, where some men would feel threatened by it. I maintain that's because they have insecurities. Larry hasn't. His inner confidence might come as a surprise to many people, because on the surface it looks as if I am the vivacious noisy one. I'm the one in the more high-profile position. But in any relationship there has to be a good listener. Sometimes I'm the raconteur, but generally we have a great back and forth.

At work Davina is different. She has a problem taking orders. Her favourite word is 'Why?' Clive is controlling and Davina wants control. She and I don't have that. Neither of us is controlling. From my point of view I don't think Davina is at all controlling. I *am* competitive, but not with Davina. She is competitive but never with me. It's very nice not to be driven into that competitive, 'I'm going to better you! I'm gonna be more successful than you!' I pray for Davina's success in film production. I wish that *True Blue* was a great hit. I wish for her success and know there are a lot of partners who wish for each other's failure, who can feel more important if the other partner is failing, who don't share the same sense of humour, who are not supportive in a true way. I don't think I'm like that at all.

The couple have both found Hollywood a creative place to live:

Hollywood is a very creative city. You walk up and down the streets late at night and hear the clatter of word processors banging out screen-plays. It's the world's most ambitious town, where everyone is striving to get ahead quickly. I felt very creative there. It's a place where you can make it huge between midnight and 3 a.m. because you had an idea and you can find a place to sell it!

(Larry.)

As a woman Davina has also found it an easier city in which to take up a powerful position:

Creative women can become powerful in the States. My creativity has been affected positively through working in Hollywood. It's given me more worldliness and business sophistication. Just from having been at what's generally considered the seat of power and having seen it from both sides of the desk you develop new kinds of knowledge. It's definitely easier to be a powerful woman in Hollywood than it is in England, just because there are many more women in the industry in important roles who are smart. There are at least three major studios out of eight right now being run by women. The Head of Production at Sony is a woman, and United Artists and Paramount have women at the top. That's an extraordinary shift over the last 10 years. In England there are subtler gender problems which I occasionally face as a male-female co-production partnership. Recently I was thrown by an incident when Clive and I as a team met this film executive. I decided to handle it and sent the executive two pieces of material. He called Clive! I thought: 'Didn't *I* send him that stuff? How odd he would call Clive!' Still, if you get in a snit about those things you'd just not get anything else done! At least on my home front

I can be a strong woman or a weak one or anything I want. If I get in a snit, Larry will get me out of it. I'd do the same. That ability to mask the other person out of a snit – and each of us has a great ability to do it – is a factor in our stability. Our willingness to do good things for each other, to get each other out of moods, to laugh together, our desire to do these things, all comes out of the great respect each of us has for the other.

Respect for her art form is what lies at the root of Davina's professional ideals.

My films weren't chosen with a sense of a grand master plan, rather they relied on an emotional and practical basis. Some films like *Britannia Hospital*, considered at the time a disaster, are now on at the National Film Theatre with the retrospective verdict of a 'masterpiece'. Essentially all the films were chosen for their creativity. *Gregory's Girl* was the one that most obviously had a vision that had to be proven to the world but that vision is somewhere in all of them.

'Vision' is a tricky word when used by a producer, for as Davina is aware such a term is more usually retained by directors:

It's a tricky path you tread as a film producer in an industry that encourages the Director to be God. Producers are like parents who rear their child or their film to school age, try to get them to the best school, then have the headmaster/director take them over and say: 'Give us your child. We shall take her/him on. Thank you, now the child is ours!' Meanwhile you're the one who's done all that work to reach that point! So there could be a clash of vision between producer and director as well as between myself and my co-producer. You have to handle it with a series of compromises.

Davina herself nurtures a quiet desire to become a film director:

I've recently directed some theatrical master classes in Los Angeles. I absolutely loved it! Larry would love to see me as a film director. For years he has said: 'You should be directing.

You're very creative.' Larry is competent enough as a person in his own skin to be able to sit back and be not only very supportive in projects I want to go ahead with but also deeply encouraging in areas where I am insecure. Directing is one such area.

I want Davina to get into more creative areas. I want her to be a director, because I think she has enormous talent but doesn't yet have the self-confidence to pursue it seriously. I encourage her. I hope she will. I want her to fulfil her creative potential.

Directing is intimidating. Part of me would love the challenge. Part of me dreads the idea of being merely competent. I'm ambitious in that I would want to be Martin Scorcese. I'd want to be distinctive. I'm afraid of being merely competent rather than 'special'. But yet I'm not ambitious enough. I'm not driven enough. Already I would like to have achieved more. It would be truly exhilarating to have made a classic the whole world knows about! What holds me back is partly the fear of being ordinary, partly the feeling that there are so many people out there who live, breathe and want nothing else in their life that I shouldn't be taking up that slot if I'm not absolutely desperate for it. It's that business of not being quite hungry enough! Have you noticed that those who inherit wealth are never as creative as those who didn't have the advantage of family money? To be a director I'd have to start again, which is healthy; in the long run it would be a good thing. But when you have a partner, a company, a salary, all ticking over it's hard to start again and face uncertainty. I should have to make a great many compromises.

'Compromise' is a term with which the couple pepper their conversation:

Over the years I've learned in the film industry that it won't be the end of the world if it doesn't happen the way you hoped! You learn as you get older to compromise more. Sometimes I want to bounce work ideas off Larry but there again there has to be compromise. It depends on whether I think he will understand the situation, whether he has had appropriate experience. I wouldn't discuss it if he was under stress; I wouldn't want him pressured with my pressure. If I'm excited about a script I'm keen for him to read it, but seven times out of ten he tends to not like what I like creatively. When we see movies we have identical reactions, but in terms of what attracts us on the page we don't always agree. It's helpful but not crucial to bounce ideas off him. More important is the *joie de vivre* he has, the sense of humour, the imagination that makes life with him stimulating.

For his part, Larry likes to share ideas:

He likes to discuss things, though he knows I don't always understand the technological aspects. I feel that in airing them he resolves things.

When Davina has time and is interested we share thoughts and ideas. From her I need the space to do my work and the understanding that it's not gonna be a nine-to-five situation – that I'll be concentrating at odd hours, that she has to be patient with me and I with her. She's in a similar situation, so it's complementary. If I were a rival film producer it would be different, it would be harder to share as we do because there would be conflict.

Do they feel they could work together?

I don't think so. The only time we came close to it, it was difficult. Larry wrote a screenplay. I found giving him comments without him becoming defensive proved an unexpectedly uphill battle!

I don't want to be Davina's creative partner. I don't want to be Davina's business partner. She and Clive have an adversarial relationship, much more highly competitive than she and I have. She's often frustrated and annoyed by him. I am a willing ear to listen to those frustrations and annoyances. I try and encourage her to be more creative. She sometimes asks my opinion of a script she's considering. I'm completely honest, so consequently she accuses me of hating most things. Not totally true. She has projects I think are hopeless and projects I think are marvellous. There's no sense in being less than honest but I suspect many partners are not honest. I couldn't imagine us trying to produce something together. It wouldn't work. But if it were a situation where she was responsible for one area and I another, let's say like her directing me as an actor, then it would work. I would have a defined responsibility, she would have her authority. But the reverse wouldn't work. She wouldn't take my direction, she'd want to be an actor and director both. She wants to be everything!

Their very different work lives have helped to establish their separate identities:

I always think of myself as being part of a couple whether Larry is there or not, yet I've never had any problems preserving my identity. I feel interdependent with him. By that, I mean I depend on Larry while retaining my own independence.

I never think about maintaining a sense of individual identity. We've been married thirty years, but we are individuals every single hour of the day! We haven't become Siamese twins though we have the little quirks of being able to read each other's minds and say, 'Wow!' We still marvel that after thirty years we share the same taste. She knows what I like. I know what she'll hate. She went to see that Marlene play. I knew I would hate it! She came back and said, 'I knew you would hate it!'

For years whilst Davina went out to an office Larry worked from home which Davina said: 'gave us enough psychological space':

In California I had a state-of-the-art recording studio in a separate office on the second floor which we built specifically for me. It was my fun and games room, with a full-size English snooker table in it! I had my own domain separate from Davina's area. A creative space where I did all my commercials. Sometimes when there weren't sufficient tools for my creative needs, I created them. I wrote imaginative computer programmes. There was no such thing as a dictionary of clichés or catch-phrases so I wrote one which I used daily to write TV commercials. Once when I was doing all the radio advertising for Universal TV I launched 'Quantum Leap'. The Head of Advertising called me and said: '*TV Guide* needs a log line. We're holding for you to produce it.' I simply went to my computer dictionary of catch-phrases, looked up time travel, third down on the list was 'An idea whose time has come'; I turned it on its ear, spoke into the phone and said, 'Time whose idea has come!' It made it to *TV Guide* and I got my $500. So creating tools is useful, but it can make you uncreative. I spent months writing a computer slang thesaurus, whereas maybe I should have written a couple of decent short stories! I'd been disappointed in the past. I thought by now I'd be a successful author, but after I had a contract for a children's novel which finally fell through I gave up on that serious writing. You could say I wasn't ambitious. Had I been I wouldn't have taken 'No' for an answer. But I needed to make money, one had to pay the mortgage, so it wasn't tenable to keep going. Maybe I was defeated by a bad experience, so I became enamoured of the computer and rechannelled my creativity.

The couple, who have a spacious apartment in London as well as a Hollywood mansion, need a large domestic residence:

This is not a marriage that could survive in a one-room apartment. In Hollywood we have a huge house. In London we found a two-bathroom, two-closet flat was essential to keep the marriage! One bathroom would be intolerable! The pathetic story is that when we first had a house with two bathrooms I said: 'We'll never use the second bathroom! We don't need that!' A month later in a hotel where our suite had one bathroom, it only took a week for me to know I never wanted Larry anywhere near my bathroom again!

Competing for a bathroom is less contentious than competing in the kitchen or the driving seat:

Our only serious fights are in the car. Davina has a mortal fear of being taken a block out of her way or going in the wrong direction! She goes ballistic if she feels I don't know the way. She'll always go mad in the car, so I'd better put up with it.

Driving is our major issue of tension. I'm a good driver but the car brings out the worst in me. It sort of becomes a war zone. Maybe it's to do with control. The only time I find Larry competitive is in the kitchen, where we are both good cooks. He likes to cook more than I do, as a result he likes to interfere. 'Oh, why are you doing it that way?' Or, 'Add such and such!' It's a primeval thing! When I'm cooking, which is only one day out of four, I want to be able to do it my way because I'm good enough to know how to do it. One night I came home and said: 'I'm cooking tonight. I'm making soup. I don't want any interference!' Just as we sat down to eat the phone rang – a crucial business call I had to take. I went into another room. When I returned, I took one spoonful and said, 'Did you put something in this soup?' He went, 'Er, er . . .' I went ballistic! Definitely a primeval thing. One's territory had been invaded!

Cooking is also part of the way they cherish each other.

The longer you're together the less romantic and more companionship-oriented it becomes, so food is part of that. Larry's not very big on gestures any more. There was a period when the gestures were heavenly. On our tenth wedding anniversary he sent me a rose to every single place I was at that day, which was a lot of places. There was one line of a message with each rose. By the time you got to the tenth rose you had the complete message. It was breathtakingly wonderful!

That they were born and raised in different cultures has made little difference to their partnership:

I've spent half my adult life in America and Larry's spent half his in England so we know how it works. The fact that we are both Jewish has overlaid other cultural differences. No matter where you're from, if you're Jewish there's that humour, which we both have, which is a wonderful immediate shorthand that unites us. It is important in our relationship, as is our Jewish taste in food! Jewish people are warm, more volatile, gregarious, spontaneous, all the things a lot of English people shy away from. Being Jewish is growing more important because as we age we start to think of old friendships and our roots.

Being Jewish also had implications for a crisis that occurred early in their marriage.

I was still enough of a conventional middle-class Jewish girl to feel you not only got married but you had children. It was the natural order of things. So when I found out I couldn't have them it was definitely a crisis. But Larry never allowed me to feel that it was a crisis in our relationship. It was a disappointment, a real disappointment, but we dealt with it together. It's interesting what you learn about yourself, because when the gynaecologist said: 'Now put your name down right now for adoption,' what came out of my mouth was: 'Oh no! I'm not interested in having children. I wanted to have a baby Larry Belling!' Was it a pure ego trip? How horrifying! Larry clearly didn't feel so strongly about just bringing up children that he thought we should go through the process of adoption. What I suspect now is that in those days I didn't have enough sense of self-esteem or confidence in my ability that I would do so well in a career that it wouldn't matter. In fact, I was furious when the gynaecologist said: 'Let's face it, it couldn't happen to a better person! It's not as if you're sitting home and knitting every day, Davina!' Actually he was trying to boost me, but then I was horrified. I was 29, already in the film industry, unconsciously I probably threw myself more into my career. I could be more focused, had less interruptions. But I look back and think maybe one of the reasons we have been so happy is that we didn't have children. There weren't those issues about how you rear them, how you educate them, how you entertain them – all the other issues that create enormous stress. It's made us focus more on each other. We've had to work out what ties us together without ever discussing it.

We wanted to have children. Davina had certain physical problems that prohibited that. When we found out she could not have them, it was a sadness, but we never let not having children become a crisis. In retrospect it may have been beneficial to our relationship. We didn't have quarrels or quandaries about how they should be raised or how much space and freedom to give them. Davina comes from Bournemouth from a particularly abusive family. I come from Oakland from a particularly permissive family. Our different views might have caused conflict.

Did the couple set out to build a long-term relationship?

When I got married, I never considered it being anything less than a permanent relationship. We middle-class Jewish boys from Oakland, California think that when you get married, you get married! We stayed married because we had a good sense of humour and the ability to ride the ups and downs, cope with the tragedies and comedies. There's no manual for being a husband. The rules are common courtesy, equality in who shares responsibility and work-load, respect for people, yes, mutual respect. I always assumed marriage is monogamous. When I heard later about those married people switching partners I found it quite distasteful. . . . It's not attractive, too sleazy, unpleasant, I've never contemplated it. It is not something I would naturally do. Our relationship is completely natural, not forced by exterior forces or people to be something unrealistic or difficult. It's a completely natural thing. I cannot imagine not being married to Davina.

We set out to build a marriage for keeps because we never thought of anything else. We came out of that era when you set out to be married to that person for the rest of your life. I assume that our marriage is monogamous. It's funny, it's never something that's been discussed. I'm not jealous or possessive. I love it when attractive young girls love Larry or make a fuss about him because I feel he's mine, isn't that terrific? I'm the one that got him! It makes me feel proud and I think he feels the same way! I was 26 when we married. I remember thinking this

felt absolutely right and comfortable, and why wasn't he a
wealthy diplomat or tycoon! Then I thought none of that really
matters. Gosh, it's nice that I'm not just a materialistic bitch,
otherwise I'd never have married him.

It is important that Davina and I share the same sense of
humour and that we understand that what we are doing is not
rocket science, is not vital in the overall scheme of things.

Our sense of humour *is* an important factor. I absolutely fell in
love with Larry's sense of humour and his voice. After 30 years
I'm still attracted to it. I still adore it. When I hear his voice on
his voice-mail at the office it just takes my breath away! It makes
up for the fact that he still comes to bed in a nightshirt, then
takes his underpants and socks off and leaves them on the floor
where they breed over the coming days!

CREATIVE COUPLE SCENE: EDNA AND DENIS HEALEY

Denis Healey, 80, former Labour Minister of Defence and
Chancellor of the Exchequer, more recently a best-selling writer,[10]
met Edna Edmunds when they were both students at Oxford
before the War.

'She had a very rosy face, was very popular, full of vitality,
known as the "Zuleika Dobson" of her time,' he recalls.

'I didn't see myself like that,' she counters:

I came from a small country school where no one had been to
Oxford. I'd been brought up a Baptist, which gave me the values
I prize now, so Oxford was all absolutely magic! I read English
but with the Spanish Civil War I got involved in politics. I met
Denis on campaigns and marches.

Their shared interests led in 1940 to a prolonged courtship
because of the War. 'I was abroad with the Army, she was teaching at Keighley. I always saw her when I came home.' During this
separation they both had affairs which they say strengthened
their love:

Once we married in 1945, having affairs never arose, I don't think it arose for either of us. I've never been tempted, whether she has you'll have to ask Edna.

I did, and discovered Edna hadn't been tempted either.

I personally see monogamy and fidelity as part of a commitment. I'm a believer in the nuclear family, which is very unpopular these days. I think a stable family background is the most important advantage parents can give their children.

(Denis.)

According to them both, their partnership is permeated by continuous love which 53 years later has an established stable family consisting of three children, Jenny, Tim and Cressida, and four grandchildren. Denis, whose writing started with a series of political pamphlets, Fabian essays and non-fiction works from a Labour perspective, has broadened his creative interests to include a best-selling autobiography, *The Time of My Life*, a book about his literary influences, *My Secret Planet*, and books on his special interests, photography and the Yorkshire Dales.[11]

Edna now has a highly successful writing and broadcasting career. She wrote and presented for Scottish Television a documentary film on Mary Livingstone called *Mrs Livingstone, I Presume*, which won the Radio Industries of Scotland award for best documentary of the year and a silver medal at the International Film Festival in New York. She followed that with another film, *One More River*, about the work of missionary Mary Slessor in Nigeria. Her book *Lady Unknown*, a biography of Victorian philanthropist Angela Burdett-Coutts, received the 1978 *Yorkshire Post* Literary Award for best first work, and has been followed by several more critically acclaimed works culminating in her recent book which lifted the veil on *The Queen's House: A Social History of Buckingham Palace*.[12]

When interviewed about her biography of her husband Tony Crosland in 1982 writer Susan Crosland said:

During the Sixties when I was writing newspaper profiles, I gave up interviewing the wives of great men. Though they understood and accepted the human foibles in every relationship, they also enjoyed the public image. When interviewed they wanted to perpetuate the image: it totally distorted the subject. I have tried to avoid the same trap.[13]

In these interviews Edna Healey avoids that trap with grace and honesty. She is realistic about the predicaments, pitfalls and patent pleasures of being one of the *Wives of Fame*,[14] the gently ironic title which she used for her own insightful biography of Mary Livingstone, Jenny Marx and Emma Darwin. She consistently illustrates the tough inner strength and sense of purpose which initially allowed her to act as 'both mother and father' (Denis's phrase) to their children, and later to emerge as a writer, broadcaster and film-maker. Throughout both her careers and in the face of her husband's, she has felt proud of their affectionate, enduring, often humorous partnership.

When discussing the difficulties of a long relationship, they both use the phrase 'a happy marriage' many times:

Love is the most important element in a marriage. Love is different from being 'in love'. That is a sort of neurosis, it rarely lasts for a very long time. Being in love with a person almost inevitably means misrepresenting them to yourself. Love develops over a period and is the one indispensable thing in a happy marriage.

(*Denis.*)

Sharing interests is central to their marriage:

When we first married Edna didn't like opera at all, whereas now she does. Painting I think she still doesn't enjoy as much as I do, it's still a passion for me. Edna's become much more keen on music than she was before. But the big interest we share apart from family and children is that we're both passionately keen on poetry, literature and theatre.

In Denis's view, what hinders a 'happy marriage' is one partner breathing down the other partner's neck:

What's essential if you've got bright people with their own

interests is that each of them has some space in their life to pursue those interests without feeling the other one is peering over their shoulder the whole time.

Denis Healey, created a life peer in 1992,[15] accepts that when one partner's interests loom larger than the other's in the life of the couple, or as in their case one partner's work is viewed publicly as having more value, the balance may shift uneasily. 'Balance' is another word the couple use consistently but view differently:

The most important thing in a couple is to achieve a balance. If you find that there is one dominant partner, don't fight against it, accept it and work at it. I mean work *with* it. For example, if there was any kind of political crisis Denis's work would always come first. I would accept it not really because of him but because of the work he did. I wrote in one of my books that the wife of a powerful man has to be wife and father too, because their absorption always is in their work. The great thing about a man is that he can be totally absorbed in his work, thinking of only one thing, whereas every woman has to think about five things at once. Achieving a balance in marriage is hard. Yes, balance is the word that comes up again and again, and it's what I say to people: don't waste emotional energy on little things, if there are little irritants . . . no, save them all up and have a good row!

(*Edna.*)

Balance is like most physical metaphors, rather a misleading thing when you're talking about relations between people. You can have very successful relations which are very unbalanced in many ways. If one person's interests are larger, it can make for a difficult marriage. Inevitably if the person is more wedded to their work than their wife – and that's not uncommon'– the most obvious single thing is that when the man gets home at night it's rather late and he's too tired to talk. His poor wife, it's her only chance to talk when he gets back. Otherwise her social life is confined to her visits to Safeway's. In our case I was very busy when I was Minister but what helped us both enormously

was that when I was Defence Secretary all our children when we
started were still at school, and our younger daughter was at
school right through the time when I was Chancellor, a good
deal later when the other two were at college. Fathers or
working wives don't have a chance to see their children off to
school but at least they tend to be there shortly after the children
finish school; but in politics, the time you're hardly ever home is
the evening because you have the votes at ten. The vital thing
was that Edna looked after the children and had to be their
father as well as their mother.

Denis's own father, 'a romantic', was away at nights and rarely
saw *his* children:

He was head of a technical college so he went off just as I got
home from school, just after five o'clock. At the weekends Dad
would always play golf, which took him away again. When I
became a parent I was very conscious of what I'd felt as a child.
I did try to see more of the children than he did, though I often
found it as difficult. What made a big difference was that
though I was terribly busy from early Monday morning till late
on Friday night I made a point of always spending weekends
with my family. We always had family holidays together,
usually camping on the Continent. If I didn't have to go out to a
dinner, I tried to have evenings with the family. The main reason
I got the reputation in politics of being a loner is that I preferred
my family to social life!

I was a little like a single parent . . . You went to the school
concerts on your own, the weddings and funerals, because Dad
had a conference. So they missed out. Except holidays, then
Denis was wonderful. He did all the things that fathers are
supposed to do. Dad for fun, Mum for comfort!

Denis's relationship with his father has had another effect on
his partnership with Edna:

My father was a little frightened of too personal a relationship
even with his wife, never mind the children. He treated them

with a sort of brutal facetiousness which I have a tendency to as well. It's escapism. He communicated more warmly with his students than he did with his children. He couldn't express his feelings directly to my mother, which was very tragic. The only time I ever saw her cry was the night of his funeral, not because she was insensitive but because she was tough; she had been a suffragette, she was like H.G. Wells' heroine Ann Veronica. But that night she really broke down. I wanted a more open and direct marriage than theirs, and I have had one.

In Denis's autobiography he points out that politicians are prone to vanity. Does he include himself?

No, I'm arrogant, not vain. Vanity is preening yourself all the time and thinking how you appear to people and trying to appear more attractive. Arrogance is exactly the opposite. You say, 'I don't give a bugger what you think – I'll do what I want!' The weakness of arrogance is it makes you insensitive to other people. You must ask the family what effect my arrogance has on my relationship at home. I think I *am* sometimes arrogant, but then Edna's a very tough character and she puts me down. There are ways I am dependent on Edna. She is very frank and honest with me if she thinks I'm being a fool or rude. She'll always tell me off, which is very helpful. Even when I argue strongly against her criticism, I usually have to admit ten minutes later that she was right.

Edna talks openly about the compromises she has made:

The compromises I've made over the years largely stem from the fact that we belong to a generation when Mum did everything. You could come in from work if you were a man and Mum would say: 'What do you want for your tea, love?' Your tea would be got! I can come in from a very hard day, but there's no question of Denis getting up and saying: 'Can I make you some tea?' He would if I asked him, but it's not automatic.

Edna several times expressed a need for women friends:

Men do irritate their wives! What women need is somebody to moan to. If you've got a sister or someone, you can say: 'My God! MEN!' My hairdresser and I do it all the time. It doesn't mean we don't love our husbands, but it's very nice sometimes to be able to say: 'MEN!' I don't have many close friends of my own that are not shared friends, and this is a real weakness in a happy marriage. My sister who is not married has thousands of friends who drop in all the time. People wouldn't drop in on us because of Denis's work. I would worry if they did, because I'd think they were disturbing him. So there is a tendency in a happy marriage for the wife (or the husband maybe) not to have so much their own friends.

Like Margaret Drabble, Edna talks frequently to her daughter:

Cressida is doing a doctorate in alternative medicine in America, but we speak a lot on the phone. She often asks me about her childhood. I do have a chatting relationship with her.

Like other interviewees, Edna feels that women communicate to women friends in a different way:

Denis hates people who chat to him. So what I need is a chatting post. This chatting post is very important, and fortunately I have a very valuable sister. She's near me in age. She's a bit clever in a sense; she's always been my admirer, stay and support. We ring each other every Sunday at five o'clock. I can say anything to her which is an important element, as I don't have the sort of friends she does. When I'm writing I don't need anything but now that my book's over I think I shall revive my friends again. It'll be important.

A difficult period for the Healeys was during Denis's Chancellorship:

I had periods of great stress when I was Chancellor. That is when of course your wife needs the understanding and doesn't feel that . . . you know, hurt if you don't express affection as much as you otherwise would. The most important thing to us is our children. I would always put the family first if there was a real clash but there was very rarely a big clash because I tried to avoid it. When you get the clash is when you're Chancellor and doing a Budget; when there's no choice, you just have to do that first.

In his autobiography Denis recalls:

Finance in those days was the last bastion of male chauvinism . . . When I was Chancellor, she could not even have an official meal with me in London. In the whole five years, she joined us at a meal in the Soane dining room at No. 11 Downing Street only three times. When I gave my major annual speech to the City in the Mansion House, she was forbidden to eat with the rest of us, and listened to the speech with the Lady Mayoress of London from a gallery above, like a medieval leper listening to a sermon from his squint.[16]

Today Denis still feels strongly about it:

The City, the financial world, in those days was almost exclusively male and even now the glass ceiling is much lower in the City than in most professions.

Edna remembers that period vividly.

As Chancellor of the Exchequer's wife I had no place whatsoever. I always say I had no more than five meals in the official dining room at No. 11 in the whole of that time! It's still bad but it was even worse then. Particularly in the City. At the City dinners there was a time when only the wives of the top table were invited and *they* were put up in the gallery. Like lepers! Looking through our yashmaks! In the end I wouldn't go because I found it so appalling!

The couple recall how hard it was for Cressida when Denis was at the Ministry of Defence:

We had to live at the Ministry in the middle of Whitehall, while

Cressida's friends lived in North London. The house was on several floors. Edna and I were on the first floor; George Thompson and his wife Grace on the second; our children on the third floor, one room of which was occupied by another Minister. They had to come down the stairs, and one family memory is poor old Cressie, her hamster dying in our bath! There's no doubt that she is the one that suffered from my political life.

It *was* hard on Cressida, coming to this great house where we all lived on different floors. Jenny and Tim were old enough to take it, she was only 12. She was so good at concealing the fact that she was lonely and isolated from her friends that I didn't realise how much she hated it until recently. We did leave her alone quite a lot. She used to sit at the window and watch people go by. It worries me now when I think of it. But she's come through all right. The other two didn't mind so much. She's very much like Denis. Strong personality, good brain but couldn't find her way in life for a long time. From my point of view and the children's there was a great deal of time when Denis was Chancellor when we became invisible. Cressida used to joke with him. She would come up and say, 'Dad, I fell out of a tree and broke my neck!' And he would say, 'Yes, darling, yes, darling.' She'd say: 'No, you're not listening, are you?' It was a very extraordinary thing – he just didn't hear. The worst thing is that he just doesn't listen to what you're saying half the time! I can't shut myself off when I'm working but he could. I'm beginning to be able to now, but the children aren't around so it's not a test. The most difficult thing for Denis to learn after he's stopped working so hard is how to listen again.

What was the most difficult thing for Edna to learn?

In politics a wife is often invisible and you learn to laugh about it. I've been in a room full of people in Downing Street when the visiting bod has been taken round, introduced to all these distinguished men and not a word about the wives! You have to laugh. It's no good getting worked up about such unimportant things. What qualities have I needed as a wife of a political public figure? What I have needed I have had. But it was in those years that I really began to think I needed to express myself.

If there is a 'listening problem', how do they communicate?

We communicate by osmosis! And by reading. We often read the same things. It's amazing when you're happily married for a long time, you don't talk about things in the same sort of way. I like never to let the sun go down on my wrath. I would never let him go out of the house having had a row, because one never knows. It's the most important rule in marriage. You have to weigh each other up. If he sees that I'm stressed, he wouldn't push me on something. Neither would I if I saw he was under stress.

In the Army Denis learned a difficult lesson, to do nothing but wait. It is a lesson which he finds useful in domestic situations:

I've a great saying that Edna and I will use: 'Let it wash over you.' When Edna went on her own to do television programmes in Africa I said, 'You're going to have the appalling situations, especially in Nigeria where everything's in chaos; you must just let it wash over you.' That's the thing you have to learn in your family life. If either of you is really unwell, you have to accept that things will be difficult until that's over, but it will pass and then change.

Change and flux are ideas on which Denis consistently focuses:

Of course everything is in flux, and you can't step into the same river twice. One change was when the children started wanting holidays on their own, and of course the teenagers rebel especially if the parent tries to guide them! I think we came to terms with that quite successfully. The other big change is from the age of 75 your faculties become less acute. Then when the children left home we were very conscious that would present new challenges and it did. Edna began to write. She'd thought about it for a long time. It's a great shame she wasn't able to

write earlier, but if you've got a husband who's not home
enough, and you're concerned about the kids, they take much
more of your time than if your husband could share the burden.

When you have three children you use up your creative
energy. There is a great deal of creative energy in women
which only comes out when their children leave home. For
years you have been listening at night for 'Mummy, Mummy, I
want a drink of water!' When they're out of the way then you
can be yourself, not the lady at the sink. That was true of *my*
generation. The important thing for our generation is to make
sure that when the children have gone you set free that
creative energy otherwise the empty nest syndrome gets you.
During the difficult days when Denis was Chancellor, I got the
idea for my first book about Angela Burdett-Coutts. That
woman became an obsession. I began thinking I really must
write. One day in the House of Lords Pearl Binder, who wrote
a book a year, said: 'Oh, for God's sake, stop talking about
writing a book! Hold my hand. Say after me: "I will go home
and write a synopsis. I will take it to a publisher tomorrow.
This I solemnly promise."' So I said all that, then I went to a
well-known publisher, fixed him with my beady eyes and said:
'Look, I've got the outline of a story. I don't know whether I
can write. But I know it's extraordinary and I've got to write
it!' He said: 'Yes. Go away and write it!' And they gave me an
advance! So I started writing at 58; since then I've written four
books, done two films in Africa, a lot of radio, and that's me
and not Denis!

What elements drew her to the subjects of her first TV script
and her best-known book, *Wives of Fame*?

I was asked to give a lecture on David Livingstone and I
suddenly realised there was a wife and nobody ever talked
about her. Everyone said: 'I didn't know he had a wife!' so I
became absolutely obsessed by the need to get Mary out of the
shadows. I said to this television chap, 'This would make
wonderful television, why don't you do it?' He said, 'Well,
why don't *you* do it?' I said, 'I've never written a script in my

life!' So he said, 'Let's have a go!' The next thing I knew I was in Africa following Mary in her ox-wagon through the desert. She was an incredible woman, but nobody knew she existed. The more I thought about it, the more I saw a pattern. So I thought I'll do *Wives of Fame*. I found the middle of the 19th century was full of these dynamic driven characters . . . there was something in the air then! The energy that these men had was very difficult to live with. I thought I'd do Socrates' wife, and Mrs Ruskin and Mrs Dickens, but finally I reduced it to three – Mary Livingstone; gentle, intelligent, relaxed loving Emma Darwin, my favourite; and Jenny Marx, the most interesting, who takes life sensibly. The jealousy of Jenny Marx meant no one wrote a life of her in English till I did. When I went to research in Moscow the Russians didn't want to know about her. You see, you've got a god and you don't want the god to be married! Since then I've written some commisioned books but I shan't do that again. Once you can say quite firmly 'This is what I am going to do' or 'This is what I'm not going to do and blow you, Joe!' then you have this new feeling of independence, which I had never really had since I was married.

An important part of Edna's creative independence is personal finance.

Earning money yourself is *terribly* important. What is so embarrassing always for a wife is having to ask her husband for money to buy his present. I now have two accounts, a joint one with him and my own personal account. I felt I wanted to have the money I earned. I know there is a little pot of money into which I can dip without reference to Denis. It's a room of one's own in a sense.

The couple do have actual rooms of their own for their literary work:

We are terribly lucky, we have more room than we can cope with. I've got my own study but Denis will tell you I spread into every corner. Writing a book I take over the dining room as well.

They read each other's manuscripts and make constructive criticisms:

She's just finished her social human history of Buckingham Palace. I read some chapters when she was polishing. She's like a new person. I long for her to write a book about her childhood because some things she has written have been moving and direct. I think she could do a wonderful book rather like Laurie Lee.

They manage to work creatively with few clashes over time or temperament:

We are now beginning to move into a very good relationship over that. Denis makes his own breakfast now. Mind you, it's a slimmer's breakfast . . . but there was a time when he wouldn't! I think my new independence has improved our partnership. I'm sure it has. He may find it irritating sometimes that I say: 'No, I'm afraid not, because I've got a conference,' but he has been tolerant and understanding. There were one or two things I ought to have gone to with him recently, but I couldn't do it with the state I was in with my book. That was OK with him. If it hadn't been OK, I would still have done it.

In what ways do the couple feel that the fact that their children now have two rather than one famous parent has been a burden?

I don't think *I* worry the children. They're very proud of me! Not everybody's got an old gran who writes a best-seller! So I don't think I'm any problem! When they were little the schoolmasters would induce in them a fear of failure. I remember Cressie saying, 'My teacher said: "With a father like yours you ought to be able to do better!"' The schoolmaster at Eton where Dickens' son Charlie was educated said: 'Consider what name you bear!' A very heavy burden! On the whole ours came rather well out of it. We love them and think they're wonderful. All our geese are swans!

Public prominence is a big burden. For Jenny at school, I don't think it was a major problem. But it was more when she went to the Froebel Institute to train to be a teacher, as I was much in the public eye as Defence Secretary. But she's extremely robust, Jen. In a sense she lets it wash over her. Tim, my boy, was at Oxford when the students at Cambridge were trying to overturn my car, shouting 'Hitler Healey' at me! A lot of his friends were anti-me because I was Defence Minister during the period of student revolutions all over the world. He found it a bit difficult to cope with. Cressida's problem was much more me not being there and her being separated from her friends. I don't think she worried too much when I was name-called. But for all of them there is the burden of fear of failure. You've got to do as well as your Dad. I don't think Jenny had that feeling particularly, but Tim certainly had.

They see themselves as a very closely interconnected couple who also enjoy time away from each other:

I like space, I think you need it . . . But if one of us is in the country and the other in town we ring each other every day, perhaps two or three times a day.

Even more, they enjoy time together:

We are very very lucky and happy at the moment and so few people get to our stage. When Denis says, 'I'm more in love with you . . .' what more could one want?

CREATIVE COUPLE SCENE: NICCI GERRARD AND SEAN FRENCH

Nicci Gerrard, 39, and Sean French, 38, the British wife-and-husband writing team who after 7 years of marriage collaborated to write the best-selling novel *The Memory Game*[17] in a mere ten months, have three distinctive voices. There is their joint fictional voice, page-turning, provocative and surprisingly unified, under the pseudonym Nicci French. There is Nicci Gerrard's passionate journalistic voice with its articulate, inquiring tone used for the insightful features and reviews she writes for the *Observer*. Thirdly, there is the quietly authoritative tone of novelist Sean French who also makes his measured mark in the *New Statesman*.

There are also their separate and combined parental voices, for children as much as books are at the heart of their firmly entrenched Proximity Couple.

The first time they met, Nicci had her two children with her:

It wasn't as if Sean fell in love with this woman, then had to cope with her children. It was like this package. People thought he was 'being wonderful'. He didn't. I didn't. Well, he was rather wonderful, but I also thought he was lucky to have them! He hadn't been married before. He was totally devoted to them immediately; he took me on as a mother. Sean's completely even-handed in the way he treats my first two and his two biological children, no distinctions. He's been exemplary.

It was a huge, complicated thing because it was clear I was meeting someone with children. We were never just a couple. The whole package was there for me. We've always been a quartet, now a sextet! Going straight into the relationship meant having to make Nicci's children's needs a priority. It was difficult physically, as immediately I lost hours of sleep. People said: 'Oh, it'll never work! They'll never see you as a real parent!' Actually it was positive. Maybe it was at a time when I was wanting children; I just got them much more quickly than normal! If you're a man and you have children, somehow you're meant to be a father, but if you're a stepfather it's an unnatural relationship so you have to make decisions about how it will work. You have to work it out, you have to create a pattern. So I think we are used to talking about things at length. Being a father is ideological, being a step-father you have to be explicit because partly it's doing things you may have to defend. I used to go to the supermarket with the older children and someone would say, 'Run back to Daddy.' They'd say, 'He's not my Daddy,' so you'd always have to explain things. They call me Sean, but I have become a kind of father figure though there are clear boundaries because Colin their father is always around. They used to call Nicci 'Nicci'; now they move between all our names. Then Nicci and I went on to have children together, so the gap is small. It's like they are all our children. We share child care but we also share a childminder with Nicci's brother who lives four doors down. We couldn't function otherwise.

Their definition of coupledom plays with ideas of interweaving and intimate connections:

My definition of a couple is two people who want to live together, are committed to share things intimately, and weave their life together. In this marriage to Sean, the meaning of a couple is different from my first marriage. Now it means we're going to be with each other till one of us dies. We've said those words. I hoped for that in my previous marriage, where I would have stayed partly because we had children. The two eldest – Edgar, 9, and Anna, 8 – are from that marriage. The two youngest – Hadley, 6, and Molly, 4 – I've had with Sean. When you're a couple with children, it's like you've almost become biologically related to their father. When I've had children with somebody it means there's absolutely no choice about the relationship. I made a choice to be with somebody, that failed, but now with Sean I try to put hope over experience. I'd already made a choice to be with him, but now we have children that's it! I'll work away and make sure it works. If you've come from a failed relationship you don't want to put yourself in a position to be hurt again, yet I must make myself vulnerable otherwise we shall not get far in our intimacy.

Their domestic life is as closely intertwined as their professional one:

There are no compartments in our life. I don't go out to work, I have the children all around. Now we write together. I see other people's lives as more compartmentalised.

(Sean.)

Because Sean works here, and I do sometimes, amidst the children, we've created a certain kind of household with an extended family. As well as my brother nearby, Sean's brothers Karl and Patrick live half a mile away, my mother-in-law lives up the road. Instead of going out into the world we've got this

community, made this into our own little world. A protected
kind of life. Instead of going out to a film, we have videos.
Instead of going out for a meal, we have takeaways. We feel
safer.

Another regular visitor to the Gerrard–French household is
Nicci's first husband.

I'm bound to see the father of my children. It's easy to finish a
relationship with someone if you haven't got to see them again
but it's very hard if you have to go on relating. It's hard to have
been intimate, then take lots of steps backwards and learn to
have a businesslike approach. When you look at them you
think you know those things nobody else knows! But we have a
very amiable, businesslike, calm and co-operative relationship,
with dry tinder underneath which we are careful never to
strike!

Once you've got children with someone on a practical basis
you're shackled together making arrangements and we just treat
it like that. Some people have awkward relationships with
previous partners, but our way is less problematic because it's
formal.

(Sean.)

Their move from separate professional lives to a new joint
career appears to them surprising yet inevitable:

It's hard enough living and working in the same house, so to
focus on a joint novel was weird because we knew the tensions.
Fortunately we had always been each other's reader. Always
shared ideas. Sean is particularly generous. There's no element
of competition. If Sean wrote a best-selling novel the world over,
I would be thrilled.

I've always shown my articles or novels to Nicci. She makes a
point of cutting me down, so we trusted each other's
judgement. But I'd retain the right to be answerable for my
material.

Why did they choose to collaborate on a *novel*?

I'd written two novels and a few other books, but this was new. I thought it would be interesting to try. Could we do this weird thing? It was an experiment. What was unexpected was that we did it! It was a surprise how it functioned, joined together, didn't seem completely absurd. You are very vulnerable, sensitive about people reading – what they say, someone changing your words. But we'd made a contract to do just that. We said both of us would have to be completely answerable for everything in it. Managing a single narrative voice, Jane, the heroine, was the easiest. Once we'd agreed on her as a person, what she felt, we fell into it. Because she was a woman I was writing in a different way. In one of my novels I had a section told in first person by a woman, but because there was my male name on the cover it was a problem. Here no one has said the female narrator isn't plausible. I've got Nicci's imprimatur; I've got this woman who can guarantee that this is what a woman will do. So that helps our joint single voice. It's as if Nicci and I went for a walk together. We have different walking styles, speeds. But together, I don't end up a mile ahead. Writing together is tossing the ball between us. There might be parts I thought were too Nicci-ish, too girlie and sensitive, so I'd think, 'Hang on a bit!' We're both professional, we know revising is crucial, that some bits which seem fantastic to you when you're drunk are so awful they've got to go.

I always wanted to write a novel. Perhaps I needed to write one with Sean, who'd already written them, before I wrote one by myself. I never felt anxious about the fact that he'd done novels. Partly literary curiosity to see if we could. Novel writing is a private, individual thing; you have to sink down, often you don't know what you're trying to get at. Could we get down to the same level ? Could we explore a shared psyche? We do have a very close relationship. I must trust Sean, because to write together in the way we have you really have to trust someone. I can't think of anyone else I could have done that with. It was revealing. It was as intimate as sex. Handing our writing over to the other person was painful – a mixture of undressing and being in an examination room. The other person doesn't just say: 'Darling, it's wonderful.' They say: 'Lovely, but we're gonna change this and that!' But having worked out the theme of memory (I became amnesiac during it), the plot, the narrator's voice, we had agreed one person would write a segment, then hand it over for the other to edit. Differences of style were ironed out in rewriting. But we had a contract that we would allow each other to rewrite. If you rewrite each other, you take away the voice of your spouse and put your own voice there. That's very significant. More significant for a woman. We further extended the contract to take equal responsibility for each other's writing. We created 'Nicci French', and we were equally responsible for her work. Partly we did it as a way of spending time together. We don't have enough of that. Writing together is sexy. It brings back the unfamiliar into a relationship. You are recreating the stranger you love. We discovered through writing together unfamiliar things. It gave us a new passion. If Sean ever wrote a novel with somebody else I'd feel terribly jealous!

If Nicci wrote a novel with someone else, it would be a bloody miracle on top of everything else! But it would be strange. Odd. It's been such an intimate thing to do, I would think: 'What is it? Why do you want to? Is it something I can't give you?'

The couple have quite different writing methods:

I need some solitude but I don't need long stretches of time. Recently I've learned how to enjoy long hours of solitude. Those days when I've nothing to do except sit and write are like a desert with rain. But I can work in snatches. I've learned to with the children. Mrs Gaskell used to work in her study while the children sat on her lap. Mary Gordon told me her ideal way of writing was a study opening into the house with the children coming in and out. I love that idea but hate the practice! Especially when the children scream and need attention. I've learned to be a tyrant with time. If someone is thirty seconds late I feel my ulcers growing! If I say I'll write a thousand words a day, I'll write a thousand words a day. It's not good for writing with

Sean because he needs long hours and space to sink down and sometimes he'll write only a hundred words a day. I would get irritable when I thought he was going to produce a thousand words. If I'd got up, got the children packed lunches, taken them to school, raced to work, delivered my copy, came back, sat down and found Sean hadn't started, sure I got irritable! That's been the most troublesome thing for me to accept because we are roped together like people climbing a mountain. I had to learn we have different ways of working and that you cannot order words.

I often find writing hard and miserable. I'm not efficient. That brings pressures when you're writing with someone. If you're very slow you're holding the other writer up. It's like crawling along a tunnel with someone behind you.

Both Sean and Nicci suffer from writer's block:

For me writer's block is like walking through treacle, facing a mountain, not knowing where the fingerholes are. I produce words but they're just meaningless. Sean used to be chronically bad at deadlines, I think he won't mind me saying this. When Sean was blocked he baked bread. The smell used to feel yeasty, comforting, but when I smelled it then I thought, 'Oh there's another deadline!' But with this family thing Sean's broken through that barrier.

I used to want to write books but never got anything longer than an article done, though I had loads of time. Then I met Nicci, had no time, totally exhausted, but was sort of unlocked! Though I'm not an organised person, when time is precious you have to organise it.

Do they see their joint writing as part of their commitment to each other?

It's been good for our marriage because it's the next stage in trusting someone. It feels like another commitment. We're absolutely tied together, contractually obliged to produce a second novel, *The Safe House*, again with a female narrator, about post-traumatic stress, which we've finished. We've started a third. Sean said recently that if one of us had an affair it would be a new story! Because there's this horrible thing that you're tied together in the public mind.

I saw the writing as separate yet part of the relationship. How you behaved in the writing was how you behaved some of the time elsewhere. We are professional, but our life together isn't only professional. I'm interested in what Nicci has to say. I tried collaborating once with a friend. It was a disaster, perhaps because we didn't have sufficient respect for each other's ideas. Nicci and I made a decision to trust each other and make it work. It worked because of the trust and because we decided it would. It's like getting married. You make that commitment.

Finances were poor when they started their novel. By its publication they were unexpectedly very well off:

We wrote *The Memory Game* when we had masses of money worries. It was like an exercise in insanity. Then staggeringly we made a £250 K advance for two books. We earned a lot of money, not enough to make the house look tidy but enough not to worry about paying bills. But we'd invested two years and total time and attention. If it had been regarded as a pile of junk, we would have just been fools. Neither of us are thrifty. He pays for some things, I pay for others. Mostly we say: 'Who's going to pay for that?'

There'd been money stresses, times when I didn't earn as much as Nicci. She took responsibility. There were moments looking at bank statements, seeing there was no money in my bank, yet the mortgage had to be paid. It's quite nice not to have to do that. We're not laughing for the rest of our lives, but for now you can really think about what you want to do! Suddenly you have freedom.

The enormous publicity they reaped has been less pleasurable than the financial rewards, though they are pragmatic enough not to complain.

When we wrote that first novel it was our secret. No one knew.
We were worried in case we were giving birth to a monster. That
would have been total embarrassment. Secrecy made writing it
a wonderful liberating tremendous game. Then it got big
publicity, the money was public property, it made me feel my
privacy was invaded.

(Nicci.)

The first book was like a game, a secret, could we do it? To do it
at all would be remarkable, amazing! The weird thing about
publicising *The Memory Game* is you have to create this line: 'Oh
it was such a fantastic marriage so therefore we can write
together!' You have to create a slightly cartoon version of your
relationship, whereas really you're like any other couple. You
have to be able to have real arguments, massive disagreements,
and manage to say, 'Well, actually that's useful' or get over
them. The second book is harder, another murder, wrongful
conviction. But it isn't a game for us.

(Sean.)

Writing together openly is harder. People say: 'You're
established! Get on with it!' We had a rule about publicity that
when reviews or interviews came in we'd look at them once,
then put them away, try and be as little affected as possible by
the bad ones. And there were some terrible things written!
There was a *Guardian* piece about how we sat down at a table to
try and find a big fat cheque to pay our children's school fees
and came up with the idea of the novel! Absolute lie. Our
children go to state schools and always will. It means you can't
believe anything! The publicity is stressful. Strange because I
believe in selling things, I don't despise marketing, but I'm
used to doing interviews not being a subject. Giving talks is
tiring, particularly when we did that marital double-act like a
parody of a happy marriage. People say: 'Are you really
happily married?' You find yourself saying smugly: 'Well yes.'
It's difficult to disentangle from real life. I feel depleted or
cheapened. You don't want to lie but you don't want to get
attached to this melodic couple who are going round sweet,
smiling and agreeing with each other! Who you are inside gets

chipped away. You just have to get on with your work and let those things drop away.

(Nicci.)

Has writing a book together submerged the couple's separate identities?

I'm not very interested in the matter of identity as a writer. I just want to write different kind of books. *The Memory Game* was seen as more of a loss for me because it came out in a woman's name. I didn't feel that. It was less exposed, a kind of relief.

(Sean.)

Independence is vital because falling in love is scary, with the impulse, for women particularly, to lose identity, merge with the other person. You feel very powerful but also powerless. I'm a very independent person. Falling in love with your children when they're born makes me feel the same way. Hurtling off a cliff. Struggling to hold back. It's good for me to go out and do my own work. I shouldn't have been able to work with Sean had I not come from a position of strength, because I'm scared of getting submerged in a relationship. A lot of women drown in relationships. I've learned to be assertive, independent, with an outside world to bring back into our relationship. That's good for us. Especially as Sean doesn't go out much. He works here and goes mad up in his attic. I have a kind of male role in this family which I didn't in my previous marriage. I earn a good salary from the *Observer*. I go to the office. I bring home more than Sean, the traditional bread. If we go out, people who don't know about us writing together or don't read books might have read a prominent feature I wrote. To them I'll be the working part of the couple. I feel a furtive mixture of anxiety for Sean, quite pleased with myself, terribly aware that it doesn't actually matter. I realise these things change with time. Sean's cleverer than me, and deeper in many ways. Next week could be the other way round, you're completely vulnerable as writers. It's interesting how easy it is to behave like a traditional man when you've got a traditional male role, being bossy, making decisions unilaterally. Thinking one has a right to be dominant in certain ways. You have power at one time or another according to status. I've become really wary of all that. I don't want our relationship pegged on status or money. I don't think it matters to Sean. That's extraordinary as it would bother loads of men. We ended up together because he's different from men like that! Sean is not a bossy dominating man, so in that way we don't replicate. Then there's the other side. There are rules made for couples like the air you breathe, you're not quite aware of them. Like I don't know how to set the video recorder. It's stupid but maybe more indicative of something else. I was the one who had the car when we first met, but he drives and I automatically step into the passenger seat. There's a way I quite like him having that male role, but I feel sheepish about it. I can't explain it to myself.

Communication is a key issue for Sean and Nicci:

Maybe we talk too much! We're so verbal! Perhaps we have an inability *not* to verbalise, not to talk through, not to analyse. Nicci is good at expressing things immediately. Sometimes I mull, sometimes I express anger or become moody. In the end it communicates itself. Partly my being a step-father has helped us communicate.

Sometimes I think we should talk over issues when Sean feels we should let them be. He thinks it's scratching a wound. I feel it's bursting a boil! Having a sexual relationship alters communication. It becomes laden with ambiguity. You're so powerful with each other, you can so hurt each other, or give pleasure. I've never had a sexual relationship in which there isn't a problem of communication to overcome. It's always difficult to talk about sex. There's always different communication between men and women. My God, I hate to use a word like 'female' but I think Sean's quite female. His life is introverted, he's ultra-sensitive, good with words, so he never uses a word meaning one thing to mean another. We're very caring, we set aside times to talk, go for a meal, or go without the children for a one-week holiday.

Compromise is a bigger issue for Nicci:

Sean is better at compromise than I am. I find it difficult. Just like my mother! I pretend I compromise, then I get my own way! I've been taught by my children to compromise and I'm keen on them compromising! A bit hypocritical!

What are the elements that make this marriage work?

A kind of honesty with each other is essential – and the ability to acknowledge our conflicts but feel we can get through them, get beyond them.

(Sean.)

What makes our marriage work is we feel equal, we do equal child care, we absolutely treat each other as equals. We share everything, we're adaptable, we help each other, we've learned the benefits of being generous with each other. Sometimes you find yourself in a relationship where you're doing the other one down, that's hell. This is the opposite. We've been good for each other. I write better because of Sean , I have better friendships because of Sean, I'm a better mother because we've helped each other.

CREATIVE COUPLE SCENE: NANCY KLINE AND CHRISTOPHER SPENCE

Nancy Kline, 51, American, writer and leadership consultant, and Christopher Spence, 53, English, founder of the London Lighthouse, had a trans-globe Intimate Commuter relationship for the first 7 years – 'the biggest disadvantage was the size of the telephone bill' – until Nancy decided to settle in England. Their second 7 years has been spent as a married Proximity Couple in Oxfordshire where Christopher though officially retired writes books, is a non-executive director of an NHS Trust and does executive coaching through Nancy's company. They are both twins, which they see as important in terms of their coupledom.

Christopher: I was in a couple with my twin. The difference between being a twin and a singleton is enormous in terms of communication. You never let issues slide. I've almost always been in a couple. Very young I was in a gay relationship which lasted 24 years, then with Nancy. So I've never not been in a couple.

Nancy: I'm the same. The expectation of intimacy, comfort, is grounded and buttressed better for a twin. I've had couple consciousness probably since birth. As Christopher indicated, maybe that comes from being a twin. I was playing couples from the time I could play anything! I had boyfriends officially from the time I was 8! I played marriage. I also had *very* close women friends who at certain stages were the most important. Did I have gay relationships? I don't think the world would have called it that. I was married before for 14 years before we divorced. I helped raise three step-children.

When Nancy, still married although not happily, ran conferences in America, Christopher, in London, still in a long-term relationship with his partner Andrew, was attracted to her through her writings. Nancy felt the same response.

Nancy: We didn't meet face to face, but I felt I knew him because I'd read his writings.

Christopher: I knew and liked her writing too. Then we met over the telephone. Then finally we met!

Nancy: I was leading a conference and he attended!

Christopher: We met in August. Nancy came on a visit in November. I went back the following January. Then it became sort of . . .

Nancy: Every day!

Christopher: We spoke every day on the phone. Then we spent a fortnight together every two months. The disadvantage was the phone bill!

Nancy: And the longing! What I learned in those seven years was if you only have a small amount of time together how to figure out what you most want to communicate. Then do it from your heart and do it satisfyingly, so you go away from a phone call filled up with good exchange and intimacy, given that you'll have to wait another 20–30 hours before you have another hour to talk. I learned also how to be in love with him and not lose myself in the process. When we'd agreed that we couldn't see each other again for X months, there were times I longed for him and missed him so much that I had to find my way out of that.

Christopher: One had to be very disciplined about making the very best of what time we had, both daily over the phone and when we were together. That discipline and the intensity enabled the relationship to grow in a steady manageable way to the point 7 years later when we decided to marry. Had we lived two doors down, either it would never have happened or it would have swamped us.

Nancy: I also had a transition to make from my first marriage to living alone, which I did during our first year, then two years later getting divorced, then deciding to marry again. But I learned not to take for granted anything wonderful.

Christopher: For three of those seven years I was still living with Andrew, which was a funny time. I always say that my relationship with Nancy was occasion rather than cause of the split from Andrew. It was time that he and I were not in that relationship but we hadn't faced that yet. My relationship with Nancy was the catalyst to do that but it took a lot of time. She was a heterosexual woman in a marriage, I was a gay man in leadership on gay issues, in a gay relationship, yet we very quickly recognised that people who felt like we did about each other married. But there was no context for that. It wasn't relevant.

Nancy: The first January we were together he said, 'People who feel this way about each other usually get married.' I said, 'I know.'

Christopher: It was good that the way forward wasn't obvious. We had to live our way, feel our way towards what was right for us. Other people saw it before we did. Before we got serious, people who knew us well thought getting married was an obvious thing to do. Long before it occurred to us, it was obvious. Because I was identified publicly as a gay man and in a gay relationship, I'd have said the pressure was *not* to marry. It was considered quite a reversal not to say betrayal on my part to do so.

Nancy: I also had a strange kind of pressure not to marry Christopher. I was very much identified with the feminist community, a strong women's rights community in America and here, who had taken a theoretical position that marriage was irrational and was always an enslavement of the woman. So for many of the seven years before we married we theorised all the time about how bad it would ever be to be married from a political point of view. It has turned out not an enslavement at all! In this day the enslavement factor is dependent hugely on the level of consciousness of the couple. Also on the extent to which both are committed to stopping any practice of sexism in their work or domestic lives. A big part of our growing together was from the beginning Christopher and I talked about gay rights and women's rights. I'd say our marriage is grounded in and permeated by that interest in eliminating sexism. It's part of our parlance and part of our normal observation.

Christopher: It's also part of our laughter!

Nancy: If one of us falls into it we laugh about it. But we do have to be vigilant. As a woman I have to stop and think, 'Am I doing this because I think I should or because I want to?'

Christopher: One example was when you were expected to and agreed to play the role of my wife vis-à-vis the Lighthouse at public events. That was hard on you.

Nancy: Yes, I did have to think about whether that would detract from my own growth or work. I'd learned to think about those things when I lived alone after my divorce.

Christopher: There was nearly three years between my separating from Andrew and Nancy and I marrying. For the first time in my life I lived *not* in a couple. My parents lived here in Oxfordshire but in a different part of the house. The richness of living alone was new, a tremendous experience. I think it led to our decision to marry. It sounds trite, but discovering how to make a primary relationship with oneself gives one a strong base.

The couple talked about the difficulties they faced when they finally decided to marry:

Nancy: We couldn't decide how to marry, where to live. Then on the phone Christopher said: 'Why don't we stop asking: 'Where are we going to live?' and start asking: 'Do we want to be married and how *could* we be married?' I thought that was a fabulous change of question. So I said: 'Yes, I do want to marry you and we can find a way.'

Christopher: We had decided to 'be married' before we decided we would live together. Initially we thought we could 'be married' but carry on commuting as before, living in both places. Our friends were exasperated! After seven years we were going to get married, but then we said we shan't live together!

Nancy: But on our honeymoon it became clear we did not want to live apart, so eventually I moved.

Christopher: There was great celebration but there was some hostility. I felt often when we were around some heavily politicised, not to say misogynist, gay men, as if I was seen to be either an intrusion or a fraud or a betrayal. But I was aware it generally came from people who didn't know us well. It wasn't easy. But as our circle grew it got easier over the years, didn't it?

Nancy: Yes, it did. I think people were confused.

Christopher: We talked about it a lot. At times when we were under a lot of scrutiny through the press, it was tense, wasn't it?

Nancy: The hard thing for me was that very few people who didn't know us wanted to understand what gay issues and gay identity meant to us. There were so many assumptions. I felt I was entering crowds of strangers who were making assumptions such as that if Christopher is gay then he's having sex with men right now, or that we can't have a real marriage, or that gay equals having sex with the same gender. He thinks people know what he means, I think they don't. That was hard for me and it wasn't so hard for him because he knew what he was doing. We didn't try and evolve a new meaning of what a gay identity could be within a marriage, we just lived what was true. When people were prurient I got angry!

Christopher: Like the time you agreed to do a newspaper interview on the basis it was about you and your new book but it turned out to be about me . . .

Nancy: Wanted to know if we had sex, that's what! I told them to get out!

Christopher: Some people from the Lighthouse came here, saw round the house, took the message back that the bed was so small we couldn't possibly be sleeping together! That made you angry.

Nancy: That made me angry. Someone told us, so later that person took the message back to the gossip network: 'lovely things go on in that bed!' so that's good!

Christopher: Apart from those annoyances, in some ways marriage didn't change anything. Our relationship was seven years established. What changed was that we actually built a home together. It represented making public something that already was.

Nancy: I think there are stereotyped views of what a couple should be like. We weren't like that. A friend of mine said something I could apply to coupledom. She said, 'I feel I should have a certain sort of holiday. I keep idealising the holiday I'm going to have, then it's never like that! What I think I need to do is to have the holiday I'm having!' A lot of couples think they should be having a certain kind of coupledom. Instead they probably should have the coupledom they're having!

Nancy and Christopher both felt that their parents' marriages had had a decided effect on their own:

Christopher: Most of us choose to model differently from the couple that produced us. We're heavily conditioned by that. Nancy and I live with our four parents, even though they're all dead now. My parents lived in this house for eleven years before they departed into nursing homes. Those were the deteriorating years of their relationship. Fundamentally they had little in common and didn't communicate well. They managed their relationship by having different interests and focusing out of it. Then when old age crept on them it caved in.

Nancy: That's a good description. My parents had a real love affair. At the level of wanting each other it was a happy marriage, they were married 53 years before they died. But I also learned by watching my mother that you sacrifice your-self pretty much wholly for the man. I watched her martyr herself and not develop in order that he would be happy. I got a mixed message. The good side of watching her with him was the joy she got in doing for him but there was also the pain. I've inherited some of that. When I was 'the wife' during Lighthouse events, I really knew how to do it. As long as I wasn't confusing that with thinking that was all I was, it was fine. Both Christopher and I saw our parents making a home and being domestic, so the home is important.

Christopher: But my mother was defiant and had a public role outside marriage, and encouraged us to go our own way while somehow staying married and running a home.

Nancy: And obeying your father!

Christopher: Yes, quite a balancing act!

Their parenting affected them in other ways:

Nancy: The first weekend that we met, Christopher and I asked each other, 'If there are going to be difficulties, what will be the key difficulty for you and what will it be for me?' It's an American–British thing which has to do with expressiveness and withdrawal. Americans are very expressive. So if I get needy to express, he withdraws. The more he withdraws, the more expressive I get. The more expressive I get, the more he withdraws!

Christopher: It's compounded by the particular type of mothering we had, which is that if her mother disapproved she with-drew. Whereas my mother would far rather you did your own thinking than agreed with her and she never withdrew.

The death of both sets of parents had critical implications for the couple:

Christopher: My parents' deaths were a big crossroads because they lived with me, then went into nursing homes, then I became primary support for my mother whom I saw nearly every day, a big investment. Nancy's parents also died, so seeing each other through double bereavements was another crossroads.

Nancy: Because we were both trained in bereavement skills it was good in a way. A bigger personal crisis was having to establish my work identity, first in Britain, then in this house instead of London. People kept assuming I was working at the Lighthouse! I had to see myself as a person in my own right in Britain, earning a living developing *my* work.

Today the couple do some creative work together. They jointly wrote a booklet: *At Least A Hundred Principles of Love.*

Nancy: The book pulls together two things the world keeps apart: social change and love. We say that intelligent intimacy is not possible in its fullest sense without social activism and leadership in the world – by leadership I mean doing your bit to make things better – and social change or leadership is not grounded enough in reality and the human spirit if it's not also inside a life that's filled with love. So you can't be a leader and have an arid unloving life, nor can you have real love unless you see yourself as having something to do with what's happening in the world. The practical side of our collaboration springs from conversations. Later we write it down. What is exciting is sharing ideas, fertilising each other's thinking. Watching the spirit of the two of us together. We are not rivalrous or competitive, we feel glad to work together, it's part of being our couple.

Christopher: We're used to critiquing each other's stuff so it's not a tense activity. It's a joyous one. I don't want our differences and individualities to be subsumed into coupledom. I think people's projections on to particularly happy couples create a danger. I was in a gay relationship where we also worked together, which was tremendously idealised by gay men which became an enormous strain. So I've been cautious about how much work we do together. I don't assume that we'll work together, but when it makes sense for us then I love to work together. I don't see a separation between our life together and our work. One flows from the other and back again.

Though they live and often work in one space, two studies and a mental set offer them solitude.

Christopher: We generally exercise separately, but always start and finish the day together. We never interrupt each other, we might say 'Hi' in passing but we're never actually on top of each other.

How important is 'success' to them?

Nancy: It matters hugely for me that my courses succeed for people, that my writing makes a difference where it can.

Christopher: I've wanted to be 'me' more than I've wanted to be successful. I found ways to be 'me' which were successful, but I would have always wanted to be myself at the expense of being successful.

Nancy: So would I! But I wouldn't have wanted to be unsuccessful in order to be myself. Some people shy away from the challenge of being successful in the name of being true to yourself. I think you can do both!

Christopher: I do too! More important than success is commitment. In one of my books I used a Goethe quote: 'Until you are committed, there is hesitancy, the chance to draw back, always ineffectiveness.'[18] That's about daring to know what you know and acting on it.

Nancy: That first weekend when we fell in love we decided we were committed to each other for ever, wherever that led. That we would follow that star without having to know. It's my belief we let it go where it was going to go because we were committed. I wanted Christopher, so where that led I followed my heart and my best thinking. But because we both believe the other should do what they really want, find the right work to engage them rather than the thing that will be most comfortable for the other, it has meant we haven't gotten subsumed.

These six couples, creative in their coupledom as well as in their work, had like Nancy Kline followed their hearts and their best thinking. This enabled their initial commitment to succeed in the face of myriad challenges and crises.

NOTES

1 Whitney Chadwick and Isabelle de Courtivron point this out in *Significant Others: Creativity and Intimate Partnership*, Thames and Hudson, London, 1993, p. 7.

2 For useful discussions see: Whitney Chadwick and Isabelle de Courtivron (eds.), *Significant Others. Creativity and Intimate Partnership*, Thames and Hudson, London, 1993; Ruth Perry and Martine Watson Brownley (eds.), *Mothering the Mind: Twelve Studies of Writers and their Silent Partners*, Holmes and Meier, New York/London, 1984; Shari Benstock, *Women of the Left Bank*, University of Texas Press, Austin, Texas, 1986; Angelica Garnett, *Deceived with Kindness: A Bloomsbury Childhood*, Chatto and Windus/Hogarth Press, London, 1984; Frances Spalding, *Vanessa Bell*, Weidenfeld and Nicolson, London, 1983; Frances Spalding, *Duncan Grant*, Chatto and Windus, London 1997; Phyllis Rose, *Parallel Lives*, Chatto & Windus 1984 Vintage, London, 1994; Nancy Milford, *Zelda*, The Bodley Head, London, 1970; Sally Cline, *Zelda Fitzgerald*, John Murray, London (forthcoming); Humphrey Carpenter, *The Brideshead Generation: Evelyn Waugh and His Friends*, Weidenfeld & Nicolson, 1990; Victoria Glendinning, *Vita: A Biography of Vita Sackville-West*, Knopf, New York, 1983; Vita Sackville-West, *The Letters of Vita Sackville-West to Virginia Woolf*, eds. Louise DeSalvo and Mitchell A. Leaska, Morrow, New York, 1985.

3 Pennebaker and Hegedus in conversation with Dennis Lim in New York, *Independent on Sunday*, 23 November 1997.

4 *Independent*, 25 November 1996.

5 Sher in conversation with Jasper Rees, *Independent*, 31 May 1997.

6 Tremain in conversation with Angela Levin, *Daily Mail*, 8 May 1997.

7 *Good Housekeeping*, January 1997.

8 Margaret Drabble to Syrie Johnson, London *Evening Standard*, 1 October 1997.

9 London School of Economics.

10 Secretary of State for Defence 1964–70; Chancellor of the Exchequer 1974–79.

11 Denis Healey, *Healey's Eye*, Jonathan Cape, London, 1980; *The Time of My Life* (autobiography), Michael Joseph, London, 1989; *When Shrimps Learn to Whistle* (essays), Michael Joseph, London, 1990;

Penguin, Harmondsworth, 1991; *My Secret Planet*, Michael Joseph, London, 1992; *Denis Healey's Yorkshire Dales*, Dalesman, Skipton, 1996.

12 Michael Joseph, 1997.
13 Reported by Philip Hoare in *Independent*, 28 August 1997.
14 Edna Healey, *Wives of Fame*, Sidgwick and Jackson, London, 1986.
15 Baron Healey of Riddlesden in the County of West York. Known as Lord Healey of Riddlesden.
16 Denis Healey, *The Time of My Life*, Michael Joseph, London, 1989, p. 417.
17 Nicci French, *The Memory Game*, Heinemann, London, 1997.
18 J.W. von Goethe in Christopher Spence, *On Watch: Views from the Lighthouse*, Cassell, London, 1996.

Background to the Research

I began this research in the United States, initially in Austin, Texas, where I carried out a pilot study. Later interviews were conducted in Burlington, Vermont, New York and Los Angeles. The research continued in Ottawa, Sudbury, Montreal and Toronto in Canada and thereafter in a range of key cities throughout Great Britain.

I interviewed 160 women and men in heterosexual couples, gay male couples and lesbian couples, then drew extensively on 80 interviews. All the participants were interviewed separately, some also elected to be interviewed together, several pairs also talked more informally about their partnership with the tape recorder running. Of the men and women who agreed to be interviewed for Chapter 9: *Creative Couples*, Sean French, Nicci Gerrard, Edna Healey, Denis Healey, Davina Belling, Larry Belling, Margaret Drabble and Michael Holroyd were all interviewed individually. Nancy Kline and Christopher Spence however chose to be interviewed together with equally good results. Initial interviews lasted a minimum of one hour per person and a maximum of three hours. All interviews were taped. Many couples were seen for follow-up interviews. All interviews were confidential. Couples whose interviews appear in the first eight chapters of the book have had their real names changed and coded to preserve their privacy. Couples in Chapter 9 chose to use their own names. Some couples had children, their own, adopted or fostered, others were childless. Partners' sexual orientations were heterosexual, bisexual, homosexual or lesbian. Interviewees included some Asians, some African-Americans, some from the Philippines and the Caribbean, some white Europeans, some New Zealanders and Australians resident in Canada, many French-Canadians, British-Canadians, North Americans, and British women and men. The respondents' religions included Jewish, Christian, Muslim, Buddhist, Hindu, Baha'i, Agnostic and Atheist. Although the study predominantly reflects the experience of white working-class and middle-class men and women, I hope there may be issues that people of colour may wish to take up.

The oldest couple were in their late 80s, the youngest in their early 20s. Longevity of each partnership ranged between 2 and 68 years, although two couples were included who at the start of the research had been together for one year.

In this as in my previous books I worked within the standard sociological and literary tradition of interactionist interviews and case study methodology. The book tapped into what Raymond Williams called 'a structure of feeling' about a certain situation, in this case coupledom. Although I offered for consideration several sociological theories about the nature of coupledom, I wove the threads from my own discoveries into a new and challenging theoretical explanation of men and women's partnered relationship to the institution of coupledom seen largely in white Western society. As in my previous studies I offered men and women the space to talk about their experience of being in a couple, in other words to tell their stories. Those stories became the starting point of my understanding.

The questions I asked which reflected issues raised by the couples included love, sex, celibacy, romance, intimacy, cherishing, monogamy, non-monogamy, celebrations, rituals, marriage, separation, divorce and break-ups. Respondents were asked to talk about sexual orientation, feminism, communication, anger, violence, sexual abuse, compromise, crises, and coping with changes.

We discussed friendships, family, ex-lovers, companionship, health, disability, bereavement, religion and spirituality. We also talked about children, child care, housework and employment.

There was a particular focus on money, power, age, race, cultural differences, social class differences, educational inequalities, politics, privacy, space, solitude, geography, commuting, long-term commitment, loyalty, betrayal, autonomy, sharing, and issues of sameness and difference. My final questions were always about their fears and hopes and the creativity within their partnerships.

At the start of each interview I asked each member of the couple three questions:

Did you always want to be in a couple?

Why did you want to be in a couple?

In what ways has being in a couple brought you benefits and in what ways has it done you harm?

Those who saw their coupledom as beneficial had little trouble in retailing the benefits for between one and three hours. Those who saw the particular couple within which they struggled as damaging assured me that it was because they were in the wrong couple, not because they were in a couple *per se*. Over 90 per cent of those couples I interviewed said they had always wanted to be in one.

The question as to why they wished to be in a couple sometimes provoked a look of incredulity or occasionally pity, as if they failed to understand why an intelligent reasonable researcher should be asking such a question. One woman's comment: 'So who doesn't want to be in a couple?' found many echoes.

To the question: 'Why be in a couple?' an instantaneous answer from a married male respondent was, 'It is a good insurance policy!' According to recent statistics, in terms of stress it does seem to be particularly good for married men, who after single women are said to have the least stress amongst groups categorised by marital status.

Many men thought coupledom, particularly with a woman, gave them a listening ear. Very few women in heterosexual couples felt that. Many women gave as a reason for coupledom the comfort of having someone you cared about close at hand, what novelist Jane Smiley called 'the brush and thump and rattle of a congenial presence in the house every day'.[1]

The question 'Why be in a couple?' arose from my starting point which did not assume that being coupled is necessarily better or more mature than being single. In our society we have millions of fulfilled individuals who are single and whose needs for affection, sexual satisfaction, companionship, intellectual stimulation, emotional nourishment and development are met without the focus on a primary relationship. Yet across the globe since ancient times, durable emotional pairing (set apart from or in addition to basic reproductive pairing) has been an awesome phenomenon eulogised by poets, and subjected to enquiry from philosophers, which demands contemporary answers as to why we pair off today.

Anthropologists and scientists suggest that over and above sexual pairing as a biological imperative for the reproduction of the species, even certain animal species pair off and become couples for their lifetime for reasons of mutual protection and companionship, just as humans do.[2]

Although in this study – unlike many of my participants – I have questioned the concept of coupledom, only about ten per cent of the interviewees knocked this sacred concept or felt they might be more content living as a single person. Those individuals who did problematise the notion of couples had either spent several years of satisfaction as single people, or were men and women with engrossing careers, independent interests, strong friendships, family, political or community networks. In general the interviewees, despite coping with conflicts, communication problems, changes, compromise and differing levels of commitment, were very optimistic about the state of coupledom today. This made it a heartening as well as intriguing book to write.

NOTES

1 Jane Smiley, *Ordinary Love*, Flamingo, London, 1991, p. 4.
2 K. Lorenz suggests that this couple relationship occurs in certain animal species both before the pair is ready to reproduce and also after reproduction ceases. K. Lorenz, *On Aggression*, Harcourt Brace and World Inc., New York, 1966.

Bibliography and Further Reading

1. BOOKS

Abbitt, D. and Bennett, B., 'Being a Lesbian Mother', in *Positively Gay*, eds. B. Berzon and R. Leighton, Celestial Arts, Millbrae, California, 1979.

Ali, Turan, *We Are Family: Queer Parents Tell Their Stories*, Cassell, London, 1996.

Ardener, Shirley (ed.), *Perceiving Women*, Dent, London, 1975.

────── (ed.), *Defining Females*, John Wiley, 1978.

Askham, J., *Identity and Stability in Marriage*, Cambridge University Press, 1984.

Bainbridge, Beryl, *Every Man For Himself*, Duckworth, 1996; Abacus, 1997.

Banks, O., *Faces of Feminism: A Study of Feminism as a Social Movement*, Basil Blackwell, Oxford, 1981.

Barrett, M. and McIntosh, M., *The Anti-Social Family*, Verso Editions, London, 1982.

Benn, Melissa, *Madonna and Child: Towards a New Politics of Motherhood*, Jonathan Cape, London, 1998.

Benstock, Shari, *Women of the Left Bank*, University of Texas Press, Austin, Texas, 1986; Virago Press, London, 1987.

Bernard, J., *The Future of Marriage*, Wales Publishing, New York, 1972; Penguin, Harmondsworth, 1976.

Bernstein, Basil, *Class, Codes and Control. Volume I: Theoretical Studies Towards a Sociology of Language*, Routledge & Kegan Paul, London, 1970.

Berzon, Betty, *Permanent Partners: Building Gay and Lesbian Relationships That Last*, E.P. Dutton, New York, 1988; Plume, USA, 1990.

―――― and Leighton, R. (eds.), *Positively Gay*, Celestial Arts, Millbrae, California, 1979.

―――― 'Achieving Success as a Gay Couple' in *Positively Gay*, eds. B. Berzon and R. Leighton, Celestial Arts, Millbrae, California, 1979.

Beyfus, Drusilla, *The English Marriage*, Weidenfeld & Nicolson, London, 1968; Penguin, Harmondsworth, 1971.

Blumstein, Philip and Schwartz, Pepper, *American Couples: Money – Work – Sex*, William Morrow, New York, 1983; Pocket Books, New York, 1983.

Boston Lesbian Psychologies Collective, The (ed.), *Lesbian Psychologies*, University of Illinois Press, 1987.

Boston Women's Health Collective, The, *The New Our Bodies, Ourselves*, Simon & Schuster, New York, 1984.

Bottomley, A., Gieve, K., Moon, G. and Weir, A., *The Cohabitation Handbook: A Woman's Guide to the Law*, Pluto Press, London, 1981.

Botwin, Carol, *Is There Sex After Marriage?*, Bantam Books, London, 1990.

Bowlby, John, *Attachment and Loss. Vol. One: Attachment*, Basic Books, New York, 1969; Penguin, Harmondsworth, 1984.

Brehm, S.S., *Intimate Relationships*, Random House, New York, 1985.

Browning, Elizabeth Barrett, 'Sonnets from the Portuguese', Sonnet XLIII, in *The Poetical Works of E. Barrett Browning*, Oxford Complete Edition, Henry Frowde, London, New York, Toronto, 1906.

Butler, Becky (ed.), *Ceremonies of the Heart: Celebrating Lesbian Unions*, Seal Press, Seattle, 1990.

Butler, P.E., *Talking to Yourself: Learning the Language of Self-Support*, Harper & Row, San Francisco, 1981.

Cameron, Deborah, *Feminism and Linguistic Theory*, Macmillan, London, 1985.

Campbell, S.M., *The Couple's Journey: Intimacy as a Path to Wholeness*, Impact Publishers, San Luis Obispo, California, 1980.

Carpenter, Humphrey, *The Brideshead Generation: Evelyn Waugh and his Friends*, Weidenfeld and Nicolson, London, 1989.

Carroll, J.B., *Language, Thought and Reality: Selected Writings of Benjamin Lee Whorf*, MIT Press, Cambridge, Massachusetts, 1976.

Cartledge, Sue and Ryan, Joanna (eds.), *Sex and Love: New Thoughts on Old Contradictions*, The Women's Press, London, 1983.

Chadwick, Whitney and de Courtivron, Isabelle, *Significant Others: Creativity and Intimate Partnership*, Thames & Hudson, London, 1993.

Chandler, J., *Women Without Husbands: An Exploration of the Margins of Marriage*, Macmillan, London, 1991.

Chodorow, N., *The Reproduction of Mothering: Psychoanalysis and the Sociology of Gender*, University of California Press, Berkeley, 1978.

Cixous, Hélène, 'Sorties', trans. Liddle, in *New French Feminisms*, eds. Elaine Marks and Isabelle de Courtivron, Harvester Press, Hemel Hempstead, 1981.

Cline, Sally, *Just Desserts: Women and Food*, André Deutsch, London, 1990.

—— *Women, Celibacy and Passion*, André Deutsch, London, 1993; Optima, London 1994; Carol Southern Books, New York, 1993; Ediciones Temas de Hoy, Spain, 1993.

—— *Lifting the Taboo: Women, Death and Dying*, Little, Brown, London, 1995; Abacus, London, 1996; Gustav Lübbe Verlag, Bergisch Gladbach, Germany, 1997.

—— *Radclyffe Hall: A Woman Called John*, John Murray, London, 1997; Overlook Press, New York, 1998.

—— *Zelda Fitzgerald: A Biography*, John Murray, London (forthcoming).

—— and Spender, Dale, *Reflecting Men at Twice Their Natural Size*, André Deutsch, London, 1987.

Clunis, D. Merilee and Green, G. Dorsey, *Lesbian Couples*, Seal Press, Seattle, 1988.

Cole, Julia, *Crunch Points for Couples*, Sheldon Press, SPCK, London, 1997.

Coleman, Eli (ed.), *Integrated Identity for Gay Men and Lesbians: Psychotherapeutic Approaches for Emotional Well-Being*, Harrington Park Press, New York, 1987.

Coward, Rosalind, *Female Desire: Women's Sexuality Today*, Paladin Books, London, 1984.

—— and Ellis, John, *Language and Materialism*, Routledge & Kegan Paul, London, 1977.

Curry, H. and Clifford, D., *A Legal Guide for Lesbian and Gay Couples*, 4th edn., Nolo Press, Berkeley, California, 1986.

Daly, Mary, *Gyn/Ecology: the Metaethics of Radical Feminism*, Beacon Press, Boston, 1978; Women's Press, London, 1978.

Darty, T. and Porter, S. (eds.), *Women-Identified Women*, Mayfield, Palo Alto, California, 1984.

de Ceccio, John (ed.), *Gay Relationships*, Haworth Press, Binghampton, New York, 1988.

Delphy, C. and Leonard, D., *Familiar Exploitation: A New Analysis of Marriage in Contemporary Western Societies*, Polity Press, Cambridge, 1992.

DeSalvo, Louise and Leaska, Mitchell A. (eds.), *The Letters of Vita Sackville-West to Virginia Woolf*, Morrow, New York, 1985; Hutchinson, London, 1985.

Dominian, Jack, *Marital Breakdown*, Penguin, Harmondsworth, 1968.

—— *Marriage and the Definitive Guide to What Makes a Marriage Work*, Heinemann, London, 1995.

Drabble, Margaret, *The Radiant Way*, Penguin, Harmondsworth, 1987.

—— *A Natural Curiosity*, Penguin, Harmondsworth, 1989.

—— *The Gates of Ivory*, Penguin, Harmondsworth, 1991.

—— *Angus Wilson: A Biography*, Secker & Warburg, London, 1995.

—— (ed.), *The Oxford Companion to English Literature*, Oxford University Press, Oxford and New York, 1996.

Driggs, John H. and Finn, Stephen E., *Intimacy between Men: How to Find and Keep Gay Love Relationships*, Plume, New York, 1991.

Edgell, S., *Middle-Class Couples: A Study of Segregation, Domination and Inequality in Marriage*, George Allen & Unwin, London, 1980.

Eekelaar, J.M. and Katz, S.N. (eds.), *Marriage and Cohabitation in Contemporary Society*, Butterworth, Toronto, 1980.

Eichenbaum, L. and Orbach, S., *What Do Women Want: Exploring the Myth of Dependency*, Berkeley Publishing Co., New York, 1983.

Ellis, Havelock, *Sexual Inversion*, Vol. 2 of *Studies in the Psychology of Sex*, F.A. Davis Company, Philadelphia, 1915; William Heinemann, London, 1944.

Elshtain, Jean Bethke, 'Feminist Discourse and Its Discontents', in *Feminist Theory: A Critique of Ideology*, eds. N. Keohane, M. Rosaldo and B. Gelpi, Harvester Press, Hemel Hempstead, 1982.

Fanthorpe, U.A., *Safe As Houses*, Peterloo Poets, Calstock, UK; Story Line Press, Oregon, USA, 1995.

Farrell, W., *The Liberated Man. Beyond Masculinity: Freeing Men and Their Relationships with Women*, Random House, New York, 1974.

Fisher, Helen E., *Anatomy of Love: The Natural History of Monogamy, Adultery, and Divorce*, W. W. Norton and Company, New York and London, 1992.

Fleming, Lee (ed.), *By Word of Mouth: Lesbians Write the Erotic*, Gynerge Books, Charlottetown, Prince Edward Island, Canada, 1989.

Foucault, Michel, *The History of Sexuality. An Introduction*, trans. Robert Hurley, Vintage Books, New York, 1980.

French, Nicci, *The Memory Game*, Heinemann, London, 1997.

Freud, Sigmund, 'Three Essays on Sexuality' in Vol. VII of *The Complete Psychological Works*, ed. and trans. J. Strachey, Hogarth Press, London, 1953.

Friedan, Betty, *The Feminine Mystique*, Penguin, Harmondsworth, 1965.

Fromm, Erich, *The Art of Loving*, Thorsons, London, 1995.

Gagnon, J., *Human Sexualities*, Scott, Foresman and Company, Glenview, Illinois, 1977.

——— and Simon, W., *Sexual Conduct: The Social Sources of Human Sexuality*, Aldine Publishing Co., Chicago, 1973.

Garcia, N., Kennedy, C., Pearlman, S.F. and Perez, J., 'The Impact of Race and Culture Differences: Challenges to Intimacy in Lesbian Relationships', in *Lesbian Psychologies*, ed. Boston Lesbian Psychologies Collective, University of Illinois Press, 1987..

Garnett, Angelica, *Deceived with Kindness: A Bloomsbury Childhood*, Chatto & Windus/Hogarth Press, London, 1984.

Gavron, Hannah, *The Captive Wife: Conflicts of Housebound Mothers*, Routledge & Kegan Paul, London, 1966.

Giddens, Anthony, *Sociology*, Polity Press, Cambridge, 1989.

Gilligan, Carol, *In a Different Voice: Psychological Theory and Women's Development*, Harvard University Press, Cambridge, Massachusetts and London, 1982.

Glendinning, Victoria, *Vita: A Biography of Vita Sackville-West*, Alfred A. Knopf, New York, 1983; Penguin, Harmondsworth, 1984.

Gottman, John, *Why Marriages Succeed or Fail*, Simon & Schuster, New York, 1994.

——— et al., *A Couple's Guide to Communication*, Research Press, Champaign, Illinois, 1976.

Gravitz, H.L. and Bowder, J.D., *A Guide to Recovery: A Book for Adult Children of Alcoholics*, Learning Publications, Holmes Beach, Florida, 1985.

Gray, John, *Men Are From Mars, Women Are From Venus*, Thorsons, London, 1993.

——— *Men, Women, and Relationships*, Beyond Words Publishing, Hillsboro, Oregon, 1993.

Hanscombe, G.E. and Forster, J., *Rocking the Cradle: Lesbian Mothers – A Challenge in Family Living*, Alyson Publications Inc., Boston, 1982.

Harne, Lynne and Rights of Women, *Valued Families: The Lesbian Mother's Legal Handbook*, The Women's Press, London, 1997.

Healey, Denis, *Healey's Eye*, Jonathan Cape, London, 1980.

——— *The Time of My Life*, Michael Joseph, London, 1989.

——— *When Shrimps Learn to Whistle*, Michael Joseph, London, 1990; Penguin, Harmondsworth, 1991.

——— *My Secret Planet*, Michael Joseph, London, 1992.

——— *Denis Healey's Yorkshire Dales*, Dalesman, Skipton, 1995.

Healey, Edna, *Wives of Fame: Mary Livingstone, Jenny Marx, Emma Darwin*, Sidgwick & Jackson, London, 1986.

——— *The Queen's House: A Social History of Buckingham Palace*, Michael Joseph, 1997.

Healey, Emma, *Lesbian Sex Wars*, Virago Press, London, 1996.

Hearn, Jeff and Morgan, David, *Men, Masculinities and Social Theory*, Unwin Hyman, London, 1990.

Hertz, R., *More Equal Than Others: Women and Men in Dual-Career Marriages*, University of California Press, Berkeley, 1986.

Hite, Shere, *The Hite Report: A Nationwide Study of Female Sexuality*, Dell Publishing Co., Inc., New York, 1976.

—— *The Hite Report on Male Sexuality*, Alfred A. Knopf, New York, 1981.

—— *Women and Love: A Cultural Revolution in Progress*, Alfred A. Knopf, New York, 1987.

—— *The Hite Report on the Family: Growing Up Under Patriarchy*, Bloomsbury Publishing Ltd., London, 1994.

—— and Colleran, Kate, *Good Guys, Bad Guys and Other Lovers: Every Woman's Guide to Relationships*, Pandora Press, London, 1989.

Hoagland, Sarah Lucia, *Lesbian Ethics: Toward New Value*, Institute of Lesbian Studies, Palo Alto, California, 1988.

Hollibaugh, A. and Moraga, C., 'What We're Rollin' Around in Bed With: Sexual Issues in Feminism', in *Powers of Desire: The Politics of Sexuality*, ed. C. Stansell and S. Thompson, Monthly Review Press, New York, 1983.

Holroyd, Michael, *Lytton Strachey: The New Biography*, Chatto & Windus, London, 1994.

Hooks, B., *Feminist Theory: From Margin to Centre*, South End Press, Boston, 1984.

Hornby, Nick, *High Fidelity*, Victor Gollancz, London, 1995; Indigo, London, 1996.

Humm, Maggie, *The Dictionary of Feminist Theory*, Harvester Wheatsheaf, Hemel Hempstead, 1989.

Isensee, Rik, *Love Between Men: Enhancing Intimacy and Keeping Your Relationship Alive*, Prentice Hall, New York, 1990; Alyson Publications, Los Angeles, 1990.

Jay, K. and Young, D. (eds.) *After You're Out: Personal Experiences of Gay Men and Lesbian Women*, Links Books, New York, 1975.

Jenkins, Mercilee and Kramarae, Cheris, 'A Thief in the House: the Case of Women and Language', in *Men's Studies Modified*, ed. Dale Spender, Pergamon Press, London, 1981.

Jeffreys, Sheila, *The Spinster and Her Enemies: Feminism and Sexuality 1880–1930*, Pandora Press, London, 1985.

—— *The Lesbian Heresy: A Feminist Perspective on the Lesbian Sexual Revolution*, The Women's Press, London, 1994.

Jivani, Alkarim, *It's Not Unusual. A History of Lesbian and Gay Britain in the Twentieth Century*, Michael O'Mara Books, London, by arrangement with the BBC, 1997.

Johnson, Anne M., Wadsworth, Jane, Wellings, Kaye and Field, Julia, *Sexual Attitudes and Lifestyles*, Blackwell Science, Oxford, 1994.

Johnson, Susan E., *Staying Power: Long-Term Lesbian Couples*, Naiad Press Inc., Tallahassee, Florida, 1990.

Keith, Lois (ed.), *Mustn't Grumble: Writing by Disabled Women*, The Women's Press, London, 1994.

Keohane, N., Rosaldo, M. and Gelpi B. (eds.), *Feminist Theory: A Critique of Ideology*, Harvester Press, Hemel Hempstead, 1982.

Kitzinger, Sheila, *Woman's Experience of Sex*, Dorling Kindersley, London, 1983; Penguin, Harmondsworth, 1985.

Kline, Nancy, *Women and Power: How Far Can We Go?*, BBC Books, London, 1993.

―――― and Spence, Christopher, *At Least a Hundred Principles of Love*, LLMS Ltd., London, 1993.

Kramarae, Cheris, *Women and Men Speaking*, Newbury House, Rowley, Massachusetts, 1981.

Kristeva, Julia, 'Woman Can Never Be Defined' in *New French Feminisms*, ed. Elaine Marks and Isabelle de Courtivron, Harvester Press, Hemel Hempstead, 1981.

Lakoff, Robin, *Language and Woman's Place*, Harper & Row, 1975.

Lamm, Maurice, *The Jewish Way in Love and Marriage*, Jonathan David Publishers Inc., New York, by arrangement with Harper & Row, 1980.

Lerner, Harriet Goldhor, *The Dance of Anger: A Woman's Guide to Changing the Pattern of Intimate Relationship*, Harper & Row, New York, 1985.

Lessing, Doris, *Love, Again*, Flamingo, London, 1996.

Lorenz, Karl, *On Aggression*, Harcourt, Brace and World, Inc., New York, 1966.

Loulan, JoAnn, *Lesbian Sex*, Spinsters/Aunt Lute, San Francisco, 1984.

―――― *Lesbian Passion: Loving Ourselves and Each Other*, Spinsters/Aunt Lute, San Francisco, 1987.

MacDonald, Barbara with Rich, Cynthia, *Look Me in the Eye: Old*

Women, Ageing, and Ageism, Spinsters Ink, San Francisco, 1983; Women's Press, London, 1983.

McWhirter, David P. and Mattison, Andrew M., *The Male Couple: How Relationships Develop*, Prentice Hall, Englewood Cliffs, New Jersey, 1984.

Mager, D., 'Out in the Workplace', in *After You're Out: Personal Experiences of Gay Men and Lesbian Women*, ed. K. Jay and D. Young, Links Books, New York, 1975.

Magezis, Joy, *Teach Yourself Women's Studies*, Hodder & Stoughton Ltd., London, 1996.

Mansfield, Penny and Collard, Jean, *The Beginning of the Rest of Your Life? A Portrait of Newly-wed Marriage*, Macmillan, Basingstoke and London, 1988.

Marcus, Eric, *The Male Couple's Guide to Living Together*, Harper & Row, New York, 1988; revised edition: *The Male Couple's Guide*, HarperCollins, New York, 1992.

Marks, Elaine and de Courtivron, Isabelle, *New French Feminisms*, Harvester Press, Hemel Hempstead, 1981.

Martin, Del and Lyon, Phyllis, *Lesbian/Woman*, Bantam Books, San Francisco, 1972.

Milford, Nancy, *Zelda*, The Bodley Head, London, 1970.

Miller, Casey and Swift, Kate, *Words and Women: New Language in New Times*, Anchor Press/Doubleday, New York, 1976; Penguin, Harmondsworth, 1976.

———— *The Handbook of Non-Sexist Writing*, The Women's Press, London, 1980.

Miller, Jean Baker, *Toward a New Psychology of Women*, Beacon Press, Boston, 1986; Penguin, Harmondsworth, 1986.

Moi, Toril, *Sexual/Textual Politics*, Methuen, London, 1985.

Oakley, A., *Housewife*, Penguin, Harmondsworth, 1974.

———— *The Sociology of Housework*, Martin Robertson, London, 1974.

———— *Becoming a Mother*, Martin Robertson, Oxford, 1979.

———— 'Interviewing Women: A Contradiction in Terms', in *Doing Feminist Research*, ed. H. Roberts, Routledge & Kegan Paul, London, 1981.

Olsen, Tillie, *Silences*, Virago Press, London, 1965.

Parker, Tony, *The People of Providence*, Hutchinson & Co., London, 1983; Eland, London, 1996.

Payne, Karen, *Between Ourselves: Letters Between Mothers and Daughters*, Michael Joseph, London, 1983.

Perry, Ruth and Brownley, Martine Watson (eds.), *Mothering the Mind: Twelve Studies of Writers and their Silent Partners*, Holmes & Meier, New York and London, 1984.

Phillips, Adam, *On Kissing, Tickling and Being Bored*, Faber & Faber, London, 1993.

―――― *Monogamy*, Faber & Faber, London, 1996.

Preston, John, *The Big Gay Book: A Man's Survival Guide for the 90s*, Plume, New York, 1991.

Price, Deb and Murdoch, Joyce, *And Say Hi to Joyce*, Doubleday, New York, 1995.

Raphael, B., *The Anatomy of Bereavement*, Basic Books, New York, 1983.

―――― and Robinson, M., 'The Older Lesbian: Love Relationships and Friendship Patterns', in *Women-Identified Women*, eds. T. Darty and S. Porter, Mayfield, Palo Alto, California, 1984.

Reece, Rex, 'Causes and treatment of sexual desire discrepancies in male couples', in *Integrated Identity for Gay Men and Lesbians: Psychotherapeutic Approaches for Emotional Well-Being*, ed. Eli Coleman, Harrington Park Press, New York, 1987.

Reibstein, Janet, *Love Life: How to Make Your Relationship Work*, Fourth Estate, London, 1997.

―――― and Richards, M., *Sexual Arrangements: Marriage, Monogamy and Affairs*, Heinemann, London, 1992.

Rich, A., *Of Woman Born: Motherhood as Experience and Institution*, Virago Press, London, 1977.

Roberts, H., *Doing Feminist Research*, Routledge & Kegan Paul, London, 1981.

Rogers, C., *Becoming Partners: Marriage and Its Alternatives*, Delacorte Press, New York, 1972.

Rose, Phyllis, *Parallel Lives*, Chatto & Windus, London, 1984; Vintage, London, 1994.

Rothblum, Esther D. and Brehony, Kathleen A. (eds.), *Boston Marriages: Romantic but Asexual Relationships among Contemporary Lesbians*, University of Massachusetts Press, Amherst, 1993.

Rush, F., *The Best Kept Secret: Sexual Abuse of Children*, Prentice Hall, Englewood Cliffs, New Jersey, 1980.

Russ, Joanna, *How to Suppress Women's Writing*, The Women's Press, London, 1984.

Saffron, Lisa, *What About the Children?*, Cassell, London, 1997.

St Aubin de Teran, Lisa, *Joanna*, Virago Press, London, 1991.

Sang, Barbara, Warshow, Joyce and Smith, Adrienne J. (eds.), *Lesbians at Midlife: The Creative Transition*, Spinsters Book Company, San Francisco, 1991.

Scarf, Maggie, *Intimate Partners*, Century, London, 1987.

Scherer, Klaus and Giles, Howard (eds.), *Social Markers in Speech*, Cambridge University Press, 1980.

Schulz, Muriel, 'The Semantic Derogation of Women', in *Language and Sex: Difference and Dominance*, eds. Barrie Thorne and Nancy Henley, Newbury House, Rowley, Massachusetts, 1975.

Segal, Lynne, *Slow Motion – Changing Masculinities, Changing Men*, Virago Press, London, 1990.

—————— (ed.), *What is to be Done About the Family?*, Penguin, Harmondsworth, 1983.

Sherfey, Mary Jane, *The Nature and Evolution of Female Sexuality*, Vintage Books, New York, 1973.

Shields, Carol, *The Box Garden*, Fourth Estate, London, 1995.

Showalter, Elaine, *Hystories: Hysterical Epidemics and Modern Culture*, Columbia University Press, New York, 1997; Picador, London and Basingstoke, 1997.

Smart, Carol, *The Ties that Bind: Law, Marriage, and the Reproduction of Patriarchal Relations*, Routledge, London, 1984.

Smiley, Jane, *Ordinary Love*, Flamingo, London, 1991.

Smith, Philip M., 'Sex Markers in Speech', in *Social Markers in Speech*, ed. Klaus Scherer and Howard Giles, Cambridge University Press, 1980.

Snitow, Ann, Stansell, Christine and Thompson, Sharon (eds.), *Desire: The Politics of Sexuality*, Virago, London, 1984.

Spalding, Frances, *Vanessa Bell*, Weidenfeld & Nicolson, London, 1983.

—————— *Duncan Grant*, Chatto & Windus, London, 1997.

Spence, Christopher, *On Watch: Views from the Lighthouse*, Cassell, London and New York, 1996.

Spender, Dale, *Man Made Language*, Routledge & Kegan Paul, London, Boston and Henley, 1980.

——— (ed.), *Men's Studies Modified*, Pergamon Press, London, 1981.

Stansell, C. and Thompson, S. (eds.), *Powers of Desire: The Politics of Sexuality*, Monthly Review Press, New York, 1983.

Stanworth, M. (ed.), *Reproductive Technologies: Gender, Motherhood and Medicine*, Polity Press, Cambridge, 1987.

Sternberg, Robert and Barnes, Michael (eds.), *The Psychology of Love*, Yale University Press, New Haven, 1988.

Stoller, R., *Sex and Gender: On the Development of Masculinity and Femininity*, Science House, New York, 1968.

Storr, Anthony, *Solitude*, Flamingo, London, 1989.

Tannen, Deborah, *You Just Don't Understand!*, Ballantine Books, New York, 1990; Virago Press, London, 1991.

——— *That's Not What I Meant! How conversational style makes or breaks your relations with others*, Virago Press, London, 1992.

Thorne, Barrie and Henley, Nancy (eds.), *Language and Sex: Difference and Dominance*, Newbury House, Rowley, Massachusetts, 1975.

Tuttle, Lisa, *Encyclopedia of Feminism*, Longman, Harlow, 1986.

Tysoe, Maryon, *Love Isn't Quite Enough: The Politics of Male-Female Relationships*, Fontana, London, 1992.

——— *The Good Relationship Guide: How to Understand and Improve Male-Female Relationships*, Piatkus, London, 1995.

Vance, Carole S., *Pleasure and Danger: Exploring Female Sexuality*, Routledge, London, 1984.

VanEvery, Jo, *Heterosexual Women Changing the Family: Refusing to be a 'Wife'!*, Taylor & Francis, London and Bristol, Pennsylvania, 1995.

Vetterling-Braggin, Mary (ed.), *Sexist Language*, Littlefield, Adams & Co., New Jersey, 1981.

Walker, Mitchell, *Men Loving Men*, Gay Sunshine Press, San Francisco, 1985.

Walter, Natasha, *The New Feminism*, Little, Brown & Company, London, 1998.

Weeks, Jeffrey, *Sexuality and Its Discontents: Meaning, Myths and Modern Sexualities*, Routledge & Kegan Paul, London, 1985.

Wells, Jess (ed.), *Lesbians Raising Sons*, Alyson Publications, USA, 1997.

Woititz, Janet, *The Struggle for Intimacy*, Impact Publications, California, 1980.

Wolfe, Susan J. and Penelope, Julia (eds.), *Sexual Practice, Textual Theory: Lesbian Cultural Criticism*, Blackwell, Cambridge, Massachusetts and Oxford, 1993.

Young, M. and Willmott, P., *The Symmetrical Family*, Penguin, Harmondsworth, 1975.

Zimmerman, Don and West, Candace, 'Sex Roles, Interruptions and Silences in Conversation' in *Language and Sex: Difference and Dominance*, eds. Barrie Thorne and Nancy Henley, Newbury House, Rowley, Massachusetts, 1975.

2. JOURNALS, PAPERS, PAMPHLETS

Black, Maria and Coward, Rosalind, 'Linguistic, Social and Sexual Relations', *Screen Education* 39, 1981.

British Sociological Association, *Report on Adultery*, London, 1989.

Cass, V.V., 'Homosexual Identity Formation: A Theoretical Model', *Journal of Homosexuality* 4, 1979.

Dailey, D., 'Adjustment of Heterosexual and Homosexual Couples in Pairing Relationships: An Exploratory Study', *Journal of Sex Research*, 15(2), 1979.

Dormor, Duncan J., *The Relationship Revolution*, One Plus One, The Marriage and Partnership Charity, London, 1992.

du Bois, Betty Lou and Crouch, Isobel, 'The Question of Tag-Questions in Women's Speech', *Language in Society* 4, 1976.

Family Policy Studies Centre, *Family Policy Bulletin*, July/August 1996.

General Household Survey, Office for National Statistics, The Stationery Office, London, 1996.

Haskey, J., 'Stepfamilies and Stepchildren in Great Britain', *Population Trends* 76, 1994.

Humphrey, Robin (ed.), *Families Behind the Headlines*, British Association for the Advancement of Science, Sociology and Social Policy Section/Department of Social Policy, University of Newcastle, 1996.

Irigaray, Luce, 'Women's Exile' (interview with Couze Venn), *Ideology and Consciousness* 1, 1977.

Kiernan, K.E. and Estangh, V., *Cohabitation*, Family Policies Study Centre, London, 1993.

McAllister, Fiona (ed.), *Marital Breakdown and the Health of the Nation*, 2nd edn., One Plus One, The Marriage and Partnership Research Charity, London, 1995.

Marecek, Jeanne, Finn, Stephen E. and Cardell, Monda, 'Gender Roles in the Relationships of Lesbians and Gay Men', *Journal of Homosexuality* 8(2), Winter 1982.

Moi, Toril, 'Who's Afraid of Virginia Woolf? Feminist Readings of Woolf', unpublished paper, 1982.

Murphy, M. and Hobcraft, J. (eds.), *Population Research in Britain*, Supplement to *Population Studies* 45, 1991.

One Plus One, Marriage and Partnership Research Charity, *Information Pack*, London, 1994.

Radford, Jill, 'Breaking Up Is Hard To Do', *Trouble and Strife* 34, Winter 1996/97.

Rankine, Jenny, 'For Better or for Worse?', *Trouble and Strife* 34, Winter 1996/97.

Selman, Peter, 'The Relationship Revolution: Is the Family Collapsing or Adjusting to a New World of Equal Opportunities?', in *Families behind the Headlines*, ed. Robin Humphrey, British Association for the Advancement of Science, Sociology and Social Policy Section/Department of Social Policy, University of Newcastle, 1996.

Smith, Dorothy, 'A Peculiar Eclipsing! Women's Exclusion from Men's Culture', *WSIQ* 1, 1978.

Social Trends 26, Central Statistical Office, HMSO, 1996.

Trouble and Strife: The Radical Feminist Magazine 34, Winter 1996/97.

Utting, D., *Family and Parenthood: Supporting Families, Preventing Breakdown*, Joseph Rowntree Foundation, York, 1995.

van de Kaa, D., 'Europe's Second Demographic Transition', *Population Bulletin* 42(1), 1987.

────── 'Emerging Issues in Demographic Research for Contemporary Europe', *Population Research in Britain*, eds. M. Murphy and J. Hobcraft, Supplement to *Population Studies* 45, 1991.

Walker, Janet, 'Changing Families: Great Expectations in Hard Times', in *Families Behind the Headlines*, ed. Robin Humphrey,

British Association for the Advancement of Science, Sociology and Social Policy Section/Department of Social Policy, University of Newcastle, 1996.